The Biblical Flood and the Ice Epoch

THE BIBLICAL FLOOD AND THE ICE EPOCH

A STUDY IN
SCIENTIFIC HISTORY

By

DONALD W. PATTEN

Distributed by
BAKER BOOK HOUSE
Grand Rapids, Michigan

Copyright 1966 by
PACIFIC MERIDIAN PUBLISHING CO.
13540 Lake City Way N.E.
Seattle, Washington 98125
Library of Congress Catalog Card No. 66-18566
PRINTED IN THE UNITED STATES OF AMERICA
FIRST EDITION 1966
SECOND PRINTING—SLIGHTLY REVISED 1967
THIRD PRINTING 1968
FOURTH PRINTING 1970
FIFTH PRINTING 1971
SIXTH PRINTING 1971
SEVENTH PRINTING 1972
EIGHTH PRINTING 1973
NINTH PRINTING 1974
TENTH PRINTING 1974

To my wife   Lorraine Louise Patten

my daughter   Judith Louise

and my sons   Richard Eugene

John Robert

William Guy

Phillip Andrew

David Paul

Thomas Wesley

Acknowledgements

THIS IS TO EXPRESS MY THANKS to those friends who have given so much help and encouragement with this book. I owe much to:

Mr. Guilford Martin, classmate in college at Montana State University, who gave me the first New Testament I was privileged to read, and who showed me both the nature and the application of the teachings therein.

Dr. C. William deCeault, mathematician and space scientist with the Boeing Airplane Company, who rendered much help and encouragement, and who gave freely of his talents and time as a scientific reader.

Mrs. Emma Hale, owner of the Chieftain Press, who helped in the technical organization of this book.

Foreword

The Biblical Flood and the Ice Epoch

*I*t takes a great deal of humility to share one's rudimentary concepts with his fellowmen. The risk of error or the embarrassment of retraction extract too much from one's reserve of pride to warrant the effort. But for those to whom a devotion to discovery, and a search for understanding spark life and bring awakeness, the jeopardy of premature exposure of ideas merely serves to test the fabric of faith and the sincerity of intellect. Mr. Patten's devotion and search are as bold as his faith and intellect are real.

To capture the essence of the author's thoughts, one will find paragraphs more significant than sentences, chapters more meaningful than the paragraphs that compose them, and the collection of chapters, the thrust of the book, more penetrating than any sub-collection of chapters.

The author considers in detail the physical context in which animal and plant life were embedded throughout the Great Flood recorded in Genesis, as well as a postulated cosmic catastrophe in which the deposition of ice on Earth was made manifest.

Microscopic disturbances of the human glandular

system are traced concomitantly with the macroscopic disturbances of the solar system. The author directs attention to the grand anatomy of mountains and the petit structure of the atmosphere.

The variety of subjects treated in context should invite study and comment from an equal variety of disciplines.

Other than for reasons of personal curiosity and academic inquiry and stimulation, one might wonder why the author occupies himself with an incident in Earth history. With rapid technological and social evolution welding the days of the present into a rigid irreversible history, with the hope and anxiety over the future dimmed by the apprehension of a nuclear miscalculation, why the concern with Earth history?

If Mr. Patten's book concerned only Earth history, the question would be valid; but this is not the case. Indeed, the book is bound together with the signature of fundamental Christian faith, the author's creed. The book is a vehicle for the mission of the fundamental Christian belief; it contends that the Bible is not only a reliable record of history, but also the foundation and substance of the future.

C. W. deCeault
February 1966

Prefatory Note

THE central proposition of this book is to demonstrate the superiority of the theory of astral catastrophism over and against the uniformitarian view of Earth history. Astral catastrophism involves occasions of sudden and overwhelming cataclysmic changes in the conditions of the Earth in a brief and limited time. Among the cataclysmic forces which engaged our fragile sphere were both gravitational and magnetic forces of planetary magnitude.

The results included tidal waves of subcontinental dimensions. We do not maintain that the period of crisis referred to in Genesis as the Flood was the first conflict nor the last; we only maintain that it was the worst. Along with oceanic tides, other results included the upheaval of tides of magma, resulting in mountain systems on a global scale and in a global pattern. There was simultaneously the dumping of a vast volume of extremely cold astral ice upon the Earth's high latitudes, but essentially in the magnetic polar regions more than in the geographic polar locations. Also there occurred a sudden and permanent change in the Earth's atmosphere, hence the Earth's climatic organization. Thus there was a new and markedly different physical environment for biological life.

Celestial Catastrophism, or as the author uses the term, *Astral Catastrophism,* involves a sudden engagement and disengagement of these forces, acting simultaneously upon each of the Earth's three fluid equilibriums—the atmosphere (air), the hydrosphere (oceans) and lithosphere (primarily fluid magma or lava).

Contents

List of Line Diagrams

List of Tables

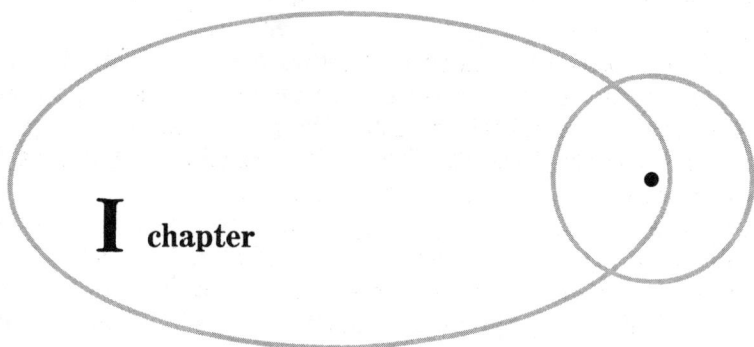

A Global Flood or a Local Flood

W HY write a book on the Biblical Flood? Has not this subject been largely relegated to academic limbo? Has not the Biblical Flood been considered by some authorities to be an event which never occurred—except perhaps in the imaginations of the ancients? Haven't other authorities considered it to be a historical fact but yet a strictly localized phenomenon? And yet has it not been considered by some others to have been a global cataclysm? While some have considered the Flood to have occurred around 10,000 or 20,000 B.C., have not others placed it at about 2,500 B.C.? Of what significance is this variation of 5,000, 10,000 or 20,000 years? Which of these views, if any, is correct, and what are the implications contained therein?

One hundred and fifty years ago, numerous controversies clouded the academic horizon, controversies which involved the leading scholars of that day. Fossils were being found in every country in Europe. Some were discovered high in the Alps, and others were unearthed below sea level, deep in German or Welsh coal mines. The fossils included remains of marine animals, mammoths, bison, giant birds, dinosaurs, exotic vegetation, and many other hard-to-classify forms. Some were tiny; many were huge. There were so many different forms and sizes of fossils that their classification became quite an art. Some were being found practically in the back yards of the leading academic figures of that day.

These abundant fossil finds demanded an explanation. Many, such as Cuvier, felt that some sort of gigantic, watery cataclysm or cataclysms had indeed engulfed the past. This possibility immediately suggested the Biblical Flood. Yet others cast about for an alternative explanation. Modern humanists, increasingly anti-Genesis in outlook, were growing in numbers and in positions of importance, especially in academic circles. To Voltaire, for instance, any mention of the Flood was offensive; it implied too much of God, or of judgment, or of the Judeo-Christian heritage. Despite evidence left by fossils and sedimentary strata, as well as literary heritages, a Biblical Flood was taboo to him, and to many others.

Voltaire was somewhat typical of the anti-spiritual humanists of his day. He was thoroughly anti-Christian and anti-Judaistic. He felt that the burial of the Bible in general, and the Genesis record in particular, would be a great service to mankind. Yet during his lifetime, most natural scientists leaned toward catastrophism. They mostly revered the Judeo-Christian heritage.

But anti-spiritual humanists, like Voltaire or Kant, usually applauded anything which tended to discredit the Genesis record of catastrophes. Thus, the doctrine of uniformitarianism was born and nurtured from the mother principle of humanism, as was the daughter principle of evolution—merely biological uniformitarianism. Evolution and uniformitarianism practically required agnosticism, and they made atheism increasingly respectable, even virile. The viewpoints of the early catastrophists became outmoded and were gradually discarded, and then they were all but forgotten. Thus our century has received an almost pure heritage of uniformitarianism, and as a consequence, is leaving a legacy of anti-spiritual humanism in various forms.[1]

Modern uniformitarianism was conceived 200 years ago, and about 100 years ago it became the dominant theory of Earth history. Its advocates maintained that our planet and our solar system have had a serene past in terms of multiplied millions of

[1]As further discussion of early humanism which was pro-spiritual and modern humanism which is anti-spiritual is reserved for Chapter XII, pp. 319-322.

years. No great, sudden cataclysms ever occurred. But is this theory defensible in the light of new evidence? Was it ever really defensible in the light of former evidence?

There are abundant evidences of a watery, global cataclysm — evidences which are not easily refuted. They are so universal, so astounding, and so inter-related that they require re-examination. How is it explained, for instance, that ancient peoples, from six separate continents, almost invariably had a Flood tradition? Why is it that ancient peoples almost always had a pantheon of sky-gods and traditions of celestial chaos? Why is it that ancient peoples all over the world, in diverse cultures possessing independent traditions, yet possessed similar traditions of cataclysms containing similar motifs? And if the ancients simply happened to have comparable or corresponding hallucinations, why, then, does our solar system also contain abundant evidences of historical astral chaos? And is it possible that our Earth could have escaped this? Re-examination of these universal evidences and their implications leads to a serious and careful consideration of the Flood catastrophe.

The evidences of a global Flood are sound and they increasingly demonstrate with drama that worldwide catastrophes have occurred. However, the Biblical Flood is far from a fully developed subject. Newer circumstances and additional evidence requires a more comprehensive review. Renewed analysis and synthesis are needed. Uniformitarianism needs to be thoroughly questioned.

Today, humanism—the adoration of homo sapiens—remains largely the attitude of our scholarly classes. This spirit of our age is reflected in our philosophies, our principles, our values and our deeds. We are asking if the humanistic viewpoint is really mature. Therefore, the objective of this work is to achieve the most critical, penetrating, systematic, analytical, and synthetical examination of the uniformitarianism which has been accomplished to date. The objective is to bring this modern hypothesis, almost a sacred cow, into the arena of test and trial; your writer is the matador and you, the reader, are the spectator.

This labor has been dedicated to young scholars. Dare to *think,* and to *re-think.* Have the courage to cheerfully challenge the current generation in its disappointing crescendo of turmoil and trouble. To use an old Latin phrase—*sapere aude.* Investigate the history of our solar system during the last 10,000 years, es-

pecially that of our fragile sphere. Examine the many traditions
of the ancients. Review the magnificent job of engraving and
etching that has occurred upon the surface of our swirling sphere.[2]
Examine these evidences carefully. Prepare to draw conclusions
that may seem at first somewhat amazing.

[2]The term "swirling sphere," or a like term "spiraling sphere," make good
alliteration in the English language. However, some object to the use of
either of these terms on the basis that they inaccurately describe the
Earth's motion around the Sun in our solar system. In this limited sense,
such a point may be valid. However in a broader sense, the terms "swirling
sphere" or "spiraling sphere" are precisely correct.

The Earth possesses four types of motion. One is centrifugal, due to the
Earth's rotation around its axis. This is at an equatorial or circumferential speed of approximately .29 miles per second. A second motion is revolving motion, due to the Earth's revolving around the Sun. This is at an
orbital velocity of about 18½ miles per second.

However the Earth possesses two additional motions. Third is galactic
motion. Our Sun and all of the members of its solar family are revolving
around our galaxy, the Milky Way, at a rate of 12 miles per second in the
direction of the constellation Hercules. Fourthly, our galaxy is revolving
through the universe, at an additional velocity of 170 miles per second in
the direction of the constellation Cyngus. Thus the term "swirling sphere"
is a good term from the galactic perspective; the term "spiraling sphere"
is perhaps superior. These terms accurately describe the Earth's motion as
viewed from the Milky Way.

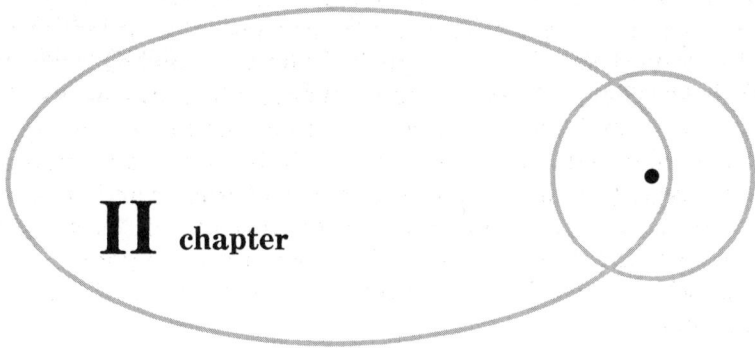

The History of Catastrophism and Uniformitarianism

A STRANGE man is entering an unfamiliar room. The lamps are turned up; the drapes are drawn. In the center of the room lies a broad-leafed maple table. Lying scattered across the broad table are some 5,000 assorted pieces of jigsaw puzzle. The man examines them and begins fitting piece to piece. Many hours pass, but little progress is made. More time passes. Intensified effort leads to increasing perplexity and vexation. There are more than four corner pieces. There seem to be too many edge pieces. Finally, a new idea streaks across the horizon of the man's mind: "Might it be that there are, lying on this table, the elements of two, or even three, puzzles?" If so, the basis for much progress is laid.

This is precisely an illustration of modern man in his search for understanding of his origin. He is trying to understand the nature of his origin in order that he may more adequately comprehend the purpose of life. It is reasonable to suppose that man's origin is related to the bewildering forces which obviously have sculptured the small spiraling sphere which he inhabits.

Actually, the Earth has had several more or less distinct ages, a fact related by the ancients of many civilizations from many continents. And these ages, cycles, or epochs were terminated and separated by catastrophes of global magnitude. While modern man assumed that he has been trying to complete one great, consecutive, interlocking, and intermerging puzzle of the past, what he has really been dealing with is a history which has been dramatically punctuated by catastrophes and abrupt termination of periods of human activity. The separated ages parallel our illustration of 5,000 pieces of puzzle, which are pieces that comprise several separate pictures, rather than one large, interlocking, merging, and consecutive puzzle. And each separate picture reveals a different facet of man's character and historical experience even as each of the pictures reveals a different scene in an unfolding drama. One of these pictures—the period of the Ice Epoch—markedly and abruptly changed the Earth's terrestrial climate.

Evidently our planet was engulfed in several celestial upheavals, some of which, having occurred within the realm of recorded history, were related in varying manners by the ancients. The Flood catastrophe of Noah's time was easily the most severe. At this time, our planet was caught within counterdominating gravitational forces and magnetic fields, resulting in (1) much tidal upheaval within our oceans; (2) surging spasms or tides of lava (fluid magma) from within the Earth's thin crust; and (3) further discharges of an electrical nature.

Until this catastrophic view of history is grasped, modern man cannot accurately conceive the perplexities, philosophies, and problems of his ancient days. Once he grasps this perspective, he can begin to understand the enormous magnitude of the forces which sculptured our sphere, as well as of our scar-faced satellite, the Moon. Then only will man be able to realize how fragile his tiny planet is and how awesome is the power of his Creator.

It should be noted that uniformitarian proponents do recognize local catastrophes on a minor scale; to this limited extent, uniformitarians do acknowledge catastrophism. Similarly, while catastrophists view the sculpturing of our sphere as having been achieved primarily by global catastrophes, they nevertheless recognize serene interludes during which the processes of climatic erosion function.

However, it is important to realize that while uniformitarians acknowledge catastrophes on a local scale, mechanical explanations have been almost completely lacking. And similarly, while catastrophists acknowledge earth-encompassing catastrophes of extreme dimensions, they also have achieved almost nothing in terms of mechanical explanations. Thus the theme of this book rests upon two important definitions of Earth history which are opposite and mutually contradictory concepts.

Catastrophism: The doctrine that changes in the earth's crust have generally been effected *suddenly* by *physical forces*.

Uniformitarianism: The doctrine that *existing processes, acting as at present,* are sufficient to account for all geological changes.[1]

This study attempts to demonstrate that uniformitarianism is not an adequate theory. Today, uniformitarianism and its daughter doctrines are essentially unchallenged and are taught as fact rather than theory. To challenge them is to invite expulsion in most academic circles; it is to cast a questionable light upon the basis of modern humanism (the mother philosophy of uniformitarianism) and it is also to question numerous other philosophies, theories, and sub-theories—including Darwinism—as well as elements of Freudianism and Marxism. It is as though such questioning were beyond the pale of knowledge. However, to refrain from questioning these systems of thought and their underlying assumptions would be to ignore an avalanche of contradictory evidence.

The uniformitarian viewpoint has traditionally held that the Flood, as recorded in Genesis and other ancient sources, is a fable, a fanciful Sumerian story.[2] This is, of course, also the viewpoint of modern humanism. This agreement between uniformitarianism and humanism is not coincidental since uniformitarianism is the daughter of philosophy of modern humanism. Thus, the

---

[1] *Webster's Collegiate Dictionary,* Springfield, Mass.: G. & C. Merriam Co., 1946, "Catastrophism," p. 169; "Uniformitarianism," p. 1093.

[2] Dolph E. Hooker, *Those Astounding Ice Ages,* New York: Exposition Press, 1958, p. 137.
   "Men of narrow, cynical minds may say the biblical story of a Flood is nothing but a fanciful Sumerian tale. How do they know? Aside from pure assumption, based solely upon imagination, they can produce no evidence whatsoever to support such a statement. On the other hand, evidence to sustain validity of the biblical story is plainly visible not only throughout the whole world, but in the heavens as well. Furthermore, the story is by no means exclusively Sumerian. It exists in the traditions of nations throughout the world—nations some of whom never heard of the Sumerians. One need not accept the biblical story as God-given to recognize that its truth is attested by much actual evidence."

Biblical Flood has not been accorded its proper importance in the history of our planet. When fully examined, the Flood event emerges not only as a severe ordeal for our planet and its inhabitants but also as the most severe disruption (extensive and intensive) which our planet has yet experienced. The Flood, the upwelling of the oceans in tidal waves upon the Earth's crust, was only a part of the global havoc of unbelievable extent. This was apparently caused by an astral catastrophe, a sudden change in equilibrium of the Earth relative to the solar system, which shall be discussed in more detail in Chapters IV, V, VI and VII.

When this is understood, it will appear that mankind indeed has had fanciful fables, but, surprisingly enough, this doctrine of 19th century uniformitarianism will perhaps emerge as the finest of these fables.

Even as uniformitarianism has been an integral part of humanism for the last 150 years, so catastrophism has been an integral part of the Judeo-Christian heritage for the past 4,000 years. Biblical events bearing upon the Flood, the fire and brimstone days of the prophets, the long and fateful day of Joshua (when the Sun and Moon apparently stood still), the celestial-oriented events at the time of the Hebrew exodus from Egypt, the earthshaking of Sodom and Gomorrah—these have all been of primary import to Judaism and Christianity. But the humanistic philosophy has been in direct contradiction to the Biblical perspective. One is oriented toward man; the other toward the Creator. As a result, humanists have had an amazing anti-Genesis prejudice, which on occasion has been the basis for some very fuzzy conclusions.

During the 18th and 19th centuries, anything which contradicted Genesis found a welcome in the great universities of Europe which were in the throes of change. One of the philosophical manifestations of this change was the ascendancy of anti-spiritual humanism over Christian philosophy.

Uniformitarianism was just such a manifestation or change; it was only one among many. However, the men who originally founded the diverging branches of natural science were not uniformitarians for the most part, but were catastrophists in the majority of instances. There was Agassiz in geology, along with Catcott, Buckland, and Woodward. There was Von Humboldt in geography, Ritter in geomorphology, Whiston, Newton, and Halley in physics, and Linnaeus in taxonomy. They had been preceded by such men as Colonna, Steno, and Grandius. And these catastrophists go all the way back to Philo, who in 30 A.D. in Alexandria, Egypt, wrote the following commentary on Earth history:

> The vast ocean being raised to an height which it had never before attained, rushed with a sudden inroad upon islands and continents. The springs, rivers and cataracts, confusedly mingling their streams, contributed to elevate the waters . . . For every part of the earth sunk beneath the water, and the entire system of the world became . . . mutilated, and deformed by the vast amputation.[3]

Especially with the great advance made through Newtonian science, and with the great prestige lent to catastrophism by Newton and his assistant, Whiston, it was generally agreed by the end of the 18th century that the Earth had been shaped by dreadful, global, watery catastrophes. But by the end of the 19th century, 100 years later, all this had changed. Uniformitarianism had come to the front. It had risen to predominance, and it proceeded to rise to the place of virtual monopoly—all in one short century. Among the leading figures in the development of uniformitarian thought was James Hutton.

1. Uniformitarian Authors

JAMES HUTTON (1726-1797). In 1795, Hutton published his major work entitled *Theory of the Earth.* In this work, modern uniformitarianism was first proposed seriously and systematically as a theory for Earth history. It was not immediately accepted, but it caused a moderate amount of speculation. Hutton was a Scotsman, a physician turned geologist. His background in astronomy was weak, and he seemed indifferent to the opinions of such men as Halley, Newton, Whiston, Cassini, Lehman, Huygens, and Wallerius concerning the catastrophic circumstances in evidence within our solar system.

Hutton remained unconcerned about the cause of the craters of the Moon, or Saturn's rings, or cometary orbits, and he was

[3]Byron C. Nelson, *The Deluge Story in Stone,* Minneapolis: Augsburg Publishing House, 1931, p. 7.

not disturbed by the fact that so many scholars taught catastrophism. Shortly after his publication, the first of the mysterious asteroids—battered fragments of a former planet—were discovered plunging through space in orbit between Mars and Jupiter. But Hutton took for granted that the Earth had never experienced catastrophes, except perhaps on a strictly local scale. He presumed the Scottish Highlands to have been uplifted at an infinitesimally slow rate, measured by millimeters over millenia and millions of years. How did he "know" this?[4] It is difficult to say. He probably inferred it from contemporary experience and concluded it as a universal principle. His work was not generally accepted, yet it intrigued some, including Charles Lyell, a lawyer turned geologist.

CHARLES LYELL (1797-1875). Lyell published three volumes entitled *Principles of Geology* (1830-1833). He opposed the catastrophic doctrine of Earth history, and he successfully advanced Hutton's theory of uniformitarianism. He set up a geological time scale, by supplying time in multiplied millions of years for any and every geological event.[5] He guessed at many things, including the dating of the Ice Epoch.

Previously, Louis Agassiz, a catastrophist, a geologist, and an outstanding scholar, had brought to attention the evidence that a great ice sheet had covered Northern Europe and Northern North America. So Lyell proceeded to date that Ice Epoch at about 1,000,000 B.C. He considered it a "recent" event, caused by falling snowflakes, descending over long periods of time.

It was later realized that certain "geological clocks" existed which could be used to indicate a date for the Ice Epoch. One such geological clock is Niagara Falls, which is receding from Lake Ontario, a lake which was formed at the end of the Ice Epoch.[6] Here, between Lake Erie and Lake Ontario, is a crystalline structure, an escarpment underlaid by soft limestone. At Ni-

---

[4]Further discussion of Hutton's approach is given in Chapter III, p. 34, footnote 2, and Chapter V, p. 72, footnote 9.

[5]Further discussion of the Lyellian time chart is given in Chapter XI, p. 301. A catastrophic time chart is also given on p. 302.

[6]Immanuel Velikovsky, *Earth in Upheaval*, New York: Doubleday & Co., 1955, pp. 161-162.

agara River and Niagara Falls, the crystalline formation has been cut and is eroding and receding from Lake Ontario toward Lake Erie. It is receding at a measurable rate. Lyell measured the lineal distance of the Falls from its original location. He interviewed the inhabitants of the area regarding the rate of erosion. They affirmed that the rate of erosion was about 3 feet per year, on the average. This rate did not check with Lyell's time scale— it indicated that his time scale was in error by 988,000 years out of 1,000,000. Therefore, Lyell impulsively concluded that the inhabitants must have been exaggerating, and he set the rate of erosion at 1 foot per year, not 3. After further calculations, Lyell announced that the Ice Epoch had ended at 35,000 B.C., and not his previous estimate of 1,000,000 B.C.

It is now recognized that both distance estimates were too low. Lyell's original estimate of time for the Ice Epoch was also wrong. Niagara Falls is retreating at a rate approaching 5 feet per year, and this is merely the current rate of erosion. Ancient rates in the decades following the end of the ice build-up were in all probability far greater. This review is not given to determine the magnitude of Lyell's error; rather it is cited so that we can recognize Lyell's attitude toward time. His theory required oceans of time because he believed that our planet had never experienced watery global catastrophes.

Hutton's views attained a modest amount of acceptance during his lifetime, but they became respectable when they were reworked, refined, and republished by Lyell some 35 years later. The relatively new geological profession at first acknowledged Lyell's ideas grudgingly, but the more humanistically oriented social sciences welcomed them. Lyell's ideas were viewed as both anti-Genesis and at the same time seemingly scientific. As modern humanism became deeply entrenched in academic circles in Europe, Lyell's ideas prospered. And then Darwin appeared, with his refined theory of biological uniformitarianism, strictly parallel to his friend Lyell's idea of geological uniformitarianism.

CHARLES DARWIN (1809-1882). Darwin studied botany and zoology, and he had an inquiring mind. His grandfather, Erasmus Darwin, a physician and amateur botanist, had established a botanical garden where he had experimented with developing new strains by plant breeding. Darwin's father also was a physician. Thus, Charles received an inquisitive attitude and a studious family heritage with a particular interest in natural science. He also took the opportunity to do a lot of travelling in areas beyond England. He crossed several oceans, as a naturalist on the H.M.S. Beagle. He viewed some of the astounding species of fauna and flora in various parts of the world. Subsequently, he became closely associated with Lyell, studying under Lyell for several years.

Darwin attempted to reconcile biology with Lyell's geological theory of uniformitarianism. This approach is the crux of Darwinism. Lyell urged Darwin to expedite the publication of his theories because others were developing similar ideas. Darwin thus spearheaded the development of the uniformitarian doctrine of biological evolution. The response was immediate. His third and most famous work, *The Origin of Species by Means of Natural Selection,* was published in 1859. The first day the publication went on the market, Oct. 1, 1859, the entire edition of 1500 was sold out. Thus it would seem that the book was received as a best seller in the popular vein more than a scientific work deserving critical examination in depth.

Since his book was completely sold out in its entire first edition on the first day of publication, one may well conclude that an excellent pre-publication publicity campaign had been achieved. This leads directly to the suspicion that this may have been the European equivalent to "Madison Avenue science" in its most proficient performance of the former century.

The relationship between humanism, uniformitarianism, and Darwinism should be noted. First of all, they are related because Darwinism sprang directly from uniformitarianism, which was fostered by modern humanism. Secondly, it must be recognized that evolution blazed the trail to further humanism and uniformitarianism. All three doctrines promoted and depended on each other. This is not unlike a backfield in football, in which one back first carries the ball while the others block, and then the order is changed in rotation. These three doctrines—humanism, uniformitarianism, and Darwinism—ran interference for each other.

The basis for Darwin's theory was threefold: (1) Lyell's uniformitarianism, (2) Lamarck's proposition of the inheritance of acquired characteristics, and (3) Darwin's own geographical observations of fauna and flora. Lyell's uniformitarianism allowed for time in inexhaustible quantities (or at least so it seemed).

Lamarck's proposition allowed for specie reorganization and translation termed transmutation (or at least so it seemed). And Darwin's travels brought the fauna of Africa, South America, Australia and other remote areas into the arena.

Here, supposedly, in Lamarckian thought was the biochemical mechanism for change and emergence, the principle of the transmutation of species. The idea ballooned immediately; it gained acceptance among academic circles rapidly. A modest amount of contradictory opinion developed, but was mostly ignored. And what little contradictory opinion existed was sporadic and rather disorganized. Agassiz, for instance, categorically objected. Pasteur also objected. Mendel, another pertinent example, was briefly heard, dismissed, and forgotten for another 40 years.

Catastrophism, along with creationism, was overruled, neglected, and then virtually forgotten by the entire geological profession. There were a few voices of objection and protest here and there. Henry Howorth, Hugh Miller and Isaac Newton Vail were examples.

A constellation of new philosophies began to emerge based, or partly based, on Darwinism. These theories, which practically burst upon the world scene, carried implications which made a climate of agnosticism nearly necessary, which also made atheism respectable. For example, Marx, in his unrestrained enthusiasm, endeavored to dedicate a book against capitalism (Das Kapital) to Darwin, a capitalist.[7] Secularism, skepticism, and cynical brands of atheism were transformed from their former lowly status into virile ideas, and they gained wide acceptance. This was accomplished although *geological uniformitarianism* is not valid, whether in Hutton's or Lyell's form or in modern dress. This has also been accomplished even though *environmental*

---

[7] In 1880, Darwin received a letter from Marx asking his permisssion to dedicate the English edition of Das Kapital to him. With courtesy, Darwin refused, not because he did not share Marx's atheism, but rather because his family and friends would not approve of so atheistic a work. (Gavin De Beer, *Charles Darwin*, Thomas Nelson & Sons Ltd., London, 1963, p. 266.)

The fact that Darwin was a capitalist must reflect Marx's intense interest and overriding enthusiasm for Darwin's biology, because Darwin in no way shared Marx's view of economics or politics. In fact both Darwin and his wife, Emma (Wedgwood) Darwin, happened to be grandchildren of Josiah Wedgwood, a famous entrepreneur, the Henry Ford of the pottery industry in 18th century England, who led a typical Horatio Alger success story of rags to great riches.

determinism is not valid, whether in Lamarck's form, Darwin's form or in modern dress.

During the 19th century, as uniformitarianism expanded rapidly (in biology and geology), humanists were greatly enthused. Catastrophists were both confused and dismayed. So were Biblical theologians. Catastrophism had been deeply interwoven into their theology. Geological catastrophists were becoming a very rare and lonely species. And theological catastrophists could not meet with secular scholars because their basis of theology was deemed insufficient, that is to say, unscientific.

Other problems also became evident during the ascent of uniformitarianism. There were repeated traditions of cosmic upheavals in virtually every culture. Among these, to name but a few, were the Chaldean, the Indo-Aryan or Hindu, the Egyptian, the Greek, the Incan, the Mayan, the Aztec, the Persian, the Roman, the Germanic, the Japanese, the Chinese, and the Polynesian. Some, like Whiston and Von Humbolt, had concluded that these traditions were related to ancient global upheavals. But after Lyell and Darwin, a reinterpretation was necessary. Therefore, the followers of Lyell and Darwin transformed these worldwide traditions of cosmological upsets into fanciful tales and ancient mythology, claiming the traditions were groundless and impossible since they could have had no physical and real basis. Certainly the planets had been regularly circling in their present orbits for untold millions of years. Certainly their satellites had regularly and unvaryingly accompanied them. Who said so? Darwin. Lyell. Hutton. Kant.

So the scholars of yesteryear assumed that there was no logical, physical, or actual basis for the ancient sky gods of so many ancient cultures. Had catastrophes been recognized, it would have led to a semi-literal interpretation, which would have led directly back to catastrophism, and then directly contradicted the plausibility of the uniformitarian approach, already considered to be above question.

Thus there was a fair amount of confusion following the rise of uniformitarianism. It was by no means restricted to the theological and geological arenas. Classicists had no recourse but to fall back on pure fancy to explain the ancient cosmic motifs. The general reaction of the mythologists and the scholars of the classics was to go along with the uniformitarian assumption. The abandoning of catastrophism has already been noted among the geologists. An additional reason explaining why there was so little resistance among the professions is the principle of conformity to the norms of scholarly society.[8]

But the reactions of conservative theologians have been more varied. Some decided to accept the uniformitarian proposition and promote the humanistic viewpoint. Some decided to reject the uniformitarian proposition and oppose the viewpoint. Others decided to ignore the contradiction. Of those who decided to reject the uniformitarian proposition and oppose it, most found that they might meet the challenge in their pulpits, but that they were nearly at a complete loss in the classroom.

Thus, following Darwin's historic publication, there was some opposing thought; but it was rapidly washed away in the flood of successive elaborations and increasing frills, which were woven into the uniformitarian proposition. Again, certain men like Agassiz, Howorth and Pasteur objected; but despite their stature, their objections fell mostly on deaf ears. Mendel, in spite of the great import of his findings, was for the time overlooked. And there were others. Nevertheless, we see that within the academic profession the objectors and protestors to the uniformitarian proposition failed, for all intents and purposes, because they gained no significant number of disciples.

Many churchmen objected vigorously, but their arguments could be dismissed because they objected on theological rather than on biochemical or geological grounds. But even so, the monopoly of uniformitarianism did not extend into all church colleges and seminaries. Here and there somebody gathered data, did a modest amount of publishing, and achieved a modest but significant following. Howorth is a good example of a catastrophist who, as a secular educator, failed to acquire a significant following. Price is a good example of a catastrophist who, as a church educator, achieved a modest but significant following.

[8]Author's Note: The tendency toward conformity is strong among the scholarly community, even though they are the first and the loudest to disdain the principle. Spengler, for instance, noticed this one generation ago in Germany, and used a descriptive term translated as "the intellectual mob." Academic men will recognize the tendency of their own community to adopt ideas en masse, while decrying the same principle in the total society. In the academic world, perhaps more than in society in general, promotions for instance, are highly dependent on conformity.

2. Catastrophic Authors

Catastrophists who have ventured to publish have been few and far between; they have gained attention only about once each decade, and invariably their motivation has been religious, the defense of the faith. In the 1910's the publishing catastrophist was Vail; in the 1920's it was Price; in the 1930's it was Nelson; in the 1940's it was Rehwinkel; and in the 1950's it was Morris. However, within the last decade, a few secular writers have also begun to publish catastrophic or semi-catastrophic material, frequently in articles rather than in books.

The catastrophic writers of the past fifty years, until the last decade, have almost invariably come out of conservative Protestant circles. It is interesting to note that no particular group has dominated. Isaac Newton Vail was a Quaker. George McCready Price was Seventh Day Adventist; Byron Nelson was Lutheran (Augustana) as was Alfred Rehwinkel (Missouri Synod); Henry Morris was Independent Baptist.

GEORGE McCREADY PRICE. Price was a prolific writer during the 1910's and particularly the 1920's and 1930's. He published three major volumes and innumerable articles. Among his publications were *Evolutionary Geology and the New Catastrophism, The New Geology,* and *Common Sense Geology.* He was considered authoritative within his own denomination, but also received a substantial response in other fundamentalist circles. He achieved no significant following in secular circles, and a certain amount of unwarranted scorn.

Price was a learned man with only a moderate academic education which included approximately three years of college, plus several years of religious education. However, it would be a mistake to underestimate the extent to which he was informed in geology. He was familiar with practically everything that had been published in geology during his time. He made extensive field trips. He compiled illustrations of fossil finds and stratigraphical formations of both dramatic interest and phenomenal length.

One significant fact about Price was his command of his field. But an equally interesting facet of him is what he failed to say. Price demonstrated the evidences of watery upheavals, sedimentary deposits, alluvial formations, and fossil finds. extensively. He considered the Flood to have been an immense cataclysm, and obviously tidal in nature. But here he went no further.

In regard to the cause and effect relationship, Price concerned himself only with effect. He looked for evidences of the Biblical Flood only in the geological formations of the Earth's crust, and neglected information filtering down from the folklore of the ancients with their astral motifs. Price looked only downward for evidences and failed to also look upward for causes. Mechanical principles involved in tidal upheaval and astral catastrophism were not considered. In this way, he partly succeeded and partly failed in his purpose. Yet in his limited success, he was more successful than any other catastrophist of his era.

As judged by a "cause and effect" analysis, Price's method of approach to catastrophism was limited to the geological *effects* of the Flood catastrophe. Nelson, Rehwinkel and Morris expanded the approach of Price by adding other categories of effects. However, like Price, they limited their approach to effects within the "cause and effect" analysis, and thereby duplicated both Price's strengths and also his weaknesses.

BYRON C. NELSON. Nelson's two major works were *After Its Kind* (1927) and *The Deluge Story In Stone* (1931). The first book principally opposed Darwinian biology, and the latter opposed Lyellian geology. The first concentrated on the contradictions between Lamarckianism (environmental determinism and Mendelianism (genetics). The second concentrated on the contradictions between uniformitarian explanations and catastrophic evidences.

In his work on geology, Nelson tended to follow quite closely the same pattern which was established by Price. He recounted the ‑innumerable truly amazing evidences of catastrophism as illustrated by the fossil record. He, too, considered the Flood to be primarily tidal, but he pursued this no further. He, like Price, considered the cause of the Flood to have been God, but he did not dwell on the means and methods God may have used.

Nelson was more concerned with additional categories of evidences. Price wrote extensively, thoroughly and quite technically on geological data. Nelson gave geology a lighter treatment, but expanded his work to include valuable data on the historical development of catastrophism. He also began to recount the existence of catastrophic themes in ancient literature and traditions of many cultures, but he did not develop this theme very broadly. In these two ways, therefore, Nelson's work was broader than Price's, although not as specialized. Hence, Price's work was more basic, while Nelson's included a more complete synthesis.

ALFRED M. REHWINKEL. Rehwinkel published, in the 1940's and 1950's, his major work entitled *The Flood* (1951). Like Price and Nelson, he was a seminary professor. His background in education was more extensive than Price's and his teaching curriculum was also more diverse. While Price wrote on geology to the virtual exclusion of other related areas, Rehwinkel kept abreast in other fields. Catastrophism was only one of Rehwinkel's projects and responsibilities. His work therefore resembles Nelson's more than Price's. It is more comprehensive, but less technical, than the works of his friend, Price.

Rehwinkel followed both Price and Nelson in considering the effects of the Flood to the exclusion of natural causes. All three considered the Flood to be tidal in nature, but considered tides only within the oceans, or hydrosphere. Beyond this they discussed none of the specifics. Had they considered causes as well as effects, many more issues would have been set forth.

Interestingly enough, all three placed the Ice Epoch after the Flood, which they dated about 2500 B.C. But again, their explanation for the cause of these ice masses is shrouded in vagueness. Price suggested very tentatively a shifting of the location of the poles. This suggestion is more significant than they probably realized. This means that they read the geological data and concluded that the ice flow from the ice mass in the Northern Hemisphere overlaid the evidences of the Flood, and thus was later in point of time.

There are many apparent difficulties in this conclusion without more specific elaborations. But it also reflects that Rehwinkel, Price, and Nelson had no basic comprehension of the mechanical cause of the Ice Epoch. And this in turn re-emphasizes that they had little comprehension of the mechanics involved in the Flood catastrophe. Thus, they also allowed themselves to be concerned only with effects, and not with mechanical causes. In this way, Price's shadow is cast strongly across the writings of both Nelson and Rehwinkel.

Rehwinkel went to greater efforts than did either Nelson or Price in documenting and analyzing the importance of ancient literature and ancient traditions about the Flood. He searched, analyzed, and compared the conclusions of many others who had encountered the Flood motif in folklores, mythologies and ancient traditions. He recounted in an outstanding way how thoroughly the Earth was blanketed by Flood traditions among tribes and cultures from every continent.[9] Thus he pointed out how the Flood is etched both in the memories of mankind and in the strata of this planet. This endeavor by Rehwinkel was particularly commendable, and it added a further advance into the scope of catastrophism.

HENRY M. MORRIS. About every ten years, it seems, a major work on catastrophism has been published. Bear in mind that secular catastrophists achieved no significant following. Nelson's work is today in its sixth printing; Rehwinkel's work is in its eighth printing; Morris' is in its fifth. Morris' major work was *The Genesis Flood* (1961), co-authored by John C. Whitcomb, Jr. Like Nelson, Price, and Rehwinkle, Whitcomb is employed as a seminary professor; he is concerned primarily with the theological implications of the Flood story in Genesis.

Morris adds to the perspective of catastrophism a different and valuable background. He is a professor of hydraulic engineering and chairman of the Department of Civil Engineering at Virginia Polytechnic Institute. This is important in that it reflects an increasing endeavor to consider the hydraulic or hydrographic effects of the Flood cataclysm. In a significant way, his work again is comparable to the works of Price, Nelson, and Rehwinkel in that it considers the effects of the Deluge to the exclusion of the astrophysical causes, or the natural mechanics.

Morris' primary contributions are twofold: his background in hydraulics brings out newer insights; and secondly, he updates the data. He is concerned about such things as atmospheric chemistry, carbon-14 datings, tree rings, meteoric dust, and the principles of sedimentation. Thus, he has followed again in the pattern of his predecessors, partly succeeding, yet, it is held, also partly failing. Part of his success is the renewed interest and attention which his work has caused.

[9]Alfred M. Rehwinkel, *The Flood*, St. Louis: Concordia Publishing House, 1951, pp. 127-176. Further discussion of this subject is also given in Chapter VIII of this volume.

However, it is held that unless the mechanical cause of the Flood is adequately explained by catastrophists, geology may easily hibernate in its present uniformitarian bed for another 100 years. But more important, catastrophists need to demonstrate the mechanics involved in the Flood catastrophe in order to deepen and broaden the entire perspective. This would be to dramatically strengthen the case of catastrophism. This in turn should simultaneously deepen the controversy with uniformitarianism and also establish a more commanding position from which to promote the catastrophic approach.

Until the cause of the Deluge is demonstrated and explained, it is held that a truly commanding position is not occupied, and catastrophic thought will not be dominant. Even though great lists of profound, contradictory evidences have been cited by men, superbly documented and graphically illustrated, this has not been sufficient to shake geology out of its bed of uniformitarianism.

There is ample evidence that within the last decade uniformitarian geology has become increasingly aware of value in catastrophic thought. It has been due in part to a slow emergence of a miscellaneous group of non-religious catastrophists and semi-catastrophists. Hapgood, Hooker, Sanderson, and Velikovsky are among this group.

C. H. HAPGOOD and *IVAN T. SANDERSON.* Hapgood and Sanderson have both written articles dealing with frozen mammoths for national magazines within the last several years. This results in a smattering of evidence being presented to the public relative to catastrophic evidences, although there has been little in the way of solid explanations. Hapgood is more of an anthropologist than a geologist. He has recognized the fact that the mammoths were quick-frozen by the millions under sudden and extremely cold conditions. He has recognized that there must have been a sudden and permanent change in the climate, from sub-tropical to Arctic. He has endeavored to explain this on the basis of a shifting of the poles, along with a possible shift in the axis of the Earth.

In this respect, his thinking is mechanically uniformitarian, although his observations acknowledge the cry for catastrophic explanations. He inferred that the cause of the Ice Epoch must have been a change in geographical location of existing planetary climates. Thus, he supposed that the cause of the Ice Epoch was falling snow, transported in the form of water vapor by planetary wind systems. This observation, along with the seeming inadequate explanation, will be considered in detail in Chapter VI.

It should be noted here that Price, Nelson and Rehwinkel all presumed the Ice Epoch was caused by snows, changed locations of planetary climates, and possible shifting in poles, and mechanically their explanations also are uniformitarian. Each of these men would have objected to being classified as semi-uniformitarian, but such is the case with respect to Ice Epoch phenomena, as will be demonstrated later.

Hapgood's approach to the cause of the Ice Epoch is not mechanically important, but his writings do reflect an increasing uneasiness among uniformitarian thinkers. Being a non-geologist, he has freely illustrated some objections to the uniformitarian approach (this is professionally easier for a non-geologist). Until geologists fully recognize the merits of catastrophism along with the demerits of uniformitarianism, men from other disciplines and professions will publish on the subject of Earth history. And thus others will receive publicity and standing which normally should accrue to geologists.

Sanderson has written articles which are probably better than Hapgood's since they deal more with the specifics of the mammoths and less with the tentative kind of explanations which Hapgood hazards. Among the articles by Hapgood is *"The Mystery of the Frozen Mammoths"* (1960),[10] and among Sanderson's is *"The Riddle of the Frozen Giants"* (1960).[11]

IMMANUEL VELIKOVSKY. The leader of modern religious catastrophism was George McCready Price. In a similar manner, Velikovsky has been the most important figure among the secularly oriented catastrophists. Velikovsky obviously relied substantially on Price in his second most important work, *Earth In Upheaval.*

Velikovsky has written four books, two of which are of major import in catastrophic thought—*Worlds in Collision*

[10]Charles Hapgood, "The Mystery of the Frozen Mammoths," *Coronet,* Sept. 1960.

[11]Ivan T. Sanderson, "Riddle of the Frozen Giants," *Saturday Evening Post,* Jan. 16. 1960.

(1950) and *Earth in Upheaval* (1955).[12] In addition he has written several articles and participated in many lectures. His primary background is medicine and his perspective is that of ancient literature. This is in marked significant contrast to the background of Price, which was in geology and theology.

There is much that is meritorious in Velikovsky's works, and especially in his first monograph. The ensuing criticisms of Velikovsky are to be construed as friendly and constructive, for not all of Velikovsky's critics have been either friendly or constructive. There are three primary areas of criticism relative to his works.

(1) His Freudian View. Velikovsky has a deep predisposition toward modern Freudianism. Simultaneously he bypasses one of our finest of heritages, the Hebrew creationist heritage, which gives us our clearest concept of origins. He is a physician who migrated from Russia after the institution of Lenin's regime. He settled for a time in Vienna, where he became a follower of Freud and of the Freudian view of man. He later settled for a time in Palestine, and ultimately in New Jersey. Velikovsky's predisposition toward the Freudian ethic has accounted for a series of errors, some of commission and others of omission.[13]

(2) His lack of Geophysical Perspective. Velikovsky possesses a brilliant mind, with the skill of genius in matters regarding ancient literature. But he bumbles and stumbles in handling matters geophysical. His genius is apparent in *Worlds in Collision*. His lack of geophysical perspective coupled with his catastrophic motivation are both evident in *Earth in Upheaval*. In this second work, he, like Price, recites the many amazing discoveries which are engraved in the crust of our Earth. But he organizes them and relates them in helter-skelter fashion, lacking prehistorical sequence, lacking climatological mechanics, lacking geophysical mechanics, and lacking other perspectives. Not the greatest criticism of Velikovsky, but surely one of the marking and meaningful criticisms is that, although he wrote hundreds of thousands of words about catastrophism, he never produced a

---

[12]Immanuel Velikovsky, *Worlds in Collision*, New York: Doubleday & Co., 1950.
Immanuel Velikovsky, *Earth in Upheaval*, New York: Doubleday & Co., 1955.

[13]One of Velikovsky's errors of predisposition is discussed in Chapter X, page 266.

single line diagram, not a single illustration, not a single tabular form. While this is a failure in presentation, it also portrays a superficiality in basic geophysical perspectives.

(3) His Overconcern With His Critics. Velikovsky was well aware that he was writing on a highly controversial subject when he discussed catastrophism, and such would be true with or without celestial mechanics. Further, he was aware of the controversy which Copernicus anticipated from his work, *De Revolutionibus Orbeum Coelestium* (On the Revolutions of Celestial Bodies). Copernicus, rather than flee his critics and rather than face the possibility of the stake, delayed writing for twenty years and publication for thirteen more years until he knew he had not long to live. Other revolutionary thinkers such as Galileo and Price have faced similar reactions and rejections. Velikovsky anticipated the pillorying which his work would receive. And as is so often the case, mostly on irrelevant bases and by people who were hardly even conversant with the specifics of the subject matter contained therein. He therefore went to great lengths, both in manuscript preparation (with ubiquitous footnotes) and in articles and rebuttals, to both appease and please his critics. This neither retarded nor lessened the blows which were leveled at his work.

What then may be Velikovsky's mistake, beyond (1) his tendency to Freudianize his conlusions and (2) his lack of geophysical perspective. It may that his overconcern with his detractors has diverted his attentions and energies, contributing to his lack of geophysical perspective. This may be a reasonably good example of the Freudian ethic, with its overemphasis on the need for social adjustment and conformity.

DOLPH E. HOOKER. Velikovsky was concerned with establishing the ancient, historical, cosmic or celestial motifs in the 1st and 2nd millenia B.C., and then, having established them, he was interested in psychoanalyzing them. Price, Nelson, Rehwinkel, and Morris were interested in evidences of global catastrophism from the 3rd millenium B.C., and then after having demonstrated them, were interested in defending the faith, in this case reaffirming the fact of a judgment by God. Hooker follows a third pattern.

Hooker is an engineer with a strong background in geology. He considered such subjects as radial patterns of ice flow, heat exchanges, juvenile waters, atmospheric canopies, rising sea levels, and flooded continental shelves. Both Price and Velikovsky were mostly oblivious to these areas, although Morris had been concerned with these areas to a greater degree. Hooker was not concerned with the Freudianism of Velikovsky, nor was he concerned with the fundamentalism of Price. He was merely content to question the prevailing interpretations of uniformitarianism, present his homework, and make no ethical or philosophical interpretations at all. Hooker's publication was *Those Astounding Ice Ages* (1958).[14]

The contrasts between Hooker, Price, and Velikovsky are rather significant in that each person has his own, unique background, and each makes his own unique contribution. Price was concerned about catastrophism from the approach of supernatural causes and natural effects. Velikovsky was concerned about natural causes and psychological effects. Hooker was concerned about catastrophism from the approach of the need for both adequate interpretations and comprehensive approaches.

Thus we have a brief history of catastrophism, which falls into four periods. The first period extends from the time of the ancients until the time of Copernicus, and more particularly, Halley, Whiston, and Newton (circa 1700). During this period, traditions of an ancient flood upheaval were ubiquitous and firmly implanted in the roots of Western Civilization. The second period (circa 1700 to circa 1860) is from Halley, Newton, and Whiston until the time of Lyell, Darwin, and Wallace. During this period, catastrophism continued to be the dominant viewpoint of Earth history, and it was reinforced by astronomical considerations, due in part to Newton and Whiston. It was during this period that astronomy and the natural sciences began to receive systematic study.

The third period (circa 1860 to circa 1960) is the time from Lyell, Darwin, and Wallace to the recent decade. During this period the uniformitarian proposition "emerged," prevailed, and soon virtually monopolized the philosophy of Earth history. The only really significant exceptions were the handful of conservative, Protestant authors, immune to the centralization of Western education and its attendant conformity, apart from the main-

---

[14]Dolph Earl Hooker, *Those Astounding Ice Ages*, New York: Exposition Press, 1958.

stream of academic thought, accepted only within the limited sphere of the English language, the Protestant faith, and the fundamentalist philosophy.

The fourth period would appear to begin with this last decade (circa 1960). As in the past, so also it is likely in the future, Earth history will continue to be a controversial and emotional issue. Criticism, as in the past, may continue to be led by idealogues, utilizing cliches, rhetoric, ridicule, scorn and propagandistic approaches more than placid compendiums of data, systematic analyses, and careful syntheses. These human traits should be recognized and evaluated in travelling the path toward mature conclusions. This, of course, is irrespective of the quarter into which any of the conclusions may lead.

3. Summary

This chapter has endeavored to briefly sketch the history of catastrophism and uniformitarianism, along with some of the leading persons involved. (It has attempted to touch on some of the background and implications.) The reader should prepare himself to examine some glaring contradictions, perhaps the most striking paradoxes in modern thought to date. It will prove interesting to catalog the abundance of modern data which contradicts geological uniformitarianism, but it should prove at least equally as interesting to examine the degree of these contradictions. Some of the assumptions of geological uniformitarianism have been wrong to an astonishing degree when viewed from any one of many angles. Thus, kind of error is one thing, and degree of error is another thing. Both need to be measured, realized and evaluated.

Lyell, for instance, originally estimated the Ice Epoch at 1,000,000 B.C., then later revised this down to 35,000 B.C. (which is still much too ancient). Here is an acknowledged error of 96%. Are other phases of geological uniformitarianism even more erroneous in degree? This possibility will be examined in Chapter V.

James Hutton's attitudes and values were being formed when he was a lad in the Scottish highlands and when Benjamin Franklin was flying his kite in a thunder storm in America— some 200 years ago—when it was assumed that there were but six planets. Unknown was the fact that there existed an Uranus, a Neptune, or a Pluto. Unknown was the fact that Neptune at that time was briefly the outermost planet rather than Pluto. Unknown were such facts as the asteroids, the icy composition of the rings of Saturn, of the eccentric orbits of meteor streams, or of the composition of the atmosphere, oceans, and crusts of the then-known planets.

And it was Hutton, the physician, who assumed uniformitarianism. In assuming geological uniformitarianism, he assumed astronomical uniformitarianism. He must have assumed that astronomical catastrophes had never occurred to any of the planets, much less to our particular planet. This assumption is quite contrary to the mythological themes of the sky gods of ancient Britain, Greece, Egypt, Germany, India, and many other cultures.

If one accepts the notion of uniformitarianism, one must be prepared to defend the concept of a serene solar system, placid for at least the last 500,000,000 years. It is our contention that the concept of a serene solar system cannot be defended at all; it cannot be defended for the last 5,000 years (much less for the last 500,000,000 years). It is to this uniformitarianism assumption that the next chapter is directed, in particular, and the total work in general.

III chapter

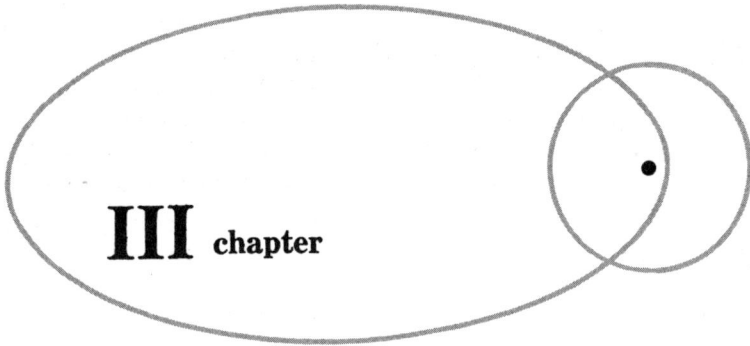

Past Celestial Catastrophies

1. Astronomy in History

UNIFORMITARIANISM has assumed that the Earth for the last several hundred millions of years, has been free from astral catastrophes. This has been an assumption of an implicit rather than an explicit kind. The reasons for this have been partly historical and partly psychological. Catastrophism has been clearly and consistently associated with Biblical doctrines. Modern humanism (not early humanism) has been clearly and consistently prejudiced against Biblical doctrines in general, and Genesis in particular. This prejudice has extended toward any ideas associated with Genesis. Catastrophism has been identified therewith. The psychological basis of this prejudice is discussed at more length in Chapter XII. The historical perspective involved is revealed in noting the relationship between Ptolemaic astronomy and uniformitarian assumptions.

This chapter will exhibit some of the shades of thought and revolutionary changes in view which occurred from the Ptolemaic system through the Copernican view to the Newtonian-Whistonian viewpoint, laying the foundation for 18th century catastrophism. Then evidences of catastrophes within our solar system shall be examined; evidence of catastrophes from beyond our solar system shall be disregarded. These evidences may indicate that one can by no means assume that the Earth was exempt from such historical cosmic conflict.

The Ptolemaic System—Claudius Ptolemy, astronomer, geographer, historian and mathematician, was among the best known of ancient scholars. He lived in Alexandria, Egypt, during the 2nd century A.D. In his work known as *The Almagest,* he compiled and summarized prevailing astronomical concepts which had been inherited from Greek thought, and through this, established what became known as the Ptolemaic System. He held that the Earth was stationary; around it revolved the Moon, Mercury, Venus, the Sun, Mars, Jupiter and Saturn in that order.

The planets revolved westward in a great circle, but also periodically retreated eastward in irregular epicycles. The description and cataloging of the epicycles became most cumbersome, particularly because the adding or subtracting of epicycles never really increased the effectiveness of the system. Nevertheless, this general system, also called a geocentric or earth-centered system, was considered authoritative by both the Islamic World and the Western World as it slipped into the dark ages of the post-Roman (Medieval) period, a time when academic activity was at a reduced level.

The geocentric proposition is an explicit theory within the Ptolemaic system. However there is also the implicit theory that celestial bodies have always maintained these circular orbits, revised only by epicycles. This presumed eternal regularity was in accordance with the assumptions of Hipparchus. This presumed eternal regularity is the second and equally significant proposition contained in the Ptolemaic system. It is an assumption, an historical assumption which disturbed Halley, Whiston and Newton much more than it did Copernicus.

The Copernican System — The Ptolemaic system was never directly questioned until the time of Nicolas Copernicus (1473-1543), and the publication of his work *On The Revolutions of the Celestial Bodies* (1543). In the Copernican system, the Sun was at the center, and was stationary. This was the heliocentric system, as contrasted with the geocentric system of Ptolemy. Around the Sun, according to Copernicus, revolved the planets in uniform and precise circles. This included the Earth and its satellite, the Moon, which revolved around the

Earth in a uniform circle. With the additional assumption that the Earth's rotation was from east to west, the daily circling of the celestial bodies was unnecessary, including their numerous epicycles; they were merely passing scenery as viewed from this rotating sphere.

The story of Copernicus is touched with the element of pathos. After much inquiring, questioning and study, both in direct observations and in searching historical astronomical records, he came to his opinion, so markedly contrary to the Ptolemaic viewpoint, which had been held for many centuries. He published his opinion in 1543, when he knew he was soon to die.

Copernicus was questioning that which was considered sacrosanct, and this new viewpoint might not be well received; indeed he knew that it would not. To say the least, this was a certain path towards controversy, and it might be the path to the stake. But following Copernicus' death, an era of increasing freedom and inquiry occurred, especially in England and Germany. Others began reviewing Copernicus' revolutionary idea.

TYCHO BRAHE—One of these was Tycho Brahe (1546-1601). Tycho adopted elements of both systems. This is curious to the modern reader; however it must be realized that, lacking a telescope, many of the calculations regarding the positions of the planets were identical in the Tychonic and the Copernican systems. Tycho adopted the view that the Earth remained at the center of the universe; the Sun and the Moon still revolved around the Earth. However, the other planets revolved around the Sun. Although this seems somewhat abstruse, nevertheless it was a major step away from the Ptolemaic system in two ways. First, it was a major revision in concept to Ptolemaic thought. And secondly, Tycho's systematic observations and accurate plottings of the progression of the planets in astronomical charts provided an operational basis for further discoveries by Kepler.

JOHANNES KEPLER—Tycho's assistant and successor was Johannes Kepler (1571-1630), who inherited the numerous records of Tycho's observations. Kepler noted many discrepancies in the Tychonic system, and adopted the Copernican system with modifications. His revisions of the Copernican system are included in his three famous laws. These laws pertained to the fact that the orbits of the planets were not circles; in all cases they were ellipses, with two foci, one of which is the Sun. He further observed that the inner planets revolve increasingly faster as they are proximate to the Sun. He further observed that the closer a planet may be to the Sun within its eccentric orbit, the faster it revolved. Further calculations showed that the squares of the periods of the various planets were proportional to the cubes of their mean distances from the Sun.

Kepler thus refined and improved the thinking of both Copernicus and Tycho. He developed principles of optics. He laid the groundwork that led to the development of calculus. He developed his three famous laws regarding planetary motions, and he laid the groundwork for Newtonian thought, and the recognition of the idea of universal gravitation. Soon, with the development of the telescope, with refinements in higher mathematics—and with the coming of such men as Galileo, Huygens and Cassini—astronomers, mathematicians and physicists firmly refuted the geocentric portion of Ptolemaic thought.

HALLEY, NEWTON AND WHISTON—Following the time of Kepler, Germany was ravaged by the Thirty Years War, and its population diminished markedly, as did its entire culture. England and France began to replace Germany as the intellectual center of the West—especially England, primarily it seems, because England offered more freedom for discussion, inquiry and publication. In the climate of England, where peace and liberty prevailed to a greater degree than on the continent, great strides in modern thought were achieved. Among the leaders of this age were three Englishmen—Edmund Halley, Isaac Newton and William Whiston—scientists and friends.

Even as Kepler went one step further than Tycho in rejecting the Ptolemaic system, so similarly Halley, Newton and Whiston went one step further than Kepler. They followed Kepler in the realization that orbits did not need to be circular, and indeed never were. Kepler showed that all orbits were ellipses. They proceeded to presume that orbits could be highly eccentric as well as mildly eccentric. They further proceeded to illustrate that in contemporary conditions, this was indeed the case, illustrated by the plotted path of comets. Further, they proceeded to form the opinion that in ancient times, larger astronomical bodies had also followed highly elliptical orbits. Thus, they rejected the second and implicit assumption in Ptolemaic astronomy, eternal regularity.

Each of these three men rejected both phases of Ptolemaic

thought. Halley (1656-1742) was the first of the three to publish (on comets) and was the first to achieve renown. Newton (1642-1727), the eldest of the three, proceeded to publish his views of planetary motion in three additional laws. This was accomplished at the suggestion of Halley, and also with a most generous offer by Halley to be responsible for the financing. Thus the *Principia Mathematica* (1687) was published, Newton became internationally famous, and England took the lead in scientific development in the Western World. With this one work, which would have gone unpublished without Halley's assistance, Newton became famous.

Halley had reviewed the astronomical records of both England and the continent. He was aware that celestial apparitions had periodically crossed the sky on historical occasions, following paths which happened to be remarkably similar to highly eccentric elliptical orbits. He began to realize that these phenomena not only possessed similar orbits, but were historically recorded in repeating cycles or periods. And when the historical cometary events of 1531 and 1607 recurred in 1682, he published his now famous prediction that this same comet would again return in 1758, and when it did, he asked posterity to remember that this prediction had been first made by an Englishman. Posterity named the comet in honor of Edmund Halley.

Halley's association with Newton was very close. Similarly Newton's association with William Whiston (1667-1752) was very close; Whiston was Newton's laboratory assistant. In addition to being versed in astronomy, mathematics and physics, Whiston, a genius like Newton, was also well versed in classical literature, classical languages (Greek, Hebrew and Latin) and in ancient history. For example, Whiston translated *The Antiquities of the Jews* by Josephus into English in 6 volumes.

Whiston came to the opinion that a large astral body, travelling in an eccentric (highly elliptical) orbit, would be sufficient to cause a great flood through tidal mechanisms. He concluded that this was the mechanism of the Biblical Flood. He further concluded that recurring events of an astral nature, involving highly eccentric orbits, were the basis for explaining later astral phenomena, cosmic traditions, celestial mythology (the sky gods) of ancient times. This included such historical descriptions as the long day of Joshua, equated to the Phaethon myth of Egypt, the Phoenix myth, the Deimos and Phobos tradition among the

Greeks, among many other traditions. He analyzed the renditions of Plutarch, Seneca, Suetonius, Virgil, Homer and many other ancient writers from the perspective that their celestial traditions were founded on historical astronomical principles. They possessed a core of truth.

In his first major work, *A New Theory of the Earth* (1696), Whiston set forth the mechanical and astrophysical theory, correlated to ancient flood dialogues, for understanding of the physical cause of the Deluge. He repeatedly attributed the physical cause to the provision of Divine Providence. This was followed by another work, *Astronomical Principles of Religion* (1717), which put greater emphasis on the scope of celestial themes in ancient mythology.[1] His works were read with much interest, especially since he was so immediately in the shadow of his senior friends, Halley and Newton.

Halley found Whiston's thesis entirely possible and historically likely. Newton, a man of stout Puritan convictions, having originally entered Cambridge to enter the ministry, also lent his enthusiasm and prestige to Whiston's remarkable effort. A few years later, in 1701, when Newton resigned his chair at Cambridge, he recommended Whiston as his successor.

The recounting of the relationship between Halley, Newton and Whiston is given in order to portray how they all rejected both the explicit and the implicit assumptions of Ptolemaic thought on geocentricity and eternal regularity. This occurred in semi-Puritan England, one generation after the era of Cromwell, Milton, Bunyan, Fox and other significant spiritual leaders. Since there was a maximum of interest in Biblical history and Biblical doctrine in this era, and with catastrophism so prominent in Biblical themes, it is apparent that here, through

---

[1] These two works of William Whiston are both available in magnified microfilm reprints, reprinted xerographically, by the Pacific Meridian Publishing Co. of Seattle. A third work by Isaac Newton, published posthumously by his sister, is also available through microfilm reprints. It is entitled *Observations upon The Prophecies of Daniel and the Apocalypse of St. John* (1733). Newton was very much a Calvinist and a Puritan. Being a scientist, he had entered into an agreement with the Royal Society to do no publishing on subjects religious during his lifetime. The Royal Society thereby hoped that theologians would not concern themselves with publishing on matters scientific. Nevertheless when Newton died, some 80% of his unpublished writings did not concern astronomy, mathematics or physics. They concerned his deep Christian faith. A very few of these have been published; many unpublished items are located at the Babson Institute.

particularly Newton and Whiston, the basis for 18th century catastrophism was reinforced.

Fossils would be found amid formations of alluvium compressed into strata. Many evidences in natural science suggesting huge watery cataclysms would be unearthed in the next 100 years. This agreed in very well with Biblical tradition and Newtonian-Whistonian mechanics. The basis for 18th century catastrophism was apparent; part of it was religious, part of it was historical, part of it was geological, part of it was astronomical. It satisfied everyone except the anti-religious or the anti-spiritual. This is to say that most but not all of the humanists of that day were pro-spiritual; examples are ubiquitous. The anti-spiritual, desiring contrary emphases and conclusions, were nonplussed. Voltaire couldn't even stand anyone to mention the Deluge.

Thus, when people began finding fossils in every province of Europe (including a location almost in Voltaire's back yard), and at virtually every elevation, the literature of Genesis was recalled. Marine fossils were found high in the Swiss Alps, the mountain backbone of Western Europe. This they attributed to the Flood. Terrestrial fossils, often of extinct forms, were found in widely separated locations, and again, this pointed to the Flood. Then, when coal miners, working in shafts below sea level, also ran into terrestrial fossils, again people recalled the Flood.

As in the case of Copernicus and Galileo, public mockery and ridicule did follow in the wake of Halley, Newton and Whiston, initiated usually by persons who hardly understood the specifics involved. However the reaction against these three Englishmen was quickly drowned in the tide of recognition; Newton was knighted and was buried in Westminster Abbey.

But then the anti-spiritual wing within humanism continued to increase, especially in the non-scientific departments of the centers of learning in Europe. This was particularly true in France, and to a lesser extent, true in England, Germany and Holland. With the anti-spiritual segment of academic figures, anything anti-Genesis was welcome; if a viewpoint seemed scientific as well, it was more than welcome.

Then Hutton proposed his theory of uniformitarianism, blithely misinterpreting and recasting evidence of catastrophic upheavals, unconcerned with narratives of ancient astral catastrophes, as recorded in Biblical and non-Biblical sources alike. Hutton bypassed conclusions of such men as Newton and Whiston, along with a host of other men emerging in the branches of natural and physical sciences. He did not concern himself with refuting their conclusions; he merely was oblivious to them.[2]

Whether consciously or unconsciously, Hutton preferred the eternal regularity which was also contained in the Ptolemaic system. This preference was more implicit than explicit; it was assumed rather than defended. Lyell's and Darwin's thought followed the same pattern. Thus there is a clear and historical parallelism between Ptolemaic thought and uniformitarian thought. Similarly there is a clear and historical parallel between ancient stories of planetary upheavals (whether Biblical or non-Biblical) and modern catastrophism.

This study proposes that the catastrophic premise is far superior to the uniformitarian assumption. Our proposition is based on a series of areas of evidence. One is the inherent validity of the Biblical record, paralleling other ancient literatures, motifs, traditions and folklores. Another is the geological record, replete with sedimentary strata, repeated universally across the several continents. But there are other evidences, of at least equal importance. They speak of ancient days when catastrophes occurred within our solar system. They speak of different kinds of astral catastrophes and of different locations of catastrophes. They hardly indicate that the Earth was exempt from such proceedings.

---

[2]James Hutton was an M.D. who, being independently wealthy, devoted vast amounts of time to the study of this new field of geology. His interest in geology was in the nature of being possessed by a hobby; others with whom he associated were academic figures and were truly professionals in that early day of geological study. Hutton became the prime figure in the early Scottish school of geology, and he confined his studies to Scotland, and particularly the Scottish Highlands. He advocated the concept of "oceans of time" for all geological events, and fortified his ideas with appeals to the rocks exclusively. This is to say he looked downward only; he did not look upward and give any consideration to astronomical data as having a possible bearing on his methodology; neither did he look backward into history and give any consideration to ancient cosmologies as having any possible bearing upon his methodology.

Hutton's error was not in his appeal to the rocks for the history of the Earth, but rather his appeal exclusively to only the rocks, and exclusively to forces which his generation had experienced and recorded. Hutton's idea of catastrophism was limited to (a) a mild earthquake, and (b) the eruption of a volcano. Hall, Lyell and Playfair followed Hutton's lead in this respect. "Nor are we to proceed in *feigning* causes when those appear insufficient which occur in our experience," said Hutton (Hutton's *Theory of the Earth*, i. p. 160, ii p. 549).

2. Past Astral Catastrophes Within the Solar System

Uniformitarianism invariably assumes, usually implicitly rather than explicitly, that our planet has never been involved in astral catastrophes, at least for the last several hundreds of millions of years, in harmony with Lyell's time chart.[3] Since Lyell has been presumed to be correct, and since no threatening catastrophe has occurred within the last several centuries, they have seen no real need to scan our solar system for contrary evidences. However contrary evidences do exist; in fact such evidences are fairly numerous. They include at least six different categories of historical astral catastrophism, evidences of which still remain in our solar system. They include:

1. Planetary Opposition (Neptune and Pluto)
2. Lunar Disarrangement or perturbation (Nereid and Triton)
3. Lunar Fragmentization (Saturn and her Rings)
4. Planetary Fragmentization (the Asteroids—Ceres, Pallas, Juno, etc.)
5. Craters (astroblemes) and an Arcuate Alignment of Mountains on the Moon
6. The Origin of Comets in the Solar System

If ancient astral catastrophism is correct, then certain elementary conclusions must follow. One refers to the position of the Earth, in a relatively inner position with respect to most of the planets, and close-in with respect to the orbits of some comets and meteor streams. The Earth, in this inner position, is among the more likely candidates for periodic visitations. The Earth's location within the solar system indicates that it would be unlikely that it would be excluded from such ancient conditions.

It appears that some substantial-sized astral bodies have travelled along highly eccentric or elliptical orbits in early times,

---

[3]Lyell's geological time chart is given in Chapter XI, p. 301. It is the policy within this book not merely to demonstrate why certain ideas or hypotheses are incongruous. This is merely replacing a poor idea with no idea. Rather the policy of this book has been to offer an alternative and better idea to what is considered a poor idea. This principle is achieved in several chapters of this work. One reflection of this principle is the proposing of a catastrophic geological time chart in Chapter XI, p. 302, immediately following the Lyellian time chart.

have crossed the orbits of the nearer-in planets, and have wrought occasional havoc in varying degrees, at varying times, and at various locations. The evidences of this belief encompasses many fields, one of which is astronomy. Following are some of the circumstances and evidences, the first of which is the historical possibility of planetary opposition, and the resultant perturbation of planetary orbits.

Planetary Interaction. When two planets approach each other, their gravities attract each other, while their magnetic fields, to a much lesser extent, also interact. The seriousness of such a clash depends on (1) the size and mass of each of the bodies, (2) the nearness of the approach, (3) the velocities of the bodies, (4) the net electrical charges of the bodies, and (5) the satellite systems which also are involved.

There is an example of this in our solar system, the most remote planets, Neptune and Pluto. Neptune's orbit has an average distance of 2,800,000,000 miles from the Sun, and an eccentricity of .009. Pluto's orbit has an average distance of 3,675,000,-000 miles from the Sun; however, it has an eccentricity of .249, the greatest among all the planets.

TABLE 1

ECCENTRICITY OF ORBITS OF
PLANETS AND SATELLITES

Planet or Satellite	Eccentricity of Orbit
Mercury	.206
Venus	.007
Earth	.017
Moon (Satellite)	.081
Mars	.093
Jupiter	.048
Saturn	.056
Uranus	.047
Neptune	.009
Nereid (Satellite)	.749
Pluto	.249
Hidalgo (Asteroid)	.656

Even though Pluto's orbit averages some 900,000,000 miles beyond that of Neptune, a considerable distance, nevertheless it approaches within 2,761,000,000 miles of the Sun once about every 250 years. It also recedes to 4,600,000,000 miles once during its year (its planetary cycle). Pluto comes closer to the Sun than Neptune once every 247.7 years. It remains the 8th closest planet for several months. This happened some 240 years ago, during the very decade that Hutton was born. It shall again recur in 1969. At this time, temporarily, we will no longer be able to say correctly that Pluto is the outermost planet.

What has happened? Nobody knows. Some believe that Pluto at one time was a satellite of Neptune.[4] They note that its rotational period, some 6½ days, is much more like that of a satellite than that of a major planet. The rotational period of the major planets (Jupiter through Neptune) varies from 10 to 16 hours—they are rotating very rapidly, particularly considering their great size. Other astronomers have noted that Pluto's characteristics are more like those of the terrestrial planets, particularly Mercury, and have disagreed about the origin of Pluto. Robert L. Forward has made the following observation:

> Apparently Pluto is a stranger which arrived in its present orbit from the regions of space. One suggestion is that it was once a moon of Neptune. There is obviously something wrong out past Uranus. It is as if Pluto had come along, interacted with Neptune, and pushed it into an inner orbit. We actually know very little about Pluto, but it is imperative that we learn more.[5]

Many astronomers suspect that something has gone wrong out beyond Uranus at some time in the past. Thus planetary interaction (Neptune and Pluto) is one of the features of the Neptune system.

---

[4]Some suspect that Pluto was at one time a satellite of Jupiter, which strayed from its original sphere. Among them is Kuiper, who considers that Hidalgo and the Trojan Asteroids as well as Pluto may once have been satellites of Jupiter. Kuiper's assumption is not widespread, however, (Gerard P. Kuiper, *Planets and Satellites*, Chicago, University of Chicago Press, 1961, p. 576.)

[5]Robert L. Forward, "Pluto, Last Stop Before the Stars," *Science Digest,* August 1962, p. 73.

Lunar Perturbation or Disarrangement. Another irregularity of the Neptune system concerns its two moons, particularly the outermost, Nereid, along with Neptune's family of comets. As illustrated in Table I the orbit of Nereid has an eccentricity of .749, which is extreme, and requires almost exactly a year (359 days) to make one revolution (one Neptune month). Nereid's motion is retrograde (east to west).

Neptune's other moon, Triton, also possesses retrograde motion. While Nereid is small, estimated at 200 miles in diameter, Triton is larger than our Moon (diameter estimated at 3000 miles and mass 1.80 larger than the Moon). Triton is the second or third largest satellite in our solar system, next to Jupiter's Ganymede and Saturn's Titan. Although Triton is larger, it is lighter than Titan. There are several satellites the size of Nereid and smaller which possess retrograde motion. There are some 17 satellites larger than Nereid, and of these, 16 possess direct (non-retrograde) motion; only Triton possesses retrograde motion. Triton is about 220,000 miles from the surface of Neptune, a distance only slightly smaller than our own Moon's distance from Earth. The fact that Triton is the only major satellite in our solar system possessing retrograde motion indeed heightens the suspicion that something has interfered out beyond Uranus.

Consider Halley's comet, one of six of the Neptune family. Halley's Comet, like Nereid and Triton, also possesses retrograde motion. Halley's comet, like most comets and planets, is an ellipse, possessing two foci. One focus or pivot is the Sun. The other is located slightly beyond the orbit of Neptune, some 3,200,000,000 miles distant. An illustration of the eccentricity of Nereid's orbit is given in figure 1. The eccentricity of Halley's Comet is illustrated in figure 2, along with orbits of three comets of Jupiter's family in figure 3.

Note the unusual features of the Neptune system: the direction of the revolution of the satellites. Neptune is the only planet known to have all satellites revolve in retrograde motion. And with Pluto, it exchanges inner positions relative to the Sun. It does seem that something historically remarkable has occurred, including

(1) causing Pluto to escape Neptune, retaining direct motion, taking the Sun for one foci and having the

second some 1,800,000,000 miles removed from the Neptune region.

(2) causing either a capture of Triton in a retrograde manner or turning it around.

(3) causing a disturbance in the orbit of Nereid, which was insufficient to allow it to successfully break out of the Neptune system.

(4) causing Halley's comet to be perturbed, in a retrograde manner out of the Neptune system, taking the Sun as one of its foci, approaching the Sun to within 55,000,000 miles, and retreating from the Sun some 3,200,000,000 miles away, taking its second foci slightly beyond Neptune's orbit.

Neptune, with a small eccentricity, is approximately 2,755,000,000 miles from the Sun and 2,680,000,000 miles from Earth at its nearest approach This is remote. Something very possibly has interfered out past Uranus. But has something also interfered in closer than Uranus? Consider the retrograde motion of Phoebe—a satellite about as big as Neried—within the Saturn system. Consider the rings of Saturn. Consider the possibility of lunar fragmentization.

Lunar Fragmentization. Perturbation and fragmentization are caused by the same principle, but at different magnitudes. Similarly, perturbations of planets and perturbations of satellites are also caused by the same principle, astral approach, only at different magnitudes. The Neptune system contains examples of historic perturbations—disarrangements of orbits, including possible planetary perturbations (Pluto), possible lunar perturbations (Nereid and Triton) and possible cometary genesis, as illustrated by the comparison between Nereid and one of Neptune's several comets, in this case Halley's.

There is a physical law dealing with the tide-raising forces of two astral bodies when they approach each other. This is known as Roche's limit. Briefly recounted, it states that when two astral bodies approach each other, the smaller one will fragmentize before collision, and the fragmentization is caused by the superior tide-raising forces of the larger of the two bodies. If the two bodies are similar in density, the smaller body will

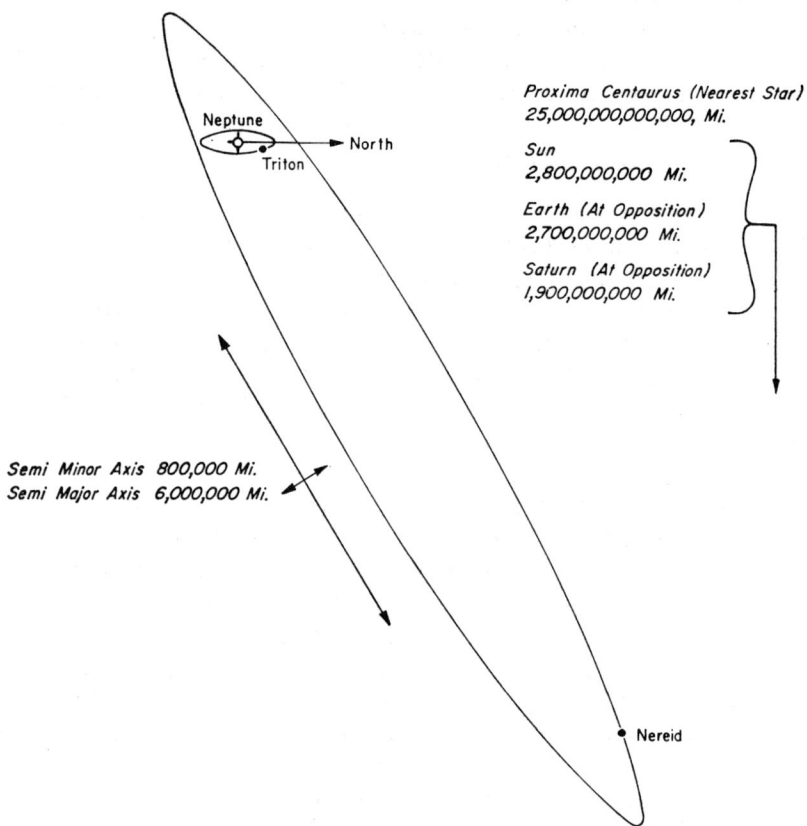

NEPTUNE'S SYSTEM
ORBITS OF NEREID AND TRITON

FIGURE 1

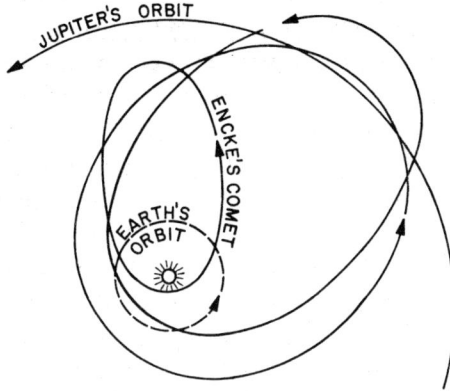

ORBITS OF THREE COMETS OF JUPITER'S FAMILY

FIGURE 2

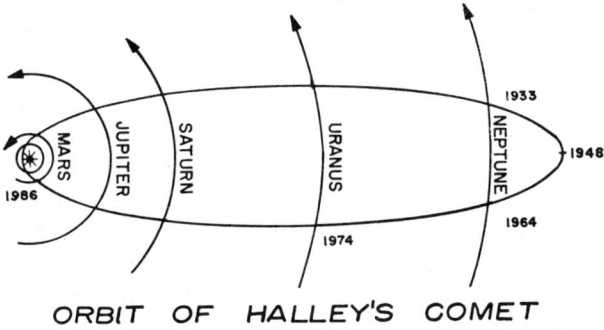

ORBIT OF HALLEY'S COMET

VARIOUS COMETARY ORBITS

FIGURE 3

fragmentize at a distance ratio of 2.44 times the radius of the larger body. This is the critical distance, in the case of Saturn, approximately 175,000 miles from its surface. The entire ring system of Saturn is 171,000 miles, 2.28 times the radius of Saturn, and entirely within Roche's limit. Taken further, such a fragmentization, if of solid material, will result in the fragments assuming orbits about the planet in accordance with Kepler's laws.

It appears that either a satellite or a wanderer within the solar system has been perturbed, and approached too close to Saturn, and fragmentized, in accordance with Roche's limit; the fragments have assumed orbits in accordance with Kepler's laws, the same laws which govern our man-made satellites.

Saturn's rings are of further interest. The outer ring is 10,000 miles wide. Next is Cassini's division, a dark band mostly void of material, about 3,000 miles wide. Inside Cassini's division is a second ring, some 16,000 miles wide. Inside this is the crape ring, the innermost, some 11,500 miles wide. Its inner edge is about 7,000 miles from Saturn's surface. The inner ring is almost transparent, and contains the least amount of material. Cassini's division is a vacant area which has occurred due to the systematic perturbations of the ring material by Saturn's nearest satellites, Mimas, Enceladus and Tethys.

In 1948, the thickness of Saturn's rings was accurately measured for the first time. They were measured to be about 10 miles thick, and 41,500 miles wide. Further data was available on the reflectivity of Saturn's rings. This then revealed the nature of the material in Saturn's rings. Previously, it had been assumed that Saturn's rings were composed of rock fragments, like the asteroids. Now it is believed that they are ice particles and not rock particles. This agrees with evidences concerning Saturn's several satellites, some of which appear to be almost pure ice (H_2O), and others of which are composed of different ices including water, carbon dioxide, cyanogen, and ammonia. Further it would appear that ices are abundant under Saturn's frigid atmosphere, ices comprising various compounds of carbon, hydrogen, nitrogen and oxygen.

Ices, in short, along with hydrogen, are the most common components of the Saturn system. Hence it is not really surprising that Saturn's rings are composed of ice; it would be surprising if they weren't. But further, this is suggestive that within the history of our solar system, at least one icy catastrophe has overtaken the planet Saturn. Could this be a clue as to the Ice Epoch which engulfed the Earth at another time in the history of our solar system? This is a subject which is reserved for Chapter VI.

What happened to Saturn? Did perturbations occur? Did they result in a particularly close approach, and fragmentation? In the case of the Neptune system, there were indications of different kinds of perturbations which included satellites (revolving around the planet), planets (revolving around the sun), and comets (revolving, in a sense, around both). But in the case of Saturn, the perturbations resulted in a greater drama than mere adjustments of orbits; they resulted in celestial fragmentations, a phenomena closely related to perturbed orbits.

In the case of the Neptune system, the distance was about 2,700,000,000 miles from the Earth at the nearest approach. Saturn averages about 900,000,000 miles from the sun (varying from 839,000,000 to 937,000,000, with an eccentricity of .056). If perturbations and/or catastrophes occurred 3 billion and 1 billion miles from the Earth, this is still rather remote. Has demonstrable catastrophism occurred closer? It was seen that lunar perturbation was one thing, and lunar fragmentization, although related, was quite a different condition. We have seen an indication (in the example of Pluto) that planets may have experienced major perturbations. But could planets also fragmentize? This question implies similar principles, but in different degrees of magnitude. Lunar fragmentization, being caused by planets, is one thing; however planetary fragmentization is quite another.

Fragmentization of a Planet. Within our solar system, there is a fairly regular ratio of increasing distances of each successive planet from the Sun. The principle also has been observed, for instance, in the satellite arrangements of the major planets. This observation parallels the planetary arrangements around the Sun. This observation of regularly increasing distances of the planets from the Sun is known as Bode's law.[6] It is con-

---

[6]There is another case, similar to Bode's law, which is also not understood, but in which a relationship, not understood, is presumed. This is the proximity of the geographical and the magnetic poles. The relationships between the geographical and magnetic poles are a subject of consideration in Chapter VI.

sidered to have a scientific or semi-scientific basis, the nature of which is not clearly understood. This was brought to public attention in 1772 by Johann Bode.

According to Bode's law, there was one vacant orbit, between Mars and Jupiter. After Bode brought this to the attention of astronomers, they turned their telescopes to this region. This was during the time Hutton was formulating his proposition of Earth uniformitarianism. Shortly the first asteroid was discovered, in 1801, named Ceres. It was observed to be some 500 miles in diameter, but irregular in albedo (reflectivity) and hence in shape. It was a fragment and not a sphere. It scintillated or varied from hour to hour in reflectivity when viewed, indicating that it rotated and possessed an irregular surface. Many more were soon discovered, also with apparently irregular surfaces.

Today, over 2,500 fragments have been identified with names and/or numbers. Estimates of the number of asteroids which are undiscovered run as high as 50,000. The circumstances surrounding this fragmentization are not known. Evidences throughout the last several decades have increasingly indicated that the asteroids are remnants of a former planet.

The asteroid fragments occur in belts, and not in an even distribution, quite similar to the material in Saturn's rings. Material in Saturn's rings has been perturbed or swept out at distances corresponding to simple fractional periods of the satellites. Cassini's division is one of these fractional distances, half the period of Mimas and one third of the period of Enceladus; also a quarter of the period of Tethys. At this region, systematic or harmonic perturbations were organized by Saturn's satellites, cleaning out these regions within Saturn's rings.

A similar condition occurs in the belt of asteroids, at distances corresponding to fractions of Jupiter's orbit. It is apparent that Jupiter has effectively perturbed the asteroids, and has cleaned out regions within the asteroid belt, at distances having a harmonic relationship to Jupiter.

A study of perturbations within Saturn's rings might indicate the date of fragmentization; however distances are too great, particles are too small, and telescopes are too inadequate to form many conclusions. However in the case of the asteroids, they are large enough and close enough to make such a study. One such study has been made, although by itself it is perhaps not conclusive. It was reported in Harper's Magazine (August 1963) as follows:

> A similar assertion that celestial disasters could have taken place when men on Earth were watching had already been made by the Harvard astronomer, Fred L. Whipple, who suggested that the swarm of asteroids which orbit between Mars and Jupiter were disturbed by a cometary collision there as recently as 4,700 and 1,500 years ago.[7]

There are traditions among ancients of explosions in the heavens. One includes a location in the zodiac known to the Romans as Cancer, or "the crab." Egyptians called Cancer a beetle, the Greeks and Chaldeans also pictured it as a crab, and the astrologically-minded Hindus called it a tortoise.[8] It is not the purpose in this chapter to introduce the cosmological themes of ancient civilizations; however it would be well to recall that in Greek legend, there were seven sisters, or planets, which were visible to the naked eye. The seventh, Electra[9] by name, could not

---

[7]Eric Larrabee, "Scientist in Collision: Was Velikovsky Right," *Harpers Magazine*, August 1963, p. 52.

[8]James S. Pickering, *1001 Questions Answered About Astronomy*, New York, Dodd, Mead & Co., 1959, p. 203.

[9]The destruction of Troy by the Greeks is both described by Homer and attributed to conflicts then going on among the contesting celestial deities who were in conflict. Among the contestants were Zeus (Jupiter), Ares (Mars), Pallas Athene (Venus) and to a lesser extent, Aphrodite (the Moon) and Hera (Earth).

Greek tradition further attributes the founding of Troy to Dardanus, whose mother was Electra, one of the seven celestial sisters, all daughters of Atlas. When Troy was destroyed, Greek mythology has it that Electra could not bear to watch, so she withdrew from the heavens, never to return.

Velikovsky has written some valuable data on this subject also, in Part II, *Worlds in Collision* (pp. 207-375). It is of interest to note that during this same century, the Hebrew fire and brimstone prophets also discussed cosmology, impending judgments, periodical in sequence. Among them are Joel and Amos, who called the nation to repentance 3 years before the great "earthquake" or "earth-shaking." Others who followed included Micah and Isaiah, the monthly prognosticator, the watchman in the night. Isaiah's cosmology is described, chapters 24-37, also II Kings 19-20. Of particular interest is a time when a blast from heaven is associated with a reversing of the sun dial and the breaching of the walls of Jerusalem, some 40 feet thick and 100 feet high, by earthquake. Habakkuk 3 among other portions of the minor prophets is remarkably descriptive.

It is of interest to note that the destruction of both Troy and the Assyrian armies (of Sennacherib) are attributed to celestial mechanics. Thus Isaiah was the prophet of crisis for the Hebrews, even as Homer was the bard of crisis for the Greeks. Some further data on this subject is presented in Chapter VIII.

bear to watch the destruction of Troy, so she withdrew from the heavens.

Here we have an example of a planet which may have fragmentized, but the matter must be considered a little further. Suggestion has been made relative to its recentness in timing (several thousand years). With regard to the rings of Saturn, in accordance with Roche's limit, Saturn was the largest participating body and the causing body. As to the asteroid fragments, which have assumed orbits around the Sun, where is the causing body? Is the tradition of Electra related?

With Neptune and Saturn, indications of astral catastrophism were reviewed, slightly less than three billion and one billion miles from the Earth respectively. The asteroids travel mostly between 200,000,000 and 250,000,000 miles from the sun (some of the asteroids have been known to pass within 10,000,000 miles of the Earth). Thus numerous asteroids are seen to be between 110,000,000 and 160,000,000 miles from the Earth (the Earth's orbit being some 90,000,000 miles from the Sun). This is an indication of astral catastrophism ten times as close as Saturn, and catastrophism of a much greater magnitude.

If it is assumed that Roche's limit and tide-raising forces were involved in the fragmentization of the asteroids (which appears logical), then we must recognize that there is no large body which today revolves between Mars and Jupiter, and which could have caused such an event. We must also recognize that there is no known astronomical or physical reason why large planet-sized bodies could not travel the same type of highly eccentric elliptical orbits which comets and meteor streams travel. This was the thinking of Halley, Newton and Whiston, long before the asteroids were discovered.

Catastrophism 3 billion miles away is one thing; catastrophism 1 billion miles away is much the same in perspective. Catastrophism 150 million miles away is something a little different; catastrophism ¼ of a million miles away would be quite a different consideration. Has such occurred? This is coming disturbingly close to our fragile terrestrial ball, as it plunges through space.

Our Scar-Faced Satellite—The Moon. Our scar-faced satellite exhibits yet other examples of astral catastrophism. The Moon has been presumed to be a solid; yet recent observations have indicated the possiblity that it may be substantially fluid like the Earth with a thin crust. Volcanic action has been reportedly observed recently. The Moon, unlike the Earth, has no atmosphere, no weather, and virtually no erosion. Ancient scars have not healed over, as they have on our planet through processes of erosion and vegetation.

The Moon has many craters, of many sizes. The craters on the Moon's side facing the Earth may exceed 30,000 in number, and range all the way from pitlets up to 150 miles in diameter.[10] The crater named in honor of Copernicus is approximately 40 miles in diameter and has an average wall height of 12,000 feet. In addition to craters, the Moon has scratches on its surface, indicative of explosions either at or near its surface, another indication of a less-than-serene history.

The fact that the Moon possesses lunar mountain ranges which duplicate the arc-like alignment of mountain systems of the Earth also enhances the totality of indications that catastrophism has indeed occurred within our solar system, and tide-raising forces within our Earth-Moon system.[11]

This chapter has already considered evidences of astral catastrophism throughout our small solar system; other kinds occur beyond our solar system. In this chapter we have considered evidences from four different regions: Neptune, Saturn, the asteroids, and our own Moon. It has considered evidences of one kind of cause (approaching astral bodies, travelling eccentric or elliptical orbits). But it has considered evidences involving two kinds of results. One result was perturbations of the orbits of the astral bodies concerned. This was a disturbance of path. The other result was tide-raising forces. This caused upwellings of fluids such as magma and/or water when at moderate intensity, but caused fragmentization when at extreme intensity. This kind of result (tide-raising forces) was an internal phenomena whereas perturbations of orbits were external phenomena. Both, however, have an identical kind of cause, but are merely different kinds

---

[10]The Moon always shows the same face toward Earth, but shows both sides towards the Sun. Recent photographs of the Moon's other side indicate that craters there are more numerous than on the Moon's earthward side. Similarly recent photographs of Mars indicate that Mars has even a higher rate of astroblemes than the Moon, possessing on occasions craters within craters within craters.

[11]The origin of lunar mountains, bearing very much on the question of the origin of our Earth's mountain systems, is discussed at length in Chapter V.

of results of different magnitudes of counter-dominating gravitational forces.

Comets. A sixth indication of astral catastrophism is in comets. Halley's Comet has already been discussed, with its two widely separated foci. Other observations relative to comets are:

(1) they tend to occur in families, with each of the four major planets possessing cometary families

(2) comets have a mortality rate—they have been observed in the process of disintegration (prime example—the comet Biela and the Bielids)[12]

(3) numerous meteor streams occur, with orbits identical to comets, and apparently are the remains of disintegrated comets

(4) comets cross orbits of nearer-in planets, and in this process are frequently perturbed

Current evidence indicates that Jupiter, our largest planet, has the largest family of satellites; it also has the largest family of comets, several dozen. Saturn, our second largest planet, has the second most numerous family of satellites and also the second largest family of comets.

What is the origin of comets?

The director of the Kiev Observatory, S. K. Vsekhsviatsky, on the basis of the rate at which the periodic comets diminish in size and brightness, argues that they are no more than a few thousand years old, and that their orbits indicate their birth by eruption from the planets, principally Jupiter.[13]

---

[12]Bielids are meteors which are associated with a meteor shower which has not been observed for a number of years. The meteors which composed the Bielid meteor shower were believed to be the debris of a comet known as Biela's comet, from the name of its discoverer. Biela's comet was observed to split in two in 1846 and vanished completely in 1865. The tiny stony and metallic fragments of which the comet's head was composed were strewn along the comet's orbit and were encountered by the Earth as a meteor shower each year for a number of years, whenever the Earth crossed the path in which the Bielids travelled. The meteor stream, however, probably because of the gravitational influence of one of the larger planets, has been scattered or diverted, and the Earth no longer has a Bielid meteor shower. Ref: James P. Pickering, *1001 Questions Answered About Astronomy*, New York, Dodd, Mead & Co., 1949, p. 203.

[13]*Eric Larrabee, loc. cit.*

It seems that the meteor streams, the fragility of comets, and the information from ancient literature indicate that comets are recent of origin. The balance of the above quotation regarding their birth by eruption, seems to be more questionable. But the mortality rate of comets is indicative of recentness. Some have suggested, as in the above instance, that they have been born within our solar system; others have suggested that they entered from beyond our solar system. In the former case, a birth is indicated; in the latter case, an entry is indicated. Both reflect astral catastrophism as a principle, with timing that may well be quite recent. Both points thoroughly contradict uniformitarian assumption, both points suggest both Earth catastrophism in mechanical principle, and Earth catastrophism in relative recentness of timing.

Summary

Examples of astral catastrophism are substantially numerous in our solar system; it is likely that existing evidences reflect only a fraction of the number of historical catastrophes. Examples have been given from four different regions of the solar system, and including some six different categories.

Our Earth is not like the huge major planets; the Earth is a small, fragile sphere,[14] spiralling through space, with a solid crust only 5 to 30 miles thick, containing oceans of hot magma within, and containing oceans of water upon it. Its crust is like a paper bag full of honey or molasses, swinging along at a rate of 1,000 miles per hour in equatorial rotation, plus 66,000 miles per hour in orbit. This neglects the galactic motion, which is much greater. The point is that our Earth's crust is markedly fragile, and this point is in contradistinction to the idea of durbility and permanence as suggested by the 19th century uniformitarians.

The fact is that the Earth has been involved in more than one

---

[14]To an aphid or a flea, an egg shell might seem quite durable. But not to a man or a predator. And to a man or a predator, the crust of the Earth seems very durable, as it indeed seemed to Hutton. However, when viewed from the enormous magnitudes of a plunging asteroid or a satellite-sized celestial body, the crust of the Earth, some 5 to 30 miles thick, is relatively insignificant. Considered in terms of these conditions, the Earth's thin crust is quite fragile, though flexible.

astral catastrophe in terms of multiplied thousands of years ago. The catastrophes have involved both counter dominating gravities (tide-raising forces) and discharging magnetic fields.

This study does not postulate that the Biblical Flood was the only one of such catastrophes, nor does it propose that the Biblical Flood was either the first or the last of them; it merely proposes that it was most severe.

We will now discuss the specifics of the Biblical Flood as given in the Genesis account. We shall consider its sudden engagement and disengagement (initiation and termination). We shall consider its tidal nature. This does not necessarily mean that the reader needs to support the spiritual implications in the Flood story; on the other hand this too may be a good idea.

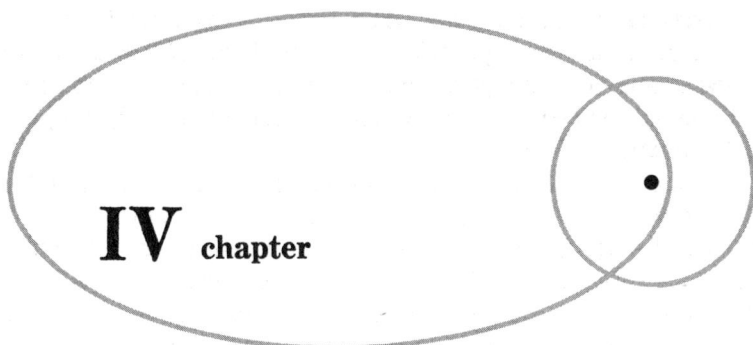

IV chapter

The Tidal Nature of the Biblical Flood

SO OFTEN THE FLOOD has been pictured as having been caused only by excessive rain. There is no better example of this than Josephus, who, never imagining any other possibility, commented as follows:

> When God gave the signal, and it began to rain, the water poured down forty entire days, till it became fifteen cubits higher than the earth; which was the reason why there were no greater number preserved, since they had no place to flee to. When the rain ceased, the water did just begin to abate . . .[1]

Modern humanistic thought had concluded that rain could never cause a flood of global magnitude such as this. Either it did not occur, or it was merely a local event, a rain-swollen flooding river system. Many have followed the notion that it may have been caused by a period of prolonged cyclonic storms. This view of course is in perfect harmony with uniformitarian thinking. Because uniformitarian views are so widely held and so infrequently challenged, the local flood concept is commonly held.

---

[1]Whiston, William (translation), *Flavius Josephus; Antiquities of the Jews,* Bridgeport, 1828, M. Sherman, p. 85.

Were the uniformitarian viewpoint correct, then the idea of a localized flood appears very logical. If the catastrophic point of view is correct, with an extra-terrestrial gravitational field approaching and affecting the Earth, then the global idea of a tidal Flood also appears very logical. If the Flood had been a local phenomenon, then any flooding must be based on climatological principles, which means rain. If the Flood were a global phenomenon, and of an immense magnitude, then oceans, gravities and tidal mechanisms were inevitably involved.

Now if the Flood had been a local phenomenon, then the accounts of an overwhelming flood might presumably have come in from one or two particular regions or localities of the Earth. Yet the accounts of an ancient Flood of continental proportions persist in over 40 different cultures in each hemisphere.[2]

Similarly, water-lain strata occurs on a global scale, and at almost every elevation, both above and below mean sea level. These facts remain indeed unexplained if a local flood concept is to be accepted. Evidences of a World Flood of continental dimensions occur both in the traditions of man and in the fossils and strata of his terrestrial domain. Furthermore, evidences of former gravitational interactions and tidal responses occur among other planets.

If the Flood were merely a minor climatological event of local significance, then nothing in all of ancient literature is more curious than the scope and the sweep of the details in this particular account of the Flood given in Genesis (Chapters 6-9). The ideas, implications, and perspectives contained in this account are very thought-provoking. It teaches that the rain was associated with the Flood, but not that rain was the primary cause of the Flood. The two phenomena were merely simultaneous.

Before we enter into a discussion of the particulars of the Biblical Flood, the validity of the Genesis account warrants comment. Here we may have an eye witness account, related and handed down, not unlike eye witness accounts found later in Genesis.[3] Later examples include Joseph's experience in Potiphar's house in Egypt, Abraham's experience on Mt. Moriah, and Isaac's

---

[2]Further discussion on ancient flood traditions is given in Chapter VIII, pp. 164 and 165.

[3]It is noted in the Genesis account of chronologies that there were nine generations between the Deluge and Abraham. Shem's age is given as 98 years at the time of the Flood. He lived a total of 600 years, continuing on some 500 years after the Flood. His 9th generation descendant, Abraham, mi-

courtship of Rebekah. A fourth illustration is the Flood story, with its precise and detailed account.

Note the manner of the logging of the events. Note also the details concerning the pitching of the ark (Genesis 7:17), the details of the dove (Genesis 8:7), the raven (Genesis 8:8), the olive branch (Genesis 8:11), and the rainbow (Genesis 9:13). Here we have a near eye witness account which has been preserved. Other ancient accounts of this catastrophe seem to have been preserved with much less precision.[4] On this basis, details

grated from Ur of the Chaldees to Palestine approximately 400 to 500 years after the Flood. Reference, Figure 25, p. 215.

Here in Palestine, one of Abraham's early experiences was his meeting with the ancient and venerable Melchisadek, to whom he tithed, and from whom he received the communion emblems. Who was the ancient Melchisadek? Henry Halley comments as follows in his Bible Handbook (Henry H. Halley, *Halley's Bible Handbook*, 1959 (22nd Edition), Chicago, Illinois).

> "Priest-King of Salem (Jerusalem). Hebrew tradition says that he was Shem, survivor of the Flood, who was still alive, earth's oldest living man, priest, in the patriarchal age, of the whole race. If so, it is a hint, that, this early, right after the Flood, God chose Jerusalem to be the scene of Human Redemption . . ."

If Halley's suspicion is correct, or nearly correct, and the ancient, venerated Melchisadek is also either Shem, or possibly Arphaxad, Salah or Eber, then Abraham's source material concerning conditions both prior and during the Flood become increasingly important. Undoubtedly Abraham, as the tither, did more than merely receive communion from Melchisadek. Undoubtedly they communed concerning their understanding of God as Creator and Lord. Undoubtedly they communed about the ancient conditions and about the then current spiritual state of the human race, the divergence of migrations of patriarchal families, and the maintaining of satisfactory historical accounts of these ancient events. Abraham's source, and renditions then became source material for Moses, who compiled Genesis.

[4] They include two ancient Assyrio-Babylonian stories—that of Ammizaduga as preserved by Asshur-bani-pal, and that of Berosus, as given in Eusebius. They include the Persian version, as preserved in the Zendavesta, and apparently also a second version has been preserved from ancient Persian folklore. A Syrian version exists in the Dialogues on the Syrian Goddess, as given by Lucian, and similar to both the account of Berosus and the Greek account, as given by Plato and particularly Appolodorus. In this account, Deucalion and Pyrrha double as Noah and his wife. Manetho, the Egyptian historian, related a Flood tradition. Livingstone, the African missionary, found a tribe called the Bermegai, relatively highly civilized, in Africa, which possessed a Flood story. Ovid gives a Roman version. The Rig Veda gives a Deluge legend in India. In China, the Deluge story includes the reputed founder of the Chinese civilization who, along with his family, escaped a deluge. Other parallel legends occur in many other cultures spread from Iceland eastward to Polynesia, and from Alaska southward to Tierra del Fuego, and the Strait of Magellan. For further reference, see Byron Nelson, *The Deluge Story in Stone*, Appendix II, (Minneapolis, Augsburg Publishing House, 1931).

can be gleaned from the Genesis story from which valid conclusions and implications may be drawn, if coupled with an adequate geophysical background.

The proposition herein set forth is that the Flood was caused by tidal movements of the oceans, tides in sub-continental proportion. Rain was also involved, but its ratio was the proverbial drop in the bucket. By carefully considering the several facets of the Flood story, and by then weighing the following reasons in tandem against the uniformitarian presupposition, a strong position may be achieved to draw firm and significant conclusions.

1. Location of the Grounded Ark: Its Elevation

And the flood was forty days upon the earth; and the waters increased, and bare up the ark, and it was lift up above the earth. And the waters prevailed, and were increased greatly upon the earth; and the ark went upon the face of the waters. And the waters prevailed exceedingly upon the earth; and all the high hills, that were under the whole heaven, were covered.
And the ark rested in the seventh month, on the seventeenth day of the month, upon the mountains of Ararat.
(Genesis 7:17-20;8:4, King James)[5]

The record of the Hebrews, corroborated by other Middle Eastern traditions, is that the Ark was grounded high in the Ararat-Caucasus-Elburz region. The elevations in this complex rise to 17,000 feet at their greatest heights. Much of the elevation is 8,000 and 10,000 feet above mean sea level. In fact, the topography of this region may be a clue as to the magnitude of the tides of the Flood era.

This region of Armenia today is controlled politically by

---

[5]Throughout this volume, various versions of the Bible have been used, particularly since clarity in language is essential in some places which does not occur in the older translations. Among the versions used are the following:
  1. Amplified
  2. Goodspeed
  3. King James
  4. New Catholic (Douay)
  5. Revised Standard
When a specific version is cited in a chapter, all of the quotations following in the chapter are from the same version unless otherwise cited.

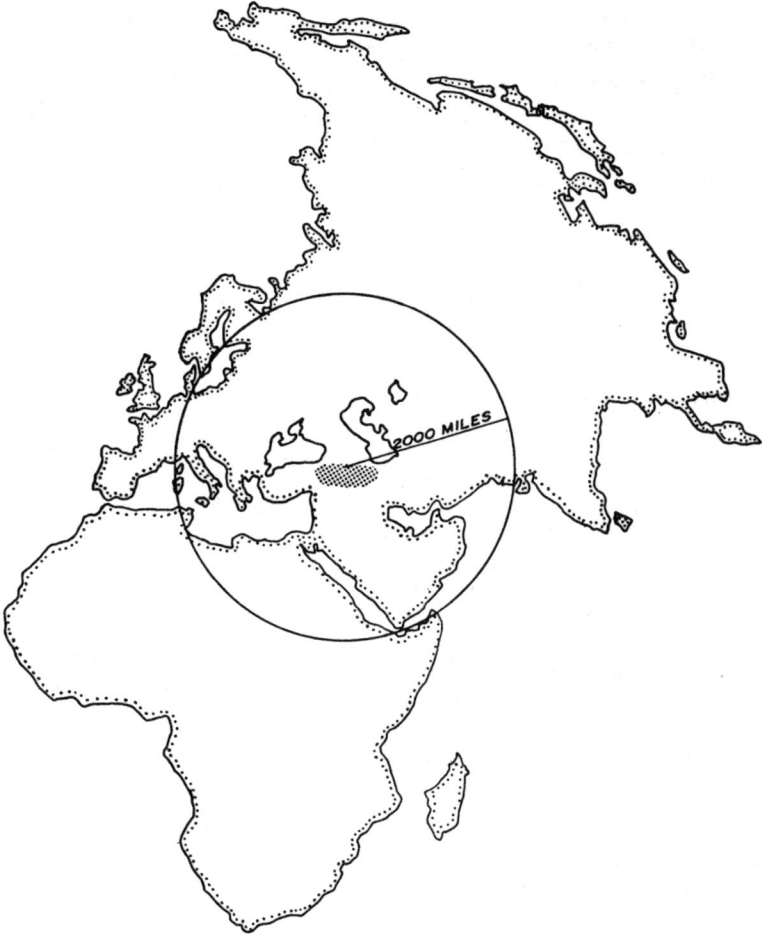

The Heartland Region of the Eastern Hemisphere

FIGURE 4

three nations: Iran, Russia and Turkey. Here are a number of interior basins which have no outlet to the sea. They contain brackish lakes, three of which are rather large, inland lakes. These lakes represent the lower elevations in this region, and they can be considered as the lowest or the minimum elevation at which the ark was grounded.

The largest of these three lakes is Lake Urmia, in Iran. It is 4,364 feet above sea level. The next largest is Lake Van, in Turkey, at an elevation of 5,260 feet. The third is Lake Gokcha (Lake Sevan), in Russian Armenia. It is at an elevation of 6,345 feet above mean sea level.

With the bulk of the topography in this region being above 8,000 feet in elevation, it is not difficult to suppose that the grounding of the Ark was at an elevation approaching 10,000 feet above sea level.[6] The ultimate resting place of the Ark has not been finally identified. Josephus reported that in his time, it had been scavenged for fetishes.[7]

The language in Genesis Chapter 7 refers to waters which increased . . . increased greatly . . . and prevailed upon the whole (visible) Earth. The waters flooded valleys, plains, plateaus and apparently mountains. This is indicative that counter-gravity or a second gravity acting contrary to the gravity of the Earth, was involved in these tidal upheavals.[8]

Tidal conditions and effects of a low magnitude are well-known, for our Moon and Sun cause modest tides on ocean beaches. Tides have the effect of both raising and lowering waters and of both raising, moving and grounding driftwood at

---

[6]The altitude and topography of the Ararat region is indicative of the elevation of the final resting place of the Ark. This is the basis for assuming tides of at least 10,000 feet, and perhaps 15,000 feet, both above and below mean antediluvian sea level.

[7]Whiston, William: Josephus p. 86.

[8]The following is contained in a letter to the author from Mr. A. James Wagner, meteorologist. "An interesting observation about which you may not be aware is that the word translated 'continually' in the King James, with reference to the retreat of the Flood waters, may be more literally rendered by the phrase 'in going and coming.' This is interesting and helpful to our belief that the main force of the Flood was tidal in nature." Dated 12/12/63, Dr. Wagner continues: "The discussion of the grounding of the Ark on the high mountain hedge of the Ararat-Caucasus group offers strong evidence of the tidal nature of the Flood. I'll bet this observation will stir up quite a storm."

or near high tide. The Ark is viewed as a piece of driftwood, an oversized barge—floating on tidal movements of subcontinental magnitude.

In such a picture the Ark would logically be stranded or grounded at or near high tide. In such a picture, it would logically be caught and grounded within a topographical barrier such as a hedge or ridge of mountains.

Had the Flood been caused by rain exclusively, the Ark (something like the Queen Mary in dimension but not in shape) would not have been floated at all. Yet had it been floated, its direction of flotation would have been downward, not upward, and toward sea level rather than toward a high group of mountains. Thus both the altitude and the rough topography, the mountainous hedge, are both significant in pointing to the tidal nature of the Biblical Flood.

Some uniformitarian-minded thinkers have considered the floating of the Ark to the Ararat Mountain region as an utter impossibility, for rain just does not accomplish this sort of thing. This is true, but the magnitude of tidal movement could have accomplished it. For instance, the tidal sweep which swamps a sand castle at the sea shore could also swamp the Alps, Andes, Pyrenees or Ararats. It is only a matter of magnitude or degree; it is not a matter of lack of mechanism. This again is a reflection of the intensity of the gravitational conflict which must have prevailed.

So far, we have noted the location of the grounded Ark with respect solely to its elevation and rough topography in the Ararat Mountains. Of equal importance is the location of the Ark with respect to its *Heartland Location*.[9]

---

[9]Mackinder, an early 20th century English geographer, specialized in a field variously called geopolitics and/or political geography. He coined the term "heartland of Eurasia." He considered this to be the region from the Caspian and Aral Seas northward and northeastward, embracing Eastern Russia, Interior and Northern Siberia, Kazakhstan Turkestan and Uzbekistan. This, he posited, was the one area on our planet which was immune to sea power and also had a pivotal location relative to the series of nations on rim of the Eurasian land mass.

Mackinder's view was posited in marked contradistinction to that of Admiral Mahan, an American naval officer and naval historian. Mahan viewed the oceans of the world as the pathways of commerce and of military movement when necessary. He viewed control of the North Atlantic Ocean and the North Sea as essential to the success of any nation, and posited that the nation which controls these waters with seapower will, more than any other, control the destinies of the nations of the world.

Mackinder,a professor at the London School of Economics, disagreed

2. Location of the Grounded Ark:
Its Heartland Location

The Ark was not floated down the Tigris or Euphrates and out into the Persian Gulf or the Indian Ocean. It was not floated down the Nile, Jordan, Indus or Volga, nor did it float out into the sea, be it the Black, the Caspian, the Mediterranean, the Persian Gulf, the Red Sea or any of the oceans. Neither was it stranded on a low-lying range of coastal hills. Moreover, it was not grounded on an interior plateau, such as the Anatolian or

with Mahan, who viewed the broad, waterless deserts as barriers, along with the numerous rugged interior mountain ranges, hindrance to transportation and agriculturally unimportant. Mackinder, on the other hand, viewed this region as unsusceptible to sea power and the nations possessing sea power. He also viewed this area as having a pivotal location relative to the many nations around the Pacific Ocean, the Indian Ocean and the Middle East. What Mackinder considered pivotal, Mahan considered a barrier. It is also of interest to note that Mahan, an American, advocated the British principle of sea power, while Mackinder, a Britisher, admired the geopolitical area of the Soviet Union.

Within the recent generation, another outspoken and compelling thinker, Colonel DeSeversky, a refugee Russian, has again disagreed, maintaining that air power—rather than heartland location or sea power—is the critical element wherein the destinies of nations will be determined. (It seems ironic that DeSeversky, a Russian by birth, admires American geopolitical position, while Mackinder, a socialist-minded English intellectual, admires Russian geopolitical position, and Mahan, an American admiral, admired English geopolitical position. It is almost as if the grass seems greener on the other side of the fence.)

Each of course is correct within a limited perspective of technology and time. It is of interest to note that the paramilitary guerilla actions of Communists in Asia, among the nations on the rim of the Eurasian land mass, is an application of Mackinder's geopolitical thinking, inasmuch as this military strategy gives the Communists the greatest number of advantages coupled with the fewest number of disadvantages.

Mackinder's geopolitical consideration of the *Heartland of Eurasia* is in marked contrast to our geophysical consideration of the *Heartland of the Eastern Hemisphere*. Mackinder considered the Arctic Ocean as geopolitically unimportant; we consider it as geophysically important. Mackinder considered the land mass of Africa as unimportant in location and unimportant in military potential; hence he limited his thinking to the "heartland of Eurasia." In contrast we consider the Eastern Hemisphere geophysically, and geophysically Africa is an important appendage to the land mass of Eurasia. Therefore we use the term *Heartland of the Eastern Hemisphere* which includes one continent and one ocean which Mackinder omitted.

It is within this *Heartland Region of the Eastern Hemisphere*, the vicinity of Armenia with the Ararat and Elburz mountains, where the Ark was grounded. This location is hardly a maritime one, to say the least; yet it is the region of the grounding of the most famous barge of ancient times. This "heartland" location is held to be a signal factor in understanding the cause of the Flood and the nature of the Flood. The *Heartland* factor is to be evaluated independently from the mountainous and altitudinous topography wherein the Ark was grounded. Both factors strongly suggest tidal mechanisms, tides of subcontinental magnitude.

Iranian Plateaus. The Ark was not stranded at or even near any maritime location.

Rather, the Ark was stranded in the second highest complex of mountains in the Eastern Hemisphere, an area second in elevation only to the Mighty Himalayas and its associated ranges. This interior region of Eurasia has been termed by early political geographers as the "Heartland" region of the Eastern Hemisphere.

Consider, therefore, the broadness of the Flood. The Eurasian land mass is the largest one on the face of our planet. It comprises about 57% of the land area of the world, including its African appendage. The Ark was grounded in the heart of this region: about 2,000 miles from the Arabian Sea, an arm of the Indian Ocean; about 2,500 miles from the Barents Sea, an arm of the Arctic Ocean; some 3,000 miles from the Atlantic Ocean; and some 5,000 miles from the Pacific Ocean.

The fact that the Ark was grounded in this heartland location similarly attests to the perspective that the Flood was tidal in nature. Had the Flood been caused by atmospheric precipitation, the Ark would have been floated downward and in response solely to the gravity of the Earth. Furthermore, any rain which fell would have been concentrated in maritime regions.

Noah has sometimes been referred to as a North Dakota sailor. His boat was a barge, and not a ship or a vessel. It apparently was not constructed at a maritime location, and it was not constructed for sailing; it was constructed for floating. Consider the Ark, rising and bounding on tidal waves of subcontinental proportions, by the following illustration of the humble tumbleweed.

On the high plains of Northern Montana in late summer, the tumbleweeds become very dry. They break off and are picked up by the hot August breezes. They roll and bounce, and bounce and roll, until they finally become caught, perhaps on a barbed wire fence, perhaps in some sage brush, or a snow fence. So it must have been with the Ark, which, like an oversized piece of driftwood or a tumbleweed, bounded along in subcontinental tides until it was caught in a topographical fence, the mountains of Ararat. This is one of the numerous reflections of the magnitude of the Flood. It is also a reflection of the global scope of the Flood catastrophe. Let us briefly consider the possibility that significance may occur in the sequence of the logged events.

3. The Logging of the Sequence of Events

Table 2 lists chronologically many significant observations of the Flood cataclysm. The record states that it rained 40 days and 40 nights (Genesis 7:17), but that the waters increased for 150 days (Genesis 7:24). Study the phrasing of the Genesis account of the action of the waters:

> The flood continued forty days upon the earth. The waters increased and bore up the ark and it rose above the earth. The waters rose higher and increased greatly on the earth; so that the ark floated on the surface of the waters. The waters rose higher and higher on the earth so that all the highest mountains everywhere under the heavens were covered. (Genesis 7:17-19, New Cath. Ed.)

Various parts of the Genesis account yield the following phrasing concerning the action of the waters:

> "The fountains of the great deep burst forth." (Genesis 7:11)
> "The waters increased and bore up the ark and it rose above the earth." (Genesis 7:17)
> "The waters rose higher and increased greatly on the earth. (Genesis 7:18)
> "The waters rose higher and higher on the earth so that all the highest mountains everywhere under the heavens were covered." (Genesis 7:19)
> "The waters rose on the earth one hundred and fifty days." (Genesis 7:24)
> "The waters subsided . . ." (Genesis 8:1)
> "The fountains of the deep and the floodgates of the heavens were closed." (Genesis 8:2)
> "The waters steadily receded from the earth. They subsided at the end of one hundred and fifty days." (Genesis 8:3)
> "The waters continued to recede until the tenth month." (Genesis 8:5)

The phrases "the waters increased greatly," "the waters rose higher," and "the waters steadily receded" are of particular interest since daily increasing and decreasing of waters is the normal description of the tidal phenomena. Tides occur twice every $24\frac{1}{2}$ hours on the Earth's surface. Tides both increase and decrease continually. Hence, the waters may have been rather accurately described as increasing continually.

Let us now examine the implications resting in the fact that sedimentary strata, in parallelism, occur on all continents.

TABLE 2

THE CHRONOLOGY OF THE BIBLICAL FLOOD

Sequence of Events	*Span of Time*
There were forty days during which the rain fell (7:12)	40 days
Throughout another 110 days the waters continued to rise, making 150 days in all (7:24)	110
The waters occupied 74 days in the "going and decreasing." This was from the 17th day of the seventh month to the 1st day of the tenth month (8:5)	74
Forty days elapsed before Noah sent out the raven (8:6-7)	40
Seven days elapsed before Noah sent out the dove for the first time (8:8). This period is necessary for reaching the total and is given by implication from the phrase "other seven days" (8:10)	7
Seven days passed before sending out the dove for the second time (8:10)	7
Seven days more passed before the third sending of the dove (8:12)	7
Up to this point 285 days are accounted for, but the next episode is dated the 1st of the first month in the 601st year. From the date in 7:11 to this point in 8:13 is a period of 314 days; therefore an interval of 29 days elapses	29
From the removal of the covering of the ark to the very end of the experience was a further 57 days (8:14)	57

TOTAL   371 days

Reprinted from The New Bible Commentary by Davidson, Stibbs and Kevan, Wm. B. Eerdmans Publishing Co., 1953. p. 85.

4. World-Wide Circumstances of Sedimentary Strata

With this possible tidal mechanism, immense pressures are realized, which become successive, twice daily as the Earth rotates, even as layers of sedimentary strata are successive. Had there been tidal conditions, with water 5,000 to 10,000 feet above sea level, pressure on the Earth's crust would have amounted to perhaps 300 tons per square foot, or 2 tons per square inch.[10] This would be sufficient pressure to compress any kind of sediment, be it sand, mud, ash or other. It would be sufficient pressure to metamorphise any of these kinds of deposits into successive strata, intermixed with occasional trapped fauna or flora, turning them not into decayed debris slowly, but turning them into suddenly and perfectly preserved fossils.

Layers of sedimentary rock, successive layer upon layer, are found on every continent, and they appear to have been laid down by immense volumes of water, and subsequently compressed by great pressures. This phenomenon, together with other data presented in this and successive chapters, makes an impressive case indeed for the possibility of global catastrophes, and of oceanic tides of subcontinental proportions and of great elevations above mean sea level.

A fifth consideration in the geophysical nature of the Flood becomes apparent as one notes the phrase "fountains of the deep," the antediluvian oceans.

5. The Fountains of the Deep (Oceans)

And in the six hundredth year of Noah's life, in the second month, and the seventeenth day of the month, the same day were all the *fountains of the great deep* broken up, and the windows of heaven were opened. (Genesis 7:11, Goodspeed)

The *fountains also of the deep* and the windows of heaven were stopped, and the rain from heaven was restrained; and the waters returned from off the earth continually . . . (Genesis 8:2-3, Goodspeed)

This phrase seemingly refers to the great oceans and seas which cover the bulk of the Earth's surface (72% in our age). Both the fluid atmosphere (rain) and the fluid hydrosphere (oceanic tides) appear to have been simultaneously deranged, but the surging, sweeping volumes of the oceanic tides were the primary cause of the Flood. It must be noted that if all the rain that the atmosphere could hold were to condense immediately, the volume of accumulated precipitation would be less than

[10]The estimate of compression at 2 tons per square inch, or 300 tons per square foot during the crescendoes of the chaotic Deluge period are caclculated as follows. Water is about 62 lbs. per cubic foot. 10,000 cubic feet of water in vertical position results in 620,000 lbs. of pressure. 620,000 lbs. = 310 tons of pressure per square foot, which is slightly over 2 tons per square inch.

12 inches at any one location.[11] In fact, if the atmosphere were composed of pure water vapor, and this suddenly condensed, it would amount to about 30 feet of water—not enough for the scope of flood which is under consideration. This would hardly be sufficient to float a small barge, much less a large one, over coastal hills and interior plateaus.

In the oceans of the Earth there are more than 200,000,000 cubic miles of water. This is enough to drown about ¾ of the present surface of the Earth, and some of it is drowned to depths of 10,000 and 20,000 and 30,000 foot depths. If, in the event of a major conflict of gravity within the Earth-Moon system, these waters could be in tidal movement. With their volume, they could indeed cause immense surges, ample to drown even the largest of the continents. The rinsing action caused by the accompanying rains would contribute perhaps only 1/10 of 1% at most to the total Flood. Thus, the breaking up of the fountains of the deep must account for the major volume of the water involved in the Flood—some 99.9% of the water.[12]

6. The Behavior of the Animals

They, and every beast after his kind, and all the cattle after their kind, and every creeping thing that creepeth upon the earth after his kind, and every fowl after his kind, every bird of every sort. And *they went into the ark,* two and two of all flesh, wherein is the breath of life. (Genesis 7:14-15, King James)

Another significant part of the Flood story is the seeming apprehension of the animals just prior to the Flood catastrophe. Animals often have been observed behaving abnormally just prior to a natural catastrophe. It is as though they can comprehend or sense beforehand foreshocks of impending earthquakes.

For example, on the afternoon previous to the eruption of Mt. Pelee on Martinique Island in 1902, an old sheepherder had observed his sheep in unusual commotion. He made his way to

[11]The total weight of the atmosphere is equal to about 30 feet of water. The percentage of water vapor in the atmosphere varies between 0 and 1½%. This is about 5 inches of water.

[12]The author's estimate of the ratio of importance of the rain to the tides in the cataclysm is about 1:2500. The rain contributed perhaps .04 of 1% of the water, and the oceans, the "fountains of the deep" contributed 99.96% of the water. The rain was a rinsing action; the tides were a washing action; both were simultaneous.

the mayor of St. Pierre and warned that something dreadful was about to happen. The mayor did not take the muttering sheepherder very seriously; however on the following day between 30,000 and 40,000 people were engulfed in pumice.

In September 1923, a severe earthquake rocked Honshu, the main island in the Japanese chain. An old Japanese priest had forecast this earthquake upon observing that a certain species of fish had been acting abnormally for months. From tradition, he knew that earthquake activity was imminent in this unstable region, known as the "Pacific Rim of Fire" where both earthquake and volcanic activity are relatively frequent.

Again, when the great earthquake occurred in Madison County, Montana, in 1959, rangers observed that birds evacuated the region on the day prior to the seismic event.

Animals spoken of in the Genesis account, domestic and probably wild ones as well, entered the Ark seven days prior to the Flood—seven days before the rain commenced and surging waters from the oceans began to heave. Apparently there were significant forewarnings, microvibrations or minute foreshocks of the coming catastrophe, seismic in nature.

If this suspicion is correct, then it would substantiate the principle that the Flood was tidal in perspective, the reaction to a gravitational conflict, an astral intruder being the mechanical cause. Oceans would begin to heave and surge in tidal movement; so also would the fluid magma (lava) within the crust of the Earth begin to surge, for all fluids would respond to the gravitational conflict. The surging and heaving of the more immense seas of magma within the crust would more than amply cause foreshocks, merely a preview to the approaching chaos.

We have considered a series of circumstances relative to the Flood. One or two alone would not be strongly indicative of the tidal nature of the Flood. But together, these six perspectives begin to be impressive; in fact, they are merely an introduction to the panorama of evidences which reflect this astrophysical basis for understanding the Flood. Had there been tides in the oceans above the Earth's crust, there must also have been greater tides of magma beneath the Earth's crust, rumbling around, heaving up and occasionally thrusting through the Earth's thin and fragile crust. With the great mass, weight and constriction involved, these subterranean tides of magma must have been immense in magnitude. It is to this subject that Chapter V is directed.

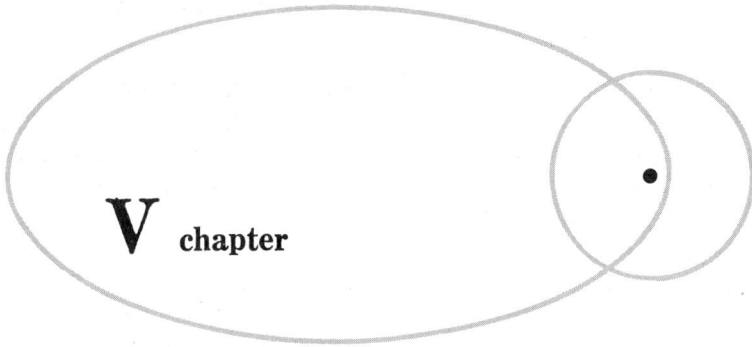

Orogenesis: The Cause of Global Mountain Uplifts

1. Geophysical Perspective of Our Small Sphere

This study contends that there was a universal, global Flood, and that it was caused by the interacting gravities of two astronomical bodies of planetary dimensions—the Earth and the astral visitor. Since the Earth possesses two fields, one gravitational and the other magnetic, there were two kinds of celestial conflict with the intruder. It appears that in one phase of this conflict, oceans heaved and ebbed in tides to a magnitude of 5,000 and perhaps 10,000 feet above and below mean sea level.

The Earth is a triple fluid; not merely a single fluid. Each of the three fluids would be in tidal upheaval simultaneously. The Earth has some 200,000,000 cubic miles of water, but this is but a drop in the bucket compared to its volume of semi-fluid magma (or lava). The Earth has a thin crust, varying between 5 and 30 miles thick. [1,2] This is quite thin when compared to the Earth's

---

[1]George Gamow, *Biography of the Earth,* New York: Viking Press, 1960, p. 85.

[2]Adrian E. Scheidegger, *Principles of Geodynamics,* Berlin: Springer-Verlag, 1963, p. 50.

diameter, about 8,000 miles. The ratio of thickness between the Earth's crust to the magma varies between 1:300 and 1:1600, something like an onionskin to an onion.

The Earth contains about 200 times as much water as atmosphere, mass to mass. The Earth contains about 1,000 times as much magma as ocean, volume to volume. And the magma is heavier. Thus there is about 5,000 times as much magma as ocean, ton by ton, or kilogram by kilogram. This gives an idea of comparisons. If we conclude that tidal activity of the oceans resulted in some 2 tons of pressure per square inch on the external side of the Earth's surface, what would be the force or the upthrust of the vastly greater magma upon the inside of the Earth's crust or skin?

The upward thrust of the magma upon the inner side of the Earth's crust must have been titanic due to the following three conditions:

1. Magma exceeds the oceans in volume (1000:1) and mass (5000:1)

2. Any tide, when constricted, will exhibit an amplification of force.

3. The direction of the thrust of the magma will be deflected by the centrifugal force of the Earth, plus any gravitational drag induced thereon.

The Volume of the Magma. Based on spherical volumes, with the diameter of the Earth about 8,000 miles, it can be seen that the oceans of magma are infinitely greater than the relatively thin and shallow pools of water lying on top of the Earth's crust. Hence the tidal upheaval from within the Earth must have been very much greater than the tidal upheaval on the Earth's surface, involving her relatively minute oceans. Therefore upheaval or thrust internally and compression externally must have been simultaneous; only their proportions were different. With this volume of magma in tidal upheaval, the Earth's crust acted something like a bellows. And the Earth's relatively shallow oceans merely washed around as the Earth's crust heaved and sagged.

The Flow of Fluids and Constriction.[3,4] Any fluid, when constricted, will exhibit a greater thrust. With respect to tides, two good examples are found in the Bay of Fundy (Nova Scotia) and the Thames Estuary (London). Here tidal forces are gathered and amplified due to the particular latitudes and the particular coastal physical geographies. Here tidal forces are amplified to an extent of being some 15 to 25 times as high as they are in the open oceanic locations of lower latitudes.

The fluid ocean is unconfined; the fluid magma is completely confined. This affects the gathering or concentration of thrust in certain belts or regions. Also the nature of water as a fluid is somewhat different than magma as a fluid. At high temperatures, magma becomes increasingly fluid, and at lower temperatures, it becomes increasingly viscous.

Iron, for instance, at surface temperatures, is brittle. However at higher temperatures, iron becomes as flexible as a leather belt. At yet higher temperatures, in its molten form, it will easily pour. At the high temperatures inside the Earth, magma has a nature which is neither exactly like a fluid, nor exactly like a solid. It is described as "plastic-like." It is something like asphalt, beeswax, honey or molasses. It will flow, but at retarded rates.

The Direction of Thrust. Due to the centrifugal force of a rotating sphere, angular momentum occurs along with the force of gravity. The Earth is an oblate sphere with the polar diameter being some 27 miles shorter than the equatorial diameter. This bulge is due to the speed of the Earth's rotation. The Earth's crust, at the equator rotates a little over 1,000 miles per hour, and the magma directly under it has a similar velocity. All magma in the various regions within the Earth has an angular momentum somewhere between these two extremes of 0 and 1,000 miles per hour depending on location.

---

[3]The viscosity of the plastic-like hot magma within the Earth's crust is complicated, due in part to different densities, pressures and temperatures in various vertical areas. Another factor which markedly affects viscosity is stress and removal of stress. Yet another factor to be considered is the centrifugal speed of the magma, and the drag induced thereon .by an approaching extra-terrestrial gravitational force. The mechanics of flow of the Earth's magma are complicated and not fully understood. For further information, see Scheidegger's *Principles of Geodynamics,* p. 106-161 and associated sources as listed.

[4]Gamow, op. cit., pp. 80-91.

This chapter will deal with the effect of an introduced gravitational force upon the magma, and the reaction of the magma upon the inside of the Earth's crust. Figure 5 illustrates the three forces conceived as having been exerted upon the Earth's magma. Force 1 is the Earth's gravity. Force 2 is the Earth's centrifugal force. Both of these combine to achieve the Earth's oblateness. Force 3 is the introduced force, which interrupted the equilibrium, previously existing between the first two forces.

The effect of the introduced force was to cause a new oblateness or bulge, of great dimensions. A second effect of the force was an induced drag on the magma in centrifugal rotation. The drag was effected in an arcuate, sweeping pattern on the inside of the Earth's crust.

Thus there were two vitally important but distinct factors, (1) the amount of the bulge due to the gravitational conflict, and (2) the direction of the bulge and its drag, related to the direction and speed of rotation.

In addition to these factors, it must be kept in mind that the Earth's thin crust or skin is considered to be as flexible as a man's leather belt. It was the give and take between these forces being alternately exerted and released within the Earth's crust upon which the explanation rests. This give and take, or alternating exertion and releasing upon the inside of the Earth's flexible crust explains both (1) the magnitude of the thrust and (2) the placement of the geographical pattern, a pattern incorporating series after series of arcuate curves which merge into one or the other of two great circle patterns.

With these factors in mind—the fragileness of the Earth, the minute thickness of its crust, the vastness of its internal oceans of magma, the velocity of its rotation, the flexibility of its crust, the confinement and the viscosity of the magma—a new orographical theory (mountain building) is about to be set forth, based on the historical probability of astronomical conflict. But before entering the proposed theory, some of the major uniformitarian theories of orogenesis will be discussed. It reveals the failure of 130 years of uniformitarian geology to produce one adequate concept regarding the origin of these great orographical systems which span our planet, and form the backbone for several continents.

EARTH   FORCES

Low tide

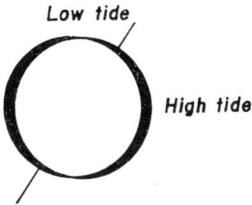

Bulging or Oblateness

High tide

Force I
Earth's Gravity

Force 2
Earth's Centrifugal Force

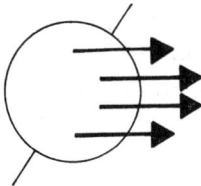

Force 3
Visitor's Gravity

FIGURE 5 — Three forces acting upon the Earth's crust during the period of celestial crisis.
        (1) The Earth's gravity
        (2) The Earth's centrifugal force, due to rotation
        (3) The Visitor's gravity
Other lesser forces included
        (4) The gravities of the Sun and Moon
        (5) The magnetic fields of these four celestial bodies

2. Uniformitarian Approaches To Orogenesis

During the last 100 years, seven major theories of orogenesis have been propounded. They are listed as follows:[5]

1. Continental Drift
2. Convection Currents of Magma
3. Differential Rotation
4. Oscillations (Undulations)
5. Planetary Contraction (Crustal Shortening)
6. Planetary Expansion
7. Polar Wandering

Several things should be noted regarding these seven theories, and their various methods in endeavoring to handle the problem of an adequate explanation for mountain-building. Note that (1) all seven theories assume Earth configuration has been a process requiring multiplied millions of continuous years, (2) forces exerted are confined to originating from within the Earth's crust, and (3) the many kinds of stress need to be explained together or in tandem. No room has been given to catastrophism or astral chaos—in accordance with classical uniformitarian approach, which assumes an unvariable solar system for as much as billions of years. All processes are assumed to have been gradual, and essentially local in scope.

Adherence or loyalty among geologists is so tenuous, generalized and non-specific that of these seven major hypotheses, few can claim as much as 10% adherence. Orogenesis is only one area of lack in uniformitarian theory; there also is no adequate explanation for the cause of the Ice Epoch; there is no adequate explanation for sudden, radical and permanent changes in paleoclimatology.[6] Evidence indicates that mammoths were frozen with suddenness and by the millions, along with associated fauna. Subtropical forests thrived where today only ice and/or permafrost prevail. None of these prime facts of Earth history has been adequately dealt with.

---

[5]Scheidegger, *op. cit.*, pp. 209-291

[6]In addition to these, there is lack of theory for the origin of coal strata and petroleum pools. Further, the Earth's mantle (crust) contains no indication as to the origin of either carbon or nitrogen, elements abundant in the atmospheres of both the Earth and the Jovian planets. See Dolph E. Hooker, *Those Astounding Ice Ages*, New York; Exposition Press, 1958, pp. 122-139.

Uniformitarianism has held a virtual monopoly in geology for a century. Having been taught uniformitarianism and having assumed uniformitarianism, modern geologists have limited their primary assumptions and exclusively confined them to the terrestrial crust and the current set of forces which occur. They have erred in not considering mechanisms reflected within our solar system as a possible region of causation.

Richard Hartshorne, one of the world's best known geographers, discusses geographical theory, the subject of geomorphology, landforms and genesis with pointed frankness:

> To the extent that the geomorphologist is primarily concerned to use landforms as the means of studying geologic processes or determining stages in geologic history, his explanatory description, as Kesseli notes, is often 'an explanation lacking a description.' Russell, as well as Kesseli, concludes that a century of geomorphology, dominated by the purpose of explaining genesis, *has failed to produce comprehensive representation of land forms for most areas of the world* . . .[7]
> These and similar protests which geographers have registered for more than a generation appear to run into a blank wall of dogma.[8]

That 100 years of geomorphology have been unproductive in explaining cause is a major criticism concerning theory in geology. Perhaps it suggests sterility of the uniformitarian approach, which has overruled and ignored astral catastrophism as a possible explanation without even revealing reasons of substance for the rejection. Astral catastrophism is a possible and probable explanation of ancient upheavals which resulted in our terrestrial patterns of mountain systems; it explains this and much more. These criticisms, leveled at the Lyellian uniformitarianism, are not mild ones.

Charles Lyell. During his time Hutton, like Lyell, ignored the possibility of catastrophism, astral or otherwise, with one

---

[7] Richard Hartshorne, *Perspective on the Nature of Geography*, Chicago: Rand McNally & Co., 1959, p. 91.

[8] Hartshorne, *ibid.*, pp. 91-92.

sweeping comment of non-analytical and arbitrary rejection.[9] But during that day, many figures in the natural sciences were by no means impressed with either Hutton or Lyell. These figures included Agassiz, Cuvier, Ritter and von Humboldt. Lyell had made a series of assumptions for which there was perilously little evidence; many of which related to time and lapses of time.

Among Lyell's assumptions were the following three. Lyell taught that mountain uplifts were (1) local in scope, (2) ancient in terms of multiplied millions of years, and (3) caused exclusively by conditions within the Earth's crust, oceans and atmosphere. We will return to these three assumptions later in this chapter. Within these three assumptions, seven theories of orogenesis as previously mentioned have been generated or derived, during one decade or another. Probably the most publicized of these was the Continental Drift Theory, still held by a handful of people.

The Continental Drift Theory. This theory was quite popular during the 1920's and 1930's. It was set forth by Alfred Wegener (1880-1930) during the 1920's.[10] This theory proposes that there were originally two great primordial continents which floated on a lava sea. These hypothetical continents, given the names of Gondwanaland and Laurasia, floated apart when the crust of the Earth was yet fluid, and before it hardened. After the crust of the Earth solidified, these floating continents were frozen in or stabilized, far from their original moorings. This theory holds, for instance, that the elbow of South America once fitted into the bend (or bight) of Africa.

No room is left for the possibility of a Mid-Atlantic range in either the North Atlantic or South Atlantic. An existing submerged range does exist, traversing both; the tips of this range are observed in the Azore Islands, the St. Paul and Peter Rocks,

[9]"No powers are to be employed that are not natural to the globe, no action to be admitted except those of which we know the principle," said Hutton. This illustrates a man whittling down history and the universe to his own preconceptions. With one flourish of the pen, he brushed aside every possibility except that which he determined to understand with his mind. Frank L. Marsh, *Studies in Creationism*, Washington D.C.: Review & Herald Publishing Assn., 1950, p. 106.

[10]Wegener, Alfred, *The Origin of Continents and Oceans,* translated from 3rd German ed. by L.G.A. Kerl. London: Methuen. 1924.

Ascension Island and Tristan De Cunha. Such submerged ranges exist not only in the Atlantic Ocean, but also in the other major oceans; the Pacific Ocean has many of them.

In addition, Wegener's theory incorrectly assumes that the underlying bedrock of the Atlantic Basin is different from the rock underlying the African and South American continents. And presumably it was similar to the rock underlying the Pacific Basin. Andesitic bedrock underlies both Africa and South America; it underlies the Atlantic Ocean as well. Basaltic rock underlies the Pacific Basin. This, among several other things, is inexplicable within Wegener's theory.[11]

The Continental Drift Theory also assumes that the Earth's hydrosphere has been constant in volume over the past many millions of years; only the continental massifs have risen or submerged. However if juvenile ice, during a past catastrophe, has cascaded in upon the Earth and added to its hydrographical reservoir, then this assumption will also be found to be in error. (This is considered in Chapter VI.) It is already well established that the continental shelves, for some reason, have been flooded and sea level has shifted from a previous lower level within recent geological times.

In summary, Wegener's Continental Drift Theory assumes that the oceanic volumes have remained constant (an assumption appears as an elementary error). It acknowledges that sediments, sea shells, and other marine materials have been found at nearly every altitude. It proposed that entire continents rose or submerged while oceans maintained a constancy in level and a serenity in terms of tides (being affected only by the Moon and the Sun).

The Contraction and Convection Current Theories. The Contraction Theory and the Convection Current hypotheses have been the more popular theories for geologists of recent vintage. Upon these two theories, and upon the balance in general, Adrian Scheidegger, a geophysicist of world renown, has made some telling statements. Hartshorne's comments were related to geomorphology (physical geography); Scheidegger's analysis of geological theory is perhaps even more revealing:

[11]Scheidegger, *loc. cit.*, pp. 10-14, 104-105.

However, the outcome of recent geophysical investigations casts grave doubts upon the contraction theory as well as upon the convection current hypothesis of orogenesis. The first of these geophysical investigations is the oceano-graphic work showing that the Mohorovicic discontinuity is not depressed beneath ocean trenches and thus dealing a severe blow to the notion of downwarping. The second is the work on faulting in earthquake foci showing the latter is, in the vast majority of cases, strike-slip and not dip-slip. This runs contrary to any idea sustained in either the contraction or the convection current theory. The third is the work on stresses showing that the Earth is subject to all types of stresses, not just one type as proposed by most theories of orogenesis.

It is therefore necessary to re-examine all theories of oro-genesis that have ever been invented, in order to determine what can be saved of them in the light of the presently available facts. If this is done, it becomes immediately obvious that *something fundamental* is wrong with each and every of the theories . . .[12]

It appears, therefore, that the problem of finding the causes of the various geodynamic features must be regarded as still unsolved. (Italics ours)[13]

Scheidegger's conclusions, like Hartshorne's and those of others, are that there is a great inadequacy in existing theory for sound commentary on genesis of mountain uplifts. Similarly, and we apprehend not coincidentally, there is also a great inadequacy of existing theory on the cause of the Ice Epoch, which shall be discussed in the next chapter.

Of the foregoing seven theories of orogenesis, all have been conceived within the womb of uniformitarianism. Not one of these major theories or sub-theories considered the possibility (and we propose the possibility) of astral catastrophism. And such a theory is most assuredly overdue.

The chief problem of the science of geodynamics is to deter-mine deformations within the Earth and upon its surface. On the surface, the present-day deformations are known and the task is to explain the latter in terms of stresses that could be considered as reasonable. In any properly

12Scheidegger, *op. cit.*, p. 289.

13Scheidegger, *op. cit.*, p. 291.

defined deformation theory, it is a matter of mathematical analysis to determine the stress from the boundary conditions. Thus, if the "deformation theory" applying to the Earth were properly defined, it would be, in principle, a straightforward (though not necessarily easy) matter to calculate the stresses from the (known) strains and then to look for causes of the latter. Unfortunately, it is a fact that the "deformation theory" applying to the Earth is not known, thus leaving the matter of finding the causes of its present-day appearance wide open to speculation. It is thus evident that the basic problem of geodynamics is to determine the proper rheological conditions in the Earth. The explanation of the present-day physiography would then follow more or less automatically.[14]

We believe considering astral catastrophim will be an initial step, *if not the step,* to offering substantial explanation for orogenesis and the geographical pattern thereof. Society has left it up to the earth-oriented geologist to determine the prime cause for orogenesis. Rather it ought to have left it up to the astronomer, the astrophysicist and the catastrophic historian. After adequate theory is established, then the geologist needs to be accountable for the local details.

3. The Geographical Pattern of Distribution of Recent Mountain Uplifts

Prior to analyzing this subject, it should be recalled that the mountain ranges of the Earth are significantly similar to the pattern of those of the Moon. Both ranges have a series of arc-like curves, although those on the Earth are more elongated. Both ranges contain dendritic patterns. In fact, the mountains of both bodies are also similar in their elevation (although the Moon is about 1/80 of the mass of the Earth and 1/50 of the volume of the Earth). Astronomers have noted this, and have suggested that similar processes were involved in their formation. This should prove to be a good clue, even though the two regions are some 240,000 miles distant.

Mountains might have been scattered across the face of the Earth in one or two of many different possible patterns, depend-

[14]Scheidegger, *op. cit.,* pp. 147-148.

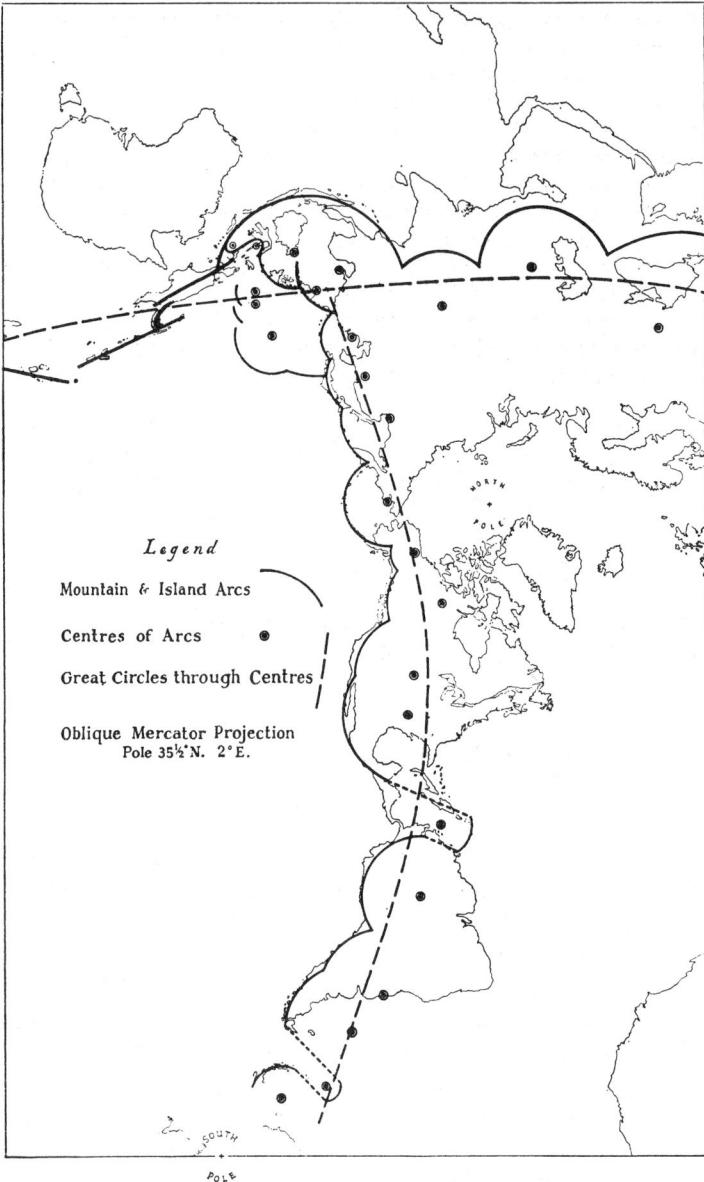

FIGURE 6 — The mountain arcs which collectively compose the two zones of recent orogenetic uplift, together with the epicenters of those arcs, and the great circle alignments
of the epicenters. The two zones are the Alpine-Himalayan zone and the Circum-Pacific
zone. (See Fig. 23, pages 158-159.) After WILSON

WILSON, J. TUZO: *The Earth as a Planet*, ed., Kuiper, p. 153, Chicago,
Ill.: Univ. of Chicago Press, 1954.

ing on cause of orogenesis. Among the possible patterns are the following:

1. Equatorial
2. Latitudinal
3. Longitudinal
4. Great Circles
5. Magnetic Equatorial
6. Magnetic Polar
7. Continental Peripheries
8. Continental Centralities
9. Random
10. Sunburst Patterns
11. Ubiquitous Wrinkles

Of these eleven possible patterns,[15] the fourth listed pattern is the pattern of recent mountain uplifts, with a qualification. Mountain arcs occur, spread across the Earth's surface. It is not the mountain arcs, specifically, which occur in great circle patterns. Rather it is the location of the epicenters of the mountain arcs which, when connected in series, presents a great circle lineal pattern. The great circle pattern does not exist once, but rather twice.[16] One system is the Circum-Pacific, and the other is the Alpine-Himalayan. Figure 6 illustrates. (Further research

[15]Mountains could have various possible geographical patterns. They could have perhaps been scattered across the face of the Earth in a random pattern, which is similar to the astroblemes (craters) on the Moon and Mars; they are not. Mountains could have occurred in sunburst arrangements, but do not. Mountains could have occurred in latitudinal or linear arrangements had a constant rate of rotation occurred along with a geographically shifting axis. Had crustal expansion been a principle, a similar pattern would have resulted. Had there been a varying rate of rotation along with a constant location in the axis, elevation from mean sea level would have varied according to latitude. Mountains could have occurred in ubiquitous wrinkles, had a universal crustal contraction been a factor. Mountains might have occurred in concentrations at continental peripheries had the Continental Drift idea been the determinant. None of these geographical patterns are the case, with one minor exception, which is the Rift Valley of East Africa. This, rather than being a formation of mountains, is the reverse; it is a cleavage rather than an uplift of the Earth's crust. This particular phenomenon does relate to limited crustal expansion, and shall be discussed or recounted in two later footnotes, one in this Chapter V, footnote 16 below, and another in Chapter X, footnote 23, p. 252.

[16]Observe that there are two great cycles, or zones of recent mountain uplifts, not one. One of the zones is the Circum-Pacific, which approaches each geographical pole within 20°, or 1500 miles. This zone generally describes the rim of the Pacific Ocean, from Antarctica and Chile, through Alaska, Japan and the Philippine Islands to Indonesia. The other zone is the Alpine-

on suboceanic mountain systems, currently being described and plotted, may reveal further arcs, curves and great circles.)

The mountain systems of the Earth are found in great scallop-like arcs, which in turn merge into greater arcs, which in turn merge into sweeping, planet-traversing circles. Their pattern seemingly is indifferent to either continental massifs or to oceanic basins; they traverse either with equal ease. This is illustrated particularly in the regions of the Western Pacific, with

Himalayan zone, which begins in the Atlantic Ocean, the Canary Islands, and Spain, and continues through the Alps, Ararat-Caucasus-Elburz group, through the Himalayas and associated ranges, across New Guinea and into the island arcs of Polynesia, including Samoa. In each of these zones of uplift, the mountain structures are similar in all respects.

This observation opens the door for a suspicion that at sometime during one crescendo of this catastrophic period, the location of the Earth's geographical poles suddenly underwent a major shift. While this does not necessarily require a shifting of the angle of the axis, which is 23½° to the perpendicular of the ecliptic, nevertheless the possibility of such a shift also exists.

Observe the location of the Alpine-Himalayan orogenetic zone, a segment of a great circle, rising some 20 and 25° above the Earth's equator, on a path quite similar to some of the space-probe satellites which have been launched within the recent decade. This zone is comparable to the plane of the ecliptic near the time of the summer solstice (June 21). At this time, the sun's perpendicular rays fall some 23½° north of the equator, due to the angle of the Earth's axis to the plane of the ecliptic. The plane of the ecliptic is the plane of the path of the Earth as it orbits around the sun. It is on this plane that vertical rays of the sun fall upon the Earth. At the equinoxes, March 21 and Sept. 21, the plane of the ecliptic crosses the equator, and the days are equal in length in both hemispheres. On the solstices, it rises 23½° above the equator into one hemisphere and alternately the other.

It is suspected that the zone of the Alpine-Himalayan uplift, similar to the plane of the Earth's ecliptic in June, and even more similar to the pattern of orbiting satellites, actually reflects the plane of the Earth facing the orbiting astral visitor, as it revolved past the Earth. The Alpine-Himalayan zone of uplift is the plane of the bulge during the crisis. But there were two bulge zones; hence the possibility of two locations of the geographical poles during the one crisis period.

If such were the case, then certain other points must be a logical consequence. One is that the Circum-Pacific zone reflects or indicates the former equatorial zone, which supposes that the geographical poles may have been previously located within 1,000 miles of Nigeria and Samoa respectively.

Additional evidence may possibly exist in research into the magnetic alignment of prediluvian lava formations. As lava hardens, the iron compounds contained therein crystallize in a pattern containing a magnetic alignment to the magnetic poles. This lava alignment does not shift later, if the magnetic poles were to subsequently shift. Since it is commonly assumed that there is a relationship, not well understood, between the proximity of the geographical and magnetic poles, such discoveries should add to a suspicion of a historical shift in location of both geographical and magnetic poles.

In such a circumstance, another condition also would necessarily follow. It involves the Earth's oblateness, which is due to its centrifugal

the numerous island chains, which are the tops of submerged mountain arcs.

Secondly, mountain systems possess dendritic patterns with auxiliary ranges, and spur ranges, separated by valleys and basins. The relationship of the main range to the auxiliary ranges is somewhat like the grain of the stock of a Christmas tree to its branches, and is particularly observable to mountain-climbers with their advantageous, panoramic views.

Thirdly, mountain systems often occur in parallelism—that is to say that major systems are frequently parallel. The Cascades and the Rockies are one example, the Sierra Madre Occidental and Sierra Madre Oriental are another example. The

motion (rotation). The Earth's equatorial diameter is 7927 miles, whereas its polar diameter is only 7900 miles, a difference of 27 miles. A change in the location of the Earth's poles implies a change in the location of the Earth's equatorial zones. A consequence then would be a shift in the Earth's oblateness to the new equatorial zone. This in turn would be facilitated by a splitting or a cleavage, a perpendicular tear in the Earth's crust, astride the equator, which would allow for the necessary expansion. Such a cleavage, due to a new equatorial zone of oblateness, could be expected to be not only perpendicular to the equatorial zone, but could also be expected to be broadest and more complex in breaching in the equatorial zone.

Such a condition closely approximates the Rift Valley of Africa. This is a cleavage which extends north and south about 5,000 miles, and is broadest in its breaching or cleavage in the equatorial zone. The Great Rift Valley possesses indications of recent vulcanism at the edges, where minor outpourings of lava occur, outpourings which are contrasted with other volcanic formations in the same region which are superimposed by alluvial strata. Other factors, such as the geosyncline of the Lake Victoria Basin, the shallowness of Lake Victoria, (279 feet deep for the largest fresh water lake on Earth), the attenuated shoreline, the precipice of Murchison Falls, where the White Nile plunges out of this basin and into the Rift Valley—a river as large as the Niagara passing with immense velocity through a precipice only 15 feet wide. Also the volcanoes of Elgon, Kenya, Kilimanjaro and Ruwenzori are related factors. Additional material on the great Rift Valley of Africa will be given in footnote 18, Chapter X, where it pertains to other data.

If this concept of a shift in location of the poles is historically correct (and geophysically correct), there may exist a clear relationship not only (1) between the Earth's equatorial plane, geographical poles and the Flood catastrophe, but also (2) between the $23\frac{1}{2}°$ angle of the axis to the perpendicular of the ecliptic and the Flood catastrophe. This is the phenomenon responsible for the Earth's climatological seasons.

This suspicion of a shift in location of the geographical poles, during the Flood celestial crisis, also suggests that the Circum-Pacific series of mountain ranges is clearly older than the Alpine-Himalayan series, older by perhaps a few months. This point bears further on a discussion toward the end of this chapter on (a) *the global scope* of the orogenetic uplifts, (b) *the direction of causation,* and (c) *the recent timing* of this astral catastrophe. Observing the phenomena of these two great circle patterns of orogenetic uplift conjointly with the celestial crisis cannot help but be stimulating and ultimately illuminating.

Himalayas and the Kun Luns are a third example. Other examples are too numerous to mention.

The recent uplifts occur in series, in scallop-like arrangements and in great circles. This is illustrated in Figure 6. The great circle alignment is formed by drawing a line through the epicenters of the arcs, often 1,000 miles from the uplift itself, and located amid broad, undulating plains, and not by drawing a line between the mountain ranges themselves. If viewed from our Moon, or man-made satellites, or some other proximate position in space near the Earth, this would appear as a straight line crossing both latitudes and longitudes.[17] This direct alignment suggests that mountain uplifts occurred (a) on an interrelated basis, and (b) on a global scope. It does not indicate that they were the result of slow forces, nor of a local scope, as asserted by Lyell and modern day Lyellians.

The Circum-Pacific uplift includes arcs which begin in Antarctica and follow the rim of the Pacific Ocean through the Western Americas, and along the eastern ridges of Asia to Indonesia. This is the so-called "Pacific Rim of Fire." It is a zone of both earthquake activity and volcanic activity, indicating that isostatic adjustments of the Earth's crust in this zone are yet being achieved; the same applies to the Alpine-Himalayan cycle. Again, this is indicative of recentness and not remoteness, as presumed by Lyell.

In our hypothesis herein set forth, a series of line diagrams is given, which illustrates a possible model—an astronomical model—for the cause of the global catastrophe. The astral intruder is shown in relation to the solar system, the Earth and the Moon. It is also shown with respect to the Earth's magnetic field. These line diagrams, as given in Chapters VI and VII, pages 118, 119, 132, 133, and 157 are presented as components of a model of Earth catastrophism, in order to increase clarity of

---

[17]A classical example of a great circle (which is merely the shortest distance between two points on a plotted sphere) is the ocean route between the Panama Canal and Tokyo, Japan. The Panama Canal is at about 9° N latitude; Tokyo is about 36° N. latitude. Many map projections indicate that the shortest route between the two is via the Hawaiian Islands in the middle of the Pacific Ocean, at a latitude of about 20° N. It would not seem that the shortest distance could possibly include latitudes north of Tokyo's. In reality, however, such is the case, due to the Earth's roundness, projected but distorted onto a plane (the map). In reality, the shortest distance between Panama and Tokyo includes a seeming detour northward to a latitude of 45° N., skirting the Aleutian Islands of Alaska.

thought. Being specific is normally superior to vagueness. There-fore a hypothetical model, a possible answer to the problem is presented in order to avoid vagueness, a trait so constantly char-acteristic of uniformitarian thought.

Any adequate theory of orogenesis must explain the align-ment of mountain systems, traversing the face of the Earth. It should also explain the similarity to the lunar mountains. But in addition, it must be able to account specifically for many kinds or types of stresses which obviously have been involved, and not just one or two kinds. This includes many types of ver-tical movements and horizontal movements. This also includes several kinds of formations. Most uniformitarian theories at-tempt to account for only one or at the most two kinds of stresses.[18]

Logically the approaching gravitational force caused a new bulge upon the Earth's surface, due to the magnitude of the new gravitational field. The new gravity exerted a pulling or lifting force upon the rotating magma, but also exerted a drag on the velocity of the magma as it centrifugally rotated around the Earth's axis.

There were new pressures caused by the tides of magma, pressures which required new adjustments and new releases. Among the new adjustments were welts or wrinkles or uplifts upon the Earth's thin skin, uplifts including both igneous and sedimentary rock alike, and in arcuate or scallop-like alignments. Another adjustment was the release of pressure by the bleeding of lava (magma) out upon the Earth's crust, forming basaltic plateaus and volcanic cones. The surging, throbbing, pulsating magma, rising to two mighty crescendoes each day, tortured the inside of the Earth's skin with a bellows-like periodicity.

The stresses must have been tremendous from the inside of the Earth; simultaneously the face of the Earth was washed twice every 24½ hours by continental tides. In addition rain (intense rain—Genesis 7:12) also occurred, further rinsing the Earth's face. Under these conditions, if water compression on the Earth's surface at "sea level" resulted in pressures exceeding two tons per square inch, pressures perhaps 100 to 10,000 times greater occurred from within. The Earth's crust was thus tor-

[18]Scheidegger, *op. cit.*, pp. 289-291.

tured from within and without simultaneously.[19]

The formation of arcuate uplifts may be accounted for in terms of the rotation of our sphere simultaneously with tidal movements of the magma. It is noticed that many of the mountain systems in the Alpine-Himalayan and Circum-Pacific Belts are parallel. The astral intruder interacted with the Earth, and revolved around the Earth in a binary manner for some 8 months, and was drawn out beyond the Earth-Moon system by the Sun in a manner described in Chapter VII. This then lays the basis for explaining the repeated parallel ranges of orogenetic uplift on a rotating planet, along with parallel and offsetting crustal trenches. Their great circle geographical pattern merely reflects the astrophysical (gravitational) nature of their cause.

Similarly, it assists in explaining the many repeated layers of alluvium, repeatedly laid down and compressed in sharply separated series, forming vertical sequences. In this way, two types of vertical movements are simultaneously explained. They are (1) the vertical upthrust or magma, forming mountain ranges, and (2) the vertical and successively layered strata, resulting from tidal deposition. Both vertical movements include shifts of fluid, namely (a) tidal magma, and (b) tidal water, both shifting in oceanic volumes. Both are explained as responses to the same gravitational interaction; both are explained as simultaneous; both parallel geological observations; both parallel elementary astrophysical principles.

Vertical movements are thus explained; however, horizontal relationships across the Earth's surface also must be recognized. The realization is that the Earth was in constant rotation, and the bulge zone (both facing toward and facing opposite the visitor) constantly shifted within the same zone of uplift. This principle assists in understanding the very apparent and very consistent horizontal parallelism of mountain ranges.

No uniformitarian theory can remotely approach the catastrophic theory with regard to accounting for either the many or the varied kinds of stresses which obviously occurred. Nor

---

[19]If the forces of pressure upon the earth's external crust, due to continental tides, were measured in tons per square inch, the alternating forces of thrust exerted upon the inside of the Earth's crust would be measured in megatons per square inch, the magnitude of thrust required to suddenly raise (and align) the Alps, the Andes, the Ararats or the Himalayas.

can any uniformitarian proposal explain either the intensity or the suddenness which were involved.

Figure 6 illustrates the mountain arcs of the world on a global basis. Figures 7 through 11 illustrate the mountain arcs of the world, region by region and continent by continent. They reflect recurring patterns around the world. Figure 12 then further illustrates these arcs on a sub-regional scale.

Figure 7 illustrates Western North America from Alaska to Mexico. Here occur differing types and heights of mountain curves. Some are primary and some are secondary; some are sedimentary and some are volcanic. Offsetting trenches are also found, parallel to the mountain arcs.

Figure 8 illustrates South American mountain arcs. The same kinds of uplifts again occur. However here is a further illustration of a reverse arc (the Caribbean region), similar to the reverse arc of the South Sandwich Islands (Fig. 6).

Figure 9 gives this arc-like alignment in Southern Eurasia. This area includes the "roof of the world," the Himalayan group, with their associated ranges. It also includes the Ararat-Caucasus-Elburz group, where the Ark was grounded, according to the Genesis account.

Figure 10 gives this arc-like alignment for Melanesia, an area mostly inundated with water. In this region, some of the deepest trenches of the Earth's crust are found, and they too are associated with mountain uplifts, with which they are parallel.

Figure 11 illustrates the great, sweeping mountain arcs for East Asia. Figure 12, the echelon structures of the East Asian Arcs, illustrates these same trends as seen on a subregional scale.

Thus it is demonstrated that mountains are not dispersed in a random pattern over the surface of the Earth.[20] They are strung out, something like the way a string of lights is hung

---

[20]Map projections, when portraying features of a sphere on a plane, always leave something to be desired, regardless of the projection. The pattern of arcs, greater arcs, and global great circles in the alignment of recent mountain uplifts is portrayed fairly well by Figure 6, page 76. It is an abbreviated oblique mercator projection, as adapted by J. Tuzo Wilson. Another map portraying these relationships is given in Chapter VII, a chapter of models. Figure 23, page 158 shows the two zones of orogenetic uplift on an adjusted polar type of projection, semi-azimuthal but semiconical. This projection was designed by Bartholomew and termed a "regional" projection, and is centered longitudinally on the longitudes of 60° W. and 120° E. Bartholomew's Advanced Atlas (McGraw-Hill), pp. 14-15.

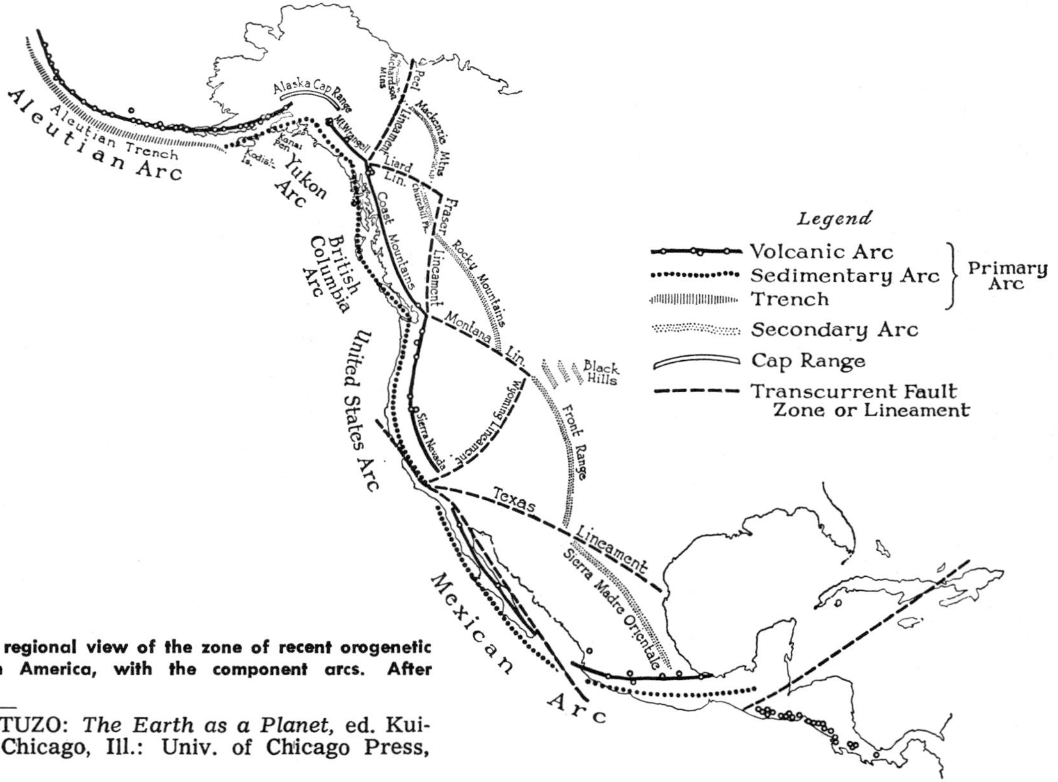

FIGURE 7 — A regional view of the zone of recent orogenetic uplift in North America, with the component arcs. After WILSON

WILSON, J. TUZO: *The Earth as a Planet*, ed. Kuiper, p. 157, Chicago, Ill.: Univ. of Chicago Press, 1954.

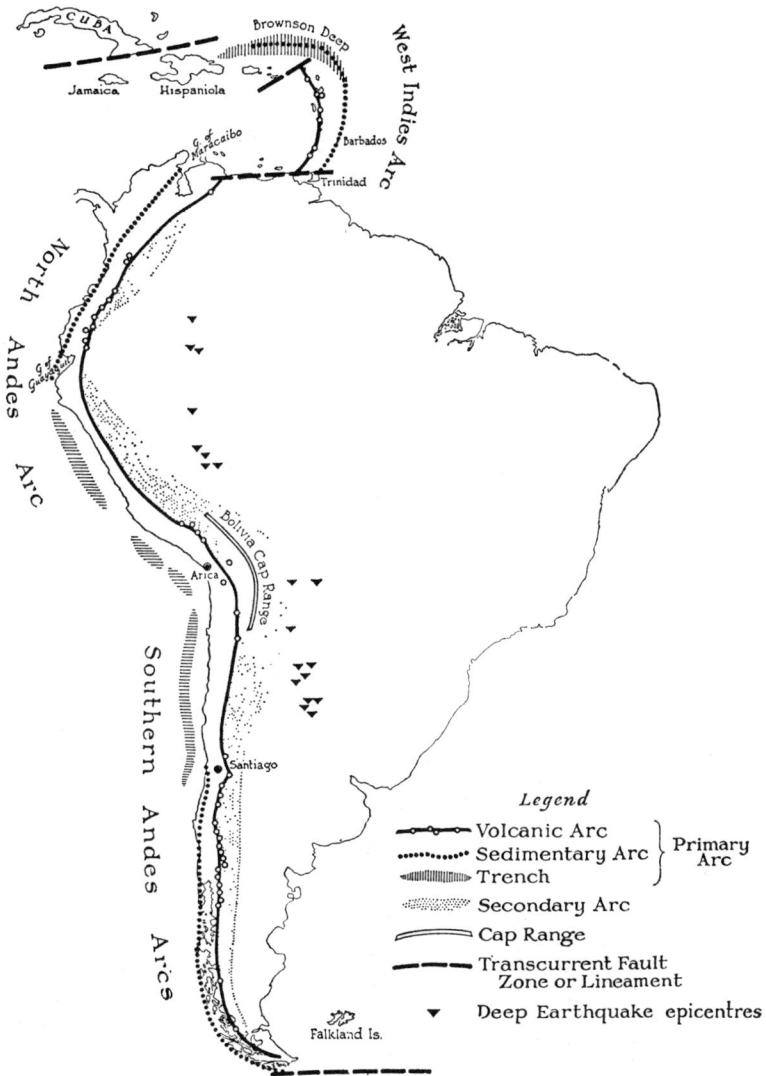

FIGURE 8 — A regional view of the zone of recent orogenetic uplift in South America, with the component arcs. After WILSON

WILSON, J. TUZO: *The Earth as a Planet*, ed. Kuiper, p. 158, Chicago, Ill.: Univ. of Chicago Press, 1954.

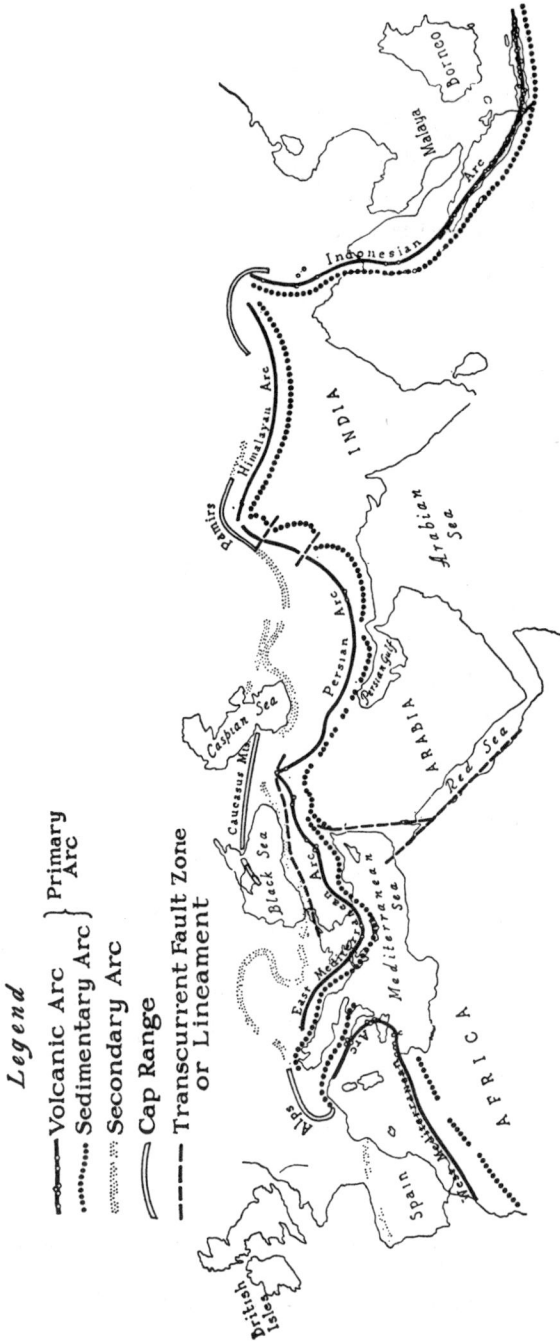

FIGURE 9 — A regional view of the zone of recent orogenetic uplift in South Eurasia, with the component arcs. After WILSON

WILSON, J. TUZO: *The Earth as a Planet*, ed., Kuiper, p. 165, Chicago, Ill.: Univ. of Chicago Press, 1954.

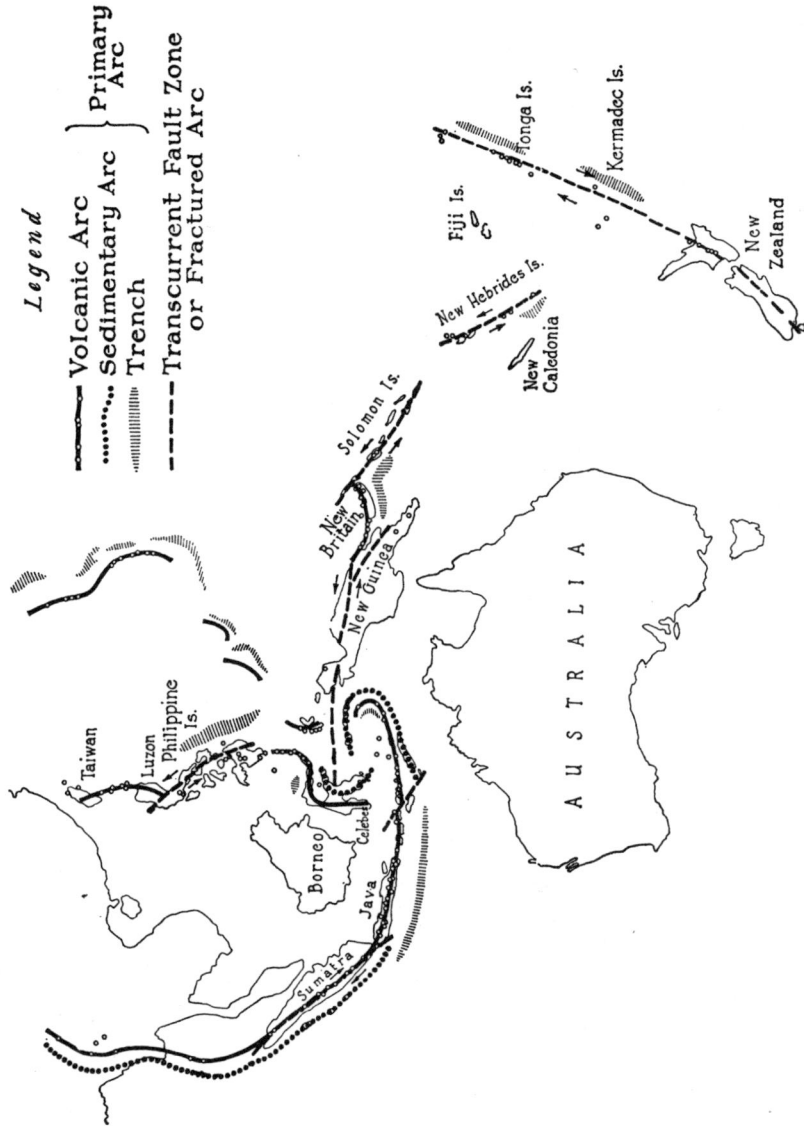

FIGURE 10 — A regional view of the zone of recent orogenetic uplift in Western Oceania, with the component arcs. After WILSON

WILSON, J. TUZO: *The Earth as a Planet*, ed., Kuiper, p. 160, Chicago, Ill.: Univ. of Chicago Press, 1954.

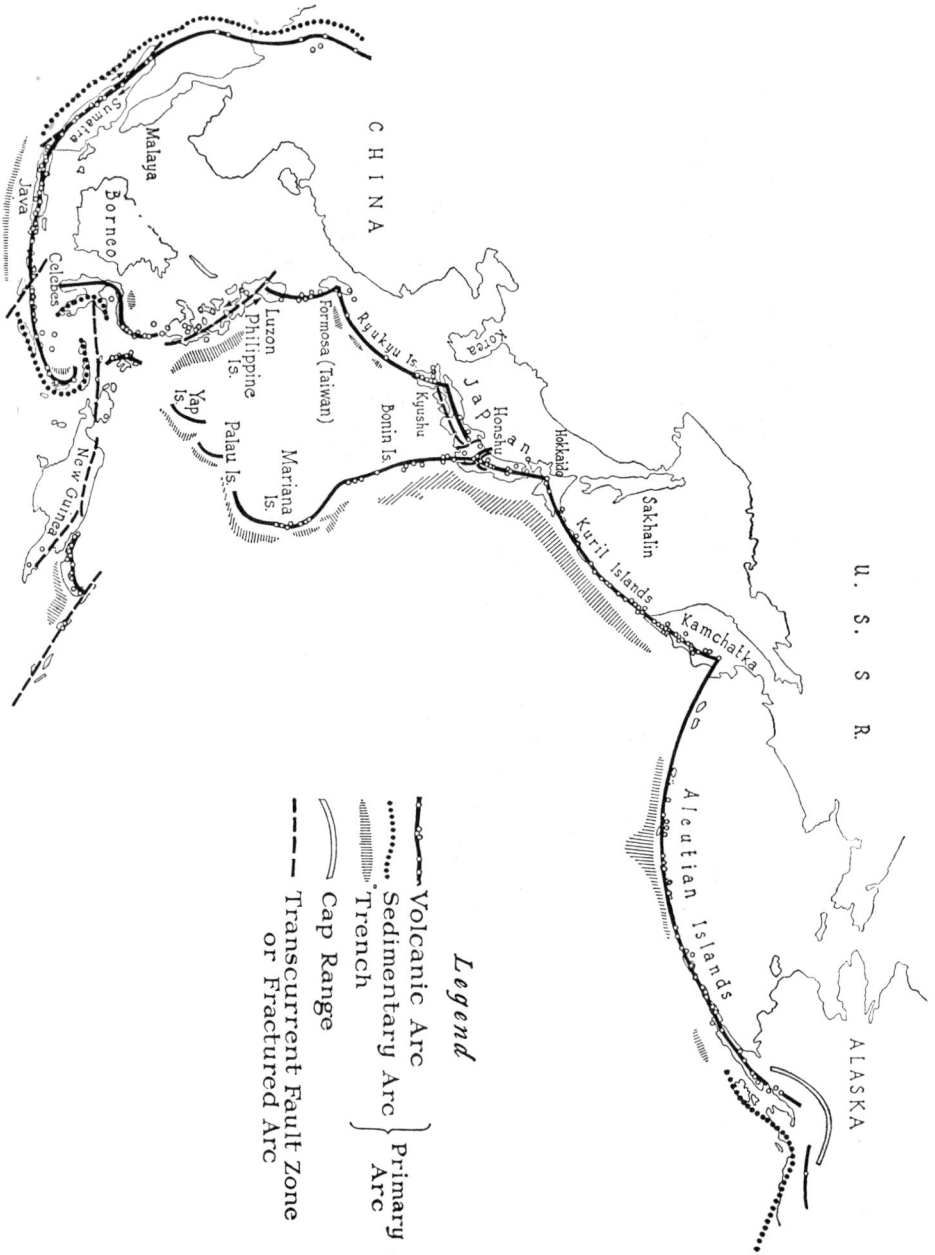

FIGURE 11 — A regional view of the zone of recent orogenetic uplift in East Asia, with the component arcs. After WILSON

WILSON, J. TUZO: *The Earth as a Planet*, ed., Kuiper, p. 163, Chicago, Ill.: Univ. of Chicago Press, 1954.

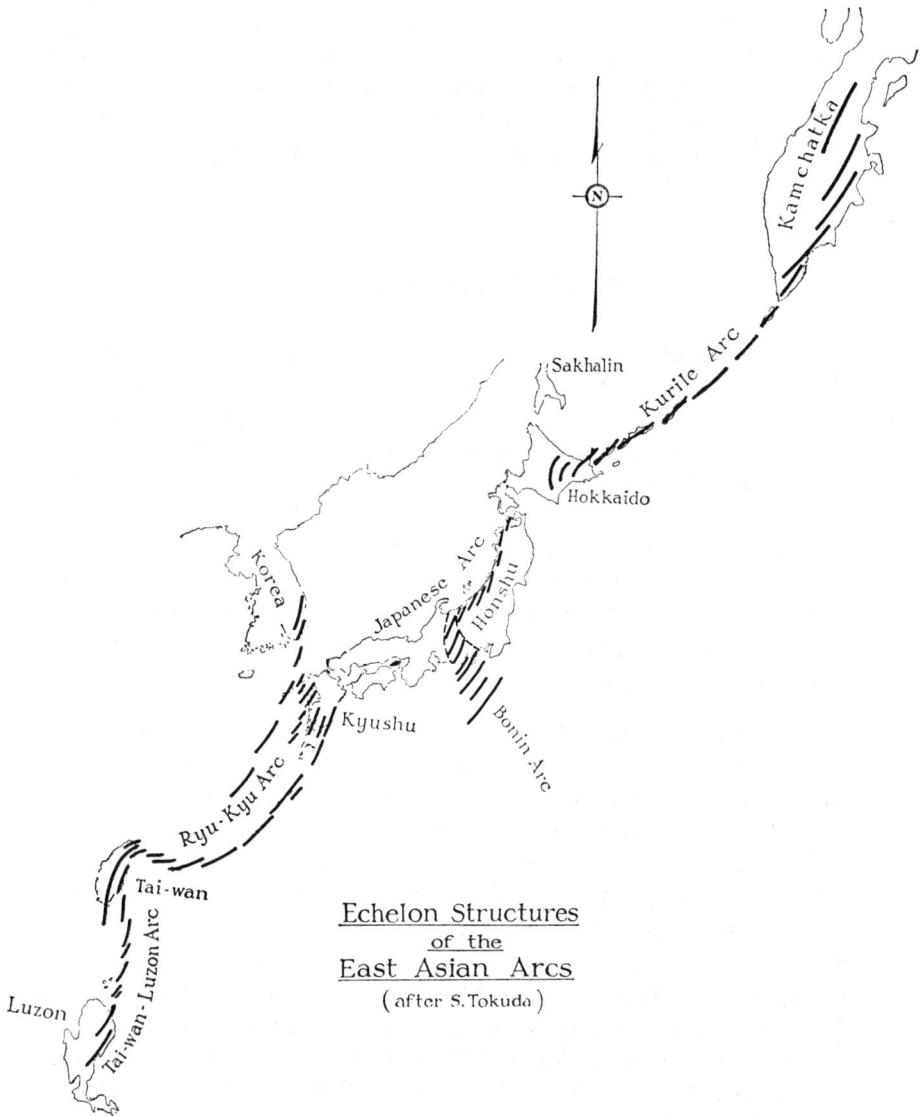

Echelon Structures
of the
East Asian Arcs
(after S. Tokuda)

FIGURE 12 — Locations of the sub arcs and structural folds of the East Asian arcs. After **WILSON.** Here are revealed sub-regional arcs within regional arcs, which are segments of a great circle alignment of orogenetic uplift, the Circum-Pacific zone. These patterns may resemble a series of strings of sausages, strung out in sequential alignment.

WILSON, J. TUZO: *The Earth as a Planet*, ed., Kuiper, p. 178, Chicago, Ill.: Univ. of Chicago Press, 1954.

around a Christmas tree, hanging from branch to branch, in arcuate curves. The entire pattern is suggestive of counter-dominating gravities, viscuous, fluid magmas, and a rotating sphere. If tidal mechanisms uplifted the mountain systems of the Earth as well as the oceans at the time of the Flood, then the geography of both hemispheres has been drastically reorganized by this celestial event.

4. The Lunar Mountains

In addition to being similar in pattern to those great ranges of the Earth, the mountain ranges of the Moon also rise to similar elevations. Our Rockies rise to 15,000 feet, as do the Sierras, Alps, and Owen-Stanley Range, among others. The Andes rise to 23,000 feet, as do the Hindu Kush, the Tien Shan and the Kun Lun ranges. The mighty Himalayas, with their sawtooth faces, rise to 25,000 and 26,000 feet, with one peak at 29,000 feet. On the Moon, the Lunar Apennines have been estimated at 20,000 feet above the mountain floor. The Leibnitz and Doerfel ranges are estimated at 26,000 feet. One peak in the Riphaen Range is estimated at nearly 30,000 feet. [21]

At the very least, the similarity of the pattern of mountain ranges, plus the similarity in their elevations, suggest a similar kind of orogenesis with the mountain systems of the Earth. The assumption has been that the Moon was more solid and less plastic-like in its internal structure than the Earth. This has recently been questioned, due to the report of some observed volcanic activity. Perhaps the Moon, like its Binary Partner, is also composed of much fluid magma. If so, the possibility is that the Moon's mountain-building processes may be similar with those of the Earth; they also may be simultaneous in timing. With all of these aforementioned features considered conjointly the whole picture becomes historically more credible (and scientifically more apparent). [22]

---

[21] James S. Pickering, *1001 Questions Answered About Astronomy*, New York: Dodd, Mead & Co., 1959, pp. 36-37.

[22] A further discussion on the relationship between history and science is given in Chapter XII, pp. 318-319.

"To look upon a landscape . . . without any recognition of
the labor expended in producing it . . . is like visiting Rome
in the ignorant belief that the Romans of today had no
ancestors." . . . William Morris Davis[23]

5. Qualifications For a Theory of Orogenesis

Any understanding of the forces which have sculptured our
fluid sphere must accommodate many qualifications, not few.
Some of the qualifications are major; others are minor; all are
significant. Those qualifications which are major to some will be
minor to others, and those minor to some will be major to others,
depending on their backgrounds and disciplines. However, all the
qualifications, not just some, must be adequately met in order to
propose an adequate and helpful theory on orogenesis.

> To sum up, it is almost inevitable to admit that the physio-
> graphic evidence regarding features on the Earth's surface
> is such that it must be assumed that some parts of the
> Earth's crust have been subject to compression (crustal
> shortening), others have been subject to tension (mid-
> ocean rifts) and yet others to shearing (fracture zones).
> MOST THEORIES HAVE BEEN PROPOSED FOR THE
> PURPOSE OF EXPLAINING ONLY ONE OF THESE
> FEATURES AND ARE THEREFORE INADEQUATE
> WITH REGARD TO THE OTHERS. A THEORY OF ORO-
> GENESIS, TO BE ACCEPTABLE, MUST BE FLEXIBLE
> ENOUGH to allow for compression, tension, and shear of
> sufficient magnitude to be produced in the Earth's crust . . .
> IT APPEARS, THEREFORE, THAT THE PROBLEM OF
> FINDING THE CAUSES OF THE VARIOUS GEODY-
> NAMIC FEATURES MUST BE REGARDED AS STILL
> UNSOLVED.[24]

The following is a list of 14 specific qualifications for an
adequate theory of orogenesis; four are considered as major or
overriding in importance, while the importance of the other ten
qualification is not to be deemphasized. Major considerations for

[23]Hartshorne. *op. cit.*, p. 106. A valuable discussion of the entire problem of
geomorphology and genesis is given, pages 81-106.

[24]Scheidegger, *op. cit.*, p. 291.

orogenesis include explanations for:
1. CORRECT SCOPE
2. CORRECT TIMING
3. CORRECT DISTANCE OF CAUSATION
4. CORRECT DIRECTION OF CAUSATION

These four overriding specifications are developed further in the succeeding pages of this chapter. Other specifications, not developed further, include:

5. The Great Circle Pattern (and epicenters of the arcs).
6. The Scallop-like Alignment.
7. Parallelism of Uplifts.
8. Parallelism of Trenches with Uplifts.
9. A Mechanism for Sudden Thrust.
10. A Mechanism for Uplifting Thrust.
11. A Mechanism for Sufficient Magnitude of Thrust.
12. A Mechanism Including Numerous Types of Stress (not just one or two).
13. A Simultaneous Mechanism for Uplifting Oceans of Magma and Water.
14. A Simultaneous Mechanism for Forming Both Igneous and Sedimentary Formations.

The existing theories, anchored to Lyell's uniformitarian assumption, attempt to explain too few of these qualifications, and those too feebly. None attempts in any way to explain all of these qualifications conjointly.

> It is therefore necessary to re-examine all theories of orogenesis that have ever been invented, in order to determine what can be saved of them in the light of the presently available facts. *If this is done, it becomes immediately obvious that something fundamental is wrong with each and every one of the theories.*[25]

In the theory of astral catastrophism, most (and indeed the author thinks all) of these clear specifications are adequately answered. Certainly the specifications involving parallelism are apparent. Certainly the mechanisms involving force are met. Certainly the features of simultaneous magma and watery tidal

---

[25]Scheidegger, *op. cit.*, p. 289.

upheaval are inherent. Incidentally (but not coincidentally) the genesis of the lunar formations are also in focus.

In this theory of astral catastrophism,[26] it is conceived that the astral visitor was involved with the Earth-Moon system for several months; it did not graze the Earth just temporarily. It perhaps revolved around the Earth twice, bringing repeated crescendoes and diminuendoes to the Earth's surface as it rotated in chaos. As Job suggested, the "pillars of the Earth trembled."[27] With each approach, a new zone of horizontal uplift occurred (the Circum-Pacific first; the Alpine-Himalayan second). And with each rotation during crisis, there occurred a new range of horizontal uplift, or a further movement of a prior uplift. Series after series of sediment was simultaneously deposited and/or compressed.[27]

Thus in the view of astral catastrophism, one section of the Alps may have been uplifted one day; another section may have

[26]A model of this catastrophic crisis is given in Chapter VII describing astral orbits and celestial regions of dominance. The model as presented suggests a somewhat prolonged period of crisis, something like 150 days and 150 nights. Although a model could be presented involving either (a) a single grazing conflict, or (b) a series of single grazing conflicts by a series of visitors, nevertheless it is concluded that (c) there was but one visitor involved, and this for a prolonged period of time. Further reference is made to Hartshorne's chapter on *Time, Genesis, Geomorphology and Geology,* pp. 81-107, with particular reference to page 90. "The test of any such theory is not in its logic but in its workability . . . Whether explanatory analysis of development adds more than it detracts from a comprehension of the existing character of a landform as an integral element in areal variation is therefore a matter of judgment, rather than logic."

[27]Job, Chapter 9, verses 5-9 (numerous other comparable examples occur in the Book of Job).

> Yes I know, it is true, but how can mortal man be right before God?
> If one should want to contend with Him, he cannot answer one question in a thousand.
> God is wise in heart and mighty in strength; who has ever hardened himself against Him and prospered?
> God, *Who removes the mountains,* and they know it not, when He overturns them in His anger
> Who *shakes the Earth* out of its place, and the *pillars of it tremble;*
> Who commands the sun and it *apparently* rises not, and seals up the stars from view.
> Who alone stretches out the heavens, and treads upon the waves and high places of the sea;
> Who made the constellations the Bear, Orion and the Pleiades, and the vast starry spaces of the south;
> Who does great things past finding out, yes, marvelous things without number.

been uplifted a few days or even weeks later. But the time lapse was measured in hours, days and weeks, and not in terms of millions, tens and hundreds of millions of Lyellian years.

Correct Scope. This catastrophist considers the Alps to have been raised up suddenly, and with great force, along with the rest of the Alpine-Himalayan and Circum-Pacific series. This was a global uplift, involving both tides of magma and the lesser but yet very considerable inundation of watery tides. Uniformitarianism considers that one portion of the Alps was raised about 185,000,000 B.C. and about 27,000,000 years later, a second portion was raised; yet a third portion was raised another 31,000,000 years later, around 125,000,000 B.C. Thus the Jura Alps, along with the marine and terrestrial fossil-bearing strata contained therein, were uplifted tens of millions of years before (or after, as the case may be) the Bernese Alps, the Carnic Alps, or the Rhaetian Alps. Hence each uplift must be viewed by implication as local in nature. The Alps collectively occupy less than .01% of the Earth's surface.

This catastrophist considers that all (100%) of the Earth's surface was affected, one way or another. In terms of scope, there is a difference between the two approaches, and the magnitude of this difference may be of equal value as to noting the basic difference itself. In terms of scope, uniformitarianism considers .01% of the Earth's surface was affected in any given year; catastrophism considers that 100% of the Earth's surface was affected in the crisis year. The differential is 99.99%. Error is one thing, and degree of error is another. Both are important, and they can hardly be each half right. One of the approaches, at least, is in extreme error.[28]

Correct Timing. By Lyell's amazing time scale, in calling for oceans of time for each minor geological event, we find again

[28]Author's Note. Error and truth are considerations which have received the widest possible treatment. Occasionally well-known thinkers will propose or suppose that truth lies about midway between two opposites. (Their number is not small.) Thus, they posit, truth and presumably progress also lie midway at a compromise between two opposing views.

For example, two children disagree on the total of 5 and 5. One claims that it is 15; the other insists that it is 55. The profound appearing thinker promptly posits that the sum of 5 and 5 is 35, midpoint between 15 and 55. Many modern thinkers take this approach. It may serve well as parliamentarianism, but this type of rapprochement, or compromise, is inadequate, to say the least, for scientific or historical research.

the Alps to be dated between 125,000,000 B.C. and 185,000,000 B.C. The author's dating of this orogenetic uplift and associated Flood is 2800 B.C., + or - 500 years. This is approximately 5,000 years ago, over and against 150,000,000 years ago. This is a differential of about 99.997%. Lyell's original placing of the Ice Epoch at 1,000,000 years ago is a difference of about 99.8%, roughly of the same magnitude.

Restated, either the catastrophist or the uniformitarian view is wrong in timing and badly wrong. Error is one thing, but degree of error is another thing. This again is error in an extreme.

Distance of Causation. In terms of distance of causation, the uniformitarian considers the cause of orogenesis to be anywhere between 25 and 2,500 miles down, toward the core of the Earth, according to the particular theory examined. In the catastrophic approach, distance was somewhere between 25,000 and 250,000 miles out in space at various stages. Again there is a differential of between 99% and 99.9%, this time in terms of *astronomical distance,* as compared to the previous differentials of scope and timing. The magnitude of these differentials is consistently similar.

Direction of Causation. Note further that uniformitarianism considers the cause of orogenesis to be straight down, while catastrophism considers the cause to be celestial, straight up. The variance verges on 180°, which is the greatest possible difference. Here the apparent error of Lyellian uniformitarianism approaches 100%. Missing the target is one thing, but missing it by 180° is quite another thing. Contrast, not comparison, is in order for these two views.

Uniformitarianism: The doctrine that *existing processes,* acting as at present, are sufficient to account for all geological changes.

Catastrophism: The doctrine that changes in the Earth's crust have generally been effected *suddenly by physical forces.*[29]

A well meaning geologist has suggested that what we need

[29]*Webster's Collegiate Dictionary,* Springfield, Mass.: G. & C. Merriam Co., 1946, "catastrophism," p. 159; "uniformitarianism," p. 1093.

is a little catastrophic-uniformitarianism. This is incongruous. We do not talk about black whiteness. We do not talk about dry humidity, nor about moist aridity. We do not use opposites to describe each other, and if we do, we create confusion and unclear thinking. Mutually contradictory adjectives cannot modify each other. And when so used, it leads to muddling, not clarification.

For example, what would be the reaction of a waitress in a restaurant, who was given a request for scrambled eggs, sunnyside up? So it is with astral catastrophism and uniformitarianism. Catastrophes have scrambled the soils and strata of the Earth's prior age and perhaps on more than one occasion. And there have been serene interludes, embracing readjustments, new norms, new climates, new erosions, new geographies. This is not catastrophic uniformitarianism; it is catastrophism, because catastrophes have been primarily responsible for the remarkable engraving and etching of our Earth's surface; the same is true with the surface of our scar-faced satellite. Since this book proposes that this remarkable sculpturing of our terrestrial home has occurred as a result of astral catastrophes, with regard to *causation, direction, scope, distance and timing,* it thereby concludes that the uniformitarian hypothesis is 100% in error. Any philosophies or views which are attached thereto must also be scrutinized and re-examined, both judiciously and meticulously.

6. A Convergence of Disciplines

This is the second of three chapters dealing with catastrophism and the Earth's three fluid components—hydrosphere, lithosphere and atmosphere. The approach of astral catastrophism cuts across lines of many disciplines, from one horizon almost to the other. It begins with the physical sciences and basic astral premises. The conflict which occurred produced conditions, effects and patterns which were vital to the re-establishment of biological life, and hence to the natural sciences.

Effects of thinking in the natural sciences have come to have immense effects in the social sciences. Examples are in the works of Agassiz, Cuvier, Darwin, Hutton, Linnaeus and Lyell. Some philosophers and social scientists have come to look to the natural sciences for its basic guidelines. And similarly, many theologians have come to look to social science for many of their guidelines. Thus uniformitarianism is more than a philosophy;

it is a cosmology, and, seemingly, a negative and a poor one. Similarly, astral catastrophism is a cosmology, and a much better one.

Among the many disciplines which are involved in this approach are astronomy, astrophysics, ancient literature, climatology, geography, geology, history, folklores and anthologies, anthropology, zoogeography and historical ethnology (survival patterns).

The catastrophic theory as contained herein, will attempt to answer some questions, and it will perhaps give rise to many more. The catastrophic theory will no doubt give rise to controversy in the geological profession. This is to be expected since geology has been hibernating in the bed of uniformitarian theory, with its anti-Genesis ideas, for over 100 years. It is stated that uniformitarian cosmology (and geology) has no adequate theory for orogenesis; this is only one major shortcoming which it possesses. The catastrophic theory as presented is not offered as being in any sense anti-geological; rather it presents to geology some new and exciting horizons to traverse, after it arises out of its comfortable bed of anti-spiritual (and anti-scientific) uniformitarianism.

An Epitaph

Which of the following six quotations makes the most fitting epitaph for 130 years of Lyellian geology?

It is therefore necessary to re-examine all theories of orogenesis that have ever been invented, in order to determine what can be saved of them. . . .[30]

A century of geomorphology, dominated by the purpose of explaining genesis, has failed. . . .[31]

It appears, therefore, that the problem of finding the causes of the various geodynamic features must be regarded as still unsolved. . . .[32]

[30]Scheidegger, *op. cit.*, p. 289.

[31]Hartshorne, *op. cit.*, p. 91.

[32]Scheidegger, *op. cit.*, p. 291.

Sterility—barren, unproductive, destitute of ideas, as, "this is a sterile essay."[33]

Unfortunately, it is a fact that the "deformation theory" applying to the Earth is not known, thus leaving the matter of finding the causes of its present-day appearance wide open to speculation.[34]

These and similar protests which geographers have registered for more than a generation appear to run into a blank wall of dogma.[35]

And as Hartshorne has stated:

The test of any . . . theory is not in its logic but in its workability. Certainly there are cases—for example, volcanic peaks, basaltic dykes or ridge-and-valley areas of folded rock in which even partial knowledge of how terrain was formed may aid the comprehension of its present character . . . Whether explanatory analysis of development adds more than it detracts from a comprehension of the existing character of a landform as an integral element in areal variation is therefore a matter of judgment, rather than logic. It is somewhat disconcerting that insistence on the value of such analyses for geography comes primarily from those who produce them rather than from those who use them.[36]

Workability is the essence of theory. While logic helps, yet as Hartshorne suggests, logic often becomes a matter of judgment. Celestial catastrophism is a theory possessing workability; it also possesses logic. In fact, it appears to be *the* correct analysis of Earth history. A model of this catastrophe is included in a series of diagrams in Chapters VI and VII.

Tides, whether of oceans or magma, are a response to a gravitational interaction of two or more fields of gravity. The Flood and the orogenetic upheaval were different phases of the counter-dominating gravities.

---

[33]*Webster's Illustrated Dictionary*, Washington D.C.: The Publishers Co., Inc., 1962, "sterility," p. 650.

[34]Scheidegger, *op. cit.*, p. 148.

[35]Hartshorne, *op. cit.*, pp. 91-92.

[36]Hartshorne, *op. cit.*, p. 90.

However, in addition to the field of gravity, the Earth also possesses a magnetic field. The magnetic field would be in counter-dominating interaction with the magnetic field of the visitor. The Ice Epoch, it is posited, was primarily related to the magnetic phase of this cataclysm. Could it be that the Ice Epoch was part and parcel of this same catastrophe? Could it be that the Flood and the Ice Epoch were simultaneous in their enveloping of the Earth?

Here is a puzzle. Price, Rehwinkel, Vail, Nelson, Howorth and Miller were correct when they maintained that there was a global deluge. They also maintained that Ice Epoch deformations overrode Flood stratigraphy. They concluded that the Ice Epoch must have occurred after the Flood, and must have been caused by postdiluvian climates. This may appear logical on the surface, but is less coherent upon further analysis.

None of them demonstrated a mechanism for the physical cause of the Flood; none of them thought in celestial terms; they thought only in terms of stratigraphy, catastrophic burial and related terms. Price suggested that the Ice Epoch, coming after the Flood, must have been caused by a sudden shift in the location of the geographical poles. He inferred that the sudden climatological change would serve in explaining the Ice Epoch phenomena. It is at this point that the author diverges with these earlier catastrophists, who upheld catastrophic thought in lonely times.

It is herein proposed that the cause or genesis of the Ice Epoch did not precede the Flood; it is also proposed that the cause or genesis did not follow the Flood. They were one and the same catastrophe. While they were simultaneous, they were of different orders. One was of a gravitational order while the other was essentially of a magnetic order.

Following the Flood catastrophe, new equilibriums were reached. It took the waters many weeks, and even months, to drain off. The zones of mountain uplift continued quaking for years and decades, even centuries, as a new isostatic equilibrium gradually was established. It took centuries for the ice masses to outflow and melt. And as the ice masses melted, they fed icy cold water into the oceans, keeping the oceans at an abnormally low temperature. And it took dozens of centuries for the oceans to gradually find a new equilibrium of temperature.

It was in this earlier postdiluvian period, when ice was

outflowing over the Flood stratigraphy, that geological ice scourings were achieved. And it was in the early postdiluvian period that the oceans, and the Earth's wind systems were much lower in temperature than they are now. This, then, was a cool, even a cold era, and it continued until new hydrographical and climatic equilibriums were gradually reached.

Nevertheless, the origin of the mountain uplifts, the Flood, and the Ice Epoch were simultaneous and celestial. It is to this second and equally important phase of the catastrophe, the glacial phase, to which Chapter VI is directed.

VI chapter

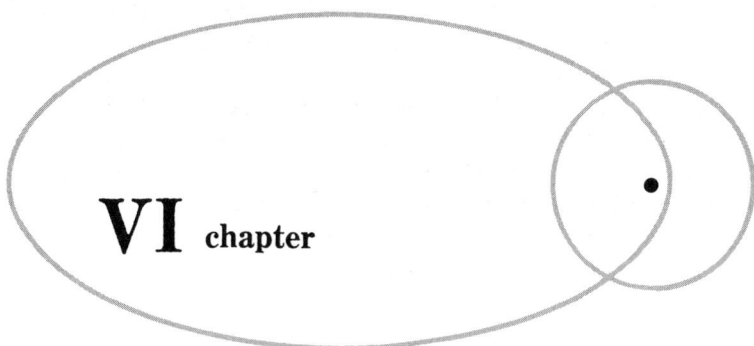

Glaciogenesis: The Cause of the
Ice Epoch

THE CAUSE OF THE ICE EPOCH is a pivotal subject in the study of astral catastrophism. Once the nature and scope of the ice cataclysm is perceived, then astral catastrophism is easily recognized, and geophysical consequences, as they apply to Earth history, become apparent.

There have been at least two icy catastrophes in our solar system. One involved the region of Saturn; the other involved the region of the Earth. The circumstance of the icy rings of Saturn is important because this may help establish a clue as to the nature of the Earth's Ice Epoch.

The rings of Saturn were originally considered to have been composed of rock-like fragments, similar to the composition of the asteroids or meteor streams. But in 1948, Gerard Kuiper measured the thickness of the rings of Saturn. They were already known to be about 41,500 miles in breadth and about 171,000 miles in diameter. There were three primary rings involved of varying widths up to 16,000 miles.[1]

Kuiper was surprised to find that the rings were only 10

---

[1]The diameter of the entire ring system is 171,000 miles. The outer ring is slightly over 10,000 miles wide, inside of which there is a dark band containing little or no material. This is Cassini's division, and is about 3,000 miles wide. Inside Cassini's division is a much brighter ring, about 16,000 miles wide. Inside this is another division, about 1,000 miles wide, inside of which is the crape ring, about 11,500 miles wide. The total ring system is about

miles thick. He was aware of the albedo or reflectivity of Saturn's rings. He immediately concluded that because rock fragments could not reflect as much light as the rings did, they must be rings of ice. Now it is generally accepted that the rings of Saturn are composed of icy particles. They are water in the solid state merely because of their great distance from the sun, and the resultant low temperature. No one knows exactly how much ice is involved in Saturn's rings. Relative to the planet Saturn, the amount of ice involved in her rings is rather negligible. Spread out evenly across her 16 billion square miles of surface, it would be of almost no consequence.

However, from the perspective of the Earth, the reverse is true. The Earth is about 100 times lighter than Saturn, and has about 1/80th of the amount of the surface of Saturn. From the Earth's perspective, there is a good deal of ice in Saturn's broad rings—enough, say, to initiate a pretty good-sized ice epoch.

The rings of Saturn are entirely within the critical distance involved in Roche's limit concerning an astral fragmentization.[2] If the material of the fragmentized body were in the solid state rather than the liquid, the gravity of the planet would prevent the coalescence, and the fragments would remain in orbits about the planet in accordance with Kepler's laws. Therefore, the origin of Saturn's rings must have been from some icy astral visitor which got too close and disintegrated under the influence of Saturn's immense gravitational field.

Are there many icy astral bodies in our solar system? Jupiter, Saturn, Uranus, and Neptune—the four major planets in our solar system—are composed of much ice (some astronomers say

41,500 miles wide. The inner edge of the crape ring is about 7,000 miles above the surface of Saturn.

Cassini's division is the primary void among Saturn's rings. It is caused by systematic perturbations caused by gravitational disturbances of Saturn's nearer and larger satellites. Cassini's division is $\frac{1}{2}$ of the period of Mimas, $\frac{1}{3}$ of the period of Enceladus, and $\frac{1}{4}$ of the period of Tethys. The gravitational fields of these three satellites swept out the original material in this region, resulting in separated rings of remaining material.

A similar illustration of perturbations has been caused by Jupiter upon the asteroid belt. At fractional periods of Jupiter, the asteroids have also been perturbed out systematically, thus leaving alternating belts containing either a concentration or a void of asteroids.

[2]A brief discussion of Roche's limit with reference to the Rings of Saturn was given in Chapter III, pp. 39 and 42. Further discussions of Roche's limit occur in numerous volumes on astronomy.

mostly of ices and hydrogen). Ganymede, one of Jupiter's moons, is considered to have a rock core and an ice crust. Io and Europa probably are composed of rock, like our moon. Callisto, some feel, is almost pure ice. Several of Saturn's satellites, like Saturn, are also presumed to be composed mostly of ice.[3]

The (1) origin of the ice in Saturn's rings seems to have been either within or beyond our solar system, from the cold and remote regions of the galaxy. The ice probably (2) approached Saturn via an orbit of substantial eccentricity, and the (3) depositing of the ice around Saturn must have been a response to the physical laws governing fragmentized particles.

Any acceptable theory of the Ice Epoch for our Earth must also adequately explain these three features: (1) the origin of the ice; (2) the method or mode of transportation of the ice; and (3) the particular location of the depositing of the ice. Although there have been numerous ideas and suggestions about the cause of the Ice Epoch which at one time engulfed our planet, all of the well-known ones have stemmed from uniformitarian thought. These theories of glaciogenesis are woven around nine major themes:[4]

1. A decrease in solar radiation.
2. The passing of the Earth through cold regions in the universe.
3. An increased eccentricity of the Earth's orbit.

---

[3]The densities of the Jovian Planets (Jupiter, Saturn, Uranus and Neptune) when compared to the density of water are 1.35, .71, 1.56 and 2.47 respectively. Saturn is the only one among them that would float in water, and may be composed of ices of carbon, nitrogen and oxygen, plus hydrogen. There is also a deep atmosphere of ammonia and methane.

The densities of Jupiter's four major satellites (Io, Europa, Ganymede and Callisto) are 4.03, 3.78, 2.35 and 2.06 respectively, considerably more than Jupiter's density of 1.35 (compared to water). This reflects that they contain probably no atmosphere, in contrast to Jupiter. This also reflects that Ganymede and particularly Callisto must be composed of rock cores and thick, deep crusts of ice. Pickering says "Callisto has a density which is very low and it may be made of ice." Thus the total composition of Callisto may not be fully known, but it seems certain that its 10 billion cubic miles of material must be mostly ice.

The densities of Saturn's six inner satellites are .5, .7, 1.2, 2.8, 2.0 and 2.4. Some are lighter than water and are presumed to be mostly · if not entirely ice. The others are presumed to contain rock cores, and deep crusts of ice, like Saturn itself.

[4]Dolph Earl Hooker, *Those Astounding Ice Ages*, New York: Exposition Press, 1958, pp. 19-20.

4. Variations in the amount of carbon dioxide in the atmosphere.
5. Variations in the directions of high-latitude ocean currents.
6. Variations in the relative proportions of land and water.
7. Variations in the angle of the axis to the plane of the ecliptic.
8. Changes in the location of the geographical poles.
9. Shifts in elevation of land areas relative to sea level.

It will suffice to merely point out that all nine themes embrace certain assumptions relative to (1) the origin, to (2) the mode of transport, and to (3) the location of the final deposition of the ice. All theories assume the origin was water vapor which had risen by evaporation from the Earth's oceans in lower latitudes. All theories assume that the method of transport was via clouds and planetary wind systems. And lastly, all theories consider that snow fell in the glacially affected areas because of the high latitude and the cold climate. These three basic assumptions are integral with Lyell's 19th century uniformitarian hypothesis.

All uniformitarian approaches presumed that snow fell unendingly over vast spans of time. Lyell first taught that the ice age ended about 1,000,000 B.C., but when it was later brought to his attention that Niagara Falls could be used as a crude natural chronometer of the ice epoch, he acknowledged 96% of the 99% dimension of his error. Since Lyell's day, a considerable volume of data has accumulated, reflecting further requirements. Following is a brief review of some ice circumstances and conditions. They involve requirements which any good hypothesis on Ice Epoch origin (glaciogenesis) must accommodate.

1. The Frozen Mammoths: An Illustration of Sudden Freezing

Mammoths were, along with mastodons, the largest members of the elephant family. They have become mummified in two manners, both of which suggest cataclysm and suddenness. In Alaska and Siberia mammoths have been mummified, apparently by the millions, both in ice and in sedimentary strata. It is as if they had been deposited in watery graves in some areas. but encased in ice in other areas, ice which has remained unmelted. Their entombment and refrigeration have been so effective that mammoth carcasses have been thawed to feed sled dogs, both in Alaska and Siberia; in fact, mammoth steaks have even been featured on restaurant menus in Fairbanks.

Every indication is that the mammoths died suddenly, in intense cold, and in great numbers. Death came so quickly that the swallowed vegetation is yet undigested in their stomachs and their mouths. Grasses, bluebells, buttercups, tender sedges, and wild beans have been found, yet identifiable and undeteriorated, in their mouths and stomachs.[5] What dropped the mammoths with such suddenness and such unearthly cold?

There is an illustration, well known and substantially recorded, which may explain this strange phenomenon. We refer to the case of ancient Pompeii, and the people engulfed therein. One observer was Pliny the Elder, a Roman naturalist, who himself lost his life in his investigation of the erupting Vesuvius. Pliny recounts that as the eruption began, many Pompeiians at first did not take it seriously; this sort of thing had happened before and had quickly settled down again. This particular time, however, the mountain continued to roar and rumble; smoke kept belching, cinders kept falling, and toxic gaseous fumes continued to be expelled in increasingly greater volumes. The people became apprehensive, and soon began to panic. In long streams they began to flee from the doomed city. As the cinders and sulphurous smoke turned day into night, and as the variable winds shifted, sudden squalls brought hot, toxic, sulphurous fumes down upon groups of fleeing refugees. Asphyxiation dropped the refugees in sudden death. Their fossil remains have been preserved by a blanket of pumice; the dying expressions yet remain on their faces, and the details in the fabric of their garments remains vividly imprinted in the layer of pumice.[6]

The excavations of Pompeii have revealed how swiftly the fleeing victims were asphyxiated, and promptly buried. In the case of the mammoths, the span of time between death and freez-

---

[5]Ivan T. Sanderson, "Riddle of the Quick-Frozen Giants," *Saturday Evening Post* Jan 16, 1960, p. 82.

[6]The fossils of these people, dead for 2000 years, have been achieved by a careful search of the ruins of Pompeii. Where a person died and was covered by pumice, the body decomposed, but the pumice did not subsequently shift. The result was a cavity in the pumice which, if filled with plaster of paris, produces a perfect specimen of the dying individuals, with dying expressions on their faces, in positions reaching for loved ones. Even the detail of the fabric of their clothes, along with wrinkles are preserved.

ing can be estimated quite accurately through an examination of the carcasses. This is determined by the extent of water separation within the cell, for water begins to separate within the cell at death, and it ceases to separate at freezing. The small extent of separated water indicates that carcasses were frozen rapidly, perhaps at temperatures below -150° F.[7]

Temperatures of this severity exist in our solar system, but not at the surface of the Earth. These temperatures exist, for example, among the frozen atmospheres of Jupiter and her icy satellites such as Callisto, Ganymede, Io and Europa. These temperatures exist among the icy crust of Saturn and her icy rings, along with such satellites as Iapetus, Rhea and Titan, to say nothing of Uranus and Neptune. If icy particles in temperatures nearing -200° F. were deposited upon the Earth from such an astral visitor, this could produce a great, icy avalanche of supercooled ice, possibly reproducing the supercooled conditions under which the mammoths so suddenly met their death. Under these conditions, even a huge, woolly mammoth would immediately perish, not to mention sheep, camels, rhinoceroses, bison, and other animals which have similarly been found encased in ice. They perished immediately by asphyxiation because, at these

---

[7]Sanderson, loc. cit., p. 82: "The Riddle of the Quick-Frozen Mammoths," Reader's Digest, April, 1960, p. 123.

It takes a great deal of cold to freeze a warm-blooded mammal. Men have been out in temperatures of -100° F. for up to half an hour without their lungs freezing. Sled-dogs in the Arctic and Antarctic have been out in blizzard conditions in temperatures well below -80° F. for many hours and even days without freezing, and admittedly moving air is more chilling than still air. In 1911 when Scott took his ill-fated dash to the South Pole, his little Shetland ponies survived until their food gave out.

At -40° F. it takes 20 minutes to quick-freeze a dead turkey, 30 minutes to preserve a side of beef. But these are mere bits of meat, not the mammoths clothed in fur, at a temperature of about 98° F. Unless we have tremendous cold outside, the center of the animal we are trying to freeze will remain comparatively warm for some time, probably long enough for decomposition to start. Meanwhile, the actual chilling of the flesh will be slow enough for large crystals to form within its cells. Neither event occurred with most mammoths, although one of them has been found by the radiocarbon dating method to be just over 10,000 years old. The flesh of many of the animals found in the muck is remarkably fresh. Frozen-food experts say they must have been frozen at well below -150° F.

Further, several studies indicate that mammoths were not especially designed for the Arctic; nor did they live in Arctic conditions. The Indian elephant, which is a close relative of the mammoth . . . has to have several hundred pounds of food daily just to survive. But, for more than six months of the year, there is nothing for any such creature to eat on the Arctic tundra. Yet there were tens of thousands of mammoths.

temperatures, their lungs were frozen solid. They dropped immediately, and death ensued very shortly.

Concerning the perishing of the mammoths, the uniformitarian approach has been non-plussed, and has had no explanation. The same applies to quick-frozen rhinoceroses, sheep, horses, oxen, lions, tigers, bison, and numerous other animals.[8]

Wrangell, the explorer, observed on Bear (Medvizhi Ostrova) Island that the soil consisted of only sand, ice, and such a quantity of mammoth bones that they seemed to be the chief substance of the island. On the Siberian mainland, he observed that the Siberian tundra was dotted more with mammoth tusks than with Arctic shrubbery.[9]

Pallas related that there was not a riverbed in all Russia or Siberia, from the Don to the Bering Strait, which did not contain bones of elephants and other animals.[10] It has been recorded that during two consecutive decades (1880 to 1900) at least 20,000 elephant tusks were taken from one single Siberian

---

[8]Charles H. Hapgood, "The Mystery of the Frozen Mammoths," *Coronet*, September, 1960, p. 76.

Hapgood, bothered by this problem, hazarded a guess as to the cause of the quick-freeze. He wrote as follows: "Only one possibility, I believe, can explain this riddle of science and with it the mysterious extinction of the mammoth. In my opinion, the climate did not change; the entire surface of the earth migrated from one climate zone to another . . ." He continues on in this vein, suggesting a shift in the location of the earth's axis. He notably fails to explain what could have caused the shift in axis, which would be something closer to the real cause. His tentative explanation is still grounded to the idea that the snow came from evaporated ocean water, and hence it is only another wrinkle or rehashing of the uniformitarian approach. Interestingly enough, catastrophists Price, Nelson and Rehwinkel also tended toward this type of explanation, which differs only modestly from the classical uniformitarian suppositions.

[9]Byron C. Nelson, *The Deluge Story in Stone*, Minneapolis: Augsburg Publishing House, 1931, p. 122.

[10]Nelson, *op. cit.*, p. 125. "The remains of mammoths are incredibly numerous in Siberia and, strangely enough, their numbers increase farther north toward the Arctic Ocean. Their bones are spread over the bottom of that ocean, where ships have dredged them up. And 200 miles to the north, in the New Siberian Islands, not much farther from the North Pole than New York is from Chicago, mammoth remains are the thickest of all."

The reason that the New Siberian Islands and other offshore islands in the Arctic Ocean were populated by fauna in that area are (1) there was a subtropical climate, and (2) oceans were lower by approximately 400 feet, resulting in land bridges not only to these islands, but also between Siberia and Alaska across what is now the Bering Strait. Africa, Europe, Asia, and North America were once an interconnected land mass in that age. South America, like Australia, was an island continent, lacking a land bridge which today exists.

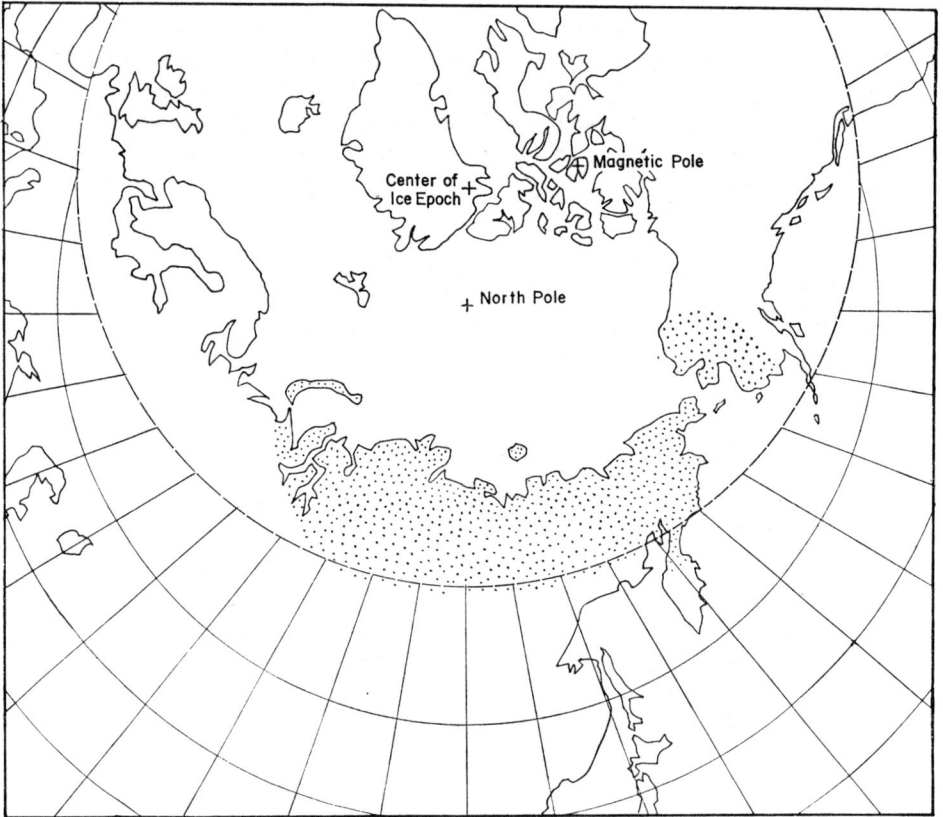

LOCATION OF THE ICE FOSSILS

FIGURE 13

ivory mine. Ivory trade from Siberia has had a long history, as old as the recorded annals of the area.[11] Traditions of Siberian ivory are at least as old as the historians of the Roman Empire.

The long series of astounding finds of icy carcasses are too voluminous to relate here. The findings of Howorth, Nelson, Rehwinkel, Sanderson, and Vail are notable. But the important thing is that an adequate explanation is needed, and furthermore, an adequate explanation should be possible. The slow snow theory intrinsic to uniformitarianism is wed to the notion that climatological bases contain the explanation.[12] In the catastrophic theory, however, the climatological approach with its various complications, is bypassed, allowing for an entirely new basis to explain the suddenness, the extremeness, the source of the ice, the simultaneous condition of icy and watery graves, and other related phenomena. This icy catastrophe was a great event in Earth history, and it was an historical event (rather than a scientific event). Some scientists may say that this sort of icy and watery catastrophe couldn't happen; the theory set forth here suggests that it did.[13]

2. The Regions of Sudden Chilling

The regions of sudden chilling occurred in both hemispheres, and mostly in the high latitudes (high latitudes relative to both

[11]Hapgood, *op. cit.*, pp. 71-72.

[12]Hapgood, *op. cit.*, p. 74. "Baron Edward Toll, the explorer, reported finding a fallen 90-foot fruit tree with ripe fruit and green leaves still on its branches, in the frozen ground of the New Siberian Islands. The only tree vegetation that grows there now is a one-inch high willow."

[13]The author took courses in geography and related subjects in two different colleges, and has discussed this problem with uniformitarians in several different departments. The tendered explanations were nearly identical. The following explanation was suggested:
Perhaps some mammoth started walking across the ice in a blizzard on a recently frozen lake. Perhaps he wandered into an area where the ice was too thin, and the mammoth fell through and drowned. Perhaps he had been carrying his breakfast of buttercups and tender sedges with him across the ice, and drowned with them yet in his mouth. Maybe through some freak of nature, his drowned body did not deteriorate, but was preserved until a permanent change of climate occurred. And possibly this sort of thing happened to thousands or millions of animals over long periods of time—animals including bison, horses, lions, rhinoceroses, sheep and others.
The author totally disagrees with such inadequate explanations, no matter how sincerely tendered, no matter how involved the path of logic may be.

the geographical poles and the magnetic poles). In Antarctica, less than 200 miles from the South Pole, Byrd found evidences of a former warm and humid climate which nurtured luxuriant forests.[14] On the island of Spitzbergen (Svalbard), palm leaves ten and twelve feet long have been fossilized, along with fossilized marine crustaceans—which could only inhabit tropical waters. This suggests that at one time the temperatures of the Arctic Ocean were similar to the contemporary temperatures of the Bay of Bengal or the Caribbean Sea. Spitzbergen is half way between the northern tip of Norway and the North Pole, at a latitude of 80° N. Today, ships can reach Spitzbergen through the ice only about two or at the most three months during the year. And in the New Siberian Islands (slightly warmer than Spitzbergen at a latitude of 75° N.), explorers claim to have found species of tropical plants encased in ice, as were the mammoths. How could this be? Were explorers spinning yarns?

Antarctica, Spitzbergen, and the New Siberian Islands are but three places where evidences occur that coldness came with extreme suddenness, wiping out a previous tropical climate with a finality that has lasted over many thousands of years. This directly leads to two queries: First, what caused the abrupt change which so dramatically froze the fauna and flora?[15] And secondly, and probably more important, what was the nature of the previous climate? This second question will be dealt with in Chapter IX, and the reasons will be given as to why an answer to this question ultimately may be the more significant. Mean-

---

[14]Dolph Earl Hooker, *Those Astounding Ice Ages*, New York: Exposition Press, 1958, p. 44, as taken from *National Geographic*, October 1935. Admiral Byrd wrote as follows:

"The rock fragments from this mountainside invariably included plant fossils, leaf and stem impressions, coal and fossilized wood. Here at the southernmost known mountain in the world, scarcely two hundred miles from the South Pole, was found conclusive evidence that the climate of Antarctica was once temperate or even sub-tropical."

[15]Reference is made to Chapter V, page 77, footnote 16. It is suspected not only that the Ice Epoch descended on the Earth suddenly from outer space, but also during the same chaotic period, the location of the geographical poles of the Earth and also possibly the angle of axis suddenly changed. The sudden descent of the Ice Epoch from outer space will assist in understanding why the freezing came so suddenly. The sudden shift in latitudes may assist in understanding why tropical crustaceans populated the Arctic Sea in the previous age, and also it may assist in explaining, in part, why frozen fauna are found in greater numbers in Siberia as the distance toward the North Pole decreases.

while, the immediate question is, what happened? Was this sudden coldness natural or unnatural, seasonal or unearthly? Uniformitarianism is hard-pressed to produce a satisfactory answer.

3. The Depth of the Ice Mass

The suddenness of the onset of the Ice Epoch has been briefly considered, relative to both hemispheres. The evidences are amazing and phenomenal. Of no less import, and of no less amazement, is the depth to which ice occurred. Sudden frost and extremely cold air are one thing; ice in depth is another thing. What was the depth of the ice mass in the Northern Hemisphere, or in the Southern Hemisphere?

It has been established, from the direction of ice flows, studies of gradients, distances, and other related data, that there were several nodes of ice on the Canadian Shield. It has further been established that the depth of ice at these nodes was between 15,000 and 17,000 feet.

In the Southern Hemisphere, a comparable circumstance apparently existed. In 1958, an ice core was taken on the Antarctic Ice Cap near Byrd Station. Drilling commenced at an elevation of 5,000 feet above sea level. The thickness of the ice sheet was 10,000 feet, and the drill went through solid ice all the way. This means that ice is not only situated 5,000 feet above sea level in the Antarctic Region; it is also resting on terra firma some 5,000 feet below sea level.[16] How is this explained?

Traditional uniformitarian thought has it that snow fell over unending epochs until ice was built up to 10,000 or 15,000 feet, after which it suddenly began to flow and/or melt faster than the rate of buildup. This is difficult to accept, for numerous reasons. For instance, uniformitarians must maintain that falling snow accomplished this both at elevations of 17,000 feet above sea level and 5,000 feet below sea level, and in both the fluid atmosphere and in the fluid ocean. Is this what we are to believe?

After all, snow when falling at or about 32° F. into brine will not sink; it will dissolve and form a sort of floating slush. And we all know what just a little bit of salt will do on a frozen pavement. The real question here does not regard whether it

[16]Hooker, op. cit., p. 68.

is ludicrous to propose that ice might be formed in brine, some 5,000 feet below sea level, by falling snow flakes. The real question is whether or not uniformitarians require us to believe other propositions equally ludicrous.

On the other hand, if it is believed that ice, descending from outer space at a superrefrigerated temperature around –200°F., caused the sudden and extreme change in atmospheric temperatures, then the sudden asphyxiation and freezing of the mammoths becomes logical. Similarly, the stacking up of ice in nodes 10,000 to 15,000 feet deep becomes conceivable. Furthermore, if this is a period of simultaneous gravitational and magnetic conflict, with tides alternately 5,000 and 10,000 feet both above and below mean sea level, then formations including ice deposits could well occur below mean sea level. And apparently this is what happened, for ice does rest on bedrock some 5,000 feet below sea level, and it has had enough coldness to overcome both the heat of oceanic melting and the heat of internal pressure. This similarly checks with mammoth fossils engulfed in ice but also in alluvium.

At this point, a further parallel needs to be seen. In the previous chapter it was pointed out that mountain uplifts, global in scope and scallop-like in alignment, traversed both continental massifs and oceanic basins with equal ease. Somewhat similarly, it seems, ice masses of vast dimensions were deposited in high latitudes (relative to both geographical and magnetic poles) indifferent to and irrespective of whether the particular area was an oceanic basin or a continental massif. This parallelism relative to orogenesis and glaciogenesis must not be overlooked.

Three perspectives of the Ice Epoch have thus far been noted: (1) The suddenness in timing, with the mammoths as the prime illustration; (2) The regions in location, with Antarctica, Spitzbergen and the New Siberian Islands as illustrations; and (3) The depth of the ice mass, with both the Canadian Shield and the Antarctic Shelf serving as illustrations. The depth of the ice on the Canadian Shield was approximately 3 miles; presumably it was originally of a similar depth on the Antarctic Continent. Next let us briefly consider the volume of ice involved.

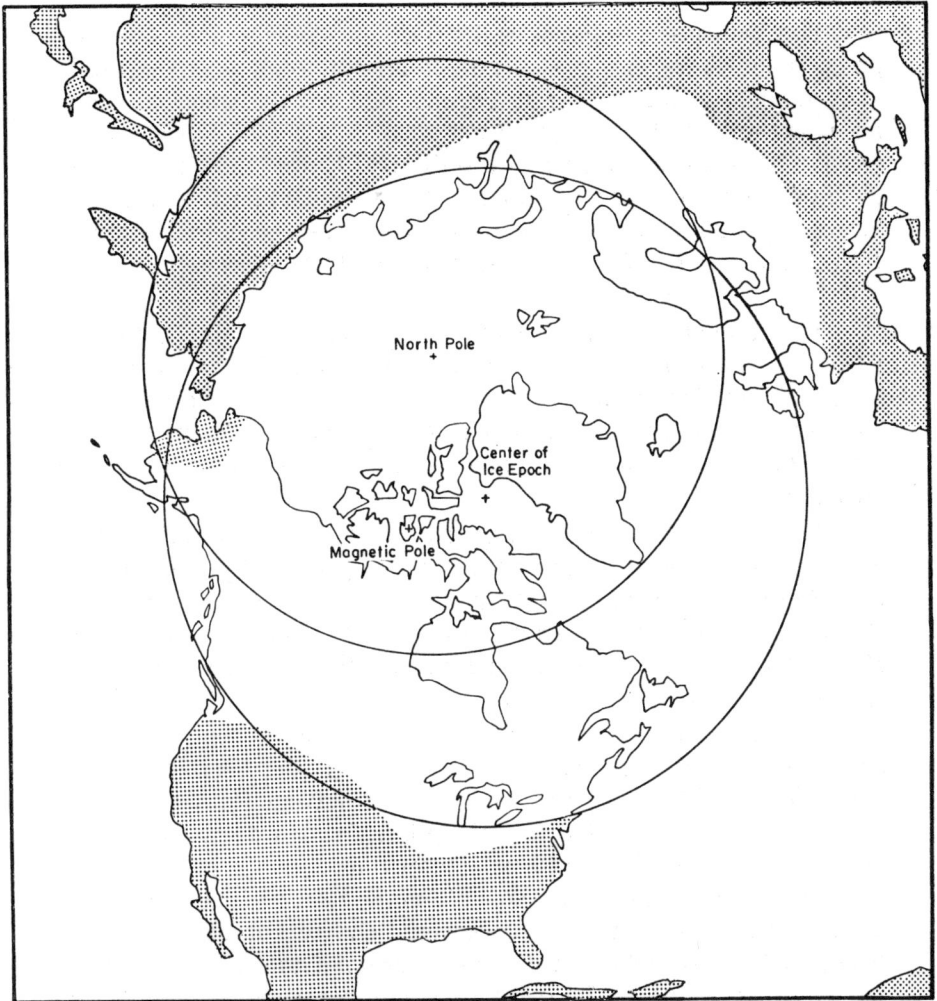

THE GEOGRAPHICAL LOCATION OF THE ICE EPOCH IN THE
NORTHERN HEMISPHERE

with regard to   (1)   the Geographical Center of the Ice Age
                   (2)   the Geographical North Pole
                   (3)   the Magnetic North Pole

FIGURE 14

4. The Volume of the Ice Mass

The ice mass is pretty well traced in the Northern Hemisphere since there is a prevalence of land at high magnetic and geographical latitudes—Asia, Europe, and North America. The ice mass extended from Eastern Alaska to Central Europe, and from the fringes of Siberia to the Central United States. Figure 14 illustrates the region involved. Note that while it is located largely in high latitude areas, it is nevertheless eccentric in location to the North Pole, but is more central to the Magnetic North Pole.

The diameter of the breadth of the ice mass was between 5,000 and 5,200 miles. The area it covered was about 17,000,000 square miles. It is equal to all of the land surface in the Western Hemisphere, including both Americas and their offshore islands. Or, on the other hand, it is equal to the continent of Asia in its entirety.

This was the area involved in the Northern Hemisphere. Presumably a nearly equal amount of ice descended in the Southern Hemisphere also. Certainly such far removed locations as Southern Chile, New Zealand, Antarctica, Tasmania, and the Kerguelen Islands indicate abundant evidences of a similar history.

The ice was approximately 3 miles deep in its central nodes, and it feathered out toward the edges. On the basis of conic volumes, the volume of the ice in the Northern Hemisphere is estimated at about 6,000,000 cubic miles. Probably a like amount was deposited in the Southern Hemisphere. This volume can be compared against the post-diluvian rise in sea level, as measured on the continental shelves. The recent rise was between 350 and 450 feet. This was a result of the melting of the ice in the Ice Epoch. The two methods of figuring the volume of the ice check out quite well.

Thus the estimate of the ice involved in the Ice Epoch in both hemispheres is between 12,000,000 and 14,000,000 cubic miles. This is a lot of ice to account for, by Earth's standards. Furthermore, here is a lot of heat transfer to explain and a lot of area as well as a lot of elevation to explain, whether above or below sea level.

The volume of heat required to reduce 12,000,000 cubic miles of water from 70° F. to below freezing and turn it into ice exceeds 3 septillion calories. This is enough heat to reduce many Earth atmospheres to absolute zero. Or in another perspective, this is enough heat loss to freeze 400 cubic feet of ice for every square foot of surface of the Earth. Imagine 400 blocks of ice, stacked vertically, for each square foot of Earth surface. This is the order of magnitude of heat exchange which somehow must be explained.

Thus far, we have discussed coldness and ice with regard to (1) suddenness of timing, (2) regions in location, (3) depth of ice, and (4) volume of ice and the magnitude of heat exchange. Twelve million cubic miles of ice is a great deal to explain. Let us now consider the geometrical shape of the ice formation.

5. The Geometry of the Ice Mass

Any acceptable theory on the ice mass must accommodate itself to the geometry of the ice formation. There were several nodes on the Canadian Shield, from 15,000 to 17,000 feet in elevation, generally about 3 miles deep at these apexes. From these areas, the ice flowed outward in a radial pattern and in every direction, corrected only by coriolis forces or local topographical features. It flowed over hills hundreds and even over a thousand feet high, and swept on over valley and dale for hundreds of miles. As it flowed, it gathered rocks, timber, and other debris which were ground and ultimately dropped at its edges, forming lateral and terminal moraines. The extent of the ice flow is determined from and orthogonal to the terminal moraines; the direction of the flow was parallel to such formations as drumlins and the lateral moraines. The path of flow is also plotted by locations of erratic boulders, striations and other methods.

According to uniformitarian theory, the ice was supposedly formed by snow, which had been transported by wind systems from moist, warm regions. The snow was to have fallen for many eons, until conditions changed and the processes of build-up were exceeded by the processes of out-flow and melting. This hypothesis does not agree with the manner of the flow of the ice mass; neither does it agree with the direction of the ice flow.

Perhaps the best illustration is found in the coldest area of the Earth, Interior Antarctica, where snow does not fall in great amounts; in fact, Interior Antarctica ranks along with the interior of the Sahara Region in precipitation.[17] It is rather at the fringes of Antarctica where substantial snows occur, for this is the region where warmer and more humid maritime air mixes with the cold, dry, interior air. A similar condition occurs in the Northern Hemisphere. The regions of abundant snowfall are mostly at maritime locations on the Arctic peripheries where warm maritime airs mix with cold Arctic airs. A saucer-shaped pattern for snowfall occurs in the Northern Hemisphere. Though more irregular, it is nevertheless similar to that in the Southern.

If falling snow is to have been the cause of the ice mass, it would be logical to presume that ice would be deepest where the snowfall was the greatest. There would be a thicker accumulation at the edges than at the interior or center where little humid air would penetrate. But geology has revealed that the ice mass was conical in geometrical shape, not saucer-shaped.

Furthermore, the pattern of ice flow also does not agree with the uniformitarian hypothesis. Today there are slow-snow glaciers in the mountains along the Pacific Ocean in Alaska, British Columbia, Washington, and Oregon, which flow in a riverine pattern, avoiding the hills and ridges and concentrating in the valleys. But the flow of ice, following its deposition in the Ice Epoch, was largely oblivious to topography until the flow feathered out at the fringes. In the more central portions, it flowed en masse over hills hundreds and thousands of feet high with seeming indifference. This is a radial pattern of flow.

A radial pattern of flow occurs when material flows outward in all directions from the center until a new equilibrium is established. This occurs, for instance, when honey is poured on bread, when milk is spilled on the table, or when pancake batter is dropped onto the griddle. Such events are sudden which cause radial patterns of flow. Gradual events cause riverine patterns of flow. The radial pattern of flow of ice from the Ice Epoch is another evidence of sudden accumulation. The illustration of the freezing of the mammoths was given to portray sudden chilling of the atmosphere; this was simultaneous with the sudden descent or dumping of great masses of ice (great volumes by Earth's standards) upon the high latitude regions.

Thus far we have considered the following features of an

---

[17]Hooker, *op. cit.*, p. 30. "The everlasting wind blowing from the pole is as dry as the winds over the Sahara. . . ."

adequate theory of glaciogenesis: (1) suddenness in timing; (2) regions in location; (3) depth of ice; (4) volume of ice and the magnitude of heat exchange; and (5) geometry of the ice mass and the radial pattern of flow. Let us now consider the eccentric location of the ice mass in the Northern Hemisphere.

6. The Eccentric Location of the Ice Mass

Figure 14 illustrates that the ice mass, rather than having been centered on the North Pole or on the Magnetic North Pole, was considerably closer to the Magnetic Pole than the Geographic Pole. Moreover, there is reason to suspect that the Magnetic Pole has migrated in post-diluvian times, having once been located in the area between Northern Baffin Island and Northwestern Greenland.

Uniformitarian hypotheses have invariably suggested that the ice mass was located in the high latitudes because that is where the climate is coldest, and where there is minimum solar radiation. This explanation fails, however, to account for the observed eccentricity in the location of the ice mass.

Notice that the ice mass appears to have missed almost all of Siberia, excepting the offshore islands. This is the coldest portion of the Northern Hemisphere in our age. Notice also that it spread out over the Central States down to the 37th latitude. This is more than half way to the equator. Illinois is about 500 miles closer to the Magnetic North Pole than is Northern Siberia. People in rural Illinois get a much better view of the Northern Lights (Aurora Borealis) than do Siberians, because they live closer to the Magnetic North Pole.

In noticing the location of the Aurora Borealis in association with the location of the ice mass, we must remember that sometimes in geography associative relationships are as meaningful as "cause and effect" relationships. The Aurora is related to the Van Allen Belts (see Figures 15 and 16) and the magnetic poles. During periods of sunspot activity, charged particles are emitted from the Sun and interact with the Earth's magnetic field. They are shunted around the magnetic field at high velocities; they are deflected, essentially by the magnetic field of the Earth. They tend to converge over the magnetic poles, and collide with atmospheric particles in the ionosphere. These collisions produce elec-

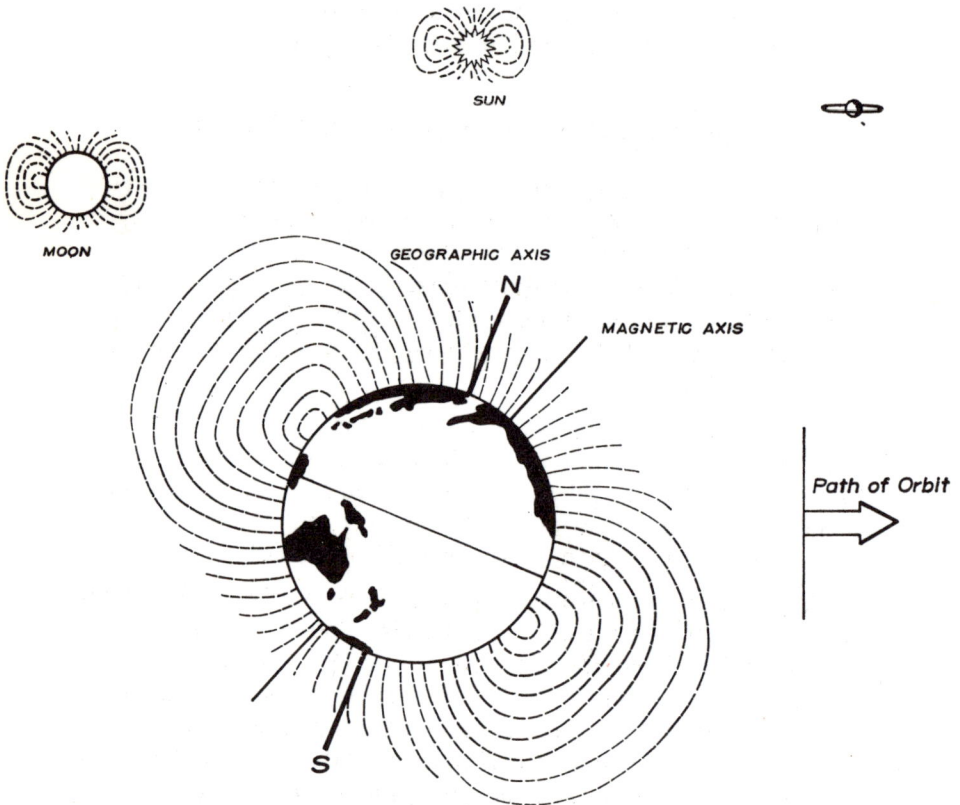

THE ASTROPHYSICAL LOCATION OF THE MAGNETIC
FIELD WITH REGARD TO:

      (1)   Geographical Axis of Earth

      (2)   the Magnetic Poles &

      (3)   the Path of Orbit

AS VIEWED FROM 180° LONGITUDE

FIGURE 15

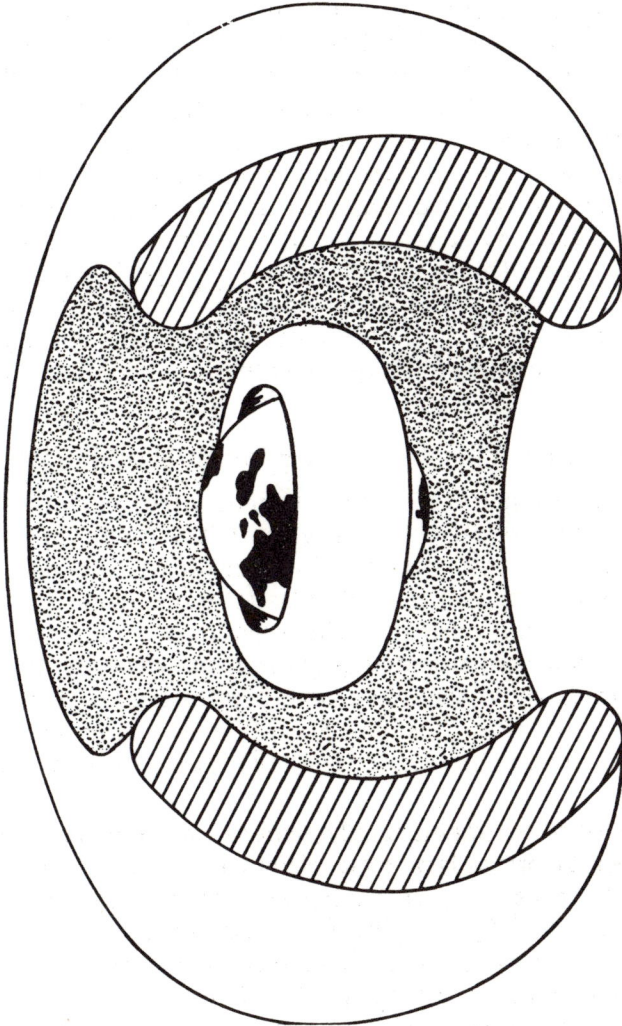

FIGURE 16

Another Perspective of the Van Allen Belts

trical changes which, in their ethereal brilliance, are termed Northern Lights. In losing velocity, the particles begin to descend.

It is our supposition that the location of the ice mass—an important factor in the astral-gravitational-magnetic catastrophe—was dependent more on the magnetic axis than the geographical axis. There seems to be a relationship, as yet not understood, between the geographical axis and the magnetic axis. However, had the magnetic poles been located in tropical climates, it is suspected that the ice mass would also have occurred in tropical climates. Therefore, the ice mass which descended largely in high latitudes offers no strength to the uniformitarian proposition, for the Arctic Circle and the Ice Epoch peripheries are eccentric to each other. The only coincidence between the two areas lies in the fact that the geographic and magnetic poles coincide within about 1200 miles of each other.

7. The Ice Cave Phenomena of Eastern Washington

It has been demonstrated that similar arcuate mountain patterns occur with equal boldness on both the Earth and her satellite. It has also been demonstrated that arcuate mountain patterns traverse both continental massifs and oceanic basins, and andesitic or basaltic regions with seemingly equal ease. It has similarly been demonstrated that immense deposits of extremely cold ice have occurred in magnetic polar regions, both on continental massifs (the Canadian Shield) and on the bedrock beneath oceanic areas (the Antarctic Shelf), also with seemingly equal ease.

Consider now yet another phenomena, namely ice sandwiched between layers of lava rock. Sedimentary rock is waterlain and usually considered as having been formed under moderate temperatures. Igneous rock is usually considered as forming under temperature conditions other than freezing. The ice which we will now examine is that found not above, not below, but between formations of igneous rock, which is normally associated with high pressures and temperatures.

In the intermontane plateau west of the Rockies and east of the Cascades, there was a great outpouring of lava during the Flood catastrophe. In some places, the lava deposits exceed 8000 feet in depth upon original bedrock. There are many successive layers of lava, anywhere from a few inches to hundreds of feet thick. They are often separated by minute layers of shale. This lava plateau covers approximately 150,000 square miles, and covers parts of five states—almost half of Washington, nearly two thirds of Oregon, and lesser parts of Idaho, Nevada, and California.

We contend that at this time of cataclysmic upheaval, lava flowed or bled out upon the Earth's surface in several parts of the world, including the Abyssinian plateau of Africa, the Deccan plateau of India, and also lesser lava plateaus in Arabia and Brazil. This outletting of lava could have been simultaneous with the deposition of the ice; however in the region of Eastern Washington, the ice deposition area coincided with the area of lava outflow.

At the northern edge of this lava plateau, inflowing ice complicated geophysical features. Great coulees were formed by rivers of flowing ice. The Columbia Valley, Moses Coulee, and Grand Coulee are several examples. Throughout this area, particularly in Northern Washington, but also occasionally in Idaho and Oregon, we find the phenomena of ice caves. Much ice remains, sandwiched in between layers of lava (of igneous origin), and that which has melted has left empty areas, the caves themselves.

When the Milwaukee Railroad was being built, section gangs discovered ice caves in the Frenchman Hills in southern Grant County, Washington, and they used them to refrigerate their beef. When road construction crews made great cuts through the lava hills of the Grand Coulee country, they again ran into great pockets of ice residing within the lava hills. In Okanogan County, Washington, in the hills above Tonasket, an ice cave exists which spelunkers have followed for 7,000 feet without finding its end.[18] And it has been reported that outside of Bend, Oregon, a man who was digging a foundation for his house encountered an ice cave.[19]

A small ice cave is located about fifteen miles downstream from Grand Coulee Dam, in the hills overlooking the Columbia River, on the Norman Alling ranch. This particular cave, a small

[18]Mr. Arthur Patten, Tonasket, Washington.

[19]Mr. Rupert Shaw, Seattle, Washington.

one, had likely been known to the Indians. In homestead days, the Allings used the cave for refrigeration, and thus ate beef during the hot summer months while their neighbors ate salt pork. Even today, by family tradition, as the family gathers on each 4th of July, one of the foremost of the festivities is the making of home-made ice cream with the old wooden bucket and crank and using fresh ranch cream and ice that is obviously old, (at least 5,000 years old) in terms of terrestrial existence.

The ice cave is at the base of a natural terrace. Rising above and over the cave is a large hill composed solely of lava and ice. Its face, almost a cliff, is over 300 feet high, and beyond that are further rises. As one stands in front of the cave, one feels the chill draft emanating. One then enters the cave—prehistoric in existence and located between layers of lava in a temperate climate. One views the massive icy stalactites and stalagmites, and is awed with wonder at the architecture and origin of these ancient ice structures.

At the base of the terrace, in addition to the ice cave, is a spring formed by melting water from the ice contained within the hill. Its temperature is a constant 34° F., summer and winter. The rate of water flowing per hour from this icy cool spring was sufficient to accommodate ranch needs, including watering of the livestock. The amount of water lost in seepage is thought to be far greater than the amount of water flowing from the spring itself. If the rate of flow of water, including both that from the spring and that lost in seepage, is five gallons per hour[20] (and since this essay recognizes the many virtues in conservatism, this estimate is conservative), then by simple calculations, at least 1,000,000 tons of ice have melted from within this one hill over the past 5,000 years. And no one knows how much yet remains unmelted; unquestionably both amounts are vast when viewed from any perspective. Recall that this ice occurs between lava formations in a climate which averages 40° F. annually and which, some 10,000 to 15, 000 feet below

[20]Mr. Arthur Kalmen, Grand Coulee, Washington. Mr. Kalmen is an employee of the Bureau of Indian Affairs for the Colville Indians, a man who is conservationist-minded, being a member of the Department of Interior. He is familiar with other ice caves in addition to this particular one on the Alling ranch and its surrounding area. Our estimate of 5 gallons of water per hour from the spring at the base of the hill containing the ice cave is considered conservative by Mr. Kalmen.

these ice formations, has temperatures which make water boil. (From within, temperatures rise rapidly in depth, increasing approximately 16° F. per 1000 feet.) For ice to maintain its state under these conditions for millenia is no small feat. The fact that the ice has not fully maintained its solid state and has partly melted is the reciprocal of the ice caves.

Does this phenomenon of ice sandwiched between layers of igneous rock seem strange? Did Wrangel's narrative concerning mammoths frozen by the hundreds of thousands also sound strange? If the proper perspective of catastrophism is considered, neither of these phenomena is impossible. Ice sandwiched in among layers of ingeous rock is really no more unusual than ice residing at oceanic depths upon Antarctic bedrock; it is no more unusual than ice residing within and around millions of mammoth carcasses.

Is it less ludicrous, or more ludicrous, to maintain steadfastly that snowflakes, falling gradually over long eras, (1) accomplished the ice and lava sandwiches of Eastern Washington as compared to (2) the achievement of forming and maintaining ice 5,000 feet below sea level in salt water or (3) the achievement of quick-freezing Alaskan and Siberian mammoths in massive numbers? Are these requirements, which are placed on the human reason, just too much? But are these the only ludicrous requirements levied on human reason by the uniformitarians?

There are many factors involved in this icy catastrophe. All are combinations of three functions acting simultaneously upon the three earthian fluids (magma, oceans, air). They are (1) astral ice, (2) heat exchange, and (3) tides. These factors include astral crisis with both gravitational and magnetic forces at work, and they include principles of orogenesis—patterns of uplifts, both on our planet and on its scar-faced satellite, the Moon. They include upwelling tides of lava (magma) plus overriding tides of oceanic source. They include astral ice, quick-frozen fauna, suddenly-drowned fauna, heat exchanges, warm oceans turned into Arctic waters, and new climates. These are all related. The effect of the gravitational forces can perhaps be isolated or separated from those of magnetic origin; the hydrographical from the lithographical or atmospheric; the orogenetic from the genesis of the ice mass; one mountain uplift from another within this period of conflict; and one glacial node from another, timewise within the crisis. However, none of these things can be disassociated from the totality of the event.

One further perspective should be touched upon to which we shall return to later. When was it that these events, particularly illustrated by the forming of the ice caves of Eastern Washington, occurred? Uniformitarian thinking originally held that the Ice Epoch occurred 1,000,000 years ago, and it still holds that the lava instrusions of Eastern Washington occurred 1,000,000 years ago. But the ice sandwiched within is only 10,000 years old, according to uniformitarianism's own revisions. And again, uniformitarianism views the Cascades as being about 150,000,000 years old; yet these ice formations are obviously interrelated.The question asked is: How long has the ice, contained within these lava hills, been melting? For 1,000,000 years? For 150,000,000 years? For 5,000 years? According to parallel data and mechanics, demonstrated in Chapters V, VII, VIII, IX and XI, a recent timing of this astral catastrophe is likely.

8. Perspectives of the Ice Epoch

Thus far, ten general conditions have been presented in addition to the three basic, overriding requirements for a good explanation of glaciogenesis. The three basic requirements for a successful theory on glaciogenesis are listed below, together with a fourth requirement, not geophysically basic but nonetheless important, the need for proper timing. The fourth requirement, the proper timing, while not essential to the understanding of the Ice Epoch mechanism however remains essential in establishing a correct historical analysis.

1. THE ORIGIN OF THE ICE
   a. *Catastrophic*   From the remote, cold, ice-abundant outer regions of our solar system or in galactic regions beyond.
   b. *Uniformitarian* From evaporated ocean water

2. THE MANNER OF TRANSPORT OF THE ICE (including both horizontal and vertical transport).
   a. *Catastrophic*   Via elliptical orbits and electromagnetic deflection.
   b. *Uniformitarian* Via planetary wind systems and precipitation.

3. THE LOCATION OF THE DEPOSITION OF THE VAST ICE MASSES
   a. *Catastrophic*   Associated with magnetic latitudes.
   b. *Uniformitarian* Associated with geographical latitudes.

4. THE DATING OF THE ICE EPOCH
   a. *Catastrophic*   2,800 B.C. +/-500 years
   b. *Uniformitarian* 10,000 B.C. +/-1,000,000 years

Over and above these four essential and overriding requirements for good hypothesis of the Ice Epoch, the following circumstances must be accommodated:

5. Suddenness and intense, unearthly coldness, as is illustrated by the very rapid death and freezing of mammoth carcasses.
6. The various locations of sudden freezing in the Northern and Southern Hemispheres.
7. The depth of the ice deposits in both hemispheres.
8. The accounting for deep ice deposits, both on continental shields and on suboceanic shelfs.
9. The area encompassed by flowing ice in the Northern Hemisphere.
10. The volume of the ice deposited in the Northern Hemisphere.
11. The magnitude of the heat exchange which occurred.
12. The geometry of the ice mass in the Northern Hemisphere.
13. The radial flow of the ice mass in the Northern Hemisphere.
14. The eccentric location of the ice mass relative to geographical latitudes and poles.
15. The ice and lava sandwiches, the ice caves of the Pacific Northwest.

This list is not exhaustive; it is merely indicative of the vast scope, of the many locations, and of the numerous ramifications involved in an adequate explanation for the Earth's Ice Epoch. Of these fifteen requirements and conditions, the first four as listed shall be considered at further length.

The Origin of the Ice. The origin of the ice is accounted for in the uniformitarian approach by the evaporation of ocean waters, a process requiring heat. The volume involved is millions of cubic miles of water, and the evaporation of this amount of water would require septillions of calories of heat.

However, what is required is a cooling principle, not a heating principle. What is required is a cooling principle in terms of septillions of calories, and accomplished suddenly (if the frozen mammoths or the suddenness of the ice flow is any indication whatsoever). Uniformitarianism not only postulates a slow rather than a sudden principle; it also postulates a heat-requiring principle rather than a heat-losing principle. The magnitude of heat exchange required for the Ice Epoch (septillions of calories) could not possibly be accomplished by the Earth's atmosphere and ocean, while in its present approximate orbit and its present approximate scheme of rotation.

The abundance of ice in the more remote areas of our solar system has already been mentioned. Most comets contain ice, and when one approaches the Sun, part of the ice melts and evaporates. In evaporation, the vapor escapes the nucleus of the comet due to its low gravitational attraction. The result is the characteristic pattern of the cometary train.

The proposition has been illustrated that Saturn had an icy catastrophe, and the contention has been upheld that some of its satellites consist of pure ice, as do some of the satellites of Jupiter. Saturn apparently possesses an outer atmosphere of ammonia and methane at extremely cold temperatures, under which is a layer of ice of unknown depth. Some astronomers have asserted, probably in error, that Saturn is solid ice below its atmosphere.[21]

While the composition of the Jovian planets (Jupiter, Saturn, Uranus and Neptune) is unknown, it seems certain that there is much hydrogen and much oxygen there, the elements which combine to form water. This is not only true for the planets, but is also true for the satellites, where ices range in temperatures from $-200°$ to $-325°F$.

When the ice masses of the Jovian planets are added to the ice resident in their satellites, it must be concluded that super-

[21]William Lee Kennon, *Astronomy*, Boston: Ginn & Co., 1948, p. 368.

cooled water (H_2O) is an abundant compound in our solar system, and much more abundant among the Jovian planets than among the terrestrial planets (such as Earth, Mars, Mercury and Venus). Supercooled ice is a very abundant substance in our solar system, the substance which was deposited upon our planet at the time of celestial crisis.[22]

It is certainly possible that a relationship exists between genesis of our Earth's Ice Epoch and the icy rings of Saturn. It has been estimated that about 6,000,000 cubic miles of ice descended in each hemisphere—a total of some 12,000,000 cubic miles of ice. Callisto of Jupiter, considered to be mostly ice, with a diameter of 3200 miles may contain 10 billion cubic miles of ice, enough for 7000 Ice Epochs just like the last one. Or tiny Tethys, Saturn's third moon, some 800 miles in diameter, may contain enough ice to supply the Earth with an Ice Epoch 100 times as massive as the one which did occur. And temperatures in these regions are between –225° and –250° F.

Nereid, which almost escaped from the Neptune system, is about 200 miles in diameter, and it might possess enough ice to equal all of the ice for our Ice Epoch. Thus, it is not inconceivable that an astral visitor from the remote areas of our solar system would possess ice. Most do, and many consist almost entirely of ice. Nor is it inconceivable that such an astral visitor could contain ice in accompanying satellites (Uranus does), in rings (Saturn does), in belts (Jupiter has belts and bands), or merely ice in its crust.

[22]*Ibid.* The estimate contained herein of the composition of Jupiter is that it may have a rock core of 19,000 miles, a surrounding ice shell some 17,500 miles thick, which in turn is surrounded by a deep atmospheric envelope, some 8,000 miles thick. Other opinions concerning the composition of Jupiter vary.

Saturn and Jupiter, with densities as compared to water, of .071 and 1.35 respectively, contain the greatest percentages of hydrogen of all the planets in our solar system, but are closely followed by Uranus and Neptune with densities of 1.56 and 2.47 respectively. Saturn and Jupiter together comprise 92% of the known (i.e. visible) material in our solar system apart from the Sun. Uranus and Neptune comprise another 7%. The 5 terrestrial planets—Mercury, Venus, Earth, Mars and Pluto, together with all of the asteroids, comets, meteor streams and satellites, comprise but a weak 1% of the material in orbit in our solar system. And many of the comets and satellites are abundant in ice, also. Therefore it is not difficult to posit that ice is an abundant material in our solar system, particularly in the satellite regions of Jupiter, Saturn, Uranus and Neptune. And the ices in these regions possess temperatures ranging from —200° all the way down almost to absolute zero.

If a specific guess needs to be made concerning the location of the origin of the ice, there are five prime possibilities: the regions of Jupiter, Saturn, Uranus, Neptune and the region beyond Neptune. It has already been observed that the Neptune region shows evidences of upheaval, with Pluto's orbit apparently having historically interacted and with the retrograde motion of Halley's Comet, Nereid, and Triton. Thus, the Neptune system cannot be overlooked as a possible region for the origin of the ice. It is more plausible to conceive that the ice came in from beyond Neptune, where billions of comets—periodic but rarely seen members of our solar system—of lengthy periods do exist[23]

The origin of the ice was not from the slowly evaporating tropical oceans over uncalculated spans of time, for this produces only a heating requirement, not a cooling requirement. This slow-process explanation not only fails to account for the extreme coldness but also it fails to explain the required suddenness of the ice catastrophe.

[23]Estimates of the total number of comets which are regular members of our solar system run as high as one hundred billion, and are far more numerous than the planets. Evidences suggest that there is a great diversity among the Sun's comets with regard to (1) eccentricity of orbit—elongation of the orbit; (2) perihelion—closeness of approach to the Sun, (3) period —time involved in one revolution, and (4) probably size also.

In eccentricity, some orbits are probably rather oval, while others are extremely elongated—more so than Halley's comet or Nereid. In perihelion a few of the Sun's comets approach as close as Pluto or Neptune. Yet fewer of them approach as close as Jupiter, and yet fewer approach as close as Mars or Earth, where the reflection of the sun's light will allow detection. In periods, evidences suggest they range all the way from a few centuries through hundreds of thousands of years, and even up to many millions of Earth years. In distance, some of them may well orbit out halfway to Alpha Centauri, the nearest star, some 4 light years away (25,000,000,000,000 miles).

As the comets approach the Sun, and perhaps approach to regions of the planets, they may be perturbed in one of three ways. They may be perturbed into (1) a hyperbolic orbit, in which case they will retreat in an orbit which never closes, and hence proceed on into the galaxy. Comets may also be perturbed into (2) closed orbits of a greater major axis, in which case their periods will increase. They may also be perturbed into (3) closed orbits of reduced period, in which case they may then orbit partly or entirely within the planetary regions. It is thought that this is the method by which the comets of Jupiter, Saturn, Uranus and Neptune have been organized.

One interesting example of cometary perturbations is the comet Wolf I. In 1875 it approached within about 1,100,000 miles of Jupiter and was disturbed. In its new orbit it was discovered in 1884. In 1922 it again passed near Jupiter, and was again perturbed—this time the perturbation almost corrected the first disturbance. In its first disturbance, its perihelion distance changed sufficiently that it could be detected from the Earth; however, in its resumed orbit, it is difficult to detect due to its distance from the Sun and its faintness.

The Manner of Transport of the Ice. The manner of transport of the ice must be considered on two levels: the horizontal (movement across the expanses of space) and the vertical (specific regions of descent). This is true in both the catastrophic and uniformitarian approaches. According to classical uniformitarian theory, water vapor was transported across the Earth's surface—both latitudes and longitudes—by planetary wind systems. Then occurred coalescence, condensation, and descent, in the form of snow. This theory has several basic defects. It has been noted that evaporation of ocean water is a heating mechanism, whereas a cooling mechanism is positively required. Similarly, the wind systems of the Earth act as a huge heat engine, responding to basic temperature inequalities, in this case caused from unequal reception of solar radiation across the latitudes. Wind systems are a response to heating inequalities, not a cause; furthermore, they are a moderating device. Winds moderate temperature differentials by mixing cold and warm air (and also dry and humid air). The uniformitarian proposition endeavors to explain cooling functions by warming mechanisms, and extreme functions by moderating mechanisms (although most of the uniformitarian theorists have not been aware of these inherent implications).

But this is not all of the incongruity. The assumption that planetary wind systems delivered the evaporated ocean water to polar regions implies a north-south movement in planetary wind systems. There are three basic types of planetary wind systems: trade winds, polar easterlies, and midlatitude westerlies. Trade winds, like polar easterlies, function primarily in an east-to-west direction. Uniformitarian thinking, however, endeavors to transform these east-west functions into north-south functions.

The second phase of transport in the uniformitarian theory implies that most of the snow fell in the regions of the nodes, where ice piled up to an altitude of 3 miles. However, these nodes were great distances from the oceans, and warm, humid air would normally drop its moisture on the fringe areas of a cold region rather than at the heart. Thus it is seen that on any one of these transporting viewpoints, uniformitarian theory extensively and consistently fails.

According to the catastrophic theory, the ice was transported across the solar system in an eccentric or comet-like orbit. It was transported from its previous orbital location or galactic region in this first phase to the Earth-Moon region. The second phase was a deflection of the cold ice particles within the Earth-Moon system by the radiation belts (Van Allen belts) of the Earth. It is thought that the particles of ice, being electrically charged, were deflected, or shunted, or redirected by the magnetic field, as are charged particles during periods of sunspot activity. The particles apparently converged over the magnetic polar regions, and in converging they bumped, experiencing intra collisions, which reduced their velocity, causing them to decelerate, and proceeded to descend. They descended over a vast magnetic polar area and concentrated in different but proximate locations or nodes during the various descents. Thus were formed the epicenters or the nodes of the ice mass. The super-cooled ice particles descended mostly in the higher latitudes because the Magnetic North Pole happens to be located only about 1200 miles from the Geographical Pole—the Earth's axis. Had the magnetic pole been located in another latitude, the Ice Epoch activity would also have been in another latitude.

Every evidence suggests that the descent of ice occurred suddenly, in great volumes, at extremely low temperatures, and over a vast area proximate to the magnetic poles. During these periods of ice descent, ice may have cascaded or descended at a rate of several hundreds of feet per hour, in the regions of the epicenters. There may have been five or six separate crescendos of ice influx spread out periodically across the first several weeks of this cataclysmic Earth crisis. The fact that ice did happen to fall mostly in higher latitudes is indicative that there is a relationship between the magnetic axis and the geographical axis.

It is also true that on the fringes of the ice mass, ice was concentrated in mountainous regions. This is substantially associated with true climatic but post-diluvian developments during a period when ice was melting, oceans were filling up with cold water, the climate of the Earth was temporarily chilled, and much snow fell as part of the aftermath of this icy crisis.

With regard to manner of transport, the first stage involved an elliptical orbit, and also involved hundreds of millions of miles of inter-planetary distance. The second stage commenced within the Earth-Moon system, and it involved tens of thousands of miles of distance and magnetic redirection. On the basis of horizontal transportation of ice across the solar system, it is recalled that clues to the cause of the Earth's Ice Epoch are

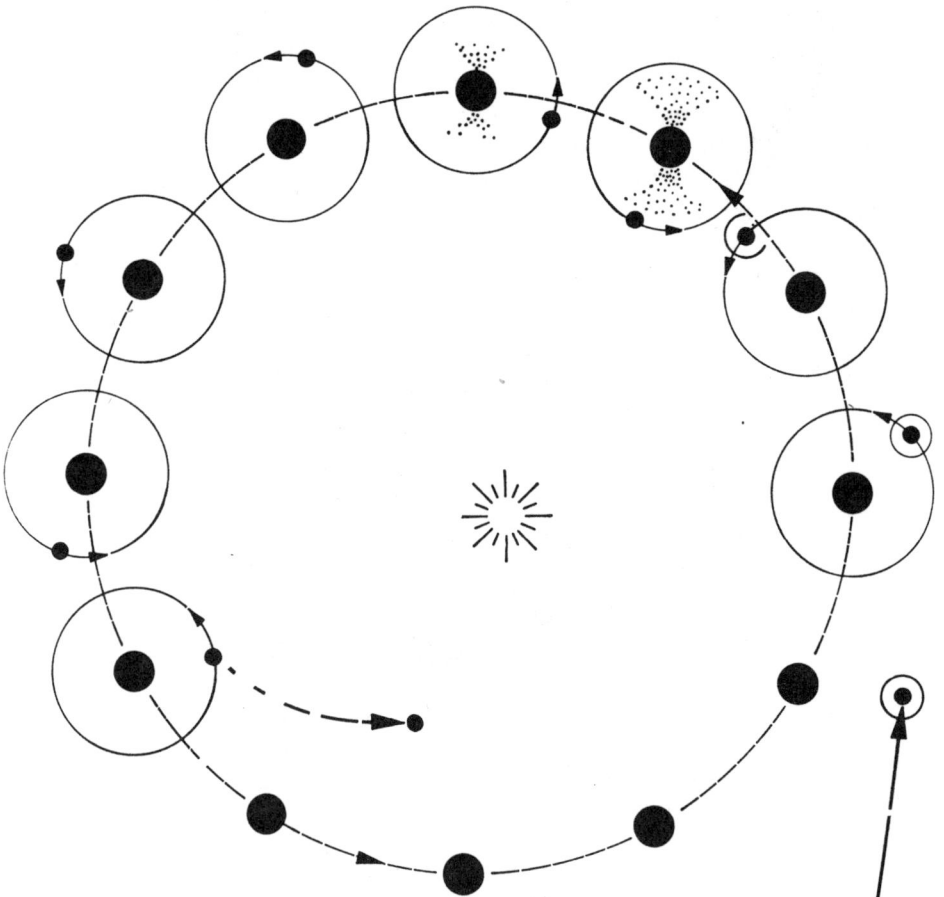

MODEL OF THE CRISIS YEAR
(FRAGMENTATION OF ICE AND
ESCAPE OF VISITOR)

FIGURE 17

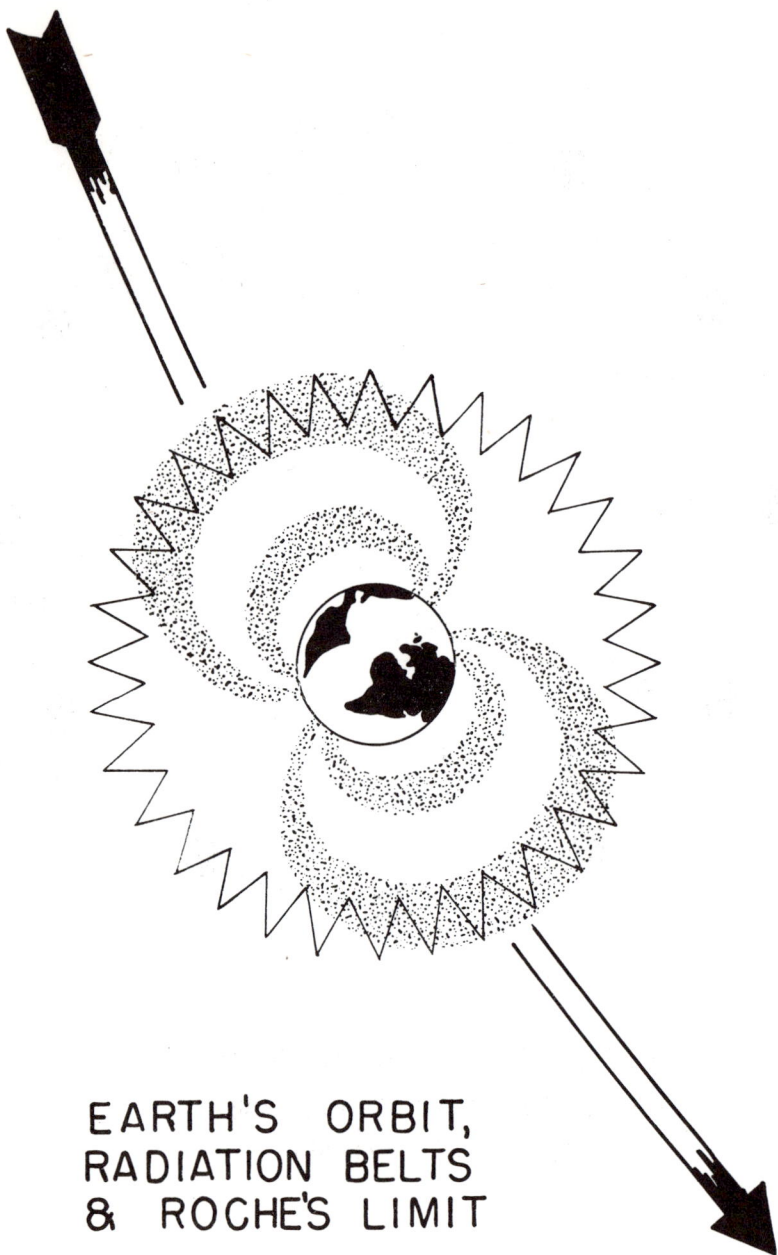

EARTH'S ORBIT,
RADIATION BELTS
& ROCHE'S LIMIT

FIGURE 18

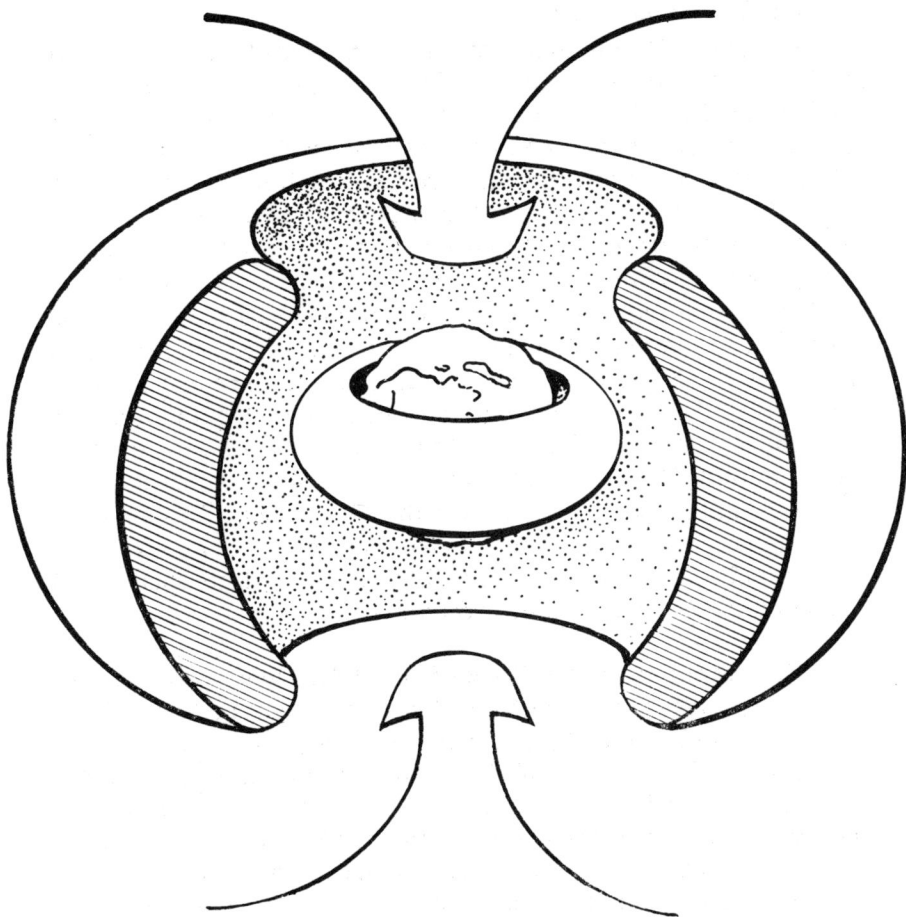

MANNER OF ICE DESCENT

FIGURE 19

similar to clues of the cause of Saturn's icy rings. And also the composition of captured material in our Ice Epoch is similar to the composition of such icy satellites as Callisto, Ganymede, Iapetus, Titan and Triton.

Chapter VII contains a model of the astral catastrophe. It includes 8 line diagrams and 40 listed categories of assumptions and conclusions, describing the catastrophe. It is thought that the duration of the chaotic conflict was five or six months, and the visitor was finally disengaged from the Earth-Moon system only after the Earth passed from aphelion toward perihelion, and only after at least two close approaches had wrought their havoc on our planet. Further particulars are contained in Chapter VII.

If the Moon had been involved in the perturbation of the visitor out of the Earth-Moon system, it would be reasonable to suspect that the Moon has gone through some of the same chaos as the Earth, and that it might have some arcuate mountain uplifts —astral battle scars similar to the Earth's. It has already been noted that the lunar mountain systems resemble our own.

It should also be noted that the Moon today has an orbit with an eccentricity of .055, whereas the Earth has an eccentricity of only .017. Is it possible that this astral conflict partly explains the Moon's greater eccentricity?

The Location of the Deposition of the Ice. Two areas of basic consideration have been discussed: (1) the area of the origin of the ice and (2) the mode of transport of the ice. This third area, the location of the deposition of the ice, is related to magnetic latitudes rather than to geographic latitudes, it being essentially a magnetic phenomenon. This is the basis for the eccentricity of the Ice Epoch area to the North Pole.

The location of the deposition of the ice is completely related to the remote astral origin and the manner of transport. It is also completely related to such factors as the geometry (conical shape) of the ice mass. It is similarly related to such factors as subsequent outflow, heat exchanges, heat equilibriums, subsequent melting, unearthly extremes in temperature of the ice, and in its sudden appearance.

Catastrophic theory can explain all of these phenomena. It can explain the presence of ice both upon continental massifs and on sub-oceanic bedrock; it also explains the simultaneous gravitational upheaval (and lava outflow) which mixed descending ice (in the peripheral regions) with upwelling magma or descending pumice. Thus is explained the ice sandwiched even to this day between inordinately cold layers of lava.

The uniformitarian approach can explain none of these adequately. It invokes climatic mechanisms to freeze mammoths by the millions. It invokes heating mechanisms (evaporation) to explain cooling requirements, and it invokes moderating mechanisms (wind systems) to explain temperatures of unearthly extremes. It has no mechanism which can account for a very minor fraction of the septillions of calories of heat loss which are involved, to say nothing of the required suddenness. Uniformitarian theory is hard pressed to adequately handle as much as one of these phenomena, much less the whole panorama in tandem. Uniformitarianism may be a magnificently successful misinterpretation of Earth history, and even in its academic success, it is hardly to be admired. But in all justice, uniformitarianism must be admired for one thing—consistency—for its errors are markedly consistent.

The Dating of the Ice Epoch. The dating of the Ice Epoch is essential for the proper reconstruction of ancient history, regarding both the Earth and its biological population. Prevailing opinion has placed the end of the Ice Epoch between 8,000 B.C. and 11,000 B.C., which is a substantial adjustment from Lyell's adjusted 40,000 B.C. or his original 1,000,000 B.C. (a date still used to explain the lava upwellings of Eastern Washington). It is obvious that recent investigations have tended repeatedly to update the Ice Epoch to a more recent time.

The dating of the Flood-Ice catastrophe, as conceived by the author, is about 2800 B.C., plus or minus 500 years. The case for the recent dating of this catastrophe is far from complete at this point; actually it has only commenced. This catastrophe included such geophysical developments as the uplifting of the Alpine-Himalayan and Circum-Pacific orogenetic zones, simultaneous with the uplifting of the Earth's oceans and the descent of the astral ice.

Among the categories of evidences to be considered is the Biblical chronology, painstaking logged, carefully preserved, and probably accurate to a high degree. Along with the Biblical account, ancient folklores and mythologies from several other continents agree with the principles and themes, contained or implicit within the Biblical account.

A second category of evidences, to which Chapter VIII is addressed, is the recent dating of subsequent celestial catastrophes, well-recorded and clearly dated within the 2nd and 1st millenia B.C. This will lead to the conclusion that disorganizations within our solar system have been recent, and it also means that the Earth has been among those bodies involved. This does much to discourage an extended or distant dating of the Flood catastrophe.

A third category of evidences is related to changes in the Earth's atmosphere from the Antediluvian to the Postdiluvian Age, and the "greenhouse effect" which dissolved at that time. The Greenhouse Effect is related to chronologies, longevities, climates, and biochemical curves, which furnish further substantiation. A discussion of this subject is reserved for Chapter IX. In total, these categories of evidences will merge into a strong web of logic encouraging a recent dating for the Flood.

And if the recent dating of the Flood is simultaneous with these glaciogenetic and orogenetic principles, as is herein affirmed, then the conclusion inevitably follows that the uniformitarian principle of dating has been conceived either immaturely or prematurely, or both.

Problems concerning prime theory of glaciogenesis and orogenesis have been mistakenly assigned to the geologist. They more properly should be assigned to the astronomer or catastrophist possessing the historical perspective of catastrophism. Once this is done, and the astronomer establishes prime theory, and the geophysicist establishes secondary theory, then the geologist is to be accountable for filling in the details of local deformation, local fossilization, and so forth.

Again, it must be emphasized that not only have geologists failed to establish secondary or local theory for Earth structures; astrophysicists and geophysicists (educated to uniformitarianism only) have also failed to establish prime theory for Earth history. It is with this in mind that Chapter VII is presented. It contains a series of definitive assumptions and conclusions, and accompanying line diagrams, which describe this event. These line diagrams comprise the model (as the author best conceives) of this, the greatest celestial crisis which our planet has thus far experienced.

VII chapter

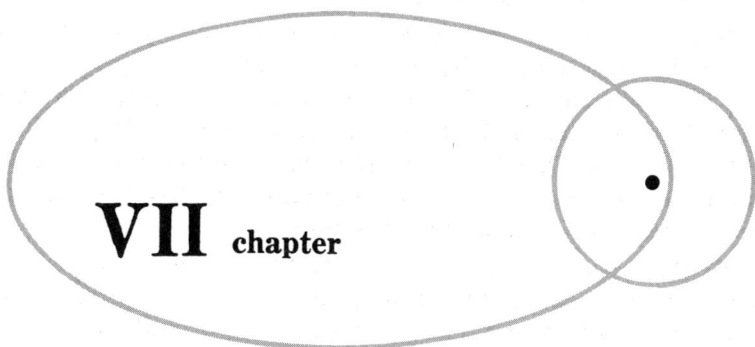

Model of the Flood Catastrophe

AMONG THE MOST severe criticisms which can be properly leveled at Flood catastrophists to date is that they fail to discuss the catastrophe in astronomical or astrophysical terms, even though they were obviously dealing with geophysical forces of planetary magnitude. A second just criticism, closely related, is that they failed to conceive of the Flood Catastrophe in terms of CAUSE as well as effect. Also, Flood catastrophists have been concerned with catastrophism almost exclusively in the third millenium B.C.

Velikovsky concerned himself with astral catastrophism in the second and first millenia B.C.[1] Among the most severe criticisms which can be justly leveled at his works includes the fact that he wrote well over a half million words, mostly on the

---

[1]In 1950, Velikovsky had published his first work, *Worlds in Collision*, by Doubleday. In his preface, he wrote as follows:

Worlds in Collision comprises only the last two acts of the cosmic drama. A few earlier acts—one of them known as the Deluge—will be the subject of another volume of natural history.

At the date of the writing of our manuscript (1966) some years later, this second work on the Deluge, which Velikovsky planned, has yet to be published. Perhaps he anticipates that this will be his finest work. Undoubtedly he has been laboring continually for nearly two decades on this forthcoming work. It is hoped that he will not fail in this effort, and the work should be of great import. It will be of interest to see how similar or dissimilar it will be in (a) subject material, (b) organization, and (c) conclusions, when compared to our work.

subject of astral catastrophism, and never produced either a single line diagram, a single map or a single table.

It may be true that Velikovsky endeavored to merge subjects which are essentially historical, but also happen to be (profoundly) scientific. It may be true that he was a good ancient historian, but not a good mathematician or astrophysicist. Even so, his characteristic of composing assemblages of words to the total exclusion of maps, line diagrams and tables of data has been a major weakness in his presentation.

In this volume, the attempt is made to avoid both of these defects. A limited number of tables are included to assist in the reader's orientation, particularly in Chapters IX and XI. A series of line diagrams is given in each of Chapters IV, V, VI and the present chapter (VII), dealing with the geography of the Ararat region, orogenetic pattern and patterns of the descent of astral ice.

In explaining the interactions of this celestial crisis, there are four celestial bodies and their four zones of gravitational dominance which must be recognized. These are:

(1) The Sun and the Sun's 25 to 40 trillion mile zone of gravitational dominance, extending outward toward the nearer stars.[2]

(2) The Earth and the Earth's 800,000 mile zone of gravitational dominance, a small enclave within the Sun's domain.

(3) The Visitor and its zone of gravitational dominance, possibly accompanied by a small, icy satellite or two.

(4) The Moon and its 50,000 to 90,000 mile zone of gravi-

---

[2]The nearest stars to our Sun are a group of three inter-revolving stars, a triple binary, known as the Centauri. This group includes Alpha Centauri, Beta Centauri and Proxima Centauri. Alpha Centauri and Beta Centauri revolve around a common center, and the distant Proxima Centauri, about 1 trillion miles distant, revolves around the inner two, or more precisely, around the common center of the inner two. Alpha Centauri is about 4.3 light years from the Sun (26 trillion miles) and Proxima Centauri is about 4.25 light years (25 trillion miles). The Sun's region of gravitational dominance is considered to extend out about half way to the nearest stars. In the direction of the Centauri about 40° from the South Pole, this is about 10 to 13 trillion miles. In the Northern Hemisphere, among the closest stars are Barnard's Star and the Sirius binary Canis Majoris A and B. Sirius is about 8.6 light years distant. The Sun's light, which takes about 8 minutes to travel to the Earth, takes about 8 light years to travel to Sirius. The Sun's region of dominance extends from perhaps 15 trillion miles to 40 trillion miles in the varying directions toward the nearest stars.

tational dominance, an enclave within the Earth's gravitational domain. [3]

The Earth's gravitational domain is not constant in size, since it orbits around the Sun in an eccentric orbit which varies between 91,500,000 and 94,500,000 miles. The Earth's field of gravitational dominance shifts about 7% in length from perihelion to aphelion and is pear-shaped, extending farther in the direction opposite the Sun than toward the Sun.

The zone of dominance of the Visitor is unknown, partly because its mass is only an educated guess, and partly because the dimensions of the zone will shift markedly, depending on its location. The Visitor may have been four times as massive as the Moon, and it may have approached the Earth ten times as closely as does the Moon approach the Earth. The contending forces involved were the staging of a four-way tug of war between the Sun, the small Earth, the smaller Visitor, and the Earth's tiny satellite, the Moon. The involvement did not result in permanent capture; the Sun finally won out.

If one concludes that this great event in Earth history, the Flood, was indeed a cosmic catastrophe, rather than merely a prolonged meteorological event, then one must conclude that its cause was gravitational rather than heat, which is the ultimate cause in floods caused by excessive rainfall (heat causing the evaporation and the organizing of wind systems). If the Flood is cosmic, it is not only a gravitational catastrophe; it is a gravitational-magnetic catastrophe, and it should be an excellent subject for a model.

Many different models might be chosen, depending upon whether analysis is limited to one or two features of this historical cataclysm. One model may seem to explain hydographical matters best; another may seem to explain orogenetical matters best; yet another might explain glacial features best. Perhaps stratigraphical features or ancient literary sources will lend themselves to yet other models. A model which is chosen from

[3]A variation in the Moon's region of dominance exists. The Moon's eccentricity is much greater than the Earth's, and is about .055. Its distance varies from 221,000 miles to 252,000. Its field of dominance extends in a pear-shaped region of 197,000-250,000 miles at perigee and extends in a pear-shaped region of 224,000-315,000 miles at apogee. This region varies between 24,500 miles to 63,000 miles from the Moon, depending on the part of the month, and the direction considered.

many possible models is designated as the *preferred* model, and it stands in contrast to the several or many rejected models.

The best model of the Flood Catastrophe will be the model which best explains a significant number of inter-related events of this crisis period on Earth history, and not merely one or two aspects. Therefore, the best model of the Flood will likely be based on the most comprehensive analysis.[4]

A case in point is the recognition that if there are tides in the hydrosphere, there must necessarily also be tides in the fluid magma, tides likely of a much greater force. The evidences of these appear in the Circum-Pacific and the Alpine-Himalayan zones of uplift, evidences which become overwhelming when ex-

---

[4]In selecting a preferred model, many features of the Flood crisis must be considered conjointly. One model may explain one or two features best, or with the highest mathematical probability. A second model may explain other features best. A preferred model is one which, in consensus, explains best all of the features. Therefore the preferred model is one which recognizes best all of the features of the Flood crisis. Among the features which must be considered are the following:

(1) The historical traditions of the Flood crisis, with the Genesis account being the best source.
(2) The repeating of layered stratigraphy of the several continents
(3) The repeated parallelism of mountain uplifts
(4) The two zones of recent orogenetic uplift
(5) The magnetic deflection and sudden deposition of astral ice
(6) The gravitational interaction involving
    a. Tides in the Earth's fluid atmosphere
    b. Tides in the Earth's fluid hydrosphere
    c. Tides in the Earth's viscuous, semi-fluid magma (or lithosphere)
    d. Impressions left upon and within the semi-solid crust (also lithosphere)
(7) The four body problem, involving
    a. The Sun
    b. The Earth
    c. The Visitor
    d. The Moon
(8) The Earth's basic conditions, which include
    a. Its mass
    b. Its orbit
    c. Its dimensions
    d. Its angle of axis to the perpendicular of the ecliptic
    e. Its location of its geographical poles
    f. Its location of its magnetic poles and field
    g. Its velocity of revolution
    h. Its speed of rotation
(9) The basic conditions of the Visitor
(10) Possibility of previous and subsequent astral crises
(11) Other factors

The line diagrams given on the following pages constitute the *preferred* model, and the remarks throughout this book are consistent with this preferred model.

amined in moderate depth. Implicit in this is the recognition that mountain-building forces are:

(1) Astral rather than exclusively terrestrial in nature
(2) Sudden rather than extremely gradual in engagement
(3) Global rather than local in scope
(4) Recent rather than ancient in terms of multiplied millions of years

These conclusions will automatically lead to a total rejection or a near-total rejection of the various and typically vague uniformitarian propositions on orogenesis.

A second case in point, beyond the orogenetical, is the glacial case, the Ice Epoch. This essay declines to use the traditional terminology of "Ice Age" because the term implies too much of uniformitarian heritages. If the Ice Epoch were a great dump of astral ice, possibly 12,000,000 cubic miles, dumped over the magnetic poles, simultaneous in timing with the Flood, involving ice at temperatures approaching absolute zero, this understanding is essential in fully comprehending the totality of the Flood event. (Incidentally, this understanding also will automatically lead to a total or near-total rejection of the various uniformitarian propositions on glaciogenesis.)

Other considerations from many disciplines, including anthology and folklores, recorded history, paleoclimatology, biochemistry and astronomy, add further perspectives which may bear upon a preferred model of the Flood catastrophe.

The model as presented in the following diagrams and categorical descriptions is a preferred model; it is not the only possible model. The preferred model may or may not be a satisfactory model. A preferred model is one which satisfies the originating one or an originating group. A *satisfactory* model (in contrast to a *preferred* model) must meet a series of requirements, scrutinies, tests, observations and verifications by others; only then does it perhaps move from a preferred model status into a satisfactory model status. A satisfactory model must meet many kinds of requirements and these requirements must include the following:

(1) Horizontal Consistency. It must have horizontal consistency with the established and understood physical principles of our universe. It must have scientific consistency. In the case of the model portrayed in the fol-

lowing line diagrams, this consistency must include:

(a) Consistency relative to principles of gravitation

(b) Consistency relative to principles of electromagnetism.

(c) Consistency relative to principles of deposition

(2) Vertical Alignment with Facts. In addition to scientific consistency, it must have historical consistency. It must be in agreement with the facts of Earth history. It need not be in agreement with the generally negative and vague interpolations and interpretations coming from uniformitarian notions; indeed, it must necessarily be in total conflict with such. However, it must be in agreement with the facts of Earth history as disassociated from the uniformitarian interpretations which have been attached thereto. Among the tens of thousands of specifics are:

(a) Sudden-drowned mammoths, numbering in millions on three continents, followed by sudden burial, compression and fossilization.

(b) Sudden freezing of mammoths, numbering in millions on two continents, followed by sudden changes in paleoclimatology and permafrost conditions.

(3) Implementation of Predictability. A satisfactory model must assist in, suggest, or even lead toward making further discoveries and observations, discoveries which in this case are historical in nature, since we are considering an historical event.

(4) Fruitfulness of Thought. A satisfactory model should be meaningful to investigating persons. It should catalyze research, ignite thought, possibly direct or focus effort. It should open new avenues of knowledge.

(5) Simplicity of Premise. A satisfactory model must contain a simple premise (in this case a simple astral crisis involving two approaches and a near capture, plus ice deposition). Although the premises for a satisfactory model must be simple, the results and conclusions derived therefrom may be neither simple nor predictable. Ordinarily the application of gained knowledge is seldom foreseen.

If a model is weighed and evaluated by one or a small group against the requirements as stated above, it may be designated as the *preferred* model in contrast to the various rejected models. If the model is scrutinized and tested by others, and substantially passes the five criteria just mentioned, it becomes a *satisfactory* model. It is found to be (a) mechanically workable, (b) generally meaningful and (c) psychologically satisfying to the uncommitted but inquiring mind. It then becomes (d) rational; only the logic contained therein has long existed, but is just recently recognized.

While a successful model should be psychologically satisfying, such satisfaction need not be universally the case. Many new ideas and discoveries, ranging from Copernicus' heliocentricity to Fulton's folly have been psychologically dissatisfying to many; however, a satisfactory model should be psychologically satisfying to the uncommitted mind, even if it may happen to contradict a century-old proposition into which nearly every philosophy of recent vintage has been rooted.

CATEGORY 1   *TYPE OF CELESTIAL BODY WHICH APPROACHED THE EARTH*

   a. A single astral body (with possible icy rings or satellites)

Rather than

   b. A two-body binary
   c. A three-body binary (a triple binary)
   d. A four-body binary (a quadruple binary)
   e. A storm of astral bodies (spheres)
   f. A storm of astral bodies (fragments)

CATEGORY 2   *MASS OF ASTRAL VISITOR*

   a. Perhaps between .05 and .10 of the Earth, like Mercury (.054)

And greater than the mass of

   b. Moon   (.012)
   c. Callisto   (.016)
   d. Titan   (.024)
   e. Ganymede   (.026)
   f. Pluto   (.033)

But less than the mass of

   g. Mars   (.107)
   h. Venus   (.814)

CATEGORY 3   *DENSITY OF ASTRAL VISITOR*

    a. Between 3.0 and 6.0 of water (water=1) like the terrestrial planets

Earth	5.52
Mercury	5.46
Venus	5.06
Mars	4.12
Io	4.03
Europa	3.78
Moon	3.32

Rather than

    b. Between 0.1 and 1.0 of water

Mimas	0.5
Enceladus	0.7
Saturn	0.71

    c. Between 1.0 and 3.0 of water, like most of the Jovian planets

Jupiter	1.35
Uranus	1.56
Callisto	2.06
Ganymede	2.35
Titan	2.42
Neptune	2.47

    d. Between 6.0 and 100.0

    e. Over 100.0

Sirius B (Canis Majoris B)	40,000 (water=1)
Van Maanen's Star	300,000
Star +70°8247	6,300,000

CATEGORY 4   *ASTRAL VISITOR CONTAINED ICE*

    a. In icy satellites, or
    b. Perhaps in icy rings

Rather than

    c. In icy belts
    d. In icy clouds

CATEGORY 5   *VOLUME OF CAPTURED ICE EXCEEDED*

    a. 12,000,000 cubic miles
    b. The volume of Phoebe, Saturn's 9th moon (diameter 200 miles)
    c. The volume of Nereid, Neptune's 2nd moon (diameter 200 miles)
    d. The volume of icy Hyperion, Saturn's 7th (diameter 300 miles)

But not

    e. The volume of icy Umbriel, Uranus' 3rd (diameter 400 miles)
    f. The volume of icy Mimas, Saturn's 1st (diameter 400 miles)
    g. The volume of icy Enceladus, Saturn's 2nd (diameter 500 miles)

CATEGORY 6   *ICE APPROACHED THE EARTH*

    a. Due to the Earth's superior gravitational force
    b. Deflected by the Earth's magnetic field (Van Allen belts)

And possibly

    c. Due to a fragmentation of an approaching icy satellite

CATEGORY 7   *GLACIAL DEPOSITION ON EARTH WAS*

    a. Sudden
    b. Simultaneous with the gravitational chaos
    c. During the initial stage only of the catastrophe (until ice reservoir was depleted)

Rather than

    d. Gradually or uniformitarianly
    e. Prior to gravitational interaction and tidal surges
    f. During the entire period of gravitational interaction
    g. After the gravitational interaction

CATEGORY 8   *ICE APPROACHED THE EARTH*

    a. As statically-charged icy particles
    b. At extremely low temperatures (possibly within 100° of absolute zero)

Rather than

    c. As uncharged icy particles
    d. As meteor-like icy agglomerates or fragments

CATEGORY 9   *DURATION OF CATASTROPHIC PERIOD WAS*

    a. Glacially, several weeks
    b. Tidally, 150 days and nights
    c. Astronomically, seven to eight months
    d. In terms of Noah's voyage, one year from embarkation to debarkation

Rather than

    e. Less than 1 day
    f. One week
    g. Forty days and forty nights
    h. One decade
    i. One century
    j. One millenium
    k. One uniformitarian era

CATEGORY 10   *DATING OF THE CATASTROPHE WAS*

    a. Approximately 4800 revolutions ago +/− 500 years
    b. Approximately 2800 B.C.

Rather than

    c. 2349 B.C.
    d. 5000 B.C.
    e. 10,000 B.C.
    f. 100,000 B.C.
    g. 1,000,000 B.C.

CATEGORY 11 *THE DIRECTION OF THE APPROACH OF THE ASTRAL VISITOR WAS*

    a. Probably in its approaching phase (to the Sun)

    b. Probably in direct motion (counterclockwise as viewed from Polaris)

CATEGORY 12 *THE SPEED OF THE APPROACHING ASTRAL VISITOR WAS*

    a. Increasing as it approached the Sun

    b. Between 1.5 and 2.0 million miles per day (Earth's speed is 1.7 million miles per day)

Rather than

    c. Below 1.5 million miles per day
      Mars' daily speed is 1.3 million miles per day
      Jupiter's is .7
      Saturn's is .5
      Uranus' is .37
      Neptune's is .16

    d. Over 2.0 million miles per day
      Venus' daily speed is 1.9 million miles per day
      The fleet Mercury (as described by the Greeks) has a daily speed of 2.6 million miles per day

CATEGORY 13 *MANNER OF VISITOR'S INTERACTION WITH EARTH INCLUDED*

    a. Nearly a temporary capture

    b. Two approaches

Rather than

    c. A single grazing approach

    d. A multiple grazing approach of a series of Visitors

    e. A permanent capture

CATEGORY 14   *CLOSENESS OF APPROACH*

    a. Perhaps between 15,000 and 30,000 miles of
       Earth

Rather than

    b. Within 10,000 miles of Earth (Roche's limit for
       fragmentation)
    c. Within 15,000 miles of Earth
       (Deimos is 14,600 miles from Mars)
       (Rings approach Saturn to 7,000 miles)
    d. More than 30,000 miles of Earth
       (Jupiter V approaches Jupiter to 112,600 miles)
       (Mimas approaches Saturn to 115,000 miles)
       (Miranda approaches Uranus to 81,000 miles)
       (Triton approaches Neptune to 220,000 miles)
       (Moon approaches Earth to 221,000 miles)

CATEGORY 15   *VISITOR'S ORBIT DURING PERIOD OF
CONFLICT INCLUDED*

    a. Perigee between 15,000 and 30,000 miles of
       Earth
    b. Apogee between 1,200,000 and 1,500,000 miles
       of Earth
    c. A period between approaches of 110 to 130 days

CATEGORY 16   *ESCAPE OF ASTRAL VISITOR WAS DUE
TO*

    a. The Earth's control over the Visitor was short
       of capture
    b. The Sun's greater control over the Visitor re-
       mained dominant
    c. The velocity of the Visitor made permanent
       capture difficult
    d. The eccentricity of the Earth's orbit discour-
       aged permanent capture
    e. The secondary perturbations of the Moon dis-
       couraged permanent capture

CATEGORY 17   *POSITION OF EARTH AT TIME OF ON-SET OF CRISIS WAS*

    a. Three or four months after perihelion
    b. Approaching aphelion

Rather than

    c. Approaching perihelion
    d. Leaving aphelion

CATEGORY 18   *PERTURBATIONS OF THE VISITOR'S ORBIT WERE DUE TO*

    a. The Earth-Moon system
    b. Primarily by the Earth

Rather than

    c. Primarily by the Moon

CATEGORY 19   *IN THIS PARTICULAR APPROACH, DUE TO ITS PROXIMITY, THE VISITOR*

    a. Used the Earth as a turnpoint

Rather than

    b. Using the Sun, as was normal
    c. Using the Moon, which was too small

CATEGORY 20   *DURATION OF THE CATASTROPHIC PE-RIOD WAS INFLUENCED BY*

    a. The perturbation of the Visitor caused by the Earth-Moon system
    b. The shortening of its major axis
    c. Its ejection from the Earth-Moon system at a velocity slightly greater than the Earth's orbital velocity
    d. Its re-engagement with the Earth-Moon system upon passing aphelion

CATEGORY 21   *POSITION OF THE EARTH DURING SEC-*
                   OND APPROACH WAS

a. One or two months after Earth's aphelion

Rather than

b. Approaching aphelion
c. Approaching perihelion

CATEGORY 22   *LOCATION OF THE VISITOR WHEN SUB-*
                   JECTED TO LUNAR PERTURBATIONS
                   WAS

a. Approximately one week from the Visitor's perigee

Rather than

b. At midpoint between the Visitor's apogee and perigee
c. At apogee
d. At perigee

CATEGORY 23   *EFFECT OF THE CATASTROPHE ON*
                   THE MOON'S ORBIT PROBABLY WAS

a. To decrease its eccentricity (currently .055)
b. To decrease its period (currently 27+ days)
c. To increase its angle to the ecliptic (currently 5°)

CATEGORY 24   *EFFECT OF CATASTROPHE ON EARTH'S*
                   ORBIT PROBABLY WAS

a. To decrease its orbital eccentricity (currently .017)
b. To decrease its period
c. To decrease its circumference
d. To reorganize the orientation of its orbital axis
e. To alter the dates of aphelion and perihelion
f. To alter the dates of the solstices
g. To alter the dates of the equinoxes

CATEGORY 25   *EFFECT OF THE CATASTROPHE WAS GREATER ON THE EARTH THAN ON THE MOON BECAUSE*

a. The Visitor approached closer to the Earth
b. The Earth had more magma to disrupt and more surface to distend
c. The Earth had oceans to disrupt
d. The Earth had atmosphere to disrupt
e. The Earth had fauna and flora to engulf in burial

However

f. The uplift of the lunar mountain ranges is attributable to the same crisis

CATEGORY 26   *EFFECT OF CATASTROPHE ON THE EARTH'S AXIS PROBABLY WAS*

a. To cause an increase in the inclination from the perpendicular to the ecliptic (currently $23\frac{1}{2}°$)

Rather than

b. To decrease the angle of the axis from the perpendicular to the ecliptic
c. To cause no change in the angle of the axis

CATEGORY 27   *EFFECT OF CATASTROPHE ON THE EARTH'S ROTATION PROBABLY WAS*

a. To increase the speed of the Earth's rotation
b. To shorten the day

Rather than

c. To reduce the speed of the Earth's rotation
d. To lengthen the day

CATEGORY 28   *EFFECT OF CATASTROPHE ON THE EARTH'S MAGNETIC POLES WAS*

a. To probably cause a relocation

CATEGORY 29   *EFFECT OF CATASTROPHE ON THE EARTH'S POLAR LOCATIONS PROBABLY WAS*

    a. To effect a shift in the location of the geographical poles

    b. To cause a location shift of the poles in a magnitude of perhaps 2500 to 3000 miles

Rather than

    c. To cause no relocation

    d. To cause a mild relocation in terms of a few dozen miles

    e. To cause a moderate relocation in terms of a few hundred miles

CATEGORY 30   *EFFECT OF THE CATASTROPHE ON THE EARTH'S MASS WAS*

    a. To increase it due to the capture of astral ice

    b. To increase it in a proportion of 1 to 2 parts per 100,000

CATEGORY 31   *EFFECT OF THE CATASTROPHE ON THE EARTH'S CRUST WAS*

    a. To cause an initial new zone of orogenetic uplift, the Circum-Pacific

    b. To cause a second new zone of orogenetic uplift, the Alpine-Himalayan

    c. To cause a bleeding of lava, forming new basaltic plateaus on several continents

    d. To cause a rash of new volcanoes

    e. To cause glacial scouring in the regions surrounding the magnetic poles

    f. To cause burying and reburying of the former crust under sediments

    g. To drown several hundred thousand square miles of crust eventually from melting astral ice.

Rather than

    h. To duplicate an earlier zone of orogenetic up-
lift (such as the Appalachian-Caledonian-Her-
zynian zone)
    i. To leave the Earth unscarred

CATEGORY 32   *EFFECT OF THE CATASTROPHE ON
THE EARTH'S HYDROSPHERE WAS*

    a. To increase the mass, approximately 12,000,000
cubic miles when the ice melted
    b. To increase its mass in a proportion of 7 to 9
parts per 100
    c. To ultimately raise mean sea level between 350
and 450 feet
    d. To cause the flooding of the continental shelves
    e. To cause an immediate decrease in the temper-
ature of the Earth's oceans
    f. To cause an eventual but marked increase in
oceanic salinity due to the new climatological
regime featuring rain and rivers

Rather than

    g. To cause a decrease in oceanic volumes
    h. To cause an increase in oceanic temperature

CATEGORY 33   *EFFECT OF CATASTROPHE ON
EARTH'S ATMOSPHERE WAS*

    a. To cause a complete condensing of the ante-
diluvian canopy of water vapor (the primeval
Greenhouse Effect)
    b. To cause a modest reduction of mass (and baro-
metric pressure) in a ratio of 5 to 10 parts per
100
    c. To cause a new heat disequilibrium
    d. To cause a new climatological regime
    e. To cause a reduced elevation of the ozone
canopy
    f. To cause a thinning of the ozone canopy

CATEGORY 34   *EFFECT OF THE CATASTROPHE ON THE EARTH'S FAUNA WAS*

a. To bury billions of specimens
b. To bring to extinction thousands of species
c. To cause a reorganization of zoogeography for those surviving species

CATEGORY 35   *EFFECT OF CATASTROPHE ON EARTH'S FLORA WAS*

a. To bury trillions of specimens
b. To bring thousands of species to extinction
c. To cause a reorganization of the florigeography for the surviving species

CATEGORY 36   *EFFECT OF THE CATASTROPHE ON MAN (HOMO SAPIENS) WAS*

a. To make his survivors very very few in number
b. To make his survivors and their early generations very catastrophic-minded

CATEGORY 37   *EFFECT OF THE CATASTROPHE UPON THE VISITOR WAS*

a. To reduce the major axis of its orbit, hundreds of millions of miles and possibly trillions of miles
b. To bring it permanently into the Sun's inner domain
c. To separate it from its pre-existing icy satellites and/or icy rings

CATEGORY 38   *EFFECT OF THE CATASTROPHE UPON THE SOLAR SYSTEM WAS*

a. To reduce the eccentricity of two of its periodic members
b. To add one to the number of planets in the Sun's inner domain

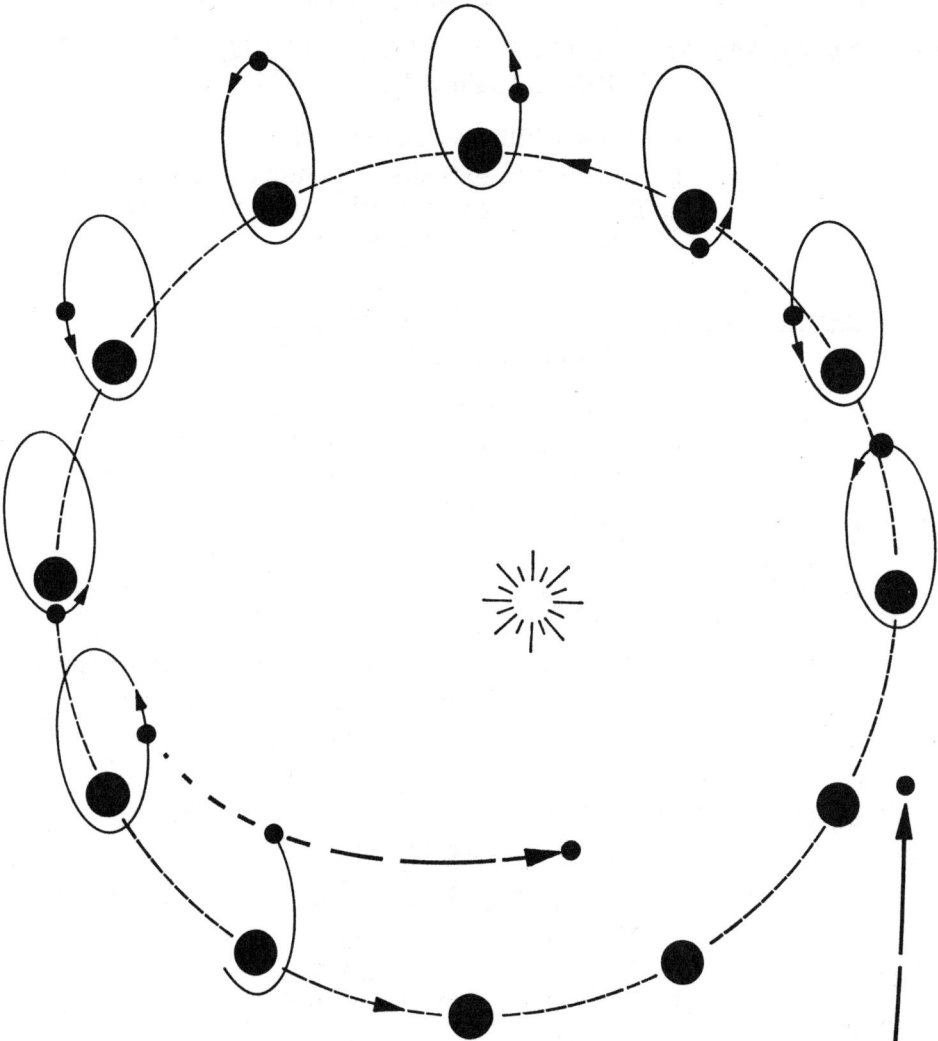

MODEL OF THE CRISIS YEAR
(ORBIT OF VISITOR)

FIGURE 20

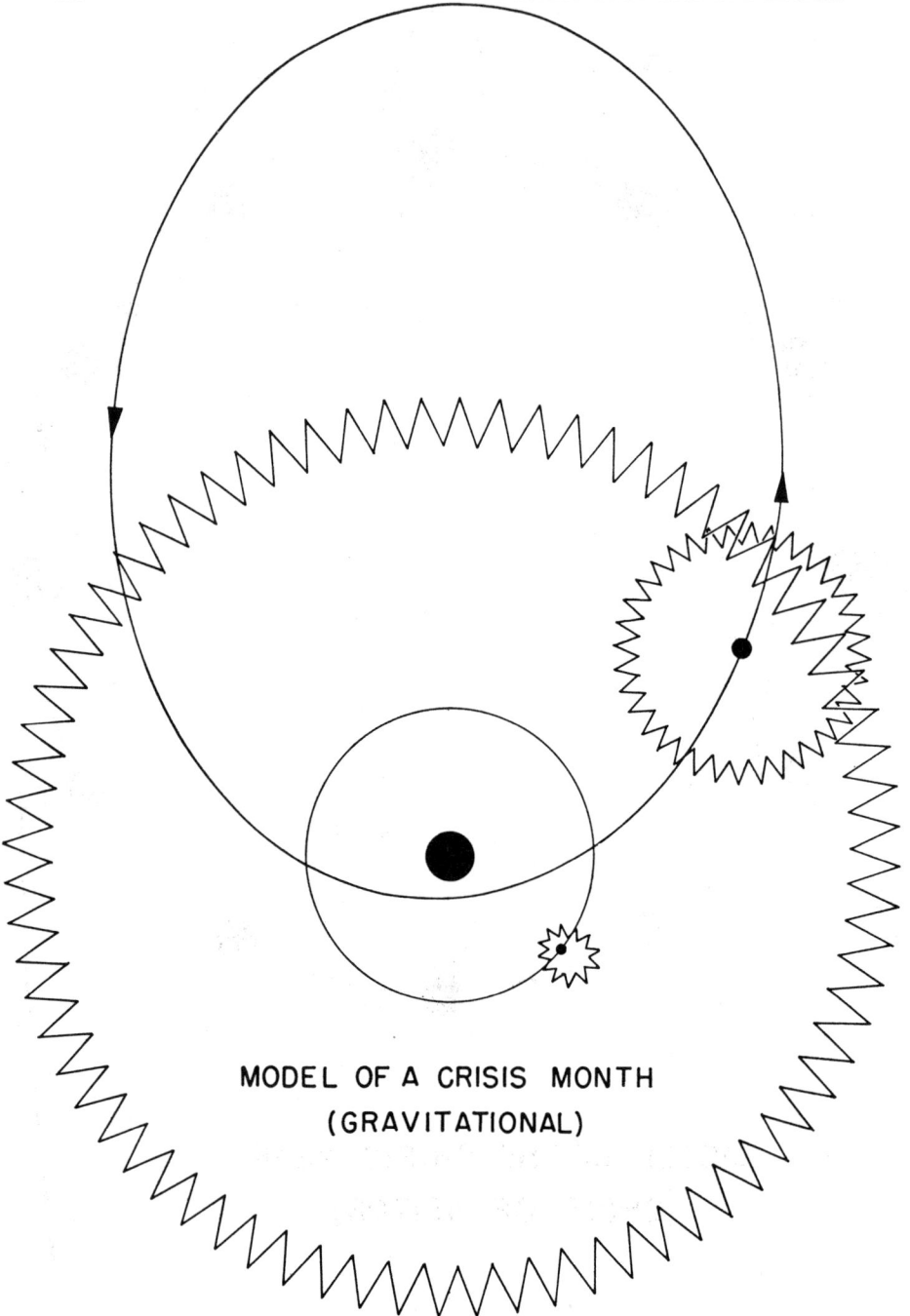

MODEL OF A CRISIS MONTH
(GRAVITATIONAL)

FIGURE 21

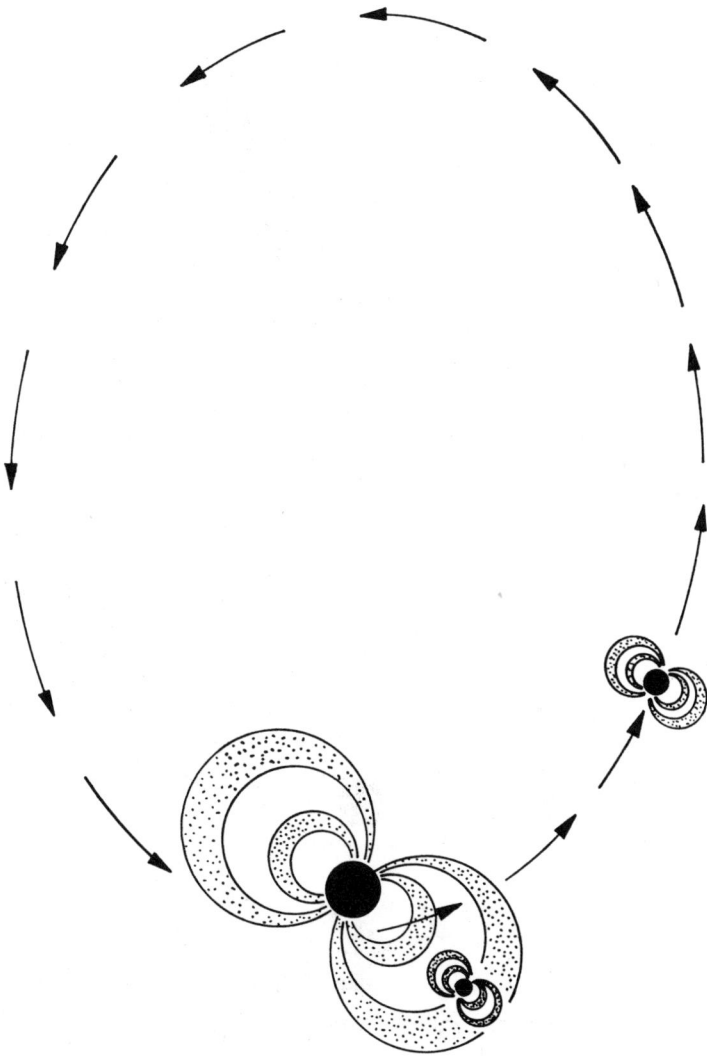

MODEL OF A CRISIS MONTH
(MAGNETIC)

FIGURE 22

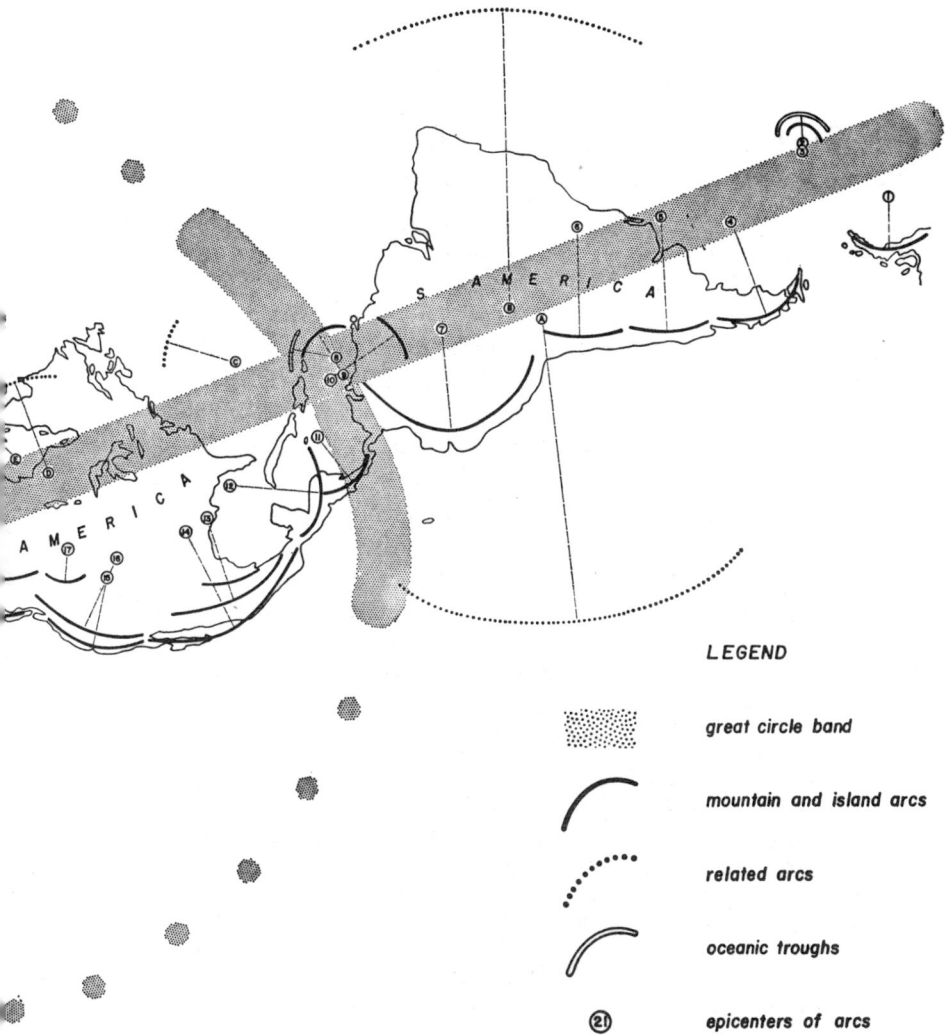

LEGEND

great circle band

mountain and island arcs

related arcs

oceanic troughs

epicenters of arcs

FIGURE 23 — The Two Zones of Recent Orogenetic
Uplift as shown by an adjusted Bartholomew projection. Reference Figure 6, page 76 and footnote 20,
page 83.

MODIFIED CONIC PROJECTION

CATEGORY 39   *EFFECT OF THE CATASTROPHE ON THE MILKY WAY GALAXY WAS*

a. Not much

CATEGORY 40   *EFFECT OF THE CATASTROPHE ON THE UNIVERSE WAS*

a. Even less

The model of the Flood Catastrophe is herein set forth. It is contained in the series of line diagrams within Chapters IV through VII, Figures 4 through 23. It is coupled with 40 listed categories of conclusions which both define and delimit this preferred model of the Flood Catastrophe, just one model among many possible models.

There may be a severe need for fresh concepts in Earth history, especially among the uniformitarian-dominated staffs of the universities of our generation. Until such ungrounded presuppositions are cast aside, little real progress will be made, and the entire matter of origins will remain a muddle. Reflections of this need are contained in the following words.

> To the extent that the geomorphologist is primarily concerned to use landforms as the means of studying geologic processes or determining states of geologic history, his explanatory description, as Kesseli notes, is often "an explanation lacking a description." Russell, as well as Kesseli, concludes that *a century of geomorphology dominated by the purpose of explaining genesis has failed* to produce comprehensible representation of landforms for most areas of the world.[5]

> These and similar protests which geographers have registered for more than a generation appear to run into a blank wall of dogma.[6]

[5]Hartshorne, Richard, *Perspective of the Nature of Geography*, Chicago: Rand McNally, 1959, p. 91.

[6]*Ibid.*, pp. 91-92.

It is therefore necessary to re-examine all theories of orogenesis that have ever been invented, in order to determine
what can be saved of them in the light of the presently
available facts. If this is done, *it becomes immediately
obvious that something fundamental is wrong with each
and every one of the theories* . . . It appears, therefore, that
the problem of finding the causes of the various geodynamic features must be regarded as still unsolved.[7]

To look upon a landscape . . . without any recognition of the
labor expended in producing it . . . is like visiting Rome
in the ignorant belief that the Romans of today had no
ancestors . . . Wm. Morris Davis.[8]

The depth of the criticisms of Hartshorne, Scheidegger and
others regarding the paucity of achievements from 100 years
of uniformitarianism are very serious, if seldom appreciated.

CONCLUSION. A preferred model has been presented
which claims to describe a realistic view of Earth history. It
claims to describe a view more realistic than that described by
other possible models of cosmic catastrophes. It claims to describe a view more realistic than the various, normally vague
propositions of uniformitarian cosmology.

If this model is valid, among the first things to go in uniformitarian cosmology (and cosmogeny) will be the Lyellian
geological time scale, a feature of uniformitarianism which pur-
ports to supply millions, frequently hundreds of millions of years
for any major development in Earth history. Within one crisis
year, as described by this model, 200,000,000 years of vague,
implausible, unsatisfactory uniformitarian fabric is compressed.
This includes all developments classified as "mesozoic" and
"cenozoic."

This model further opens the way to conceiving an earlier
catastrophe, possibly when the Earth became a dump or "void,"
and darkness may have been upon the face of the deep (Genesis
1:2). A possible earlier catastrophe, coupled by related evidences,
might bring some interesting things to light regarding "paleozoic" events, events which purportedly required almost 400,000,-
000 years.

[7]Scheidegger, Adrian E., *Principles of Geodynamics,* Berlin: Springer-Verlag, 1963, pp. 288, 291.

[8]Hartshorne, Richard, *loc. cit.,* p. 106.

This preferred model presents a new theory[9] of Earth history. If this preferred model, or any other model is mechanically workable, generally meaningful and psychologically satisfying, it is viewed as rational. And yet if it is found rational, it does not suddenly make the Flood account in Genesis rational; that account has been rational for 5,000 years. Only the rationale contained therein has been unrecognized by many recent, semi-rational academic figures who allow only uniformitarian assumptions. Hence, the rationale in this model does not "prove" the Flood; it merely proves the irrationale of the uniformitarian proposition.

This catastrophic perspective leaves the model-maker in a unique position; he becomes markedly skeptical of the professional skeptics. He recognizes that all of German rationalism and its atheistic tendencies are grounded to uniformitarian cosmology, which in this case was organized by Kant (in his work *General History of Nature and Theory of the Heavens*, 1755). Kant required billions of years for the formation of the Earth or the birth of the Moon, as well as other developments in Earth history. Upon this basis he posited his non-theistic rationalism, a basis which is most inadequate (as will be reviewed in a later chapter.)

This then drives the model-maker to the question as to whether German rationalism, based on seemingly irrational assumptions, can be rational? This problem devolves into an even larger one. The question becomes, "Who is rational in this age of so-called rationalism?" "Who is the genuine skeptic in this age of professional skepticism?" And then there is its converse, or reciprocal question, "Who has been mostly gullible in this

[9]The term "new theory" is a relative term. Another concept, rather similar but in embryonic form, was set forth in 1696 by William Whiston, only 9 years after the publication of *Principia Mathematica*, authored by Isaac Newton and published by Edmund Halley, the classic work establishing the nature of gravity. Whiston was a personal friend of Halley; he was the laboratory assistant of Newton, and succeeded Newton to his chair in mathematics at Cambridge. This is the same William Whiston who translated the works of Flavius Josephus from Greek into English. Whiston was an astronomer and mathematician; he was also an ancient historian and classicist; he was well-acquainted with the histories and cosmogenies of the ancient Egyptians, Greeks, Hebrews and Romans. Whiston, like Newton, was a Puritan. Whiston's two leading works were *A New Theory of The Earth* (1696) and *Astronomical Principles of Religion* (1717). Whiston's work, along with Newton's endorsement, contributed heavily to the development of 18th century catastrophism.

catastrophic-uniformitarian matter regarding Earth history?"
And which is the truly liberating viewpoint, Catastrophism
(which contains certain creationist implications) or Uniformitarianism (which contains certain atheistic implications)? These
may be questions which are anything but new, but yet are new.
These are questions upon which the ancients also invested much
intellectual energy.

It may be that the readership, particularly those dedicated
to research, imbued with curiosity, and receptive to catastrophism, should think increasingly in terms of models for their
research into Earth history.

> The test of any such theory is not in its logic but in its
> workability . . . Whether explanatory analysis of develop-
> ment adds more than it detracts from a comprehension of
> the existing character of a landform as an integral element
> in a real variation is therefore a matter of judgment,
> rather than logic.[10]

Workability is essential; when something is demonstrated
as workable, logic or rationale usually follows. This is the learning process.

The learning process is one which has been sometimes easy,
but more often difficult for various generations. This chapter
opened with twin sets of criticisms. One was relative to the learning process, and the failure of Flood catastrophists to view catastrophism in terms of CAUSE as well as effect. Another was that
Flood catastrophists limited their perspective to the 3rd millenium B.C.

A second set of criticisms concerned the valuable but not
entirely satisfactory works of Velikovsky. He thus far has limited his writings to catastrophism in the 1st and 2nd milleniums
B.C. But he has not brought forth line diagrams, maps, models
or even tables to support his thesis.

Celestial catastrophism in the 1st and 2nd milleniums B.C.,
if factual, does nothing to weaken our case concerning the mechanics of the Flood catastrophe; simultaneously it does nothing to
weaken our case for a recent dating (2800 B.C.) of that catastrophe. It is to this theme of postdiluvian catastrophism to which
Chapter VIII, in its brevity, is directed.

---

[10]Hartshorne, Richard, *op. cit.*, p. 90.

VIII chapter

Astral Catastrophism In Ancient Literature

The Geographical Distribution of Ancient Flood Traditions

THE PURPOSE OF THIS CHAPTER is to demonstrate that ancient astral catastrophes, or threatening astral catastrophes, continued to plague mankind and his planet for perhaps 20 centuries following the Flood catastrophe, and this theme permeated ancient literatures, architectures, cosmologies, folklores and religions. The geographical distribution of these ancient traditions illustrates that elliptical orbits and a semi-orderly solar system were a recent but historical condition in our small corner of the galaxy. An understanding of the principle of the astral motif in ancient sources will contribute to and undergird an understanding of the mechanics of the Flood; and similarly, an understanding of the mechanics of the Flood will prepare for a broader and deeper understanding of the geophysical and psychological crises of ancient civilizations, where cities were destroyed periodically by earthshakings and then rebuilt upon their own rubble.

Experiences of a great Flood were recorded in the traditions from every continent, Antarctica excepted. Various scholars in the past have noted and correlated this phenomenon. The following list is not to be considered exhaustive; it is merely representative of the societies possessing Flood traditions:

TABLE 3
EASTERN HEMISPHERE

Asia	Africa	Europe
Andamanese	Bermegai	Druids
Armenians	Carthaginians	Germans
Assyrians	Egyptians	Greeks
Babylonians	Hottentots	Gypsies
Chaldeans	Sudanese	Icelanders
Dravidians		Laplanders
Hebrews		Lithuanians
Indo-Aryans		Norse
Japanese		Romans
Kurnai		Slavs
Mongols		Voguls
Persians		Welch
Phoenecians		
Phrygians		
Syrians		
Tatars		
Toradjas		

WESTERN HEMISPHERE AND OCEANIA

North America	Indonesia and Polynesia	South America
Algonquins	Bataks	Arawaks
Arapahoes	Dyaks	Cauras
Athabascans	Fijiians	Incas
Aztecs	Hawaiians	Maypures
Cherokees	Melanesians	Mechoachens
Crees	Menankabans	Tamanacs
Eskimos	Micronesians	
Klamaths	New Hebridese	
Kolushes	South Polynesians	
Kwakiutls		
Lenni Lanapes		
Mayans		
Michoacans		
Papagos		
Pimas		
Snoqualmies		
Texpi		
Tlingits		
Toltecs		

The post-diluvian theme of astral chaos or threatening astral havoc includes motifs of fire and brimstone: comets, earthquakes, meteors, pestilences, tumults, and earthshakings. These events do not mean that another Flood recurred, but they do indicate that this kind of astral phenomenon persisted over many centuries. If there were eccentric orbits, persistently intersecting orbits, conflicts, and near oppositions, then catastrophes would be mathematically inevitable. This phase of ancient history strengthens the case of the astrophysical mechanism of the Flood.[1,2] The only variables would be the type of havoc, the intensity of the chaos, and the location of the occasion, which would vary from time to time, and from opposition to opposition.

Since this subject is a monumental one in its own right, for the sake of brevity this chapter will consider only a few areas, among which will be India, Japan, Mexico and Peru, and the Middle East.

The Astral Motif In India

India has been settled historically by two major races: the Aryans and the Dravidians, both of whom had their principles

---

[1]Alfred Rehwinkel and Richard Andree in particular have gathered a substantial amount of material on Flood traditions. Among others who have worked on the same subject are Baron Alexander von Humboldt, James G. Frazer, Sir Henry Howorth, Hugh Miller, Byron Nelson, Harold Peake, Johannes Riem, George Smith, Lowell Thomas, Isaac Newton Vail, and William Wundt.

Richard Andress (1835-1912) was a German geographer who, along with his wife Marie, a folklorist, claimed to have compiled Flood traditions from 88 different cultures and societies—42 from Eastern Hemisphere and 46 from the Indian cultures of the New World. Von Humboldt, one of the outstanding geographers of the early 19th century, did his field work in the Orinoco Region of South America. Later, after comparing his findings of Flood traditions with other studies, he came to two conclusions. His conclusions were (1) that the traditions of the Flood were global in geographical distribution, and (2) that the more primitive the culture, the more vivid or emphatic the traditions of an ancient Flood were apt to be.

[2]The nearer to the Sun a planet or comet is, the more rapidly it revolves, and for planets, the more abbreviated is its orbit. A plane perpendicular to the zodiac is crossed by Mercury once every 44 days. The same plane is crossed by Venus once every 112 days. For Earth, Mars, Jupiter, Saturn, Uranus, Neptune and Pluto, it is once every 183, 343, 2,166, 5,381, 15,344, and 25,106 days respectively. This illustrates how much more activity there is in the regions nearer the Sun, and how much higher is the chance of conflict with a random comet with the inner planets. This principle, however, is countered by the distribution of distances of known comets at perihelion. Most do not approach the Sun within the ranges of the inner planets.

of astral worship. The sky gods of the Aryans were quite comparable to the celestial pantheon of the Persians, the Greeks, and the Phoenecians. For instance, the Indo-European Dyaus Pitar was the Aryan or Indian counterpart for the Greek Zeus, the Roman Jupiter, the Egyptian Horus, and the Babylonian Bel.

The Indo-Aryans migrated into Northern India at approximately the same time Abraham was migrating westward toward Palestine from the famed Ur of the Chaldees, some 4,000 years ago. The Aryans spoke a language related to Old Persian and Sanskrit. Concerning the similarity of their sky gods with those of other peoples of the Middle East, E. O. James makes the following comment:

> The mighty warrior, Indra, the god of the thunder, had his headquarters in the atmosphere, between sky and earth, and Agni, the god of fire, was all pervading as the wind. Behind all these celestial gods was the ancient Indo-European Dyaus Pitar, the counterpart of the Greek Zeus and the Roman Jupiter.[3]

The Dravidians were also to be found with astronomical and astrological themes in their literature and religion. They were concerned about perishable versus imperishable worlds, about ages, catastrophes, cycles, and new ages, and they were also concerned about mathematics, causes of natural phenomena, planets, orbits, and zodiacs.

The astrologer was an important person in ancient Hindu life. This astrology motif recurs among such peoples as the Chaldeans, Druids, Egyptians, Germans, Greeks, Incas, and Mayans, all of whom also had astronomer-priests and astrologically oriented oracles. In Hinduism, the Sun, the Moon, the movements of the planets, the zodiac, meteor showers, earthquakes, and eclipses were (and still are) areas of fear, of worship, and of study. This is a holdover from ancient times when astral catastrophes, or impending catastrophes, were very imminent concerns.

During these times, astral catastrophes periodically threatened to occur. Their close approach might well be associated with great destruction; cities might be ruined, oceans might surge, fire and brimstone might again rain from the sky. Their

[3]E. O. James, *The Ancient Gods*, New York: G. P. Putnam's Sons, 1960, p. 75.

approach or regress, night after night, was very much visible, and it was to these celestial bodies that the Hindus offered their propitiations. Kenneth W. Morgan has given the following description:

> Eclipses of the Sun or Moon are times of great importance in the life of the Hindus. Mythologically it is said that the eclipses are caused by the demon Rahu. At the time of the churning of the oceans to make nectar, which would have given immortality, Rahu tasted the nectar without permission. When the Sun and Moon called this to the attention of Vishnu, the god immediately cut off Rahu's head, but since he had drunk the nectar, his head became immortal.
>
> The head was placed in the heavens, and Rahu was allowed as a means of revenge on the Sun and Moon *to approach them at certain times, and thus render them unclean* so that their bodies at those times would become black and thin . . . During the eclipse, conch shells are sounded, devotional songs are sung, and the women bathers utter shrill cries, all of which are considered to be auspicious and help drive Rahu away from the Sun or Moon. (Italics ours)[4,5]

Rahu is parallel in motif to celestial concerns of other ancient religions. Rahu may refer to a historical semi-regular or periodical wanderer within our solar system. For instance, the story of the Phoenix in Egyptian mythology carries all of these elements of the Rahu story. Similarly, the story of Sosa no wo no Mikoto in Japanese mythology carries these elements, as does the ancient Druid traditions of the screeching witch, periodically crossing the heavens on a celestial broomstick and threatening the inhabitants with dire calamities, fearful and evil. Again, the Aztec counterpart of this theme is Quetzalcoatl, a deity described as a fierce, feathered, flying serpent, periodically threatening to engulf the world in fire. The dragon in Chinese folklore also has comparable elements in its theme.

Thus, Hinduism, in being nature-oriented, was like so many of the ancient religions. However, two kinds of nature were

---

[4]Kenneth Morgan, *The Religion of the Hindus*, New York: Ronald Press, 1953, pp. 94-95.

[5]The nectar of the mythology of India bears a striking, even a suspicious parallel to the ambrosia of Greek mythology, the manna of the Hebrews, and also the heavenly nectar in the Japanese tradition.

involved within its orientation to nature worship. One involved the worship of astral phenomena which were comparable to the Apollo, Pallas Athene, Minerva, Hera, Aphrodite, Ares, Electra, Deimos, Phobos, Zeus system of the Greeks. And the second involved nature worship relative to geophysical phenomena—it included worship of winds, typhoons, oceans, thunderings and lightnings, rain, mountains, rivers, and seasons. And again, Greece, for instance, had a parallel complement of nature gods, oriented to the geophysical as well as to the astronomical.

The religious life of the Hindus, therefore, involved idolatrizing of the geophysical elements upon our own planet and also of themes celestial. Both involved nature worship; one was terrestrial; one was astral. They worshipped both phases of nature because it was nature that they couldn't understand, and hence it was nature that they feared.

Ancient people oriented many things toward astral phenomena. Architecture is an illustration. Many ancient peoples had obelisks, sun caves, sundials, sun temples, solar discs, solar and lunar calendars, and they observed solar and lunar festivals. The Egyptians, Druids and Mayans all built temples architecturally planned so that the first rays of the Sun on the autumnal and vernal equinoxes would fall upon the altar at the heart of the temple.[6] The Egyptians built one such temple on the west bank of the Upper Nile, above Luxor; the Druids at Stonehenge, some 3,000 miles distant, as did the Mayans some 8,000 miles distant.

Thus, there seems to have been an historical concern that was in reality based on these ancient periodic astral catastrophes, and on whether the Earth's orbit remained regular or became perturbed. Calendars of the ancients were confused from time to time. For instance, ancient Syrian sundials prior to the ninth century B.C. point about 1° away from true east. Originally, archaeologists concluded that the ancients were poor mathematicians. They weren't. Early Babylonian astronomer-

---

[6]The sun temples were constructed so that the first rays of the dawn of each morning approaching the equinox would fall deeper into the dark heart of the temple. If the first rays of dawn failed to fall on the heart of the temple on the expected day, the equinox, it indicated either (a) that their calendar needed a readjustment, or (b) a perturbation of the Earth had occurred, which again would call for an adjusted calendar. If the first rays of dawn succeeded in falling on the heart of the temple on the expected day, this was reassurance that the gods were sufficiently in celestial harmony that another regular year had been experienced.

priests had mastered some phases of calculus. It would appear, for instance, that our 360° circle is actually based on the ancient Babylonian calendar involving 360 days in the solar cycle.[7]

The Astral Motif in Japan

As in so many areas of the world, Japan's supreme deities were also nature-oriented. They represented terrestrial (or geophysical) nature, such as mountains, oceans, winds, and seasons. They also represented celestial nature. Some of the ancient Japanese traditions were codified in the Nihongi where there is a tradition of creation which is remarkably similar to that in Genesis. There is also a tradition of a rupture between the sun-god and the moon-god. This is somewhat similar to the Hebrew tradition in the time of Joshua and of the extended day in which meteorites (fire and brimstone) rained from above, and the Sun and Moon were in irregular motion—again comparable to the Egyptian story of Phaethon, being drawn across the sky in a solar chariot by steeds gone wild.

The tradition of the Japanese Soso no wo no Mikoto is comparable in theme: a wandering and vicious, evil, and astral principle, periodically afflicting one generation and then another. Note the similarities in themes:

> They next produced the moon-god . . . His radiance was next to that of the sun in splendor. This god was to be the consort of the sun-goddess, and share in her government. They therefore sent him also to heaven.
> Next they produced the leech-child . . . They therefore placed it in the rock-camphor-wood boat of Heaven, and abandoned it to the winds. Their next child was Sosa no wo no Mikoto . . .
> This god had a fierce temper and was given to cruel acts. Moreover he made a practice of continually weeping and wailing. So he brought many of the people of the land to an untimely end. Again he caused green mountains to be-

---

[7]It is suspected that a slight change occurred both in the location of the poles and in the orbit of the Earth during the 8th century B.C., at which time the year changed from 360 to 365¼ days. This was not the result of one conflict, but rather was the net result of several conflicts. One of these conflicts was prognosticated by Amos. Another, described in retrospect by Zechariah (ch. 14) is described with even greater clarity by Josephus (IX-X-4), and a third is described by Isaiah (24:20, 37:36, 38:8).

come withered. Therefore the two gods, his parents, addressed Sosa no wo no Mikoto, saying: Thou art exceedingly wicked, and it is not meet that thou shouldst reign over the world. Certainly thou must depart far away to the Nether Land. So they at length expelled him.[8]

The Astral Motif in Mexico and Peru

Astral themes seem to be equally in evidence in the Western Hemisphere as in the Eastern Hemisphere. Evidences are particularly clear among the Aztecs, Incas, and Mayas, since their cultures were more highly developed; yet similar themes are in evidence among many more primitive Indian tribes. For instance, there is the story of the Indian boy who tried to rope a rabbit and roped the Sun instead, and brought it back a little way.

In the Mayan religion, the most important deities were the Sun, the Moon, and the planet Venus. This, of course, is directly parallel to the deities of Phoenicia, Egypt, and Babylonia. Eric Thompson describes something of the Mayan religion as follows:

> The Aztecs believed that the world had been created five times and had been destroyed four times, the present age being the fifth. Each age had been brought to a violent end, the agents being respectively ferocious jaguars, a hurricane, volcanic eruptions, and a flood. Traditions that have survived among the Maya on the number of creations and destructions of the world are somewhat at variance. That we are now in the fourth age is the view expressed in two sources. Nevertheless, it is probable that Maya belief was in agreement with the Aztec in assigning the number five to the present age.[9]

Aztec and Mayan traditions, like that of the Hindus, were concerned about world ages, cycles, catastrophes, and new ages. The structure of their astral temples reflected this, as did that of so many other ancient peoples. Their mathematics and their religion also reflected their concern with astral cosmology.

---

[8]W. G. Aston, "The Age of the Gods," *The Nihongi* (Chronicles of Japan From Earliest Times to A.D. 697), London: George Allen & Unwin Ltd. 1956), pp. 19-20.

[9]J. Eric S. Thompson, *The Rise and Fall of Maya Civilization*, Norman, Okla.: University of Oklahoma Press, 1954, p. 226.

In South America, the Incas built the capital of their immense empire at Cuzco, high in the Peruvian Andes. The center of Cuzco was their temple, along with the palace. At the center of the temple was a huge image of the Sun. It was made of solid slabs of gold and was placed on an altar. Within this splendid Inca temple, the mummified bodies of the Inca chiefs were placed on great golden chairs. The high point of the religious year was celebrated by the gathering of the priests and temple virgins in a great formation to repeat their sacred vows to their great god, the central body in our solar system, also known as Apollo in Greece. Similar themes of worship occurred in Memphis in Egypt, where sacred vows were made unto Ra, the sun-god of Egypt.

When Pizarro arrived in Cuzco, he was overwhelmed. He had heard stories of golden splendor at Cuzco. But being essentially barbaric and mercenary-minded, he was interested only in plunder and lacked an appreciation for historical or artistic values. He had all of the priceless items of Cuzco melted and shipped in galleons to Spain where they were converted into coin. Only the surrounding traditions remained, and many of these were preserved only piecemeal.

Another Inca tradition goes as follows:

> Perhaps the stories about the ancients were right . . .
> Legend says that in those days of the jaguar-faced gods
> called huaca, the Andes were split apart and the Callejon
> was formed, when the sky made war on the earth. [10]

The Egyptian traditions are similar; only the god was hawk-faced, and he periodically flew across the celestial sea, bringing fire and smoke and occasionally earth quakings with his flight. Again the phoenix tradition is one of these comparable themes. And similar traditions occur regarding an interruption in the Sun's progress and natural calamities among the Arapahoes, the Comanches, the Polynesians, the Snoqualmies, and the Tlingits, to name but a few.

The purpose in recounting these ancient astral themes is three-fold. One is to establish that astral phenomena, such as eccentric orbits, cosmic chaos, and planetary oppositions, were

[10]Bart McDowell and John E. Fletcher, "Avalanche: 3500 Peruvians Perish in Seven Minutes," *National Geographic*, June 1962, p. 871.

not limited to the Flood era. Another purpose is to establish that ancient astral traditions were independent and global rather than interrelated and regional in derivation. A third purpose is to establish that these traditions were deep and persistent, even though they are three and four thousand years old. All of these considerations do not directly concern the century of the Flood; yet these themes reinforce the mechanism or the principle needed to properly understand the cause and scope of the Biblical Flood. Thus, the astral catastrophe known as the Flood was not the last encounter of the Earth with elliptically traveling astral phenomena. It was merely the worst.

The Astral Motif in the Middle East

The Middle East is the region of the cradle of Western Civilization. It was in this region that the Ark landed and its passengers disembarked. It was here that Western Civilization was re-established, and it was from here that the Western World was repopulated with people of Caucasian phenotype. It was here that Caucasian peoples multiplied and migrated, and it was here that they worshipped, speculated, counted, measured, and wrote.

There have been numerous sources of information on the ancient conditions in the Middle East which have been lost or destroyed; among those which have survived are the writings of Moses (Genesis, Exodus, etc.), Job, Josephus (The Antiquities of the Jews), and the Psalms. Moses, the author of Genesis and Exodus, has already been considered briefly in Chapter IV regarding his source material on the Flood. We turn now, and again only briefly, to a consideration of Josephus, the historian, and his source material.

JOSEPHUS. Josephus' account of the times of the Flood and early post-diluvian times is more extensive than that of Genesis. It is interesting to note that Josephus had acquainted himself with Flood stories of other Middle Eastern nations through literature which is no longer extant. Some of his comments reflect ancient concern with regularity versus irregularity of astral phenomena and our solar system. Other comments regard whether or not another Flood might recur. Both types are most significant, and each reflects catastrophism in its own way. Our first quotation regards the Flood; the second regards post-diluvian conditions several centuries later:

> However the Armenians call this place * * * * *, the place of descent, for the ark being saved in that place, its remains are shown there by the inhabitants to this day.
> Now some writers of barbarian histories make mention of this flood, and of this ark; among whom is Berosus the Chaldean. For when he was describing the circumstances of the flood, he goes on thus: 'It is said there is still some part of this ship in Armenia, at the mountain of the Cortyaeans; and that some people carry off pieces of the bitumen, which they take away, and use chiefly as amulets, for the averting of mischiefs.' Hieronymus the Egyptian also who wrote the Phoenician Antiquities, and Manaseas, and a great many more, make mention of the same. Nay, Nicolaus of Damascus, in his ninety-sixth book, hath a particular relation about them; where he speaks thus: 'There is a great mountain in Armenia, over Minyas, called Baris, upon which it is reported that many who fled at the time of the deluge were saved; and that one who was carried in an ark and came on shore upon the top of it; and that the remains of the timber were a great while preserved: this might be the man about whom Moses the legislator of the Jews wrote ... [11]

But let no one upon comparing the lives of the ancients with our lives, and with the few years which we now live, think that what we have said of them is false; or make the shortness of our lives at present an argument, that neither did they attain to so long a duration of life, for those ancients were beloved of God, and (lately) made by God himself; and because their food was then fitter for the prolongation of life, might well live so great a number of years; and besides, God afforded them a longer time of life on account of their virtue, and the good use they made of it in astronomical and geometrical discoveries, which would have not afforded the time for foretelling (the periods of the stars), unless they had lived six hundred years, for the great year is completed in that interval.
Now I have for witnesses to what I have said, all those that have written Antiquities, both among the Greeks, and Barbarians; for even Manetho, who wrote the Egyptian history, and Berosus, who collected the Chaldean monuments, and Mochus, Hestiaeus, and besides these Hieronymus the Egyptian, and those that composed the Phoenecian history,

[11]William Whiston, *Flavius Josephus; The Antiquities of the Jews,* Bridgeport, Conn.: M. Sherman, 1828, pp. 85-86.

> agree to what I here say: Hesiod also and Hecataeus, and
> Hellanicus, and Acuslaus; and besides these Ephorus and
> Nicolaus relate, that the ancients lived a thousand years.
> But as to these matters, let every one look upon them as
> they think fit.[12]

If Josephus is to be trusted (and few ancient historians
were more thorough), then the ancients were not inclined to doubt
whether or not there had been a great, overwhelming and universal Flood. They may have debated the dating of it. They may
have wondered as to which part of Armenia contained the remains of the Ark. And it is known that they did debate the
proper names of the survivors of the Ark and the migration
patterns which ensued. For instance, the Hebrew gives the leader's name as Noah, whereas the Greek gives it as Noeus and then
seemingly combines or confuses the story with an ancient King
Deucalion and his wife. The Babylonian account gives the name
of the builder of the Ark as Ut-napishtim, and another account
gives it as Xisuthrus. Interestingly enough, the Aztecs have a
similar story of two persons who survived in a boat which landed
on the mountainside after the rain stopped. The Aztec name for
the survivor was Coxcox.

Now it also appears that the ancient Chaldeans built ziggarats as something more than architectural feats; they built them
in response to a pervading Flood psychology. The Chaldeans did
not debate whether or not there had been a Flood. They debated
whether or not there might be another. And if there were to be
another, they would need a place of great elevation for refuge
from the flat plain of the Tigris-Euphrates Valley. In order to
be ready to cope with it, they were going to build mighty mounds
for safety. One of these was the Tower of Babel, which, interestingly enough, had an astral temple at its top, the climax of the
endeavor:

> Now it was Nimrod who excited them to such an affront
> and contempt of God. He was the grandson of Ham, the son
> of Noah, a bold man, and of great strength of hand. He
> persuaded them not to ascribe it to God, as if it was through
> His means that they were happy, but to believe that it was
> their own courage which procured that happiness.
> He also gradually changed the government into tyranny,

[12]Whiston, op. cit., pp. 87-88.

seeing no other way of turning men from the fear of God,
but to bring them into a constant dependence upon his
power. He also said "He would be revenged on God, if he
should have a mind to drown the world again;" for that he
would build a tower too high for the waters to be able to
reach; and that he would avenge himself on God for
destroying their forefathers.
Now the multitude were very ready to follow the determination of Nimrod, and to esteem it a piece of cowardice to
submit to God; and they built a tower, neither sparing any
pains, nor being in any degree negligent about the work ...
It was built of burnt bricks, cemented together with mortar,
made of bitumen, *that it might not be liable to admit water.*
(Italics ours)[13]

Again it is interesting to note that it was not a historical
Flood which they debated; it was the possibility of another one
which they feared. And this quotation is also interesting in philosophical ways. It seems that man had his difficulties even in those
early post-diluvian days. Among those difficulties was the struggle of the traditional faith of a holy Creator and Judge versus
the corruption of this into idolatry and a humanistic pantheism.
Another struggle was the retaining versus the abrogation of
personal freedom. As civilization developed in this valley, so
also did idolatry and tyranny arise.

And it was this tyranny, but even more particularly the
engulfing idolatry in Ur, the jewel of the Chaldees, which pro-
voked Abraham to protest. Josephus gives to us a bit of Abraham's not-so-serene life as a citizen of Ur of the Chaldeans—a
recount of some of Abraham's difficulties prior to his migration
to Palestine:

Now Abram, having no son of his own, adopted Lot, his
brother Haran's son, and his wife Sarai's brother; and he
left the land of Chaldea, when he was 75 years old, and at
the command of God went into Canaan, and therein he
dwelt himself, and left it to his posterity. He was a person
of great sagacity, both for understanding all things, and
persuading his hearers, and not mistaken in his opinions;
for which reason he began to have higher notions of virtue
than others had, and he determined to renew and to change
the opinion all men happened then to have concerning God;
for he was the first to venture to publish the notion that

13*Whiston, op. cit.,* pp 88-89.

there was but one God, the Creator of the universe; and that as to other gods, if they contributed anything to the happiness of men, that each of them afforded it only according to his appointment, and not by their own power. This his opinion was derived from the *irregular phenomena that were visible* both at land and sea, as well as *those that happened to the sun and moon,* and the heavenly bodies thus: 'If (said he) these bodies had power of their own they would certainly take care of their own regular motions; but *since they do not preserve such regularity,* they make it plain that so far as they cooperate to our advantage, they do it not of their own abilities, but as they are subservient to him that commands them, to whom alone we ought to justly offer our honour and thanksgiving.' For such doctrines, then the Chaldeans and the people of Mesopotamia raised a tumult against him, he thought fit to leave that country; at the command, and by the assistance of God, he came and lived in the land of Canaan; and when he was there settled, he built an altar and performed a sacrifice to God. (Italics ours)[14]

In Abraham's time, there must have been, even as Josephus indicates, a concern about celestial bodies and their motions and periodicity. Some bodies were observed as regular and predictable; some were observed but their periodicity or predictability was not understood. These early Mesopotamian scholars, in their study of mathematics and the stars, had discovered some of the principles in both geometry and calculus, but so far as it is known, they never grasped the principle of gravitation. It is interesting to note that Newton also studied mathematics and the solar system, and he conceived the idea of universal gravitation after inventing differential calculus, integral calculus, and the binomial theorem—all of which assisted him in his understanding of gravitational law.

Like the Hindus, the Chaldeans drifted into the tendency to worship that part of nature which they failed to understand. They pantheized the planetary system. This is the source of the ancient sky gods which occurred throughout this entire area. Abraham determined to worship the Almighty, the Creator, and objected to the pantheizing of these bodies into nature worship. The Creator, rather than the created, merited man's worship. Abraham was lonely in his convictions, and he emerges as one of

[14]*Whiston, op. cit.,* pp. 94-95.

those persistent, stubborn, and even cantankerous individualists
of history—a protestor and reformer. He might be classified as a
twentieth century B.C. non-conformist who, though his life was
filled with difficulties and trials, yet was great among the greatest.

Abraham was concerned about the irregular phenomena
which occurred among the heavenly bodies: periodicity, planets,
cometary phenomena, and other related conditions. In fact,
Josephus relates that when Abraham temporarily migrated to
Egypt, he was considered an authority from the Chaldees concerning matters astronomical, historical, and mathematical.[15]

THE PSALMS. It is being shown in the Psalms that catastrophism is in evidence among many of the portions of the
Hebrew scriptures, the Old Testament, just as it is in evidence
among the literatures of the non-Hebrew ancients. We have just
considered some of Josephus' accounts, and now turn to the
Psalms, where again is found the catastrophic motif.

The Psalms date from different periods. Many are Davidic,
some are from the period of the Exodus. Among the Exodus
Psalms which contain the catastrophic motif are Psalms 46, 68,
74, 78, 97, 104, and 114. The following are excerpts:

> God is our refuge and strength, a very present help in
>   trouble.
> Therefore we will not fear though the earth should change,
> Though the *mountains shake in the heart of the sea;*
> Though its waters roar and foam,
> Though the *mountains tremble with its tumult.* (Psalm
>   46:1-3 R.S.V.)

> O God, when thou didst go forth before thy people, when
>   thou didst march through the wilderness,

---

[15]*Whiston, op. cit.* pp. 96. Abraham conferred with each of them (the leaders
of Egypt) and confuting the reasonings they made use of, every one for
their own practices, he demonstrated that such reasonings were vain, and
void of truth; whereupon he was admired by them, in those conferences,
as a very wise man, and one of great sagacity ,when he discoursed on any
subject he undertook; and this not only in understanding it, but in persuading other men also to assent to him. He communicated to them arith-
metic, and delivered to them the science of astronomy; for before Abram
came into Egypt they were unacquainted with those parts of learning for
that science came from the Chaldeans into Egypt, and from thence to the
Greeks also.

The *earth quaked,* the heavens poured down rain, at the
presence of God;
Yon *Sinai quaked* at the presence of God,
the God of Israel. (Psalm 68:7-8)

Thou didst divide the sea by thy might;
Thou didst break the heads of the dragons on the waters.
Thou didst crush the heads of Leviathan,
Thou didst give him as food for the creatures of the
wilderness.
Thou didst cleave open springs and brooks;
Thou didst dry up ever-flowing streams.
Thine is the day, thine also the night;
Thou hast *established the luminaries and the sun.*
Thou hast *fixed all the bounds of the earth;*
Thou hast made summer and winter. (Psalm 74:13-17)

He *divided the sea* and let them pass through it,
and made the waters stand like a heap.
In the daytime he led them with a cloud,
and *all the night with a fiery light.*
He cleft rocks in the wilderness,
and gave them drink abundantly as from the deep.
He made streams come out of the rock,
and caused waters to flow down like rivers. (Psalm
78:13-16)

The Lord reigns; let the earth rejoice;
let the many coastlands be glad!
Clouds and thick darkness are round about him;
righteousness and justice are the foundation of his
throne.
Fire goes before him,
and burns up his adversaries round about.
His *lightnings lighten the world;*
the earth sees and trembles.
The *mountains melt like wax* before the Lord
before the Lord of all the earth. (Psalm 97:1-5)

Bless the Lord, O my soul! O Lord my God, thou art
very great!
Thou art clothed with honor and majesty,
Who covered thyself with light as with a garment,
Who hast stretched out the heavens like a tent,
Who hast laid the beams of thy chambers on the waters,
Who makest the clouds thy chariot,
Who ridest on the wings of the wind,
Who makest the winds thy messengers, fire and
flame thy ministers.

Thou didst set the *earth on its foundations,*
    so that it *should never be shaken.*
Thou didst cover it with the deep as with a garment;
    the waters stood above the mountains.
At thy rebuke they fled;
    at the sound of thy thunder they took to flight.
The mountains rose, the valleys sank down to the place
    which thou didst appoint for them.
Thou didst set a bound which they should not pass,
    so that they might not again cover the earth.

Thou hast made *the moon to mark the seasons;*
    the sun knows its time for setting.

May the glory of the Lord endure for ever,
    may the Lord rejoice in his works,
    who looks on the earth and it trembles,
    who touches the mountains and they smoke! (Psalm
    104:1-4, 5-9, 19, 31-32)

When Israel went forth from Egypt, the house of
    Jacob from a people of strange language,
Judah became his sanctuary, Israel his dominion.
The sea looked and fled, Jordan turned back.
The *mountains skipped like rams,* the hills like lambs.
What ails you, O sea, that you flee? O Jordan,
    that you turn back?
O mountains, that you skip like rams? O hills, like lambs?
Tremble, O earth, at the presence of the Lord,
    at the presence of the God of Jacob,
    who turns the rock into a pool of water,
    the flint into a spring of water. (Psalm 114) (Italics
    ours)

At the time of the exodus from Egypt (Exodus 7, 8 and 9), the following themes, considered by Velikovsky, occur in a catastrophic syndrome, and lead to the suspicion that here is another celestial crisis, awesome and destructive:

(1) A universal red dust, possibly iron oxides, covered the land.
(2) Meteorites (hail mingled with fire) repeatedly shelled and wasted the land.
(3) Repeated earthquake activity occurred, leaving most buildings in shambles·
(4) The crescendo of the earthquake activity occurred at the tenth plague, the climax.

(5) An extended, unusually long period of night, as if the Earth's rotation temporarily was interrupted, the ninth plague.

(6) Renewed volcanic action from within the Earth's magma, as illustrated by the Mount of Lawgiving.

(7) Possible tidal phenomenon on the Red Sea, allowing it to remarkably open (allowing the Hebrews to pass across) and, six hours later, its remarkably rapid resurgence, engulfing the pursuing Egyptian army.

(8) A most remarkable astral phenomena, a "cloud by day" but a "pillar of fire" by night, passing not through Egypt, but rather, over Egypt.

This catastrophic motif, found in Exodus, seems to be given in a repeat performance, not quite as severe, not quite as long, but nevertheless something of a return engagement, some 50 years later, as reported by Joshua, standing on Mount Perazim, overlooking the Valley of Gibeon. Note the parallel themes:

(1) Earthquake activity, one seeming illustration being evidenced in the collapse of the walls of Jericho.

(2) Meteorites (astral hail mingled with fire) falling in devastating proportions, and concentrated in certain locations while avoiding others.[16]

(3) An extended, unusually long period of day, as if the Earth's rotation were again temporarily interrupted.

(4) Only this time it was during the Palestinian daytime, as contrasted with the extended nighttime during the previous crisis.

(5) The observed disturbance of the ordinary course of the Sun *and Moon,* a phenomena so similar to the Phaethon

---

[16]In many places in the Biblical narrative, where catastrophic themes are involved, later translators have groped for words to translate that which they failed to comprehend. The terms "blood" and "pestilence" are repeatedly used. Blood is like iron dust, which oxidizes into a crimson color, and this may have some relationship to the Red Sea, so named when it may have literally appeared crimson. Pestilence is more on the order of bolides or meteorites, a somewhat larger scale item of similar astral origin. Note, for example in Psalm 91, the term "noisome pestilence."
Surely he shall deliver thee from the snare of the fowler, and from the *noisome pestilence* . . .
Thou shalt not be afraid of the terror by night; nor of the arrow that flieth by day; nor of the pestilence that walketh in darkness; nor of the destruction that wasteth at noonday.

story from Egypt, where the celestial steeds, drawing the heavenly chariot, suddenly went wild.

(6) "They fought from heaven; the stars in their courses (or paths) fought against Sisera"—a theme so strikingly similar to Homer's interpretation of celestial events and Earthian repercussions during the Greek-Trojan conflict and the destruction of Troy.

These observations obviously deserve fuller comment; however, this chapter endeavors only to emphasize the presence of a catastrophic theme rather than endeavoring to portray the full scope of these circumstances.

Here again, as in the traditions of India, Greece, the Aztecs, and other ancient peoples, is seen a concern about periodicity, planets, celestial paths, watery upheavals, earthquakes, volcanism, and related phenomena. These are among the earliest literary observations which remain in the possession of the human race, now some 35 to 40 centuries removed from that era. Very possibly the earliest of all extant literature is the Book of Job which similarly contains data about trembling mountains, circuits of heaven, names of astral bodies, and the shaking of the foundations of the Earth.

JOB. Job, like Abraham, was another twentieth century (B.C.) non-conformist. He lived in the western portion of Arabia. Job's attitude toward astral idolatry appears to have been similar to that of Abraham, for he also objected to the pantheising of the solar system in Arabia. God alone was to be worshipped:

> If I beheld (as objects of worship) the sun when it shone, or the moon when I was walking in its brightness; and my heart has been secretly enticed by them, or my mouth has kissed my hand (in homage to them); This also would have been a heinous and principal iniquity . . . (Job 31:26-28, Amplified)

Just as Abraham was concerned about regularity versus irregularity of the movements within our solar system, so was Job:

> God, who removes the mountains, and they know it not, when He overturns them in His anger. Who shakes the earth out of its place, and the pillars of it tremble; Who commands the sun and it apparently rises not, and seals up the stars (from view); Who alone stretches out the

heavens, and treads upon the waves and high places of the
sea; Who made (the constellations) the Bear, Orion and the
(loose cluster) Pleiades, and the (vast starry) spaces of the
south. (Job 9:5-9, Amplified)

There are other similar passages in the Book of Job which
discuss the former Flood, the stars, the circuit of heaven, and
the trembling of the crust (pillars) of the Earth. One of the
more interesting portions is found in chapter 38:

Canst thou bind the sweet influences of Pleiades, or loose
the bands of Orion? Canst thou bring forth the Mazzoroth
in his season? Or canst thou guide Arcturus with his sons?
Knowest thou the ordinances of heaven; canst thou set the
dominion thereon in the earth? (Job 38:31-33, Amplified)

A reference has already been seemingly made to the Milky
Way (Job 9:9). Here, in chapter 38, Pleiades, Orion, and Arcturus appear to be bodies moving across the zodiac. Among the
three, note, Orion was visible with bands. Arcturus was visible
apparently with its sons, or luminaries, or satellites. What
could this mean? This question is much deeper than might appear on the surface. And what about Mazzaroth and its irregularity versus its periodicity? It is known, for instance, that the
Greeks had names for both of the moons of Mars (Deimos and
Phobos) which were discovered in 1877 by Asaph Hall. The
Greeks also had a name for a planet, not now extant, named
Electra. As has been mentioned in an earlier chapter, the Greeks
explained her disappearance from the heavens by saying that
she withdrew at the time of one of her conflicts with Ares.

Interlude: Recognition of Scientific Validity
of Ancient Cosmology

At this juncture we shall consider events some 3,500 years
after the time of Job which may shed further light on the circumstances which Job considered and to which we shall return
for further consideration.

HALLEY, NEWTON AND WHISTON. Edmund Halley had
posited the periodicity of comets, even as Copernicus had posited
the heliocentricity of the solar system a century previously. Having searched the astronomical records which he could locate in

both England and Germany, he came to the conclusion that comets were not occasional celestial phenomena, but regular members of our solar system, even as planets were. Halley had traced records back 1,500 years to come to this conclusion.

Meanwhile, his friend Newton was discovering several forms of calculus in his endeavor to measure and calculate the orbits of the planets. Having noticed that all bodies move more rapidly when nearer the Sun, and that this applied to each planet within its particular elliptical orbit, Newton came to the understanding of gravitation. His conclusions, set forth in *Principia Mathematica*, had been based in part on his understanding of Kepler's laws regarding planetary motion and particularly the third law.

Both Halley and Newton had gone farther than Copernicus, who had rejected the Ptolemaic notion that the Earth was the center of the solar system. But Ptolemy had also implied that the motions of our solar system were regular and everlasting. Halley and Newton, also William Whiston, his assistant, all rejected this second assumption of Ptolemy. They all presumed that the past of our solar system may have been markedly different from the present arrangement.

Whiston's writings upon the catastrophic circumstances and the astral nature of the Flood upheaval established some basic concepts for eighteenth century catastrophism and were a decided advance. Newton and Halley followed Whiston's conclusions in ancient cosmology even as Halley and Whiston followed Newton's theory in gravitation.

JONATHAN SWIFT (1667-1745). The Halley-Newton-Whiston breakthrough in astronomical, historical, and mathematical knowledge was a major event of that century. This is perhaps best illustrated by Jonathan Swift, a novelist, political malcontent and contemporary of Whiston's in London. Swift wrote many satires, one of which reflects Whistonian thought, and more. It is *Gulliver's Travels,* with its famous story about the Lilliputian, a race of six-inch pygmies, and with its essay about the Laputans, an imaginary race of people on the other side of the world who were more intelligent than the Europeans. They had developed superior telescopes; and with their telescopes they had discovered two moons orbiting around Mars which were unknown to Europeans.

Swift proceeded to describe the circumstances of these

mythological moons orbiting about Mars. He described (1) their sizes, (2) their respective distances from the planet, and (3) the direction of revolution of these moons in their orbits. In his imaginative essay, Swift stated that the inner moon revolved about Mars faster than the planet itself rotated. Thus, said he, to a Martian it would seem to rise in the west and set in the east. Each of these three sets of conditions comprised the situation discovered some 150 years later by Asaph Hall in 1877.

Swift's allegorical essay is related by a skeptical but astounded modern, scientific writer, Isaac Asimov, in a current volume on scientific thought, as follows:

> This is an amazing coincidence. Of course, Swift might have reasoned as follows: It was known that Earth had 1 moon, Jupiter had 4 and Saturn had 7 at the time he was writing his book. It was reasonable to suppose that Saturn might have an 8th moon hidden somewhere and, in that case, if Mars had 2 moons, there would be a nice list of numbers.
>
> As one moved outward from the sun, beginning at Earth, the number of moons for each planet would be 1, 2, 4, 8. Then too, the moons of Mars would have to be small and close to the planet, or even Europeans with their "poor" telescopes would have discovered them.
>
> So far, Swift's thinking can be followed. However, his guess that Phobos would rise in the west and set in the east because of its speed of revolution is uncanny. It is undoubtedly the luckiest guess in literature.[17]

Asimov assumes that Swift was guessing. Actually, Asimov is doing the guessing. Furthermore, he is rationalizing, and his rationalization may be far from satisfactory. Whiston and Swift both lived in London for over fifty years of their lives, and contemporaneously. They were both educated men and writers. They were both idealists and men with sufficient courage to qualify as non-conformists (Whiston in mathematics, astronomy, classics and theology and Swift in literature and political science). London in 1726 was a city of about 300,000, comparable in size to metropolitan Tacoma, Washington; Grand Rapids, Michigan, or Charlotte, North Carolina. It is reasonable to sup-

[17]Isaac Asimov, *The Kingdom of the Sun*, New York: Collier Books, 1962. p. 126.

pose that the two men may have been acquaintances, and, indeed, may have been very good friends.

Swift probably got much of his material for his imaginative essay from Whiston and, rather than guessing, he seemed to be interpreting ancient Greek cosmology rather correctly.[18] He believed that there had been several irregularities in the solar system and at least one had involved Mars. He, like Whiston, realized that large bodies as well as small bodies could travel in eccentric orbits, following Halley's thinking. Halley did not really discover the periodicity of comets, for Seneca had reported that the ancient Babylonian astronomers were of this opinion. Halley, in reality, only affirmed what Seneca had reported.[19]

This study suspects that Asimov had guessed about Swift

---

[18]Swift also may have read the ancient Greek cosmologies as well. The Greeks had named the two steeds of Ares at least 3,000 years prior to Asaph Hall. Hall, in deference to classical Greek mythology, named the two steeds of Mars (Ares) in accordance with their ancient names, Deimos and Phobos, meaning "fear" and "panic."

Job describes Arcturus with its two sons. Homer described Ares with its two steeds, at a time during which the Trojan war was, in their minds, a war between the celestial dieties of Athens and Troy, a war whose fortunes depends on such astral conflict. This was also the same age in which Amos, Isaiah, Joel and Micah were uttering their prognostication of judgments and the need of spiritual growth. Their prognostications or prophecies took the form of blasts from heaven (Isaiah 37), "blood," earthquakes, falling fire and brimstone, pestilence, tumults, vexations and a similar array of phrases.

Sometimes these phrases were not well understood by later generations, and were translated with a sort of biological implication (such as "blood" and "pestilence", whereas their origin was astral in nature, as is shown frequently in the context.

These are the same times in which Isaiah describes the Earth as wandering like a drunkard, a day in which Northern Palestine more than Southern Palestine was afflicted (Isaiah 9). These were days, Isaiah reminded his people, which were similar to those of the long day of Joshua (Is. 28:21). Not only at this time were the walls of Troy shattered with earthquakes; similarly we find that the great walls of Jerusalem, 30 feet thick and 100 feet tall, were breached, and the aqueducts were also broken.

More can be set forth on this theme; however it is obvious why the Greeks named the two mythical steeds of Ares (Mars) "fear" and "panic."

[19]Mary Proctor, in her volume *The Romance of Comets* makes an interesting statement together with a possibly erroneous rationalization or conclusion: "It was not till the time of Halley's comet in 1682, that modern astronomy began to consider the question of the possibly periodic character of cometic motions with attention. (For my own part, I reject as altogether improbable the statement of Seneca that the ancient Chaldean astronomers could calculate the return of comets.) Mary Proctor, *The Romance of Comets*, New York: Harper Bros., 1926, p. 103.

rather than probed into catastrophic theory because his mind
was subconsciously conditioned by the prevailing uniformitarianism. Asimov was assuming, whereas Swift and Whiston were
basing their conclusions on correct interpretations of ancient
Babylonian, Egyptian, Greek, Hebrew, and Roman cosmology.

JOB. We will now return to our original point of departure,
Job, chapter 38, where Job is discussing "Arcturus and his sons,"
This portion is requoted:

> Canst thou bind the sweet influences of Pleiades, or loose
> the bands of Orion? Canst thou bring forth Mazzaroth in
> his season? Or canst thou guide Arcturus with his sons?
> Knowest thou the ordinances of heaven; canst thou set the
> dominion thereon in the earth? (Job 38:31-33, Amplified)

Let us examine the term "Mazzaroth." In Hebrew, "roth"
means beard and "mazza" means star. We seem to have here a
descriptive term: the bearded, or hairy, star. This is descriptive
of cometary phenomena. Orbits were understood only with diffi-
culty by the ancients. Highly eccentric orbits were the most
difficult of all to understand, partly because of the chance of
being disturbed by some of the larger and remoter planets, such
as Jupiter and Saturn. Comets would disappear into the remote
oceans of our solar system, and then they would return with
renewed brilliance—sometimes in the same orbit and sometimes
not, sometimes on schedule and sometimes not—a generation or
so later. Apparently, bodies following highly elliptical orbits at
that time were of sufficient mass to threaten and occasionally
disturb the Earth.

One or two involvements with a large celestial body and the
resulting celestial havoc would be remembered as a dreadful
ordeal. An approach of even a major comet would be a dire por-
tent. Fear and wonder of such encounters form the basis of the
astrology and the sky-gods of the ancients and reflect the motivation of their astrally oriented religious architecture. For this
reason an astral observatory or planetarium was reportedly built
at the top of the Tower of Babel. For this reason Stonehenge
was built. And this ancient concern for understanding the ordinances of heaven was fully shared by Abraham and Job. One
difference, however, was that these early patriarchs were determined to maintain the traditions, the standards, and the faith of

their forebears. Another great difference, in harmony with the one already described, was the religious determination of the Hebrews to keep records without alteration or loss. Priests and scribes were careful that not one mark of punctuation should be misplaced in the copying of manuscripts. And their emphasis on accurate transcription allowed the scriptures to survive, whereas the valuable Sybilline and Delphine oracles, as well as the Egyptian oracles at Memphis and later Alexandria did not survive the ravages of time.

The Book of Job, therefore, is one of the most profound of all works of literature. It is profound in its spiritual values. It is equally profound in its contemporary observations for that early patriarchal age. Consider, for instance, the animals discussed in the dialogue: the lion, the ass, the cow, the ox, the jackal, and the ostrich. These animals do not exist in Arabia today; rather, they are often found in the savanna grassland climate of East Africa. This is because the climate of Arabia at that time was cooler and more humid since the oceans of the Earth were yet cold from the melting of the ice mass. Because there were cooler oceans, there were cooler planetary wind systems. The climate was more temperate than arid, and there was more rain and less evaporation. This is but one of the many indications that the Ice Epoch was simultaneous with the Flood, a magnetic phase of that global catastrophe.

Let us return briefly to a passage in Genesis:

> And unto Eber were born two sons: the name of one was Peleg; for in his days was the earth divided. (Genesis 10:25, Amplified)

This particular Eber may be the origin of the word Hebrew; that is to say, Eber was four generations from Noah, even as the aforementioned Nimrod was three generations from Noah. And at this early date, approximately 200 to 300 years after the Flood, it is believed that the ice sheet had substantially melted. The oceans, in receiving this juvenile water, increased and flooded the continental shelves. It was in this age that the seas found their new mean sea level. Rising waters divide lands, as was described, whereas diminishing waters would have united the lands.

Scriptures also state that the southern end of the Dead Sea region (Sodom and Gommorah's hinterland) was well watered, undoubtedly meaning that it was skillfully irrigated. Today this region hardly possesses an itinerant wadi, much less a creek or river. It is one of the hottest and driest parts of the Earth. Likewise, rivers are frequently mentioned in Job's Arabia, rivers which are no longer in existence. Snows, also, are occasionally mentioned. Three such significant passages are found in the Book of Job:

> Have you entered the storehouse of the snow,
>   or have you seen the storehouses of the hail,
>   which I have reserved for the time of trouble,
>   for the day of battle and war?
> From whose womb did the ice come forth,
>   and who has given birth to the hoarfrost of heaven?
> The water become hard like stone,
>   and the face of the deep is frozen. (Job 38:22-23, 29-30,
>   God's first speech to Job, R.S.V.)

This is another indication of the Ice Epoch and its rather recent demise. What further evidence is required to conclude that the Arabian peninsula, along with other regions in a similar latitude, had a more temperate climate at that time? And does not this suggest an historical shift in climatic zones? And what, then, would be more likely to cause a shift in climatic zones than a shift in the temperatures of the oceans?

For instance, even in Roman times it is recorded that olive groves extended 100 miles into Cirenaica (Eastern Libya). Today, this region has been engulfed by the expanding Sahara desert. It is also well established that the immense Sahara desert is also expanding on its southern flanks in the Sudan. Similarly, it is well recognized that the higher latitude land masses (such as Scandinavia and the Baltic Regions) have experienced a historical warming effect. The reason appears to be that the Ice Epoch was simultaneous with the Floodtide Cataclysm. It took many months for the waters to drain off the Earth. It took many decades and possibly several centuries for the ice to outflow from its concentrations. It took several centuries for the ice to melt sufficiently for the new mean sea level to be achieved. But it took many centuries and, in fact, several millenia, for the ocean to achieve a new temperature equilibrium. And temperatures of the oceans are the primary determinants for the temperatures of the Earth's planetary wind systems. Thus, the shift in historical climatic zones, as indicated in Job and elsewhere, serves as a further evidence of the totality of the Flood and Ice Cataclysm, commonly known as the Biblical Flood.

Throughout the Book of Job evidences of the concern of the ancients about the ordinances of heaven have been found, including planetary movements, lunar movements, cometary movements, and references to the Deluge. Elihu, in his attempts to explain natural and spiritual principles to the stricken Job, and comfort him, acknowledged the wondrous powers of God in nature, as follows:

> By the breath of God ice is given, and the breadth of the waters is frozen over. (Job 37:10, Amplified)

This very likely refers to ice formed climatologically, as are snows and frosts. However, in the Lord's speech in Job 38 is found the following, which hardly suggests climatological ice, especially coming as it does just prior to the discussion of the constellations, of Mazzaroth, the sons of Arcturus, and of the ordinances of heaven:

> Out of whose womb came the ice? And the hoary frost of heaven, who has given it birth? The waters are congealed like stone and the *face of the deep is frozen*. (Italics ours)

Again note that ice here is termed in association with the constellations, the periodic and semi-periodic astral phenomena, and the ordinances of the heavens in contrast to the ordinances of the Earth.

There is ample evidence that civilization after the Flood developed very rapidly, and for reasons in part given in Chapter IX. There is ample evidence that not only were the Chaldean ancients well versed in geometry, astronomy, and even in some forms of calculus; there is also ample evidence that they understood a good deal about structural engineering (the Babylonian ziggarats and the Egyptian pyramids serving as illustrations). Further, this study posits that in the age following the Flood-Ice catastrophe, when the ice mass was yet melting and when Chaldean climates were cooler, moister, and more temperate, exploring parties very likely had been sent out and had given reports of the vast icy reaches in the north, where the "face of the deep was yet frozen." Thus, although the Book of Job is profound in its spiritual context, it is equally profound in its historical scope of analyses and observations of matters astronomical, geophysical, climatological and zoological.

Concerning further observations in matters zoological and astronomical, review God's first speech in Job, chapters 38 and 39. Animals are used broadly, denoting only the regional ecology of that day. In chapters 40 and 41, however, Behemoth and Leviathan are discussed—they have been mistranslated as "hippopotamus" and "crocodile"; they carry a much different meaning.

William Ward, who hardly has any idea of the catastrophic picture of these times, has nevertheless made the following observation in his excellent work:

> The detailed descriptions of these two animals, occupying most of two chapters, seems exaggerated and out of place here . . .
> The descriptions are not of ordinary animals, as in God's first speech, but are of two symbolic creatures which played a most significant role in ancient mythology. The great sea monster was a symbol of the primeval chaos God had to conquer to bring his creation under control. One of the earliest stories of the creation was of God's destroying the monster of the deep, Tiamat, or Rahab, or Leviathan, representing the primeval chaos, to make the universe an orderly one under his control. This story is often referred to in ancient apocalyptic literature and occasionally in the Old Testament.[20]

The descriptions being made are comparable to Quetzacoatl of the Aztecs, Sosa no wo no Mikoto of the Japanese, Rahu of India, and some of the Greek mythology. Tiamat or Rahab appears to be complementary to the dragon motif of China, to the celestial witch motif of the ancient Druids of Great Britain, and to comparable motifs which have a global distribution.

Thus it can be understood why Phoenicians were concerned about erecting planetariums on hilltops to worship Astarte and Baal; why the ancient Chaldeans erected ziggarats in the Tigris-Euphrates Valley and built astral temples at the apexes. Astral themes permeate ancient traditions, and we see why the sky-gods of these various peoples may have differed a little in detail, though not in theme. Although this chapter has given no room for discussion of the astral traditions among the Germans, Norse,

[20]William B. Ward, *Out of the Whirlwind*, Richmond: John Knox Press, 1958, p. 103.

Icelanders, Polynesians, Melanesians, and others, these cultures also had their celestial pantheons and their traditions of world destructions.

The Significance of Catastrophic Motifs in Ancient Literature

Today, we use a term called "imagination" to describe something which is conceived, and does in fact exist, but is not easily perceived. We also use a term called "fancy" for something purported to exist which in fact does not. Are these ancient astral mythologies, then, imagination or fancy? It is feared that too often these mythologies have been relegated to mere fancy, whereas they in reality had a core of historical truth involving celestial mechanics. They were the best explanations ancient man could give to describe and understand his times and the causes of catastrophism which troubled his centuries.

Both the capacities and the times of the ancients have been greatly underestimated by the moderns. It has been shown that motifs of cosmological traditions are present on every continent, Antarctica excepted. The astronomical themes inherently correlate with mechanics of the Flood catastrophe. Since the sequence of ancient times is often garbled in ancient legends, folklores, and literatures, and since an understanding of such a sequence is necessary for comprehension of ancient times, here is presented an approximate time scale for post-diluvian astral catastrophism:[21]

Diluvian Catastrophe	2800 B.C. +/– 500 yrs.
Mosaic-Joshuaic Cycle	1450-1400 B.C. +/– 50 yrs.
Amos-Homeric-Isaiahic Cycle	775- 700 B.C. +/– 15 yrs.

Following the Flood catastrophe, the fifteenth and the eighth centuries B.C. were the ones in which major catastrophes overtook and shook the Earth, providing the major source for fire and brimstone perspectives of the ancients. Other centuries in which catastrophes threatened were the twenty-first, the twelfth, and the eleventh centuries B.C. [22]

[21]For a further sketch of catastrophic time-chart, reference is made to Chapter XI, p. 304.

[22]Biblical references are Genesis 19, I Samuel 7, and II Samuel 24.

Some of the purportedly great thinkers of the nineteenth century, following Ptolemaic thought with regard to ancient conditions, thought that they had discovered a great new truth, the uniformitarian proposition. Ptolemy's assumptions of geocentricity were in error. Similarly, his assumptions of Earth regularity (uniformitarianism) were also in error. But Ptolemy had no telescope, no calculus, no computers, little in the way of travel, and meager libraries. That his assumptions were erroneous is understandable and even forgivable.

Halley, Newton, and Whiston made great steps toward correcting the Ptolemaic viewpoint of uniformitarianism, even as Copernicus made great steps in correcting the Ptolemaic viewpoint of geocentricity. Why then did the nineteenth century humanists fall back into the Ptolemaic error? And why has the twentieth century similarly become so dominated by this apparent absurdity? And how important is this uniformitarian error? These are questions which will be considered prior to the conclusion of this volume.

First, however, a further analysis of catastrophism and uniformitarianism is in order. Catastrophism has been discussed relative to evidences beyond our planet and evidences within our planet. Catastrophism has been discussed relative to matters gravitational and matters magnetic. Catastrophism has been discussed relative to tides (upheavals) in both oceans of water (hydrosphere) and in oceans of magma (lithosphere).

But the Earth is more than a two-component fluid; it is a three-component fluid. It is composed of hydrosphere, lithosphere and atmosphere, man's essential habitat. A derangement of man's atmospheric environment could be the most profound effect of a cataclysmic period. It is to this subject, that of paleoclimatology and atmosphere, that the next chapter is directed.

IX chapter

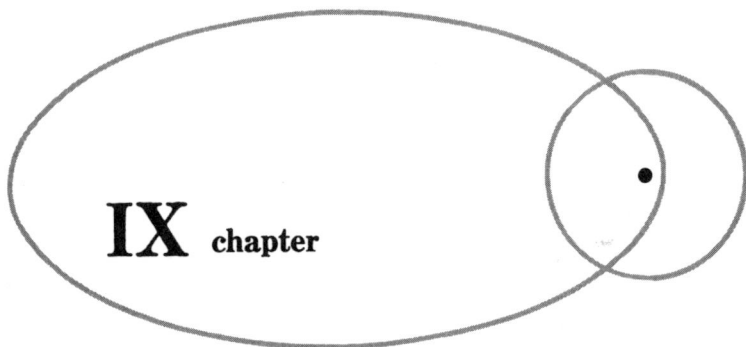

The Greenhouse Effect:
The Antediluvian Canopy

ASTRAL CATASTROPHISM has been considered thus far in various ways. Chapter II considered its historicity in modern thought. Chapter VIII considered these motifs in ancient thought. Astral catastrophism has been considered from the evidences which are beyond our Earth but yet resident within our solar system. It has also been considered from evidences from the sphere of our own planet. It has been considered with respect to two of the three fluids—fluid components of the Earth, the fluid hydrosphere (the oceans), and the fluid lithosphere (the magma).

In a brief summary, the Earth is a three-component fluid, and of these components, the atmosphere is both the least massive and the least restricted. It is the least stable and most easily subjected to change. The atmosphere, weighing about one-millionth of the total weight of the Earth[1], is also man's essential

---

[1]The weight of the envelope of air above the Earth's surface is 14.8 lbs. per square inch—a total of 5×10^{15} tons. This is about equal to 30 feet of water, distributed evenly across the surface of the Earth. This, while a substantial tonnage, is less than one millionth of the weight of the Earth as a whole. The weight of the lithosphere is about 99.8% of the total; the weight of the lithosphere and hydrosphere combined is about 99.9999%. One millionth or otherwise, the atmosphere is far and away the most critical part of man's terrestrial environment. Moderate changes in the atmosphere could have drastic effects upon the biological habitat. Atmosphere, weightwise, is relatively nothing, but for biology, it is the most important of all portions of the terrestrial picture.

habitat, because it is within the Earth's atmosphere that he breathes and lives.

Tidal effects have been considered with respect to the hydrosphere—the global floodtides having been the reported phenomenon. Tidal effects have been considered with respect to the magma — the globe-encircling arcuate uplifts, the Earth's recent mountain systems, having been the result. Evidence indicates that there also has been a reorganization of our atmospheric envelope at the time of the Flood crisis, a reorganization which took its effect in at least five ways:

1. A lowering of barometric pressure.
2. A change in the mix or proportions of gases.
3. The disestablishment of a heat equilibrium, causing a horizontal reorganization of the Earth's climates.
4. The disestablishment of a heat equilibrium, causing a change in magnitude of vertical turbulence in the Earth's troposphere, stratosphere, ionosphere, and exosphere.
5. A shift in the level of actinic radiation at the Earth's surface.

Thus, each of the Earth's three fluid components was profoundly affected. As far as gross weight, force, or thrust are concerned, the greatest change occurred within the shifting magma. As far as aquatic life is concerned, the changes in the hydrosphere (including salinity and temperature) were of primary concern. But as far as man is concerned, the changes in the atmosphere have easily produced the most extensive, long-range effects.

It is the author's contention that, prior to the Deluge, the Earth possessed a primordial vapor canopy, in some ways similar to that surrounding Venus today. The canopy of Venus consists primarily of carbon dioxide and hydrocarbons, with some water vapor. It is supposed that the Earth's primordial vapor canopy was composed mostly of water vapor, some carbon dioxide, and virtually no hydrocarbons. Even as the surface of Venus is hidden from the telescope and from the rays of the Sun, so in the previous age was the surface of our Earth also shielded from the direct rays of the Sun. This water vapor canopy condensed out at the time of the Flood-Ice Cataclysm.

1. The Primordial Canopy

There are two sources supporting the conclusion that a primordial canopy existed. It has been discussed in the early chapters of Genesis in various ways. The Biblical rendition states, clearly and repeatedly, that the climatic regime was not only different, but much different. This is also maintained or indicated in numerous other ancient traditions. Secondly, geological findings compare and harmonize with these evidences and reinforce this conclusion.

If the Earth had a water vapor canopy prior to the Deluge, it is a very easy matter to understand why the canopy condensed and was eliminated at the time of the Flood cataclysm. Ice was captured in avalanches of charged particles, forming the Ice Epoch. Ice particles form the perfect nuclei of condensation. Had there been a primordial canopy of water vapor, and had the Earth captured a substantial amount of ice in particles at the time of the Deluge, the water vapor canopy would have been completely condensed out of the upper atmosphere. It could not have been otherwise.

Similarly, there are several reasons for concluding that there was much more available carbon dioxide in the atmosphere in that earlier era. One evidence is that during the Flood cataclysm, much vegetation was buried. Vegetation which was buried by alluvial action resulted in just that much less carbon available to today's atmospheric carbon cycle.

THE DESCRIPTION IN GENESIS. The Genesis account makes the following statements which have implications relative to the antediluvian climatology:

> And God said, Let there be a firmament (the expanse of the sky) in the midst of the waters; and let it separate the waters (below) from the waters (above). And God made the firmament (the expanse) and separated the waters which were under the expanse from the waters which were above the expanse. And it was so. (Genesis 1:6-7; Amplified)

> When no plant of the field was yet in the Earth, and no herb of the field had yet sprung up, the Lord God had not (yet) caused it to rain upon the Earth, and there was no man to till the ground. But there went up a mist (a fog-

vapor) from the land, and watered the whole surface of the ground.   (Genesis 2:5-6; Amplified)

I set my bow [rainbow] in the cloud, and it shall be for a token or sign of a covenant *or* solemn pledge between Me and the Earth. And it shall be that when I bring clouds over the Earth, and the bow [rainbow] is seen in the cloud, I will [earnestly] remember my covenant *or* solemn pledge, which is between Me and you and every living creature of all flesh, and the waters shall no more become a flood to destroy and make all flesh corrupt. . . . (Genesis 9:13-15; Amplified)

The first quotation directly suggests that there was a water vapor canopy in the upper atmosphere at all times. No blue sky was ever seen until after the Flood. In this section of Genesis, not only are the oceans divided from other oceans by continents, but also the upper atmosphere (water vapor canopy) is separated from the lower atmosphere (the firmament). There were waters above the firmament and waters below the firmament, the canopy and the ocean. A separation of the atmosphere seems clearly indicated.

The second quotation states in definite terms that the Earth was watered abundantly, though not by rain. It was watered in a different manner than today, when the Earth is watered primarily by rain and somewhat by dew. It is believed that in this earlier age a dew regime was the only mechanism by which the Earth's surface was watered.

The third quotation reflects that rainbows are a result of the prismatic effect of bending of rays of light through water droplets. Rainbows can only occur after rains, and require the direct action of sunlight. This time immediately after the Flood was the first time that rainbows were observed. This again suggests that direct sunlight and blue skies, along with water droplets in the atmosphere, were new phenomena.

In Genesis 2:8-14, a swampy type of river hydrography is alluded to. Four major rivers met at the Garden of Eden. The type of hydrography here described suggests a similarity to the lake country of northern Minnesota and Manitoba, where water is in great abundance and swamps are numerous, but where there is so little gradient that the flow of water is very sluggish.

The primordial canopy was thus organized quite differently from our present atmospheric regime, water vapor within the atmosphere being one component of difference. This antediluvian condition was similar to that found in the atmosphere of Venus today which has a remarkably reflective canopy. This reflectivity in scientific terminology is called "albedo." The albedo of Venus is 76%. The albedo of the Earth, with its reflective oceans, its white polar ice caps, its mid-latitude snows, and its low-latitude, light-tan deserts, averages about 39%. The albedo (reflectivity) of the relatively dark face of the Moon, by comparison, is but 7%. Mercury is about 6%.

Assuming that Earth had a canopy similar to Venus, the effects would be very great, not only in the area of climatology but also in the penetration of actinic radiation. Before considering some of the specific circumstances of the canopy, it would be well to note some evidences in geology which parallel these findings.

ANTEDILUVIAN CLIMATOLOGY. It has already been noted that sub-tropical conditions have been ascertained from geological discoveries in all lands surrounding the Arctic Ocean. These lands include such places as Alaska, Canada, Nova Zemlya, the New Siberian Islands, Severnaya Zemlya, Siberia, and Spitzbergen. Palm leaves and marine crustaceans have been found entombed in strata on Spitzbergen, 800 miles from the North Pole, indicating the previous existence of a tropical or subtropical climate. Admiral Byrd wrote about some similar findings in a protruding mountain range, some 200 miles from the South Pole on the Antarctic subcontinent:

> The rock fragments from this mountainside invariably included plant fossils, leaf and stem impressions, coal and fossilized wood. Here, at the southernmost known mountain in the world scarcely two hundred miles from the South Pole, was found conclusive evidence that the climate of Antarctica was once temperate or even sub-tropical. [2]

Temperature is but one consideration, and consideration of *humidity* is quite another. For instance, most tropical and sub-tropical areas today are composed of either desert or steppe climates. Northern South America and Southeastern Asia are the exceptions in equatorial humidity. Africa has about five times

---

[2]Dolph Earl Hooker, *Those Astounding Ice Ages*, New York: Exposition Press, 1958, p. 44; ref: *National Geographic*, October, 1935.

as much desert as rain forest; it also has much more steppe land than savannah grassland. The example of desert-like Australia is even more extreme; perhaps 5% of Australia can be classified as humid, whereas about 75% is desert or semi-desert.

In today's climatic regime, hot climates do not necessarily imply humid climates; in fact, the trend is toward the opposite, as, for example, Mexico. In the fossil record of the antediluvian era, however, desert-like conditions are not found.

Consider, for instance, the Rocky Mountain region of the United States, the intermontane region between the Cascades and the Rockies. This includes part of British Columbia, Eastern Washington, Eastern Oregon, Idaho, dry Arizona, drier Nevada, and parts of Colorado and New Mexico. This is distinctly dry country in which nature has preserved numerous fossils of both fauna and flora. Many varieties of both deciduous and coniferous trees (including the curious ginko tree) occur in the fossil record, indicating a climate of lush vegetation and reflecting excellent conditions of humidity, in addition to a favorable temperature gradient. Fruit trees with ripe fruit (encased in ice) have been found in Arctic zones, but luxuriant vegetation has similarly been found fossilized in sage brush and cactus country; moreover, this is true for deserts on five continents.

It appears that these conditions are not a result merely of a shift of various regional climates; rather, they seem to be the result of a different global climatology, a different organization of the atmosphere surrounding our planet.

2. The Composition of the Antediluvian Canopy

The composition of the antediluvian canopy should be considered in terms of pressure and in terms of components, or the proportions of gases.

BAROMETRIC PRESSURE. In our age, atmospheric pressure, as measured with reference to sea level, averages 14.8, or nearly 15 pounds per square inch. It is thought that the atmospheric pressure in the antediluvian age was greater; in fact, it is likely that the pressure was one to three pounds per square inch greater. Today, it is known that man can work under much greater pressures than this daily as well as over a period of years

without apparent adverse effects. Underwater diving also illustrates how much pressure the human body can tolerate.

However, the human body cannot accept pressures radically
smaller than the pressure of 15 pounds per square inch of our
present mixture of atmosphere. At elevations over 14,000 feet,
there is plenty of oxygen in the air to breathe. The critical problem is that it is unavailable to the human lungs due to the lack of
pressure and the construction of the lungs. But if oxygen were
present (under greater pressure) in even smaller proportions
than our present atmosphere, it would still be equally available
and usable for physiological requirements. Thus, the apparent
slightly greater atmospheric pressure in the antediluvian world
posed no problem for human survival.

THE MIX OF GASES. The second perspective from which
the composition of the antediluvian atmosphere should be considered is its mix of gases. Today, the atmosphere contains gases
in the following proportions:

TABLE 4

Nitrogen	77%
Oxygen	21%
Water Vapor	0-1½% (variable)
Argon	1%
Carbon Dioxide	¼%
Miscellaneous gases	¼%

It is possible that the antediluvian regime had the following proportions:[3]

TABLE 5

Nitrogen	70-75%
Oxygen	18-20%
Water Vapor	5-10%
Argon	1%
Carbon Dioxide	½-1%
Miscellaneous gases	¼-½%

The Earth's atmosphere contains a very small proportion of
carbon dioxide; however, this does not mean that it is an insig-

[3]The proportion of water vapor to the other gases in the antediluvian atmosphere is not known. The author's estimate is 5-10% of the total volume.
Similarly the proportion of carbon dioxide is not known, but may have
been in excess of 1%.

nificant gas. It is as necessary to all plant life as oxygen is to animal life. Carbon alternates between atmospheric circulation (as carbon dioxide) and plant fixation (in organic compounds). At the time of the Flood, a vast amount of carbon was buried, and in being buried, became locked out of the carbon cycle. Along with greater humidity, the greater availability of carbon dioxide in the earlier age was an additional reason why plant life was denser and more luxuriant.

3. The Greenhouse Effect

A third reason plant life was more luxuriant in that earlier age has to do with the proportions of carbon dioxide and water vapor in the atmosphere, the principle of long-wave radiation of heat from the Earth, and a Greenhouse Effect. The Earth receives short-wave, medium and long-wave radiation from the Sun during the day. It converts this into long-wave radiation which it re-radiates into space, during both the daytime and the nighttime. The emission of heat is in long-wave rays, which are efficiently captured by either water vapor or carbon dioxide, particularly carbon dioxide. Hence, an increase of either water vapor or carbon dioxide in the atmosphere will tend to recapture radiated heat and create a Greenhouse Effect which creates an increasing uniformity in temperature within the atmosphere between day and night and also between summer and winter.

If there had been a canopy of water vapor enshrouding the Earth during the antediluvian period, this would have greatly reduced temperature differentials at the Earth's surface. Today, because the Sun's radiant energy shines directly on the Earth's surface, and because it shines unequally in strength on the various latitudes, the Earth's atmosphere acts very much as a great heat engine. The planetary winds function to equalize or moderate these differentials in temperature and pressure. The pressure differentials accompanying the temperature differentials cause the flow of air.

The Earth today has several types of winds. One group is the planetary wind system, which includes trade winds, mid-latitude westerlies, and polar easterlies. Another type is the seasonal monsoon, a periodic wind which is caused when a continent either heats up or cools off much faster than the surrounding oceans.

A third type is the diurnal land and sea breeze. It is similar to the monsoon in that it is caused by a differential in heating of the land relative to the surrounding water; however, this is a daily rather than a seasonal type of wind. It is also local rather than continental in scope.

If there were a canopy, comprised of relatively large amounts of water vapor and carbon dioxide, enveloping the Earth (a circumstance similar to that of Venus), the result would be a near-temperature equilibrium. This is for two reasons. One is the high reflectivity, or albedo of the canopy. More solar radiation would be reflected. The second reason is the efficient capture by the atmosphere of long-wave radiation of the planet, the Greenhouse Effect. If there were temperature equalities, there would be no planetary wind systems, no trade winds, no mid-latitude westerlies, no monsoons, and no land and sea breezes. And this appears to have been the case.

The significance of this wind system is made manifest in study of the relationship between wind and rain. There are three types of rain: convective, cyclonic, and orographic. Each is based on various combinations of winds, temperatures, and elevations. But all are based on flowing air, or winds. Thus, if there were a canopy, there would be no temperature differential, which means there would be no winds, which in turn means no rain.

And as a consequence of no rain, there would be a very poorly developed or primitive arrangement of river systems, because river systems are based on rain and run-off, which are in turn based on wind systems, which in turn are based on temperature inequalities.

The Biblical record, like the geological record, indicates that the Earth in the antediluvian era was a luxuriant place for flora (vegetation). It was anything but desert-like. And it was anything but ice-bound. Yet the Biblical record specifically states that there was no rain; rather, the Earth was abundantly watered by mist or dew at night:

> But there went up a mist (a fog-vapor) from the land, and watered the whole surface of the ground. (Genesis 2:6; Amplified)

If there were a canopy of water vapor, the water vapor would have been an abundant atmospheric constituent. It may have been as much as 5 to 10% of the total, compared to the present 0 to 1½%. Under these conditions, humidity, even in the daytime, would have been at a near maximum, and temperatures would have hovered constantly near dewpoint. But with the coming of night, the temperature would have dropped perhaps a degree or two and dewpoint would be quickly reached. At this time, a thick, somewhat chilling, clammy and uncomfortable layer of dew would begin to form. And with the vast volume of available water vapor in the air, the layer of dew may have been rather thick.

In today's climatic regime, dampness versus dryness of a climate is evaluated in two ways: the amount of rainfall, plus what dew may occur, measured in inches; and the measured evaporation potential. For instance, 10 inches of precipitation will grow wheat in Alberta; 25 inches may be insufficient in West Texas. This is due to the high rate of evaporation. The evapo-precipitation ratio is the important feature, along with tempera-ture, in evaluating a particular climate. Under the circum-stances of the canopy, with humidity continuously hovering near 100%, evaporation would be at a minimum, and the Earth would be abundantly watered by the dew or the fog-like mists forming in the evening.

There are other features of this antediluvian era which must be considered along with the foregoing observation of relative humidity, dewpoint, and the canopy. First is the phrase, "the cool of the day" which is found in Genesis 3:8 with the discussion about the Garden of Eden. This apparently was the period toward dusk, after the temperature slid below dewpoint, and the clammy dew had started to gather. The chilling coolness was related not to gross declines in temperatures but rather to saturation, or dew point. This may have been the "cool" of the day.

Secondly, it is of interest to observe the habitation of the so-called cave men, whose homes have been discovered and stud-ied in France, New Mexico, Spain and other areas. Today, such caves are among the chilliest and most inhospitable places for human habitation. If they are inhabited at all, it is ordinarily by animals. However, traces of antediluvian man, antediluvian art, antediluvian hardware, and antediluvian bonfires have been per-sistently found in or near caves. Why? Very likely the antedi-luvians, in building a bonfire at the mouth of a cave, could there-by maintain the temperature above dewpoint all night and thereby increase their comfort. Undoubtedly, cave regions in this era were centers of culture. Climate and comfort, more than protection from predators, were reasons for such fires.

There are also persistent traditions in folklore of both hemispheres of an age when the sky hung very low—a condition similar to the observation given in Genesis of the division of the waters above the firmament from below the firmament.[4] How conclusive are these evidences? Each is not conclusive in and by itself. But the principle of the primordial canopy draws from numerous different bases, locations, observations, and records which verify a general pattern involving a completely different organization for the climate of our planet, a climatic regime superior in most ways to that of today.

Is a canopy possible? Yes. Venus has one. Another planet (Jupiter) has belts. Yet another (Saturn) has rings. Yet another (Mars) has ice caps. Jupiter apparently possesses great oceans of ammonia and an atmosphere of methane and hydrogen, while our own planet possesses immense reflective oceans of water, repeatedly covered and uncovered by cyclonic systems which swirl across its atmosphere. The condition of Venus illustrates that a canopy is possible. The summary of evidences herein presented in abbreviated form indicates that a canopy of water vapor (and some carbon dioxide) was probable in the earlier age.

4. A Primordial (Hydrocarboniferous) Catastrophe Prior to the Flood

It is proposed that the antediluvian canopy condensed with the intrusion of particles of astral ice, and that this was one phase of the Flood catastrophe. This subject of the atmosphere of the Earth has a greater significance, and a more striking history, than any of the areas thus far presented. In Figures 6

---

[4]The Genesis account states that it rained for the first 40 days and nights of the Floodtide Cataclysmic Crisis. It also indicates that rain was a persistent and steady phenomenon rather than an intermittent and insignificant phenomenon. Undoubtedly the bulk of the rain which fell was a result of the condensing of the canopy, and this is a further indication of the bulk of water in vapor form which was "above the firmament" in the Antediluvian Age. If it took 40 days of rain (approx. 1000 hours) to condense out the canopy, it is conceivable that our estimate of 5 to 10% of water vapor in the antediluvian atmosphere may be conservative. This estimate of 5 to 10% is equal to about 1½ to 3 feet of liquid water. This estimate concludes that there was between 18 and 36 inches of rainfall, on the average, during the first 40 days of the Flood cataclysm.

through 12 in Chapter V (Orogenesis), a series of arcuate curves, spanning our globe, was given as one great evidence of a global cataclysm involving gravitational conflicts and tidal upheavals of magma. Figure 24 now gives a similar pattern, relative to the Appalachian Mountain uplift of the Eastern United States. Here again, the same pattern of arcuate uplifts occurs, lower, to be sure, but nevertheless comparable in alignment or pattern. Other mountain ranges, lower and more eroded, seem to be of this same era, including the Caledonian Mountains of Scotland and the Ural Mountains of Russia. These uplifts suggest that at least one earlier catastrophe, probably more, overtook the Earth prior to the age of the antediluvian world.

There are various reasons which serve as grounds for this suspicion. One is the orogenetic observation just mentioned. Another is our atmosphere. Our atmosphere today contains inert nitrogen, that is, N_2. N_2 comprises about 77% of our atmosphere, and it comprised nearly as much in the antediluvian age. Where did the nitrogen come from? The crust of our Earth—the rocks and volcanoes—contain no clue. Our Earth's oceans also contain no clue. Yet great oceans and atmospheres of nitrogen are found in various compounds such as ammonia, beyond the asteroids in the atmospheres of Jupiter and Saturn. Compounds of nitrogen are also found in the trains of comets. They include ammonia, cyanogen, hydrides of nitrogen, ionized carbon monoxides, ionized hydroxyls, ionized nitrogen and various of the lighter hydrocarbons. Perhaps the Earth's nitrogen, like the ice, came from an extraterrestrial source in an earlier primeval catastrophe.

Furthermore, it is to be noticed that coal beds occur horizontally in broad series of strata, often alternating with shales, sometimes limestones. Sometimes there are fifty or more alternating layers.[5] The Appalachians are replete with examples. Sometimes the layers are a few inches thick; occasionally they are many feet. But they seem to have been laid down horizontally. They seem to have been laid down through fluid mechanisms. They seem to have been laid down alternately. They seem to have been laid down by similar mechanisms from continent to continent, and on something approaching a global basis. Again it seems that tidal mechanisms were involved.

[5]See footnote 6.

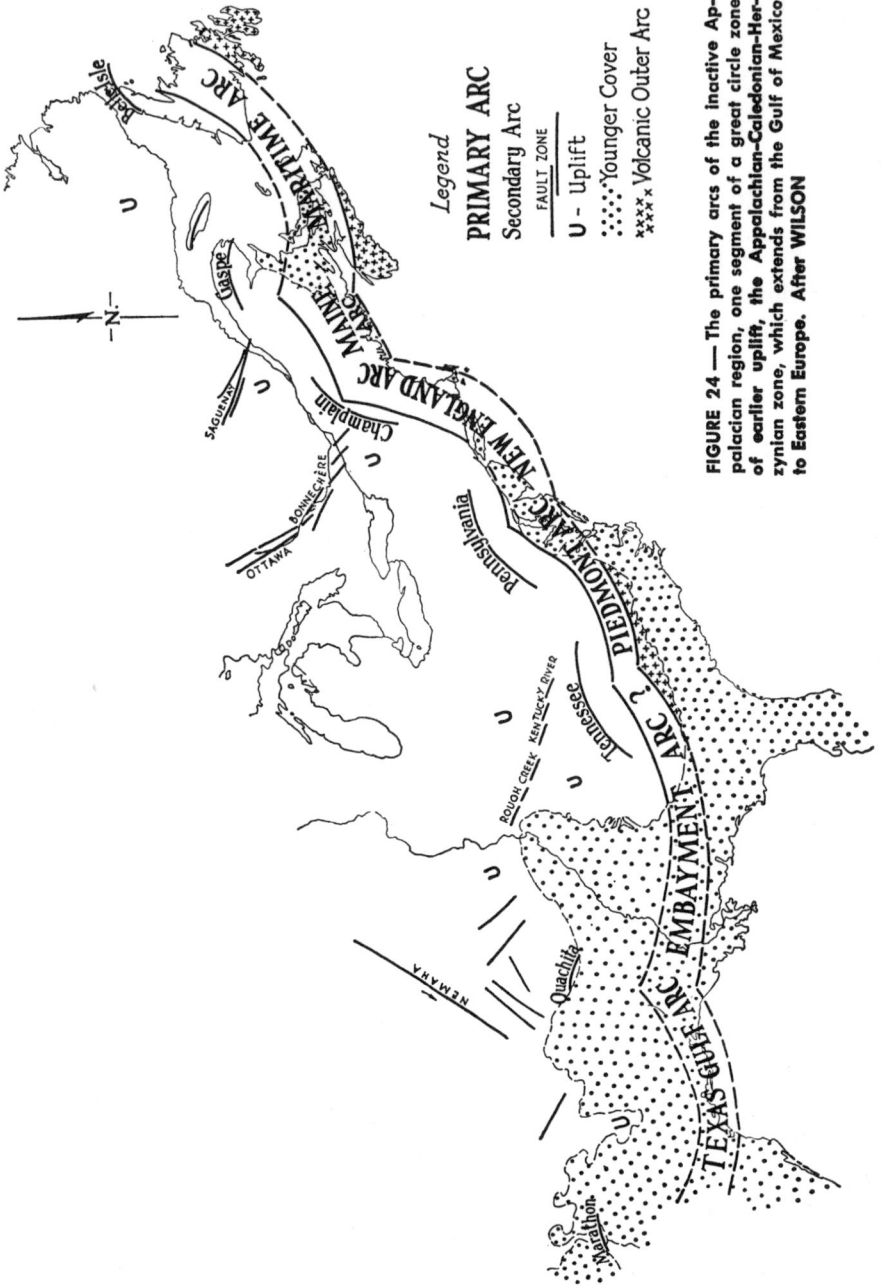

FIGURE 24—The primary arcs of the inactive Appalacian region, one segment of a great circle zone of earlier uplift, the Appalachian-Caledonian-Hercynian zone, which extends from the Gulf of Mexico to Eastern Europe. After WILSON

WILSON, J. TUZO: *The Earth as a Planet*, ed., Kuiper, p. 176, Chicago, Ill.: Univ. of Chicago Press, 1954.

These are grounds for suspecting at least one primordial catastrophe before the era of man. At that time or during those times, the Earth may have captured materials including ammonias, cyanogens, hydrides of nitrogen, hydroxyls, light and heavy hydrocarbons, ionized carbon monoxides, and nitrogens. These compounds are found in the trains of comets and also in the atmospheres of the Jovian planets. These will break down into nitrogen, carbon dioxide, and water.

Some of the hydrocarbons which may have been captured were gaseous, like methane; others were liquids, and others were heavier tars. Some became compressed by diurnal tides and formed coal strata. Thus, this earlier primordial hydro-carboniferous catastrophe or catastrophes may well assist in explaining the following:

1. The large proportion of nitrogen (N_2) in our atmosphere.
2. The great amounts of water in our oceans.
3. The successive layers of coal strata, often alternating with shales.
4. The deposition and percolation of petroleum into substrata pools.

Another illustration might come from Carbon 14 tests of petroleum. Petroleum deposits are supposedly paleozoic for the large part. This means they are supposedly in excess of 200,-000,000 years in age, according to classical uniformitarian chronology. Dr. W. F. Libby tested some petroleum from the Tampico region of Mexico in 1952. His results show an age of thousands, but not millions, of years. This deposition upon the Earth may have been as late as 20,000 B.C.[6] Petroleum, like coal and limestone, contains very little Carbon 14 or its ash byproducts.

It is important to differentiate the Primordial Carboniferous

---

[6]"The possibility that Earth's petroleum deposits could have come from outer space was laughed at when suggested by Velikovsky; it is now put forward by others in perfect seriousness. Hydrocarbons similar to petroleum derivatives have recently been found on meteorites, and an extraterrestrial origin for all petroleum was proposed recently in *Nature* by A. T. Wilson of Victoria University, New Zealand. Oil was believed, when Velikovsky wrote, to be millions of years old. There is of course a method, based on the radioactive decay of the carbon isotope 14, for dating organic materials. When Velikovsky asked its inventor, W. F. Libby, for a Carbon 14 test of petroleum, he was told that one had already been made; it had been reported in *Science* in 1952 and showed the age for samples from the

Catastrophe from the later Flood Catastrophe as related in Genesis. For if the primordial catastrophic approach is also correct, then immediately the genesis of the antediluvian atmospheric canopy can be postulated. Within the Earth's atmosphere reside four principal elements in varying proportions: carbon, hydrogen, nitrogen, and oxygen. Two of these, hydrogen and oxygen, comprise the principal elements in the Earth's oceans. They also were the elements in the "waters above the firmament" prior to the Flood as described in Genesis.

The crust of the Earth contains many oxides, such as aluminum, iron, calcium, and silicon, and it might suggest the origin of a portion of the oxygen in the Earth's oceans. But the crust of the Earth fails to give a clue as to the bulk of the hydrogen as well as the origin of the other gases. It does not point toward the origin of either carbon, hydrogen, or nitrogen. However, the regions beyond Mars and the asteroids do point to a possible common origin of each of these, in addition to more oxygen.

And with the possible deposition on the surface of the Earth by an earlier catastrophe of ammonias, cyanogens, hydrides of nitrogen, hydrocarbons, and hydroxyls, there would immediately

---

Mexican Gulf in the thousands, and not millions of years." (See *Harper's Magazine*, Aug. 1953, p. 48-55.)

The author does not advocate the adoption of Velikovsky's views *en masse* or *per se*, without revision, reworking, re-examination, and further analysis. On the other hand, Hooker discusses coal strata as follows:

In Westphalia, there are 117 beds of coal, one above the other; in South Wales, 100 beds; in Nova Scotia, 76 beds; in Pennsylvania and other coal regions all over the globe there are multiple layers of coal, always with sedimental strata of clay, shale, limestone, etc., in between. These rock vary in thickness from a few inches to hundreds of feet. Coal strata vary from paper-thin to many feet in thickness. . . . Coal seams 50 feet thick are not uncommon. (Hooker, *op. cit*. p. 128-129.)

Hooker, like Velikovsky, proceeds to point to the solar system for the area of origin for Earthian carboniferous deposits, including petroleum pools. However, his approach is more conservative, less dramatic, more specific, and less controversial. Both, however, have their good points. The adoption of Hooker's views are not urged *per se* either; he makes certain obvious errors. For further germane points, see Hooker's volume.

It should be pointed out, however, that along the regions of these earlier pre-deluge uplifts, such as the Appalachian cycle, coal strata, both folded and unfolded, are common, as are (to a lesser extent) petroleum pools. The crust of the Earth gives no clue as to where the carbon in the hydrocarbons originated; and the Earth's crust has been the exclusive area of investigation for the uniformitarian school of thought, which today has nowhere near a remotely sensible explanation. Hooker and Velikovsky, looking toward the methanes and heavier hydrocarbons in other regions within our solar system, both have good points.

have been a great oxidization or burning across the face of the Earth. The result of the burning would be water, water vapor (H_2O) and carbon dioxide (CO_2). The nitrogenous compounds would have decomposed and reduced to N_2. The result for our atmosphere was the production of oxygen (O_2) water vapor (H_2O), carbon dioxide (CO_2), and inert, diatomic nitrogen (N_2).

Some of the water vapor became part of a permanent shroud or canopy—permanent with respect to that earlier age. Much of the carbon was deposited in layers or pools. Here occur the basic elements provided for life as we know it, with our Earth's unique biological organic chemistries, based ultimately on carbon dioxide, nitrogen, oxygen and water.

This consideration does in no way bar as impossible the principle of chemical reactions in the atmospheres of the colder planets; however, it presupposes that such reactions must be based on chemistries other than water, oxygen and carbon dioxide. But primitive chemical reactions (based on chemistries of ammonias, cyanogens, and the lighter hydrocarbons) could occur. The relatively weak rays of the Sun in those areas will still cause chemical reactions in the upper atmospheres.

The sudden and chaotic occurrence of the earlier Primordial Hydrocarboniferous Catastrophe could have provided the Earth with much of its atmosphere—its carbon and nitrogen, plus abundant amounts of hydrogen and oxygen. Even as it is concluded that the Floodtide Catastrophic Period was one in which the Earth received substantial volumes of ice from outer space, so it is similarly concluded that the Primordial Hydrocarboniferous Catastrophic Era was one in which the Earth captured hydrocarbons and nitrogenous compounds.

(A discussion concerning the timing of the Primordial Hydrocarboniferous Catastrophe, along with the Flood Catastrophe, is given in Chapter XI, in the section which discusses the Lyellian Geological Time Chart and a Catastrophic Time Chart.[7]

---

[7]For further explanation of the concept of the Catastrophic Time Chart is reserved for Chapter XI. Note that the Carboniferous Period, embracing both the Mississippian and Pennsylvanian Periods, has been well-named if poorly dated by Lyell. Similarly note that if this Catastrophic Time Chart is even approximately correct, it rather tightly boxes in Darwinism with its requirements of oceans of uninterrupted geological time. However, this does not concern the writer, since he apprehends that both catastrophism and Creationism are facts. This opens up the possibility that Darwin may have made as many errors as did Lyell.

The Lyellian concept of oceans of time for every local uplift is cast into a full comparison with catastrophic contradictions.)

The heavier hydrocarbons in the form of tars which may have been captured, were stratified by alternating tidal action. They became compressed into seams of coal, alternating between layers of limestone, shale, or sandstone. Other hydrocarbons, lighter in weight, liquid in state, may have percolated through the Earth's upper crust and gathered into subterranean petroleum pools.

The Earth then became a dark, hydrocarboniferous dump at the time of the earlier catastrophe or catastrophes. Part of the surface tar (bitumen) from that period may have been utilized by Noah and his sons for the pitching of the Ark (Genesis 14). Bitumen was also gathered several centuries after the Flood in the oil-rich Mesopatamian Valley. It was used at that later time to pitch the Tower of Babel so that it, too, like the Ark, would be impervious to water if another Flood might recur (Genesis 11:3). Similarly, bitumen was reported in the slime pits of Sodom and Gomorrah (Genesis 14:10) at a time which may have just preceded a rifting of the Earth's crust in that region.[8] Thus, it is posited, some 10,000 or 20,000 years ago, our planet may well have been the scene of a dark, celestial, carboniferous dump. This might help explain why horizontal seams of coal, like subterranean pools of petroleum, contain virtually no Carbon-14 (along with limestones). Perhaps this is how our antediluvian canopy originated, with its abundances of water vapor and carbon dioxide, merely oxygenated hydrogen and carbon. Our planet may have become literally a dark dump or void, a contention suggested in Genesis 1:2.[9]

> The Earth became without form and an empty waste (or void), and darkness was upon the face of the very great deep. (King James)

[8]A discussion of the rifting of the Earth's crust is given in Chapter X, Page 252, footnote 23. This subject is also mentioned in Chapter V, page 77, footnote 16.

[9]This observation that the Master Architect has fashioned creation from such a catastrophic dump or void is held to be a brief and dim, yet valuable reflection of the glory and magnificence of our Maker. And it can be seen why the Floodtide Cataclysm, while being neither the first nor last of the Earth's geophysical crises, nevertheless was the worst.

5. Ozone, an Atmospheric Radical

Thus far the canopy (the Greenhouse Effect) has been discussed, with its resultant heat equilibrium relative to the Earth's climate, in which neither winds, rains, nor mature river systems played a prominent part. This was a result of a horizontal wind equilibrium—an absence of horizontal wind systems which today sweep across the face of the Earth in the fashion of land and sea breezes, hurricanes, typhoons, monsoons, blizzards, cyclonic storm fronts and trade winds.

However, if there was a horizontal wind equilibrium in the Antediluvian Age, similarly there also must have been a near equilibrium vertically with a minimum of convection (turbulence) between the exosphere, ionosphere, stratosphere and troposphere. This is to say that our modern epoch must experience more mixing of gases between the zones of the Earth's atmosphere.

Is the upper atmosphere (the stratosphere, ionosphere and exosphere) composed any differently from the troposphere, the Earth's atmosphere at or near ground level? This has been a question of importance to modern astrophysicists and meteorologists, concerned with such items as men plummeting through electrically charged fields (Van Allen Belts), formation of weather patterns and their relevance to jet streams, and even the consumption of pressurized stratosphere on jetliners.

In the upper atmosphere, the solar wind beats down unrestrained upon the atmosphere until the solar rays, especially of the ultra-violet frequency, strike the oxygen molecules and ricochet. When they strike the nucleus of the oxygen atom in just the right way, they will split the oxygen molecules (O_2). The free oxygen atoms immediately recombine into another form of oxygen known as ozone (O_3).

The ozone in the atmosphere is concentrated in the upper atmosphere zone where these reactions mostly take place. Although the content of ozone in the atmosphere is extremely small, its influence is out of all proportion to the quantity involved. The molecules of ozone, formed by the solar wind, possess the property of absorbing radiations of wave lengths less than 3,000 A° (Angstrom units), which means that the layer of ozone effectively shields the Earth's crust from the majority of the Sun's ultra-violet range of radiation.

The Earth's shield of ozone is a canopy which is invisible to the human eye (the human eye sees radiation only in wave lengths between 3,000A and 8,000A). The ozone canopy is a vital factor in the composition of our outer atmosphere. If it did not occur, and the short-wave rays of the Sun could beat down directly upon the Earth's crust, there would be a sudden extinction of all life processes on the Earth's surface.[10]

There is no certainty that throughout the previous ages, the ozone shield has remained constant in quantity, altitude, or effectiveness. It would seem that the ozone shield in the Antediluvian Age was more effective than is the current ozone shield; moreover, the ozone shield was reinforced by a water vapor shield, which has already been discussed (the waters above the atmospheric firmament, as related in Genesis). Over and above this, there was a greater amount of atmospheric carbon dioxide also.

Ozone occurs in its greatest amounts, or proportions, at altitudes between 50,000 and 80,000 feet, and in volumes of 3 parts per million. This proportion is a balance between the effect of the solar wind, which creates ozone, and the effect of the Earth's long-wave radiation, which acts as a catalyst and turns ozone back into its normal diatomic state of O_2 (oxygen).

TABLE 6

Rare Gases in the Atmosphere	Parts per 10 Million
1. Neon	181
2. Helium	52
3. Methane	15
4. Krypton	11
5. Hydrogen	5
6. Nitrous oxide	5
7. OZONE—variable	
(at sea level)	1.4
(at 80,000 feet)	10 to 30
8. Xenon	1
Approx. Total	280-300 ppm

In the antediluvian atmosphere, which contained more water vapor and carbon dioxide, it may well be that the effect of

[10]"The ozone layer is thus a buffer between the continuance of terrestrial life as we know it at present and sudden extinction by the short-wave rays of the Sun against which we have no physiological protection." W. M. Smart, *The Origin of the Earth,* Baltimore: Penguin Books, 1959, p. 56.

the Earth's long-wave radiation of changing ozone (O_3) back to oxygen (O_2) was also increased in the lower atmosphere, but was decreased in the upper atmosphere, allowing for a greater canopy of ozone to form at upper atmospheric levels.

It is viewed that the water vapor canopy worked two ways. It prevented the Sun's short-wave radiation from reaching ground level. In this way, it buttressed the effect of the ozone canopy, which the human eye cannot see, since our eyes see only wave lengths from 3,000 to 8,000 Angstrom units.

But the water vapor canopy not only shielded the Earth from solar radiation; it similarly shielded the outer ozone layer from the Earth's long-wave radiation. It was a buffer zone in the atmosphere. The Earth's long-wave radiation is what causes the ozone (O_3) to recombine back to its normal diatomic state of oxygen (O_2). A reduction in the Earth's long-wave radiation at upper atmosphere levels, absorbed by the intervening water vapor canopy, possibly allowed for an even thicker ozone canopy than exists in the present age. Thus the ozone canopy more effectively shielded the Earth from the solar wind in the Antediluvian Age.

The water vapor canopy caused a near temperature equilibrium at ground level, where the atmosphere is thickest. The temperature equilibrium reduced horizontal turbulence to the extent that wind was very slight. The temperature equilibrium also reduced vertical turbulence. Therefore it is contended that the earlier atmosphere actually contained a thicker ozone canopy at the upper atmosphere levels than does the Earth in the present age; nevertheless, the ratio of ozone at ground level was also reduced as compared to current conditions. Thus the ratio of ozone at the Earth's surface in the previous age may have been measurable in parts per billion or even less, as contrasted with the present age in which it is measurable in parts per ten million.

It has been pointed out to the author that, under these conditions, Carbon-14, an atmospheric radical of carbon, would perhaps also be formed in even greater volumes at upper atmospheric levels; however, it too, like ozone, would not experience the convection (turbulence) of the present modern era. It would remain in its higher concentrations at the upper levels, and would similarly exist in even lower proportions at ground level than in the present age. One of the assumptions in the Carbon-14 dating mechanism is that the level of Carbon-14 has remained constant in the atmosphere over the ages—an assumption over which Dr. Libby, its discoverer, has been somewhat uneasy, and apparently for good reasons. This could conceivably throw Carbon-14 datings for events earlier than the 2nd millenium B.C. into a new light.

The proportion of ozone in the upper atmosphere varies considerably. It is greater in the ionosphere above the magnetic poles than in equatorial magnetic latitudes. It varies during the peaks and troughs of sunspot activity. It varies due to both horizontal and vertical turbulence at upper atmospheric levels. It will average between 10 and 30 parts per million at 75,000 feet; but at the Earth's sea level, it averages about 1 part per ten million. Under the conditions of the Antediluvian Age, it may have occurred in proportion of a few parts per billion at sea level. The significance of this factor is seldom realized, but shall be further considered later in this chapter.

6. The Primordial Canopy and Actinic Radiation

Actinic radiation is a term which encompasses the various kinds of short-wave radiation: cosmic rays, X-rays, and ultra-violet rays. The author's conclusion is that the level of actinic radiation at the Earth's surface was reduced in the Antediluvian Age. Part of the reason for this conclusion was the *water vapor canopy*, and part of the reason was the greater effect of the *ozone canopy*.

These shields, along with the differing mix of gases in that atmosphere, and the different climatic regime, constituted a self-perpetuating balance or equilibrium much different from the current conditions.

Ultra-violet light, for instance, affects bacteria, and is an effective germicidal agent. Ultra-violet light also penetrates the human skin, and is significant in the production of Vitamin D. It apparently also has a complicated relationship with the rate of metabolism. Both of these in turn affect calcification and tissue wear. These in turn have cumulative effects upon the process of aging.

7. The Curve of Declining Longevity After the Flood

Figure 25 illustrates the declining curve of longevity of man following the collapse of the Antediluvian Canopy. This curve is

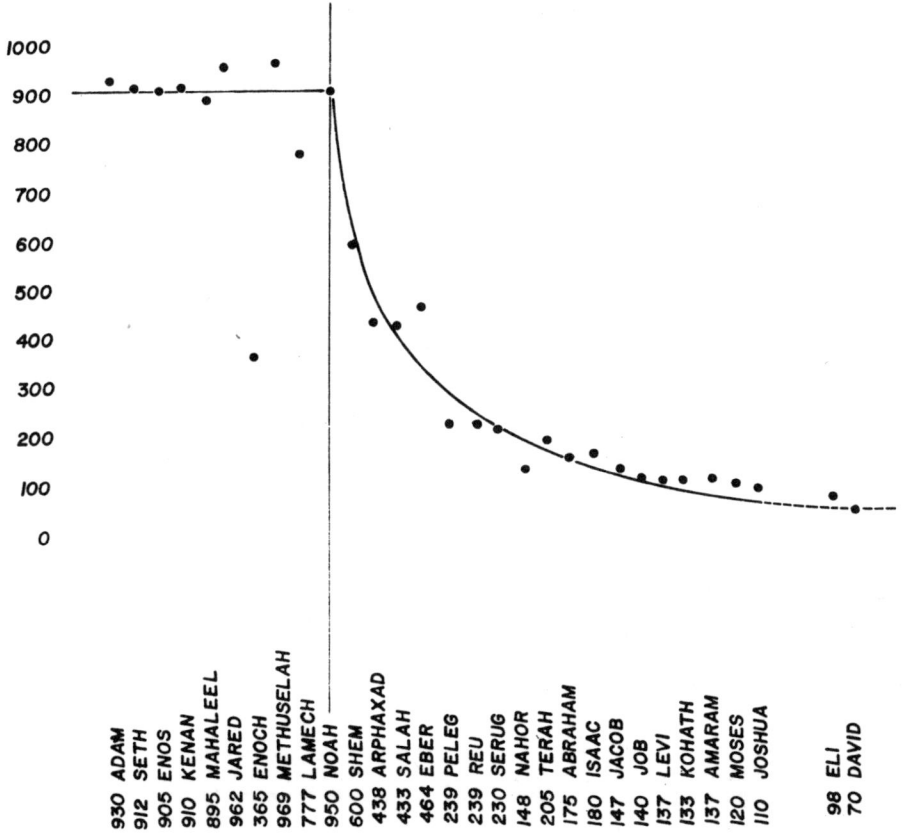

CURVE OF DECLINING LONGEVITY

ANTE-DILUVIAN AND POST-DILUVIAN PATRIARCHS

FIGURE 25

recorded in the chronicles of Genesis. The resultant curve is a biochemical curve involving over 1500 years of history, and over 30 generations until the new norm was ultimately reached. This logging of the ages of the post-diluvian patriarchs is one of the formidable but unexplained facts of Genesis. This includes the "beget" and "begot" chapters which have seemed so repetitious and boring to the casual reader, chapters which in reality are among the most important of all ancient literature.

Ancient longevity is a tradition not only in Genesis but also in many other independent folklores and literatures of the ancients. [11] Only in Genesis has there occurred a carefully preserved account.

This curve required over 30 generations and more than 1500 years until the new norm of "three score and ten" years was reached by the descendants of Noah. This curve suggests that cumulative factors rather than single factors were involved in causing the change in the rate of aging. This curve is a common type of decay curve, and can be duplicated in many other chemical or electrical experiments. It can be plotted when a capacitator is discharged and a new norm is ultimately reached. It can be plotted by subjecting bacteria to mild (and non-lethal) levels of germicidal ultra-violet radiation. It can be achieved by subjecting fish to ozonated water.

It should be observed that the abscissa of this curve is not calendar years but is rather number of generations, and in this sense it is a semi-chronological graph. If this biochemical curve contains any meaning at all, its implications are immense. It im-

---

[11]The ancient Rabbis considered that they were the stewards of Divine oracles, and took extreme care in preserving these documents, and also in copying them. It is common knowledge that they would copy a manuscript, perhaps one entire book of the Old Testament, and then count the Hebrew characters in both the original manuscript and the copy. The count would have to agree. Then, the middle or median character of each manuscript would have to be located. These too would have to agree in each copy. If they didn't, it meant that somewhere, a comma, a dot, a jot, a dash, a character of some kind had been either introduced or omitted. The erroneous copy would then be promptly destroyed, because they were stewards of "The Word of the Lord." Through this type of painstaking care, and with this type of psychology, we have received in the Hebrew account of ancient times, renditions which are only mildly garbled, and are essentially undiluted source material within the sphere of the topics discussed. Had the ancient Sybillene oracles, the Delphine oracles, or the Egyptian oracles been preserved, they too would undoubtedly be valuable source material.

plies that with a reorganized atmosphere, both climate and longevity could be either markedly improved or deranged.

Interestingly enough, it has also been found that ozone, an extremely toxic gas, can accomplish this same "transient decay curve" chemically upon human cell tissue. Ozone is a chemical radical which, when ingested through the lungs and into the blood stream, can be bound by hemoglobin, distributed throughout the human body, and diffused to the cells as a substitute for oxygen. Here it is received as an over-oxygenated substance.

> Laboratory studies with ozone have shown that this molecule reacts with amino acids and proteins, with nucleic acids and their derivatives, and with other compounds all of which are biologically essential.[12]

Ozone, a radical form of oxygen, can also disrupt chromosomal material, something accomplished chemically which may also be accomplished physically by ultra-violet radiation. Following are some excerpts taken from reports of laboratory tests of human cell cultures immersed in water ozonated at a rate of 8 parts per million:

> The investigations reported here are an extension of this work to demonstrate the activity of ozone against human cells in culture . . . Table 1 and Figure 2 represent the results of exposing cultures of KB cells to 8 parts per million by weight of ozone in oxygen for 5 and 10 minutes. . . This investigation has demonstrated that exposure to ozone is capable of producing chromatid breakages in human cell cultures, which are apparently identical to those produced by X-rays.[13]

In the above study, by Fettner, Figure 2 was a plotting of the findings. The resulting curves were also of the transient decay type, strikingly similar to the one in Figure 25 concerning decline in longevity of our own race following the Floodtide Catastrophe, and the resultant breakdown of the primordial canopy.

Ozone, even when ingested in parts per 10 million, has a tiny, but nevertheless toxic effect, and as a chemical radical, will

[12]USAF School of Aerospace Medicine 61-54, March, 1961, p. 1.

[13]Robert Fettner, *Nature,* London: May 1962, Vol. 194, p. 793.

react and injure many types of tissue, not excluding germ (repro-ductive) tissue.[14]

Ozone, like ultra-violet radiation, will disrupt genetic mate-rial, and this might occur to any cell. A very limited number of studies have been undertaken, which have been concerned with the toxic effects of ozone upon lung tissue in industrial regions, and also the effect of ozone upon thyroid tissue. More studies of greater breadth and depth may reveal some most interesting data, data which may be very latent in significance. [15,16]

It should be pointed out that if this understanding of the toxicity of ozone is correct, even in such minute proportions as exists in our atmosphere, it is a subject for concern. It is a prob-lem more for long-range concern than short-range concern, be-cause the effects of excessive ozone would appear to be cumu-lative and permanent and not immediate in its effect.

The conditions in the earlier Antediluvian Age were much

[14]It should be noted by way of interest that according to the Genesis log of ages, in the early postdiluvian centuries, the first half dozen generations may have all died at approximately the same time. If this logging is substantially accurate (and it so appears) this indicates that if ozone is the major factor in causing a decline in longevity, its proportion in the lower atmospheres increased for many years until the new equilibrium was established. It further suggests that the biological changes which followed (1) may be markedly cumulative, and (2) may include dele-terious changes on the intracellular level. In intracellular biochemistry, the ozone radical, when delivered in lieu of the normal diatomic oxygen mole-cule, will react variously with intracelluar materials.

[15]There has been a paucity of studies made of ozone with respect to the human physiology. This study suspects that ozone is a major factor in the general aging processes and in the breakdown of tissue. This study suspects that further experimental analysis may reveal that ozone (tria-tomic oxygen) when delivered and utilized within cell tissue, being an over-oxygenated material, will cause abnormal chemical reactions, occasionally harmful. Among the potentially harmful effects could be the damaging of a cell, transforming it from a healthy, productive one into a deformed, semi-parasitic one, potentially a virus-encouraging condition, potentially a cancer-encouraging condition. It is forecast that triatomic oxygen will be found as an aging factor in the environment of our era, and moreover, triatomic oxygen may be found to affect lipids more than proteins, and pro-teins more that nucleic acids. If such is eventually confirmed through lab-oratory analysis, then studies in historical catastrophism, and the ancient curve of declining longevity, along with the contemporary factor of atmo-spheric ozone, contain biochemical implications which might be of major import in understanding our environment.

[16]By way of interest, the normal respiration rate is 18 to 20 breaths per minute. Thus an individual will inhale the equivalent of one breath of pure ozone every 60 days.

different than in today's atmospheric environment, and were for the most part better, if we consider longevity to be "good."[17]

The human body absorbs or ingests material in three ways. These three ways are (1) through the skin (ultra-violet radiation), (2) through the lungs (oxygen, ozone, and sometimes carbon monoxide), and (3) through the stomach (the diet).

Thus far it has been stated that there was a different (and reduced) level of ultra-violet radiation in the Antediluvian Age. There was also a different mix of gases, and a different barometric pressure. These features pertain to sunlight and ingestion through the skin and lungs.

Similarly, there seemingly was also a difference in the diet of fauna in the Antediluvian Age in the following respect: the dispersion of minerals. Minerals are dispersed through soils and solutions by running water. Minerals are collected in solutions, and our oceans with their great concentrations of salts are the leading example. Interior basins such as the Aral Sea, the Dead Sea and Great Salt Lake are other examples.

With little running water, and little leaching of the soils,

[17]If this is the correct understanding of the Antediluvian Age, and the wealth of time which ancients possessed, then man at that time possessed a wealth modern man lacks, namely time. The modern age, in which technology is mushrooming, has resulted in man being wealthy in other ways, in terms of knowledge, money, credit, political power and services.

In the earlier age according to the Genesis account, man with his wealth of time, promptly abandoned his concern about his Creator. The Earth soon became "filled with violence" and "corrupt." Today, with the opening up of another kind of wealth—a wealth of inventions, energies and knowledge—the Earth has somewhat similarly become "corrupt, and filled with violence." This tendency has not diminished as atheistic and semi-atheistic ethics have increasingly prevailed.

Thus it is debatable whether wealth is good for man, be it a wealth of money, economic power, political power, or (as in the case of the antediluvians) in terms of time. These wealths frequently turn men from faith, honor and humbleness toward less desirable and more vicious, violent principles—more akin to the flesh than the spirit. Thus a wealth, even in terms of time, may or may not be "good," even as it is with money or power. It is a matter of values, and application, which in turn hinge upon matters of faith.

Faith is again a matter of anticipations and conclusions relative to (a) the destiny of the race, and/or (b) the destiny of the individual soul. Both of these are related to the understanding of origin, and Creator along with Creation. Shortness of life keeps man perpetually living on the brink of eternity, in contrast to the longer-lived antediluvian ancients. Conceivably the limitations and restraints contained therein prevent man to a degree from abusing and misguiding his fellow man, and the currently existing lack of longevity therefore might conceivably be classified as "good." It is a matter of values and viewpoints.

and with the water table constantly high, there would be little in the way of dispersion of solutions, and little in the way of dispersion of trace minerals in water. It is thought that such elements as bromine, cadmium, calcium, chlorine, chromium, cobalt, copper, fluorine, iodine, magnesium, manganese, potassium, selenium, zinc and others were less available in the previous age. And this was especially true in "heartland" or landlocked areas in contrast to maritime areas.

Many trace elements are vitally required by the human physiology, and it cannot function either effectively or durably without them. However, it also appears that other trace elements effectively poison the human physiology. Iodine illustrates the former case; cadmium the latter case.

The subject of the differential in dispersion of trace elements is an additional consideration which may bear heavily on longevity differentials plus an assortment of other physiological differentials between the two ages.

8. Traditions of Longevity

The tradition of longevity among the ancients is a universal phenomenon. It occurs in Greek mythology where the ancient gods such as Prometheus take a position comparable to antediluvian patriarchs such as Enoch or Methuselah in the Hebrew account. Egypt, Syria, Persia, and India all possess similar traditions of a long-lived race during a previous age. This principle is unfortunately garbled, and often takes the form of folklore in more primitive cultures. Being vague rather than specific is the rule, except in the Hebrew account. However many of these ancient traditions were at one time clear to the ancients, and those sources have been lost. Josephus was familiar with many of those accounts, from historians of several ancient cultures, and wrote as follows:

> But let no one upon comparing the lives of the ancients with our lives, and with the few years which we now live, think that what we have said of them is false; or make the shortness of our lives at present an argument, that neither did they attain to so long a duration of life, for those ancients were beloved of God, and made by God himself; and because their food was then fitter for the prolongation of life, might well live so great a number of years; and besides, God afforded them a longer time of life on account of

their virtue, and the good use they made of astronomical and geometrical discoveries, which would not have afforded the time for fortelling the periods of the stars, unless they had lived six hundred years, for the great year is completed in that interval. Now I have for witnesses to what I have said, all those that have written Antiquities, both among the Greeks and Barbarians: for even Manetho, who wrote the Egyptian history, and Berosus, who collected the Chaldean monuments, and Mochus, Hestiaeus, and besides these, Hieronymus the Egyptian, and those that composed the Phoenecian history, agree to what I here say: Hesiod also, and Hecataeus, and Hellanicus and Acusilaus, and besides these, Ephorus and Nicolaus relate, that the ancients lived a thousand years. But as to these matters, let every one look upon them as they think fit.[18]

It has been noted that the Genesis account very formidably states that longevity was normal in the Antediluvian Era, and its decline was regular (and not sudden) following the Floodtide Catastrophe. These other ancient chroniclers, with whom Josephus claimed much familiarity, gave a similar story.

While we may not agree with Josephus' reasoning as to why the ancients lived longer, the fact is that he had a strong conviction about the matter. Josephus, like others, made some premature conclusions. One was that rain, since it was associated with the Flood, caused the Flood—a premature conclusion. Josephus considered the food of the earlier age as the superior factor; rather it may have been the atmosphere which was breathed (in general), and the absence of the ozone radical (in particular). Secondly, however, a reduced level of trace elements in the diet may have also been an additional category of factors.

There seems to be three general ways in which the ancient chroniclers erred about the extended lives of their ancestors. First of all, the later historians did not understand that which they were trying to report. This was a major handicap, and led to inaccurate interpolations. Secondly, historians (not unlike other human beings) have a tendency to exaggerate. But in the astrologically minded India, a third factor also may have occurred.

In India, where a tropical climate prevailed, including minor temperature differences between seasons, it is suspected that cer-

[18]Josephus, *Antiquities of the Jews*, pp. 87-88.

tain ancient chroniclers used a dicalendar system—some counted with lunar cycles and others with solar cycles. (Even among the Hebrews of ancient times, the festivals of the new moon rivaled the annual feasts in importance.)[19] It is suspected that in India, earlier chroniclers counted in terms of the lunar cycle; later chroniclers counted with solar cycles, and did not realize the difference. Thus months became interpreted as years. In this way exaggeration also occurred, even though there is a core of truth in their understanding of ancient longevity, of zodiac-related catastrophes, of ages, cycles and previous ages.

Traditions of longevity among the Hindus for the earlier age ascribe ages of 10,000 and 15,000 years. Berosus, the Babylonian historian of 300 B.C., basing his history on the archives from the Temple of Marduk, copied the names, in sequence, of the Pre-Flood kings, Alulim through Xisuthros and ascribes ages of 18,000 through 60,000 years for them. (And "in the time of Xisuthros, the Great Deluge occurred.") Our conclusion is that exaggerating occurred in counting, estimating, copying, and confusions occurred among counting systems; nevertheless, there is a core of truth also in the chronicles of Berosus.

Further implications drawn from the biochemical curve of declining longevity, as plotted from the Genesis chronicles, are vast. One implication is that the re-establishing of a canopy similar to that of the previous age is by no means impossible. Such a development could rejuvenate the climate of the Earth, and could cause the desert to again bloom as the rose. Vast barren regions like the Sahara could again become fertile. This has demographical (population) implications. On the other hand, whether such a re-establishing of the ancient longevity would be desirable, at the present state of man's spiritual development, is questionable.[20]

[19]Five of the seven annual feasts of the Hebrews in the post-Mosaic times were concentrated around two annual events, each six months apart. The first two feasts of the year were within the first 8 days following the vernal equinox (the Passover and the Unleavened Bread). The last three feasts were concentrated within the 15 days of and including the autumnal eqinox (the Trumpets, Atonement and Tabernacles).

[20]The prophet Isaiah looked backward (in a sense) to the Earth's prior antediluvian climatology, as he understood it. He then projected a similar climatology for a coming millenial age, and this is reflected in his prognostications relative to both climate and longevity.
"And the desert shall rejoice, and blossom as the rose; it shall

At this juncture, toward the close of this 9th chapter on the Greenhouse Effect, the trend of the book begins to take a wide turn, not dissimilar to that of a baseball player, rounding third base and heading for home plate. Up to now, the discussion has been centered around considerations which were astrophysical and geophysical in the history of our planet. It has concerned such physical matters as ammonias, asteroids, atmospheres, carbon dioxides, comets, electro-magnetic fields, forces, interacting gravities, ices, meteor streams, monsoons, oceans, orbits, ozones, planets, satellites, space, tides, vulcanism and water vapor.

But the line of demarcation between the physical (the astrophysical and the geophysical) and the biological has now been reached. The discussion enters into the biochemical realm.

Lyell's (geological) uniformitarianism is seen as hopeless. Does Darwin's (biological) uniformitarianism have a basis apart from its Lyellian foundation? From now on, the discussion shall

---

blossom abundantly. . . ." Isaiah 35:1, 2a.

He seemingly anticipates a rejuvenation of the Earth's climate which formerly existed in desert-like Arabia and the Sahara. A rejuvenation of the Earth's climate along lines of antediluvian climatology could restore dozens of millions of square miles to productivity. Concerning a restoration or partial restoration of longevity, he wrote:

"There shall be no more (in Jerusalem) an infant that lives but a few days, or an old man who dies prematurely, for the child shall die a hundred years old, and the sinner who dies when only a hundred years old shall be accursed . . . for like the days of a tree shall be the days of my people . . . Isaiah 65:20, 22.

Isaiah, a prophet and cosmologist, was simultaneously a dark pessimist, and a profound optimist; he was a pessimist regarding the immediate, short-range destiny of his people, so engrossed in anti-spiritual values and polytheism. But he was even more optimistic regarding the ultimate or long-range destiny, both for his own people in particular, and for the human race in general.

He apprehended a period of dismal crises and desolating turbulences for the immediate future of his people, the leaders of whom were so anti-spiritual in values, and so inclined toward a negative pantheism. This differs but little from our own century, where leaders are mostly engulfed in anti-spiritual values, along with atheistic, semi-atheistic and uniformitarian philosophies. It hardly takes a prophet to forecast a similar culmination of wars, desolations, destructions and increasing crises for our century, unless the leaders were to happen to exchange anti-spiritual values for pro-spiritual ones, an event which is rare (but not unheard of in history).

Even as Isaiah foresaw an increasing anti-spirituality in his own age, a rising tide which would crest only with destruction, so he also foresaw an eventual age when pro-spiritual ethics would replace anti-spiritual ones, an age when universal peace would exist conjointly with universal justice and universal longevity. This may have been the age our Lord had in mind when he discussed a time when the meek more than the brazen would inherit the Earth.

consider such subjects as apes and alleged apes, catastrophism and cave wall art, chromosomes and genes, Darwins and dinosaurs, cross-breeding and in-breeding, alluvial fossils and ice fossils, saber-toothed mesonyxes and saber-toothed smilodons, twenty-foot bears and twenty-inch dragon flies, genetical disorders and endocrine disorders, acromegalics and cretins, mutations and transmutations. Thus the subject of Lyell's uniformitarianism is left behind, and the more famous subject of Darwin's uniformitarianism, usually termed "evolution," comes to the front. This is always a controversial and emotional subject, and is usually discussed in a quasi-scientific manner. What is its foundation—how strong is its defense—to what is its real appeal?

It has been proposed that physical uniformitarianism, whether celestial or geological, is inconsistent with observation both astronomically or geophysically. Nor does it make sense when one views the astral and catastrophic motifs which saturate ancient folklores, histories, literatures, religions and architectures. Uniformitarianism is incompatible with the Biblical narrative. It does not adequately interpret the atmosphere, hydrosphere or lithosphere of our planet. It does not account for the magnitude of force required for orogenesis, nor for the patterns of global arcuate uplifts (nor the parallelism also involved). Uniformitarianism fails to explain the basis for sudden changes, whether orogenetic, glacial, flood-tidal, or climatic.

Uniformitarianism does not explain the amazing mixtures of strata which occur, such as the ice and lava sandwiches of the Pacific Northwest. It fails to explain the immense pools of petroleum which underlie much of our great Southwest. It fails to explain the origin of the great seams of coal, both folded and unfolded, which lie astride the Appalachian uplift on our Eastern seaboard. Uniformitarianism fails to explain the rich, many-specied fossil finds of aquatic animals, covered over with sedimentary strata in our semi-arid mid-continental Great Plains states, the very heart of the North American continent.

Geological uniformitarianism, even in its vaunted near-monopolistic position in academic circles, is totally lacking in mechanics, and therefore, must be considered an absurd hypothesis. But what about biological uniformitarianism? Can Darwinism stand apart from its Lyellian foundation? The next chapter is directed to a systematic analysis of the strengths and weaknesses of this famous hypothesis.

X chapter

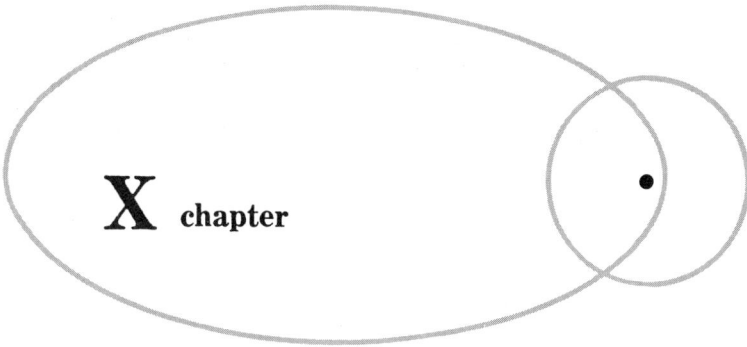

Biological Uniformitarianism
(Darwinism)

Requirements of Darwinism

DARWIN ENDEAVORED to adopt or reconcile Lyell's geological time scale and uniformitarian theory to biology. In this way, Darwinism (evolution) can be considered a daughter theory of uniformitarianism. This Darwinian endeavor became famous in *The Origin of Species By Means of Natural Selection* (1859). This hypothesis, modified and reworked by others in later decades, became a virtual doctrine for a collection of modern antispiritual philosophies, just as Genesis has served as a doctrine of origin for the Judeo-Christian collection of philosophies.

This chapter shall probe into the various assumptions, and subtheories of Darwinism, even as the previous chapters have been concerned with some of the assumptions of uniformitarianism. Darwinism is actually a complex of assumptions, which were amalgamated by Darwin.

There are seven major assumptions or subtheories within the Darwinian premise. Six are basic assumptions, and one is of overriding central importance—something like a Greek temple, supported with six vertical pillars, but containing a seventh central overriding horizontal beam. These seven subtheories, embracing various assumptions, are as follows. The central or overriding assumption is listed last.

1. Geological Uniformitarianism   ) Relates to
2. Survival of the Fittest   ) Catastrophism

3. Environmental Determinism   ) Relates to
4. Natural Selection (Inbreeding)   ) Genetics

5. Comparative Embryology   ) Empirical

6. Missing Links (Apemen)   ) Relates to
) Endocrinology

7. The Requirement of a Biochemical
   Mechanism

The first six of these subtheories, or preliminary assumptions, are supposedly vertical pillars of support, and the seventh, the principle that every biochemical process requires a mechanism, is the overriding subtheory. Of these seven subtheories, the sixth is essentially post-Darwinian, although Darwin briefly discussed the subject.

How many of these seven subtheories need to be valid in order to provide effective support for the theory. What if only five, or three, or one of these seven theories are found to be valid? What if none are found valid? Does the encompassing theory of Darwin remain valid?

Certain hasty claims might be made to the effect that catastrophism destroys the heart of the Darwinian premise. This would be an overstatement. Rather in a precise analysis, catastrophism pitches a second hard strike against the evolutionary theory. Genetics has already pitched a first hard strike against it. Astral catastrophism is the second strike, as shall be shortly demonstrated. But it is not a third strike. Nevertheless, a second strike opens the way for a possible third strike. And so astral catastrophism opens the door for more extensive probings. And such deeper probings just could possibly result in a resounding third strike.

Frequently, history has supported the saying: "Necessity is the mother of invention." During the middle portion of the 19th century, many were teaching some idea or other regarding spontaneous generation of life and emergence from small and inferior forms to larger and superior forms, an idea to which bacteriologist Pasteur strongly objected. This idea has been woven into Greek literature, and into the deep reaches of Greek philosophy. Anaxamander, some 2500 years ago, had taught this, as had Plato.[1]

The anti-spiritual, "enlightened" scholars of yesteryear were searching for an alternative to the proposition of Creation as set forth in Genesis. To them, Darwin's evolutionary premise sounded scientific; therefore it was considered and propagated as a scientific doctrine. What Darwin had accomplished was to provide what purported to be a biochemical mechanism for views of emergence which were already being advanced.

Thus Darwinism, without being rigorously tested, was presented to the world in the triple garb of rationalism, science and truth. The purpose of this chapter is to review the rationalizing, to test what part if any of the theory is demonstrably scientific, and to ascertain whether the Darwinian hypothesis is indeed myth or truth.

In like manner, Ptolemy's *Almagest* had sounded scientific in his day, and Ptolemy was considered a sancrosanct authority for fourteen centuries. His thesis had appealed to the prevailing views of his day. That Ptolemy's views happened to be in error did not prevent them from being accepted. Yet had they been tested with sufficient rigor, other views would have replaced his.

It is with the above in mind that the Darwinian hypothesis is reviewed. When, in the Ptolemaic system, unsatisfactory circumstances kept arising, new explanations were given which satisfied the moment but which eventually complicated the total picture. For example, planets in their procession around the Earth suddenly reversed directions. This was explained by adding a few epicycles from time to time. And so it has been with Darwinism. Difficulties have arisen. How have these difficulties been met? Have they been satisfied with fact or with additional unverified hypotheses? Do they appeal to historical assumption, philosophic doctrine or scientific reality?

By examining the inner machinery of the Darwinian hypo-

---

[1] Among other Greeks of the era of the 4th and 5th centuries B.C. who taught one form or another of emergence were Anaximenes, Aristotle, Empedocles and Epicurus. John W. Klotz, *Genes, Genesis and Evolution*, St. Louis; Concordia Publishing House, 1955, p. 22.

thetical superstructure, and by applying a little stress here and there to each of the six supporting subtheories, and by examining any presence or absence of valid historical and scientific explanation, this hypothesis will inevitably emerge either stronger as a result of testing or clearly weaker as a result of probing.

Thus Darwin's six assumptions, or subtheories shall be cast into three categories: (1) geological catastrophism, and Earth history, (2) genetics and biochemical processes of heredity and (3) endocrinology and biochemical balances.

If, say, two of these supporting subtheories of Darwinism are found to be in shambles, what does that do to the total strength of the superstructure? If four of the supporting subtheories are found to be simply untenable, then does the superstructure become a good candidate for academic abandonment? And what if six are found to be invalid? The forthcoming analysis will investigate this possibility, and will examine each subtheory in the light of historical and modern scientific findings.

1. Geological Catastrophism and Darwinism

Subtheory 1: Geological Uniformitarianism. Darwin considered the proposition of *GEOLOGICAL UNIFORMITARIANISM* fourth in his series of assumptions; here it shall be considered first, because the main thrust of this volume has been to establish the lack of validity of this premise. Again, the definitions of uniformitarianism and catastrophism are reviewed:

Uniformitarianism: The doctrine that existing processes, *acting as at present,* are sufficient to account for all geological changes.

Catastrophism: The doctrine that changes in the earth's crust have generally been effected *suddenly by physical forces.*[2]

Lyell's ideas relative to time were at least as poor as Ptolemy's, but Ptolemy, with his lack of data, had a better excuse for error. Darwin, who was intimately associated with Lyell for about two decades, worked as his assistant for several years fol-

---

[2]*Webster's Collegiate Dictionary,* Springfield, Mass.: G & C Merriam Co., 1946 "Catastrophism," p. 159; "Uniformitarianism," p. 1093.

lowing his excursion on the H.M.S. Beagle (and prior to his marriage). He was coached carefully by Lyell in uniformitarianism. It was during this era (1837-1839) that Darwin's hypothesis took its essential form.

Lyell with Darwin rejected and ignored the views of his contemporaries on catastrophism, and thus they each had no understanding of the forces which have shaken our planet, brought forth an Ice Epoch, upthrusted mountain systems, and caused surging oceans of subcontinental magnitudes. They had no understanding of a previous era and another climatic regime in that era, the Greenhouse Effect. Nor did they have any understanding of the meaning involved in such a gross change in our atmospheric habitat.

Furthermore, Lyell and Darwin neither had any understanding of either (a) Catastrophism as a principle in Earth history, or (b) at least two separate and distinct catastrophic periods, one of which included the rise of the Alpine-Himalayan cycle and the Circum-Pacific cycle of mountains, and the other in which other lower ranges were raised. Lyell and Darwin didn't understand the fact of catastrophism; neither did they understand the timing of Earth catastrophes. The Flood Catastrophe may have occurred less than 5,000 years ago, and the earlier catastrophic age may well have ended as recently as 20,000 to 10,000 years ago.

This writer dated the Flood Catastrophe at 2800 B.C., plus or minus a few hundred years. A prior catastrophe, having occurred before the creation of higher life, has been projected, and both completely contradict Lyell's time scale. The dating of this primordial catastrophe was 10,000 to 20,000 B.C., plus or minus a few thousand years.

Ten thousand years is ample time for the establishment of the antediluvian species, via methods of serial creation from region to region. Although it is ample time for creation, it is so little time for evolving that if it is correct (or even nearly correct), it confines and strains the Darwinian requirement for time to the point of absurdity.

Within this last decade, many men in the natural sciences have sensed the poverty of the uniformitarian proposition. It is hardly a secret that men, particularly within the geological division of the natural sciences, have been searching for some method to let catastrophism in through the back door, yet without giving any credit to Genesis. With such an approach, a paradox is being developed which may well be increasingly difficult to solve. [3, 4]

When one considers the many marvelous species on our planet and the more numerous species on our planet prior to the Flood Catastrophe, it is thought that any chance construction—even oblivious to the time element involved—of such extremely complicated biochemical mechanisms as the simpler, one-celled animals cries out for the conclusion of a Divine Architect, whether or not the Creator is associated with the Judeo-Christian interpretation.[5] But if the time element is regarded, and if geological (astral) catastrophism is credited, and geological uniformitarianism is disallowed, there is very little room left for Darwinian emergence.

Subtheory 2: Survival of the Fittest. This is a premise which Darwin dwelt upon at length particularly in the fourth chapter of *The Origin of Species*. He taught that the most adaptive strains and the most prolific strains of animals survived, and that the weakest and the least adaptive did not. Often, to the

[3]Eric Larrabee, "Scientists in Collision: Was Velikovsky Right?" *Harpers Magazine*, August, 1963, p. 51.

[4]*Newsweek*, December 23, 1963, p. 48.
   Catastrophism is a fighting word among geologists. . . . It was a major line of thought for a few decades last century, but a vigorous counterattack by the naturalists against the supernaturalists eventually pushed it aside. But now many geologists believe the counterattack may have been all too vigorous. In their haste to reject the hand of God, they have passed over some solid evidence that could help improve their understanding. . . . As a result, many geologists at a recent meeting . . . were advising the rehabilitation of catastrophism, without recourse to a supernatural agent.
   Author's note: Some uniformitarian geologists, in making a slight retreat from their uniformitarian dogma, have come up with the term "catastrophic uniformitarianism." This is a case of having one opposite modify another, like black whiteness and humid aridity, terms which confuse rather than clarify. This is something like a person at a restaurant ordering "scrambled eggs, sunny side up." One can have scrambled eggs in one order and eggs sunny side up in another order. But one can hardly have scrambled eggs, sunny side up. So it is with uniformitarianism and the scrambled strata of our planet.

[5]It is well established that the internal structure and organization of the simplest one-cell organism, or even a molecule within a one-cell organism is more complex by several magnitudes than the organization of our solar system. Hence it might be easier to establish satisfactory theory for the origin of the solar system than to establish satisfactory theory for even the simplest of nature's organisms. Yet the diversity of modern thought on cosmogony indicates that there is a lack of consensus on this (relatively) simple problem.

average reader, the fittest have been identified with the most ferocious—those animals which could most easily defend themselves from their enemies. These were often the animals at the top of the food pyramid: the lions, the tigers, the wolves and other great predators. This is an over-simplification of the Darwinian view.

This study appeals to the only known historical principle to compare modern species with earlier species. This is the fossil record, and one brief look into the fossil record will result in perhaps a surprise. The fittest (either as Darwin defined them or as others have defined them) mostly did not survive. In many fossil beds, remains of numerous carcasses are found both disjointed and piecemeal, jumbled in an unsorted fashion. These carcasses have obviously been impounded by a great watery upheaval. There is no evidence that these animals were inferior or not adaptive. There is substantial evidence that they were caught and trapped. The fossil beds include animal remains, in unsorted fashion, both great and small, both carnivorous and herbivorous.

There is little evidence that they were inferior to their modern counterparts, or less adaptive; in fact there is evidence to the contrary. These animals were mostly larger than their current surviving species, and were apparently well-fed. While there is no evidence that they were inferior as adjudged by Darwinian definitions, yet there is evidence that they were unable to climb or fly away from the Flood when it came. They were simply victims caught and engulfed in cataclysmic conditions; their carcasses were deposited, often disjointed and littered in watery dumps with many other parts of carcasses. Overlaid strata and subsequent Earth tides buried the carcasses in strata and compressed the strata. The carcasses became fossilized.

In some fossil beds in mid-America, 60% of the species found therein are today extinct; 40% are extant. In other fossil beds, as high as 75% and 85% of the fossil forms found therein are extinct, and as low as 15% are extant. And contrary to the Darwinian proposition, those fossilized forms are in most cases larger and more impressive than their current counterparts, which have survived. How can they be presumed to be inferior? Actually if size and specialization mean anything (and it did to Darwin), the fauna of our current age are the fauna which, in comparison, must be considered as inferior.

There are numerous examples. One is the modern elephant,

found in both Africa and India. He is dwarfed by the fossil imperial elephant, which in turn was smaller than the hairy mammoths or the woolly mastodons. Ostriches have been found in fossil form; their size is comparable to the modern giraffe. Fossil pigs have been found as large as rhinoceroses. Fossil sloths have been found fossilized, some 18 feet tall, and bears, some 20 feet tall. Some fossil bears, by comparison, make the Alaskan Kodiak bears appear as dwarfs.

Bears, elephants, ostriches, pigs and sloths are mostly herbivorous in their diet. Is this same principle relative to size true among carnivorates (meat-eaters)? There is the example of the saber-toothed mesonyx. He was a wolf, somewhat larger than a Great Dane, and at least twice as large as a modern timber wolf. Another example is the smilodon, a large saber-toothed panther. It too was bigger and more ferocious than its modern counterpart. And there was the saber-toothed tiger, again not smaller, but larger than its modern counterpart.

The same principle holds true for birds, insects and reptiles. Birds with 20 and 30 foot wingspans are known in the fossil record. Dragonflies with wing spans of 20 and 30 inches are known in the fossil record. Reptiles 75 and 85 feet long, and weighing 40 and 50 tons are also known in the fossil record.

Turtles thrive in protected habitats. Darwin was most impressed by the turtles on the Galapagos Islands, where they possessed a marine reserve, protected from their natural predators. South Dakota and Nebraska are not known for their protected marine location, nor their humid climate, which turtles require to thrive. Furthermore, their continental location would hardly qualify this area as a protected reserve from their predators. Nevertheless in this location, cold in the winter and arid in the summer, fossil turtles have been found some 12 feet in diameter. They would make any of the Galapagos Island turtles look like dwarfs.

And concerning the numerous dinosaurs, some were herbivorous; others were carnivorous. Some were a few inches tall, and others were very tall and bulky. Some were aquatic while others were terrestrial. Some had horns, some had spiny spikes, some had extravagant coats of horned mail. None were "fit" to survive by Darwinian theory. All were engulfed, drowned, buried, compressed and fossilized according to catastrophic theory.

But then, let us for a moment suppose that Darwin's guess

about *"Survival of the Fittest"* was correct. Interesting questions have already been posed from the geological view. Some further questions of interest might be posed from the geographical view. The horse became extinct in the Western Hemisphere if the fossil record is to be trusted, but it survived in the Eastern Hemisphere. The elementary conclusion is that conditions occurred allowing it to be "fit" in one hemisphere but not in the other. And what of the camel? The camel became also extinct in the Western but not in the Eastern. What then of the musk ox, which became extinct in the Eastern but not the Western? And then, what of the rhinoceros, which is found in the Western Hemisphere only in zoos or in fossil form? Saber-toothed tigers have been found, among other places, in the La Brea tar pits near Los-Angeles. Was this form not fit to survive in the Western Hemisphere? But was fit to survive in the Eastern? The elephant apparently survived in two places in the Eastern Hemisphere, but not in any place in the Western, while the mammoths and mastodons became extinct in both hemispheres.

What do these conflicting patterns indicate? They indicate that many animals became engulfed in huge, watery or icy cataclysms, were drowned, buried and fossilized. This indicates that the Flood was indeed global and tidal. But beyond that, what do these opposing or conflicting geographical patterns of survival show? They show nothing, in terms of the Darwinian hypothesis. [6,7] Actually, Darwin's idea is sufficiently abstruse, when com-

---

[6]This argument is made to point up the catastrophic view which Darwin and Lyell completely rejected. One should not ignore these Darwinian proposals, a portion of which (when satisfactorily qualified) contain validity for serene interludes. Darwin proposed three principles for survival: ferociousness, mating precocity and adaptiveness. These three pyramids have been merged into one by subsequent writers who often tended to oversimplify. Our argument is directed to the view that it was the catastrophic principle which mostly determined which species survived and which did not. The Darwinian proposal is viewed as a minor determinant when it is properly qualified, which seldom is done. It is not a major determinant.

Furthermore, this argument or any argument must respect the principle that Earth history is viewed with a catastrophic camera. Species which perished in catastrophes have been recorded in the fossil record, and man has some limited idea as to how many, how large and how diverse were the types which perished therein. Animals which perished during interludes have not been preserved in fossil form. No one has any idea as to how many of the created species disappeared in the serene interludes where Darwinian thinking, if properly qualified, applies. These two principles apply on a global basis, but perhaps even more incisively on a regional basis, inasmuch as it would appear that Creation has been

pared to actual findings, that it makes a poor explanation for nearly everything in the fossil record.

Darwin's hypothesis does not align with the fossil facts. Nevertheless, it needs every opportunity to establish itself. And therefore other questions are in order.

Seemingly, the finest of the ancient herbivorates were the mammoths and mastodons. This is ruling out the much larger variant forms of dinosaurs, such as the ceratopsians (horned dinosaurs), the ornithopods (duck-billed dinosaurs), stegosaurs (plated dinosaurs), and the giant sauropods (including the 87½ foot diplodocus). This is also ruling out such fine mammals as the baluchitheriums, the brontops, the megatheriums, and so forth. This is overruling some fine-looking rhinoceroses, some with two horns, some with one horn, and some rhino-like forms with no horns at all. The mammoth, certainly one of nature's finest herbivorates, failed to survive.

But what then of nature's finest carnivorate? Again, deference is made from the giant carnivorous dinosaurs, such as the allosaurus, tyrranosaurus and the gorgosaurus. Deference is made from the mesonyx, and smilodon, among other forms. The saber-toothed tiger is often considered as the carnivorate su-

accomplished both in great diversity and variously across the regions of the Earth.

[7]This abbreviated analysis of conflicting geographical patterns of survival, relative both to extant and extinct species, is sufficiently complicated and diverse that one is faced with the question of what do they prove, beyond catastrophism. It is concluded that this zigzag pattern proves nothing; however, Darwin endeavored to conclude or infer principles from a pattern which was random, and proved nothing for his thesis. However, when catastrophically cast, the subject of migrations of races, migrations of languages and zoogeography is a fascinating consideration.

This zigzag pattern of survival perhaps is overplayed because it discusses survival patterns in the Eastern and Western Hemispheres, a division which did not exist in a continental sense in the previous age. During the previous Antediluvian Age, sea level was several hundred feet lower than in the current age. The Bering Strait between Alaska and Siberia was an isthmus, and it contained a humid, subtropical climate. Thus in the previous age, both Africa and North America were appendages of the Eurasian land mass. Antarctica, Australia and South America were isolated island continents. Even today the similarity of the extant species of Northern Eurasia and North America are quite similar. The existing species of Australia, South America and sub-Sahara Africa, on the other hand, are quite dissimilar. Thus even though the zigzag pattern of fossil finds and specie survival was a bit overplayed, nevertheless it is more logical to account for the diversity of species between the continents, particularly the island continents, in terms of Creation, diverse among the regions.

preme in pre-historic times. Why was he unfit to survive as a species?

Nature's finest herbivorate, the mammoth, and nature's finest carnivorate, the saber-toothed tiger, have been considered. There is a third category, the omnivorates. This includes animals which eat both plants and animals, and usually insects as well. A bear is an omnivorate. A pig is an omnivorate. And there are some fine-looking bears and pigs in the fossil record.

But according to prevailing opinion, nature's finest omnivorate was neither the bear nor the pig. It was Homo sapiens, according to man's opinion. And according to the records of Homo sapiens, both in folklore, on paper and in stone, he too just barely survived. This story comes not merely from just one region of our globe, but rather it occurs independently on several continents, and in almost the same way.

This Flood motif, or Flood story, involving a universal flood which either engulfed or nearly engulfed the tops of the higher mountains, occurs in the cultures of the world in a geographical pattern approaching universality. It often involved a large barge or boat, used to escape the Flood. If Homo sapiens just barely survived, according to his own records, and if this concept is repeatedly verified by geological data, then wherein is Darwin's assumption sound? It is no sounder with regard to *Survival of the Fittest* than was Lyell's assumption regarding *Geological Uniformitarianism*. In numerous cases, the "fittest," so called, simply failed to survive.

Two of the seven pillars of Darwinism have been examined and they are found to be so feeble that they cannot contribute any support for the total hypothesis. Rather, these two assumptions may be myths, involved in a possible myth complex. Astral catastrophism has engulfed and swamped both.

Even as astral catastrophism contradicts the Lyellian phase of Darwinism, are there other areas of research and study which support another phase of Darwinism, say, the Lamarckian phase? Does Mendelian genetics contradict and thereby discredit Sir Charles' ideas, or does genetics harmonize and thereby undergird the Darwinian-Lamarckian propositions? What is the import of genetics upon, say, *Environmental Determinism,* or upon *Natural Selection?* It is to this second couplet of assumptions, Lamarckian rather than Lyellian, to which attention is now directed.

2. Genetics and Darwinism

Subtheory 3: Environmental Determinism. Not all of Darwin's thinking was based on Lyell by any means. Actually, far more was based on Lamarckian ideas, which were part of the Darwin family heritage.

Lamarck proposed the idea that conditions in the environment control and govern changes (the hypothesized transmutations) in the natures of animals and plants. This was supposedly through the increased or induced use of certain organs, and the disuse followed by atrophy of others. Hence, characteristics were mysteriously acquired, developed, and transferred to the offspring in some vague feed-back mechanism, a notion which he believed and termed "pan-genesis." This, of course, is completely mistaken and such has been conceded even by most Darwinians for the better part of 50 years.

Although a portion of Darwin's thinking was based on Lyell, his writings reflect an even greater dependence and development of Lamarck's principles of hypothetical transmutation of species. Erasmus Darwin, Charles' grandfather (1731-1802) had a botannical garden in which he had experimented with plant breeding and inbreeding, and he originally had been searching for the very principles which Mendel ultimately discovered. Erasmus Darwin, however, had proposed ideas similar to Lamarck's. This was a significant factor in the heritage of Charles Darwin, who was merely bringing these ideas, or at least the leadership of them, back into the family.

Lamarck's proposition of acquired characteristics was formerly used to explain the Negroid color of people living in the tropics. It was proposed that the greater volume of sunlight brought out blackness (melanism) in the skin. Similarly, this understanding was proposed as an explanation for baldness. Men became bald because their ancestors wore hats too often, and the function of the hair atrophied. Neither explanation has the slightest degree of validity, for both baldness and melanism are controlled through the genes and chromosomes, something about which little was known in Darwin's time.

Since Lamarckian thought has been completely discredited by genetics, modern Darwianians normally tend to underemphasize the influence of Lamarck upon Charles Darwin.[8] But Charles was profoundly influenced by both his own grandfather and Lamarck and their ideas of *Environmental Determinism*. The thinking of Charles Darwin and Lamarck is not easily separated, as is evidenced by an analysis of Darwin's writings.

Although the idea of *Environmental Determinism* is not creditable, there are significant overtones in non-scientific areas which cannot be rightfully overlooked. *Environmental Determinism* may be poor genetics, but it is doctrinaire to Marxism. Marx's enthusiasm over the thrust of Darwin has already been mentioned in an earlier chapter, along with his offer to dedicate· the English edition of his book *Das Kapital* to capitalist Darwin.[9]

Marx took Darwin's "science" two steps further, one step including incorporating Darwin's uniformitarian views with Feuerbach's atheistic theology.[10] A uniformitarian doctrine of atheism resulted. A second step, then, was to replace the Creator with a new godling, the "enlightened," intellectual communist. Marx theorized that if the environment can change and deter-

---

[8]In Darwin's *Origin of Species,* 23% of his paragraphs relate to matters Lyellian in theme whereas 77% relate to matters Lamarckian. In his second most famous work, *The Descent of Man and Selection in Relation to Sex* (1871), about 8% of his subject matter is Lyellian and 92% is Lamarckian. Although the relationship between Lyell and Darwin was very close, the relationship between Lamarck's ideas and Darwin's, when studied objectively, can hardly be minimized. After Darwin published his work *Origin of Species* in 1859, Lyell followed with a work in 1863 entitled *The Antiquity of Man* which allows, through comparison, for the Lyellian theme to be factored out of Darwinian thought. Most of Darwin's discussion, including all relating to biological function, are Lamarckian.

[9]That Marx would dedicate this kind of a book (against capitalism) to a capitalist (Darwin) reflects that Marx may have been concerned more about negating spiritual principles than negating economic principles. Marx's enthusiasm is due to the thrust of implications contained therein, and not to the logic contained therein. Darwin refused the "honor," not because he didn't share Marx's atheism, but rather because his wife didn't; furthermore, his friends, the dilettante set of London society, mostly heirs, did not look upon this sort of thing as proper.

[10]Gertrude Himmelfarb, *Darwin and the Darwinian Revolution,* New York: Doubleday, p. 387. "Edward Aveling, Karl Marx's son-in-law, came away from a conversation with Darwin shortly before his death complaining of his parochialism in regarding himself as an agnostic rather than an atheist. Aveling consoled himself, however, with the thought that 'Atheist' is only 'Agnostic' writ aggressive, and 'Agnostic' is only 'Atheist' writ respectable—on which Francis Darwin rightly commented that it was precisely the difference between aggressiveness and unaggressiveness that distinguished his father from the class of thinkers to which Dr. Aveling belongs."

mine the future of a strain, it can do the same thing for Homo sapiens, another species of animal. Thus, by taking command of the environment and by selecting changes, intellectual, atheistic man could take control of the direction of biological change (as well as economic, philosophical and political change). Man could thus control the future if a total monopoly of control could be established. (Marx insisted on a total global monopoly and nothing less.)

In this tyrannical way, a class of intellectual atheists might become their own godlings, controlling the future of the race even as an irrigating farmer can choose seed and direct paths of water flowing into his fields. The direct social and philosophical implications of this anti-scientific doctrine of *Environmental Determinism* are seldom appreciated by non-Marxians.

Here was the supposed biochemical mechanism for evolution. For fifty years this was considered the most brilliant part of the Darwinian hypothesis. But when DeVries rediscovered the Mendelian principles of heredity, he exposed what was considered the strongest part of the Darwinian hypothesis as the weakest. It was the first to be discredited.

For some six decades now, Darwinism has lacked a creditable mechanism. Usually a theory without a proven mechanism is considered an uncertain thing; yet among anti-spiritual humanistic thinkers, nothing is more certain than Darwinism. Thus, while humanists have applauded and aggressively promoted the evolutionary theory, they simultaneously have been oblivious to "details." The Mendelian laws, governing heredity, have clearly invalidated the notion of *Environmental Determinism;* they simultaneously are very severe on the Darwinian notion of *Natural Selection.*

Subtheory 4: Natural Selection (Inbreeding). One of the several ways in which Darwin considered the subject of sex and selection was through a study of inbred pigeons. Darwin observed that pigeons from many different regions of Europe possessed accentuated and varying characteristics. He postulated correctly that an historical phenomenon of inbreeding had occurred. He then postulated, again correctly, that inbreeding was the cause of specializing of strains. He further continued, this time with error, by saying that inbreeding was good, especially among superior specimens.

Darwin advocated inbreeding as the best means to develop superior strains. The idea that inbreeding concentrates hereditary characteristics is correct, but the idea that inbreeding is a beneficial principle is false. Darwin thought that changes in heredity were 50% favorable and 50% unfavorable. With inbreeding, and the matching of characteristics, this process of change, of both favorable and unfavorable, could be accentuated.

It is true that inbreeding does induce changes in appearance and qualities of strains. It is also true that nothing debilitates a strain faster than inbreeding. Conversely, nothing revives it faster than cross-breeding. We know this now because man has learned many of the principles of heredity, and the nature of mutations.

Mutations, it is now understood, are not superior. The germ tissue, and the organization of the molecules within the cells are sufficiently delicate and precise that any disruption, such as damage to a gene or shearing of a chromosome, is almost sure to be in the direction of disorganization and imbalance, that is to say, inferiority. One of the most striking examples of collective mutations are the mutations induced in massive amounts by the undersea atomic bomb at Bikini Atoll. The genetic results included abundant deformity and sterility among the fish population. Mutations, it is now known, are rarely adaptive, sometimes neutral, often harmful, and occasionally lethal. They are never described as "superior."

It is further known that mutations, in almost every case, are recessive rather than dominant. They are not expressed when paired with a normal gene, which is the dominant one. Darwin thought changes due to inbreeding would be sometimes superior, and sometimes inferior, and in arithmetically equal ratios. This is far from the case. They are sometimes adaptive, but more likely are neutral or inferior in a proportion greater than 99% of the time.

Mutations are deranged genes and they may be inherited generation after generation. Ordinarily, they are not expressed because they are paired with a normal gene, which is dominant. But when inbreeding occurs, defective mutations are matched in increasingly higher proportions the closer the relationship of the parents become. Inbreeding is the process of matching defective mutations and the results frequently include biological weakness and deformity of any among the many body organs. Monstrosities are frequent. Albinism, diabetes and hemophilia are only three examples of this phenomena. Discoveries of new mutations, sometimes inherited by entire races, are being discovered almost every month, and the physiological areas which they control are very diverse, affecting different parts of the physiology in many different ways.

Darwin presented his hunches about heredity as scientific findings; they were not very scientific. His lack of knowledge in these matters is understandable; his lack of humility in propagating his views is hardly understandable, if he is considered a scientist. If he is considered a propagandist rather than an educator or scientist, then his assertiveness and almost messianic self-assurance becomes understandable. With his self-assured attitude, he considered verification unnecessary. And without verification, other academic figures promoted Darwin's ideas vigorously.

The cultural climate of the period following Darwin's publication is deftly described by Hugh Iltis in his volume, *Life of Mendel.*

> The psychological law that the contents of consciousness are sharply restricted applies, not only to individuals, but to generations; and since the consciousness of the epoch was entirely filled by the flood of ideas contained in the Darwinian theory and its consequences, people would not trouble themselves to make a place in their minds for the profound and peculiar ideas of Mendel, even though these were concerned with a kindred field.

> The basic notion of Darwin's doctrine was *the variability of the species* whereas the basic idea of Mendel's (though none of Mendel's hearers or even the lecturer himself had clearly recognized this) was *the constancy* if not *of the species, at least of their elements or characters,* and the heredity factors producing these. . . . The trouble was this, and this only, that the time was not yet ripe for the understanding of Mendel's law either in Brunn or elsewhere. (Italics ours)[11]

In Darwin's endeavor to join the ideas of survival and animal conflict, he constantly dwelled upon the subjects of in-

[11]Edward C. Colin, *Elements of Genetics,* Philadelphia: The Blakiston Co., 1949, p. 93.

breeding, mating, sex, sexual characteristics, sexual ratios, and so forth.

In so doing, he appealed for his theory of emergence to such esoteric examples as mating among hermaphrodite sea slugs, the mental powers of dragonflies the love antics of the umbrella bird, sexual colors among spiders, and the protruding posteriors (buttocks) among Hottentot women. These are the kinds of examples which he used to "prove" his hypothesis.

Darwin endeavored to merge the ideas of organic transmutation, prolificness and survival, and he constantly, chapter after chapter, returns to and reiterates himself on subjects relating to sex, such as the fight among the cocks for the hen.

It must be kept in mind that Darwin lacked catastrophic perspectives as well as genetical perspectives. He also lacked endocrinological perspectives, of which sex is a part. It cannot be denied that there is some validity in this area, more related to the survival of individual animals than to survival of the strain or the entire species. However, Darwin had little else on which to base his appeal. Therefore it is contended that he markedly and repeatedly overemphasized this area.

However, in this overemphasis he opened the door to another development in modern thought, that through which the sex-oriented Freud entered.[12] Freud rejected the principles of the Judeo-Christian ethic even as Marx did. However, he also rejected the methods and objectives of the Marxians. Among the three figures in the 19th century who successfully organized entirely new views of man (Darwin, Freud and Marx), Darwin is to be considered the central figure, for both of the others took ideas and views from Darwin. Darwin's influence upon Marx was primarily in the area of *Environmental Determinism*. And

[12]Richard LaPierre, *The Freudian Ethic*, New York: Duell, Sloan & Pearce, 1959, p. 55. "Some of Freud's critics have thought that the popularity of Freudianism stems from its preoccupation with sex; and it has been remarked that, although Freud did not discover the causative basis for human action, he did succeed in deifying the lowest common denominator. The ancient Greeks deified sex in the person of Aphrodite; but she was a happy and playful goddess, not a grim and destroying force. Moreover, the Greeks had many other gods. *To Freud, sex was all, or almost all.* It is doubtful, however, that Freud's engrossment with sex explains, even in part, the popularity of the Freudian doctrine. The explanation lies, as will be shown in due course, in the fact that Freud's idea of man has acquired functional value; it has, in recent years, given men a justification for some of the more significant of the changes that they have been working out in our society. And in so doing, it has no doubt contributed its force to the other forces that have been inciting these changes."

Darwin's influence upon Freud was primarily in the area of *Sex and Selection*. The introspective Freud wasn't much interested in economics or political upheaval.

DARWIN'S MARRIAGE. Darwin relied upon Lamarck very strongly for his biological assumptions. His interest in Lamarck, paralleling his grandfather's curiosity in biology, was pronounced at an early age. Following his voyage on the H.M.S. Beagle, he not only studied under Lyell, but had a renewed interest in Lamarck's works. He paid many compliments to Lamarck in his later life, and in his later writings. But the greatest compliment he paid to Lamarck was when, at 30 years of age, in 1839, he "selected" his wife. Darwin lived as he taught. He taught inbreeding, and he inbred.

He considered himself to be superior. He also considered his wealthy cousin, Emma Wedgwood, another grandchild of the famous potter, Josiah Wedgwood, to be superior. He proposed. She accepted. They brought into the world ten inbred children. Darwin presumed that if two "superior" humans who were closely related mated, the chances for markedly superior offspring would be excellent.

From Darwin's letters and manuscript, *Notebook on Transmutation of Species,* it can be concluded that Charles and Emma, at their wedding breakfast, discussed such romantic subjects as inbreeding of animals, inbreeding of plants, transmutation of species, mating like with like, and never planting cauliflower and turnips which are unlike, in the same garden patch.

It is obvious that Charles mystically believed in the transmutation of species, although this had (or has) never been demonstrated. His ideas required such a process. It is also obvious that neither he nor his cousin Emma knew what they were talking about. Darwin not only advocated inbreeding for himself; he did for others also. When his youngest sister Caroline also decided to marry a cousin in 1838, Darwin not only was glad, but also gave his authoritative biological approval.[13,14] Today, neither one of these marriages would be allowed by law.

[13]Gertrude Himmelfarb, *Darwin and the Darwinian Revolution*, New York: Doubleday & Co., 1962, p. 131.
In November, 1838, two years after his return from the voyage, he became engaged to his cousin, Emma Wedgwood. Emma, then thirty-one, a few months older than Charles, was the youngest daughter of his uncle Josiah,

According to Erasmus Darwin, Charles' brother (his uncle and grandfather were also named Erasmus), there was a definite question of biological weakness within the Darwin family, epilepsy being reported among other maladies. Charles' answer to this was to improve the strain through inbreeding.

> The dread of hereditary ill health was not entirely illusory . . . And as it happened, of his ten children, one girl died shortly after birth, another, the much-beloved Annie, died in childhood, his youngest son, Charles, was a mental defective who lived only two years, Henrietta had a serious and prolonged breakdown at fifteen, and three sons suffered such frequent illness that Darwin regarded them as semi-invalids. Even if all these ailments were not the constitutional disorders he took them to be, they were real enough to warrant some amount of anxiety.[15]

Darwin's last son, Charles Jr., was born a mental defective and died 19 months after birth, just 14 months prior to the publication of *Origin of Species*. One wonders how Darwin could have had a more dramatic signal to check and recheck his ideas on inbreeding and natural selection. And with this degree of inbreeding, one can easily suspect that Mary Eleanor, who lived only three weeks, may also have had grave hereditary disadvantages.

In the case of Darwin's inbred children, they had only six great-grandparents. Normally, children have eight. Josiah Wedgwood Sr. and his wife doubled on each side. Darwin's mother had been Susanna Wedgwood, and his uncle was Josiah Wedgwood Jr., Emma's father (and now his father-in-law as well). Josiah Wedgwood Sr. had been a famous entrepreneur in

and their childhood ties had recently been drawn closer with the marriage of her brother to Charles' sister Caroline. It was so much a matter of course that a Darwin should marry a Wedgwood that the only thing in doubt was which Darwin and which Wedgwood it would be.

[14]Himmelfarb, *op cit.*, p. 16.
   "As Freud felt obliged to psychoanalyze himself, so Darwin conscientiously sought in himself the hereditary influences he found so readily in plants and animals."
   Author's note: Whereas Darwin advocated the idea of inbreeding in animals and plants, so also he advocated this deleterious principle to his sister and to his cousins.

[15]Himmelfarb, *op. cit.*, p. 137.

the pottery-making industry (Wedgwood china) of 18th century England, having taken a commanding position not unlike that of Henry Ford in twentieth century America.

The fact that Josiah Wedgwood Sr. and his wife served on both sides of the family tree meant that each child inherited 50% of their genes from both of these great-grandparents. Each person has two sets of chromosomes and genes. Thus, the Darwin children had 12 gene pools from which to draw, rather than 16. This means that after pairing, Darwin's children possessed an average of 12½% identical pair of genes.[16] Many of these genes must have been recessive mutations, normally dormant but under these conditions, expressed. This proportion is somewhat aggravated by the fact that Josiah Wedgwood Sr. is known to have been himself somewhat inbred, coming from the village of Burs-

---

[16]There are many examples in history of inbreeding in various degrees. For instance, the leading family of Great Britain, Prince Philip and Queen Elizabeth, are fifth cousins (kissing cousins); this is not considered sufficiently close for biological peril. Mating among third and second cousins, however, raises the possibility of biological peril to prominence.

Mating among first cousins, as in Darwin's case, or his sister Caroline's case, results in the offspring having identical genes in a ratio of 1 to 7. Many of these genes are expected to be recessive mutants. Mating of uncle-niece, or nephew-aunt, raises this ratio to 1 to 3 (25%). Mating among siblings, almost the worst possible kind, raises this ratio 1 to 1 (50%).

Darwin correctly noted that inbreeding does tend to accentuate characteristics, and bring out new traits, latent in the mutant recessive genes. This was his only consideration, and he assumed that new traits would emerge in a rate of 50% favorable and 50% unfavorable. His own inbred sons possessed many identical pairs of mutant genes. The fact that four of them became reasonably successful does not indicate biological strength; it indicates academic and economic strength which prevailed over the inherent biological weakness.

There are better-known illustrations of inbreeding than Darwin's children. Among the biological Caesars following Tiberius, inbreeding and incest were common. Caligula and Agrippina are among the better (or worse) examples. The inbred Caligula considered each of his three sisters, at one time or another, as his legal wife, Agrippina being one. The insane Caligula was succeeded by Claudius, whose wife was Messalina. The inbred Agrippina was simultaneously Messalina's aunt and niece. Agrippina proceeded to poison her second husband, Crispus, frame Messalina, marry the Emperor Claudius, and poison Claudius. In marrying Claudius, she became the successor of her deceased aunt-niece. In one of her previous marriages, she bore Nero, who went on to other accomplishments, few of which are praiseworthy.

The 19th century also has a famous example. He came from a small town on the Austrian border, mountainous country where inbreeding in many communities was common. The responsible party was Herr Heidler who, although married, impregnated his servant girl, who also happened to be his niece. He proceeded to divorce his first wife, and marry his niece. From this second union came a series of miscarriages, as well as

lem where intermarriages were common. His parents apparently had been second cousins.[17]

If Darwin was not a good biologist, he was an original thinker with an encyclopedic mind. He could catalog vast groups of biological data, even if he couldn't draw correct conclusions from that data. Darwin was not afflicted with shyness as was Newton, Orville Wright, Einstein, Edison or Steinmetz. Darwin's traits rather were presumptiveness, self-assertiveness, and audacity, among others. His presumptiveness, allied with his increasing atheism and the admiration he received from others, merged into an interesting and fairly predictable complex. His uniformitarian friends began to consider Darwin as the new Copernicus of biology, and Darwin was disposed to agree with them.

He was quick to act the part and play the role to the full. He was not one to wait and check results, investigate and analyze, while others might move into this dashing role which he thoroughly anticipated. And others, including Gray, Hooker, Huxley,

---

one son and one daughter. The son's name was Adolf Heidler (Hitler). As a youth, Hitler displayed a physical sickliness and a mental instability; it is also granted that he displayed some remarkable abilities, including an incredible will. In his later years, his paranoia verged on insanity, somewhat comparable to Caligula and Agrippina.

In comparing the inbred Hitler and the inbred Caligula or Nero, it is of interest to note that they each possessed great egos, strong wills, a flair for oratory, a love of parades, an interest in arts (music, painting, sculpture) and a liking for the macabre. Consider Hitler's attitude toward the Jews, so similar to Nero's attitude toward the early Christians. Consider Hitler's willingness to blame the Reichstag fire on the Jews without evidence, and Nero's willingness to implicate the Christians in responsibility for the burning of much of Rome — not because they were responsible but because they were worthy of death anyhow. Further, the Roman Senate finally took steps successful in getting rid of their near-maniac Emperor, a step which sorely tempted the German general staff also.

This footnote is not made for the purpose of psychoanalyzing inbreeds. Our purpose is secondarily to point out a reason, seldom evaluated in terms of its true significance, as to why Hitler was so obsessed about pure blood, German marriages, and the Aryan race. Almost inevitably biographers of Hitler note his inbreeding, but fail to relate it to his biological weakness, to his psychological eccentricity, or to his racial obsession.

However, primarily this footnote is to demonstrate why Hitler or his sister, or Caligula or his sisters, are better examples of Darwin's deleterious biology than were Darwin's own sons or nephews, merely because of the higher intensity of inbreeding. History records that Frau Heidler had a series of five or six miscarriages; undoubtedly this was due to the inbreeding factor in part.

[17]Himmelfarb, *op. cit.*, p. 15.

Lyell, Spencer, and Wallace were working with this same thesis.

Something of this trait is also seen in the publication of his book. His social life centered around his inner circle of friends and the dilettante society of London's younger scions. He was a popular lecturer, and he knew how to choose contacts. Before his book came out, advance raves were publicized. The first edition went on sale on October 1, 1859. By 6:00 P.M., October 1, 1859, all orders had been filled, standing line customers had been served, and the entire edition was sold out. The unemployed Marx very likely was among those who stood in line on that day to receive his copy. In another 70 days, a second edition of another 1500 had been sold out. Europeans may not have a word for this kind of operation, but in the United States, this is known as "Madison Avenue science."

This illustrates the effectiveness of the pre-publication promotion and publicity. It reflects assistance he received from such figures as Gray, Hooker, Huxley, and Lyell. It reflects the enthusiasm with which the book anticipated and generated. It also reflects how uncritically it was received by most.[18] The rising tide of intellectual anti-spiritual humanism would bring Darwin along, riding at the peak of its rising crest, which Darwin correctly anticipated.[19] Marx, in his lazy poverty and in his atheistic

---

[18]"Huxley and Hooker were Darwin's advance guard, with Lyell bringing up the rear. But it was not long before others joined the ranks. By March 1863, enough had committed themselves, to one degree or another, for Darwin to draw up a table of organization of the names and professions of fifteen of his prominent adherents. One of these . . . observed hopefully that as species emerged from the war of nature, so truth would emerge from the intellectual collision precipitated by his work." Himmelfarb, op. cit., p. 266.

[19]When the slightly-known Pasteur wrote Darwin of his biological objections, his correspondence was ignored by Darwin. When the leading geologist and zoologist of that age, Louis Agassiz, organized a series of lectures refuting Darwinism at Harvard. Agassiz' reputation was badly mauled by lesser scholars. The title of Agassiz' unfortunate series of lectures was "The Structure of Animal Life, a series of lectures on the Power, Wisdom and Goodness of God, as manifested in His Works."

The great enthusiasm and seeming gullibility which Darwin's works received, coupled with a modest amount of challenging and checking, indicate the mood of many academic figures, and it also reflects their aggressiveness in promoting their anti-spiritual conclusions. Within a few decades, challenging Darwin was identified with committing academic heresy, and penalties for such non-conforming heresy were repeatedly invoked. Darwin correctly foresaw this role. He did not foresee the related but contradictory conclusions of Mendel or DeVries, however.

dream world, was raptured by the implications proposed by this revolutionary naturalist.

This brief discussion of Darwin, his heritage, his career, his marriage, his inbred children, his travels, his associations, etc., are essential in understanding his hypothesis and the series of assumptions upon which his hypothesis is based. There is much that is left unsaid in this brief resume concerning his college life, his travels on the Beagle, his infection with trapanosomes and his health, his economic life, his married life and his wife's evaluation of her husband.

Perhaps it should be included that Emma Darwin never was strongly sympathetic with her husband's endeavors or his atheism although she loyally took care of him. After he died, and their son Francis undertook his famous father's biography, Emma refused to allow some of Darwin's more extreme antispiritual statements to be included. But from this, it is further suspected that Darwin was more of an anti-spiritual propagandist than a scientist.

Darwinism has been presented to the world as a scientific proposition; therefore it must stand the tests of scientists more than of educators, philosophers or skilled propagandists. Genetics has pitched a first hard strike against the Darwinian hypothesis. It rejects the two Darwinian assumptions of *Environmental Determinism* and *Natural Selection* (Inbreeding, whether historically random or intentional). The importance of this is seldom realized. *Environmental Determinism* supposedly was the finest point Darwin made; it was the first one to fall. But here was the supposed mechanism for emergence. With its rejection, Darwinism has no mechanism. Certainly genetics, undergirding the idea of the stability of the species rather than the variability of the species, gives no assistance.

Formation or malformation of the organs of the physiology are controlled not only by the genes, but also by the system of endocrine glands. If genetics does not allow the Darwinian assumptions, perhaps an alternative area will assist.

Thus far, genetics has pitched a first hard strike against the Darwinian proposition. Astral catastrophism has pitched a second hard strike against the Darwinian proposition. A second strike does not eliminate a batter, but it opens the door to a sudden third strike, and a third strike does mean elimination. It is to the area of endocrinology that attention is now directed.

3. Endocrinology and Darwinism

Subtheory 5: Comparative Embryology. The principle of recapitulation (ontogeny recapitulates phylogeny) went out a generation ago, and it hardly deserves consideration in equal status with the other five "pillars of support." This idea observes that there is a parallelism in the development of mammalian embryos. The same organs all develop in a similar, sequential pattern. The eyes, for instance, appear at comparable stages, as do teeth, tails, and other organs. This, it formerly was held, was another evidence of Darwinism.

Without contradictory data, this elementary observation might seem to support Darwinian thought. On the other hand, it might easily lend support to the proposition of a common Architect of all life, a common Creator. Every architect or builder proceeds in sequential patterns, even though the particular plan varies. Thus, *Comparative Embryology* is a philosophical and speculative matter—an empirical matter—and not a scientific matter.

Five of the seven pillars of the Darwinian superstructure have been examined and none thus far have been able to bear the stress of the briefest analysis. Two are left. One proceeds deeper into the field of endocrinology. The other, the overriding requirement of a biochemical mechanism, will also be examined. How strong and impressive is the famed superstructure of Darwinian thought when one peeks under the trappings and the imposing facade, and when one tests the structural strength?

Subtheory 6: Apemen. (Missing Links). Endocrinology is the study of glands and hormones and their effects on the organs within the body. It includes both fetal and post-fetal stages. Since the *Apemen* proposition cites skeletal systems— bones and dentition—as its basis for concluding emergence, it is to the endocrine branch of medicine to which our attention is now directed. It is the endocrine system which controls both the formation and/or the malformation of the skeletal system.

The skeletal systems of the fossil men are clearly out of scale and proportion with the skeletal systems of modern man. Furthermore, they resemble in certain ways the skeletal systems of apes, and are thus reasoned to be an intermediary step. This explanation offers an easy, logical, progressive, and uniformitarian pattern which at first appears fairly simple. But upon closer scrutiny, it may be not quite that simple.

In both prenatal and postnatal stages, the development of the skeletal system is dictated by the genes, but is organized by hormones secreted from the endocrine glands. Other physiological systems such as the circulatory system, the digestive system, the muscular system, the nervous system (including the brain), and the reproductive system are also affected by hormones. A hormone imbalance or malfunction in the fetal stage could result in malfunction of any of these systems or organs, not just the skeletal system.

Proponents of Darwinism have grossly neglected this basic approach and have been content to measure the prognathous jaws of antediluvians, along with apes, humans and monkeys, and have proceeded to make premature conclusions. They have been content to take the external measurements in terms of millimeters of brain cavities, clavicles, dentition, mandibles, and supraorbital ridges. They have then made comparative lists, drawn up tables of measurements, and have proceeded to draw conclusions which may be quite superficial.

The proper approach to the *Apemen* proposition must be concerned with biochemical mechanisms, and in this case, endocrinology is basic. Darwinists have illustrated that fossil men possessed apelike skeletal characteristics in varying degrees. This is partly true, but the uniformitarian assumption of a transition from apehood to manhood must be tested. It must not be accepted in such a rudimentary way.

(A) ACROMEGALY. It very easily can be demonstrated that twentieth century men, possessing no apelike genes, may—due to a certain type of endocrine disorder—develop "apelike" characteristics in their skin, hair, metabolism, and skeletal system. This is known as *acromegaly*. It is caused by the abnormal resumption of growth hormone after maturation. A reactivation of this particular function of the pituitary gland—the master gland—causes renewed bone growth. Since at maturation the epiphyses close (the bones fuse), they can no longer elongate and therefore must grow by thickening. The cause of acromegaly is not well understood, but malfunctions in pituitary tissues may be one cause. Today, this skeletal malformation occurs in about one person in 10,000, in males and females in equal ratios, and usually in persons in their twenties and thirties—about one or two decades after maturation.

The description of a person afflicted with acromegaly sounds like a description of Neanderthal Man, and the changes are not merely limited to skeletal malformations.

In the following excerpts from medical textbooks, there are similarities of the descriptions with *Apemen*. Since acromegaly is considered a basic physiological imbalance, it is medically classified as a retrogressive development. Here is a case which the medical profession describes as retrogression, a case strikingly similar to what Darwinists term evolution:

> As in many endocrine types, there is considerable resemblance among all acromegalics. The large extremities, awkward movements, thickened features, and drooping shoulders with hands falling near the knees in advanced cases, give the picture of Simian (*apelike*) man, and where gigantism has preceded the acromegalic changes, of a primitive ape-like giant. Great strength, however, may give place to exhaustion and weakness in the later stages . . .

> The skull is considerably thickened, the ridges becoming very prominent, and the external occipital protuberance enlarged. The cranial sutures may be obliterated. Even more marked are the changes of the facial bones: thickening and enlargement of the zygomatic arches, of the malar bones, and especially of the lower jaw, which becomes prognathous through overgrowth and also through changes in the temporo-manibular joint. The teeth become spaced wide apart as the jaw increases in width. The clavicles are thickened, and the antero-posterior diameter of the chest is greatly increased . . . [20]

> The patient with fully developed disease presents a striking appearance which, when once seen, is never forgotten. The hands become large due to a broadening and thickening of the fingers and palms, so that they assume a "spade-like" appearance. They feel stiff and clench with some difficulty. The facial features coarsen, the lips thicken, while the nose becomes large and bulbous. The head increases in size and the supraorbital ridges become prominent and overhanging. There occurs a protrusion of the lower jaw, the so-called "prognathism," due essentially to thickening

[20] A. Stuart Mason & G. I. M. Swyer, *Major Endocrine Disorders*, Fairlawn, N.J.: Oxford University Press, 1959, pp. 15-17.

> and overgrowth of the mandable. As a result, the teeth become widely spaced and override the upper dentition . . . The patients frequently stoop due to kyphosis associated with enlargement and thickening of the vertebrae . . . They are sullen and vacillating, although mentally quite alert and normally endowed. [21]

Post-Darwinian evolutionists have assumed and taught that Neanderthal proportions are due to some admixture or transmutation of apelike genes. They have further assumed and taught that these proportions, formed by some transmuted ape genes, have been modified by some as yet unascertained biochemical mechanism. But Neanderthal Man is an excellent parallel to the modern description of acromegaly. [22]

If antediluvians commonly had acromegaly, they would have appeared "apelike," yet possessed no ape genes whatsoever. Other "apemen" seemingly were afflicted with acromegaly, but this may have been complicated by further endocrine disorders, such as hypothyroidism. What post-Darwinian evolutionists propose as emergence has no biochemical basis, but similar conditions are found, in easily documented medical data, in retrogressive or imbalanced forms of man.

Neanderthal Man, Peking Man, Zinjanthropus, and other fossil men, involve matters quite beyond merely skeletal proportions. Neanderthal Man, for instance, was found under glacial till. Any explanation of the total picture must include not only his variant skeletal formation, but also a good analysis of the cause of his abnormal entombment—in this case the catastrophe of the Biblical Flood and the Ice Epoch. Peking Man was found within a thick layer of compressed alluvium in the heart of the

---

[21]Louis J. Soffer, *Diseases of the Endocrine Glands*, Philadelphia: Lea & Febiger, 1956, pp. 103-104.

[22]John W. Klotz, *Genes, Genesis and Evolution*, St. Louis, Concordia Publishing House, 1955, pp. 198-199.
   "In recent years a wrestler by the name of Maurice Tillet, known professionally as "the Angel," achieved considerable notoriety. Not only did he win a number of bouts and gain recognition in that way, but his physical appearance attracted considerable attention. Apparently he suffered from acromegaly, an endocrine disorder. As a result his head and his face became very large, his hands and his feet thickened, and his torso, too became broadened. Certainly if his bones were fossilized, it is not hard to believe that they might be regarded as those of a pre-human form. And yet M. Tillet was a 20th century human being, and a cultured, well-educated member of our society at that."

arid zone of China. Any full discussion of Peking Man must include the total picture which includes the deposition (and very possible drowning) of this antediluvian in the heart of arid Asia, and such theory must therefore account for vast volumes of water in this now arid and distinctly non-marine location.

Zinjanthropus involves another situation. This form was found in Tanganyika, Africa, on the edge of one of the spurs of the Great Rift Valley. Zinjanthropus was found in alternating and successive layers of shales and volcanic ash. Even as any explanation for Neanderthal Man must explain glacial till and the Ice Epoch, so any explanation for Zinjanthropus must explain shales caused by tidal activity on massive scales along with simultaneous massive volcanic eruptions. Gravitational disturbances of a celestial nature and simultaneous upwelling of fluid oceans and magma can account for this kind of phenomenon.

How old was Zinjanthropus? Dr. Leaky, following classical Lyellian thinking, and the Lyellian time scale, says 1,700,000 B.C., adding a little to Lyell's classical 1,000,000 B.C. for safety. However, the catastrophic thesis is that the orogenetic and hydrographical phenomena which entombed Zinjanthropus burst forth on our planet something like 5,000 years ago.[23]

Thus, it is to be pointed out that the fossil men and their

[23]The Rift Valley is a wrenching or a cleavage of the Earth's crust. It extends for some 5,000 miles, and is between 5 and 50 miles wide. Particularly in the equatorial zone of Central Africa, its pattern becomes highly complex and dendritic, a further indication that the crust of the Earth was literally torn by internal stresses requiring expansion.

The northern extremity of the Rift Valley is in Syria, between the Anti-Lebanon and the Lebanon Mountains. It runs southward between Israel and Jordan, forming the Jordan Valley trench, and includes the Sea of Galilee, the Dead Sea and the Gulf of Aqaba. It continues in the Red Sea trench, and enters Africa proper in Ethiopia, opposite the confluence of the Gulf of Aden and the Red Sea. Here it proceeds up and across a mountainous plateau, 5,000 to 7,000 feet above sea level. A series of small lakes stud the cleavage. In Kenya, Uganda, and Tanganyika, the Rift Valley becomes wider and more complex as it approaches the equator. It surrounds the Lake Victoria basin. In Kenya and Tanganyika, Lakes Rudolf, Naivasha, Natron and Eyasi stud the eastern rift. The larger lakes of Albert, Edward, Kivu, Tanganyika and Rukwa stud the wider western rift. They merge in Southern Tanganyika, near Lake Nyasa, and the merged Rift Valley continues southward into Mozambique.

This is the major rift valley of the Earth; a second one, also perpendicular to and astride the equator, has been detected in the submerged Mid-Atlantic Range. The specific cause of the Rift Valley has yet to be established. Our conclusion is that its cause was the shift in location of the geographical poles in the time of the Floodtide Cataclysm, about 2800 B.C. The dating of the rifting of the Earth's crust is later, due to the sub-skeletal abnormalities cannot be considered to the exclusion of the forces which entombed them, no more than can the mammoths, dinosaurs, or other fossil types. Could it be that fossil men lived in a markedly different physical environment, even as has been suggested in the preceding chapter? Could it be that their atmosphere was reorganized in at least five different ways, compared to the present atmosphere? Is there a relation between this earlier physical environment and differing endocrine re-

sequent isostatic adjustment of the Earth, in its requirement of a new zone of oblateness.

In Chapter V, it was illustrated that there were two great cycles of orogenetic uplift, the Alpine-Himalayan zone and the Circum-Pacific zone. This, among other reasons, led to the suspicion that there had been a dislocation of the geographical poles (and also probably a shift in the angle of the Earth's axis) during the Flood cataclysmic period. Here, in the Rift Valley, is another strong indication of a dislocation and relocation of the Earth's geographical poles.

The Earth is an oblate spheroid, and it rotates with a circumferential speed of over 1000 miles per hour at the equator, and with a circumferential speed of nothing at the poles, and with intermediate speeds in intermediate latitudes. One result of this is that the Earth's equatorial crust has bulged, due to the centrifugal motion of the magma. The equatorial diameter is 27 miles greater than is the polar diameter. If there were a relocation of the poles, there would necessarily be a relocation of the equator. And with the Earth in rotational motion, there would necessarily be a relocation of the equatorial bulge zone. This requires an expansion of the Earth's crust, a cleavage or a tearing perpendicular to the equator, and wider in the equatorial zones than in the sub-tropical extremities. The Rift Valley of Africa not only fulfills the requirements of being (1) perpendicular to the equator and (2) widest in the equatorial zone, but it also is (3) most complex (and dendritic in pattern) in the equatorial zone. This orogenetical cleavage, coupled with another similar one in the Mid-Atlantic Range, coupled with the two zones of orogenetic uplift, linked with astral catastrophic thought, is suggestive that there was a major relocation of the Earth's axis, and the two geographical poles, during the Flood catastrophe.

Further factors which also point in this direction are such physical features as (a) the geosyncline of the Lake Victoria Basin, (b) the shallowness of Lake Victoria—the second largest lake in the world, with an area of 26,828 sq. miles and a maximum depth of but 270 feet, (c) its attenuated coast line and (d) its numerous islands, all reflecting a minimum of erosion, as if the basin had been filled up within recent times. Further related factors are the recent volcanic formations of (e) Elgon, (f) Kenya, (g) Kilimanjaro— Kibo and Mawenzi, (h) Ruwenzori, between Lake Albert and Lake Edward—Margerita and Alexandra—the so-called "Mountains of the Moon." Also (i) on the edges of the Rift Valley are outpourings of lava which are not covered by alluvium, again indicating a date of volcanic bleeding subsequent to the Flood. Other physical features suggesting a recentness are (j) the soda lakes and (k) Murchison Falls. Here the White Nile, a meandering river over 1300 feet wide, suddenly plunges over the edge of the geosyncline, and into the Rift Valley. The narrowest part of the crevasse or fissure of Murchison Falls is 15 feet wide, and through this crevasse, the entire White Nile flows, needless to say at a tre-

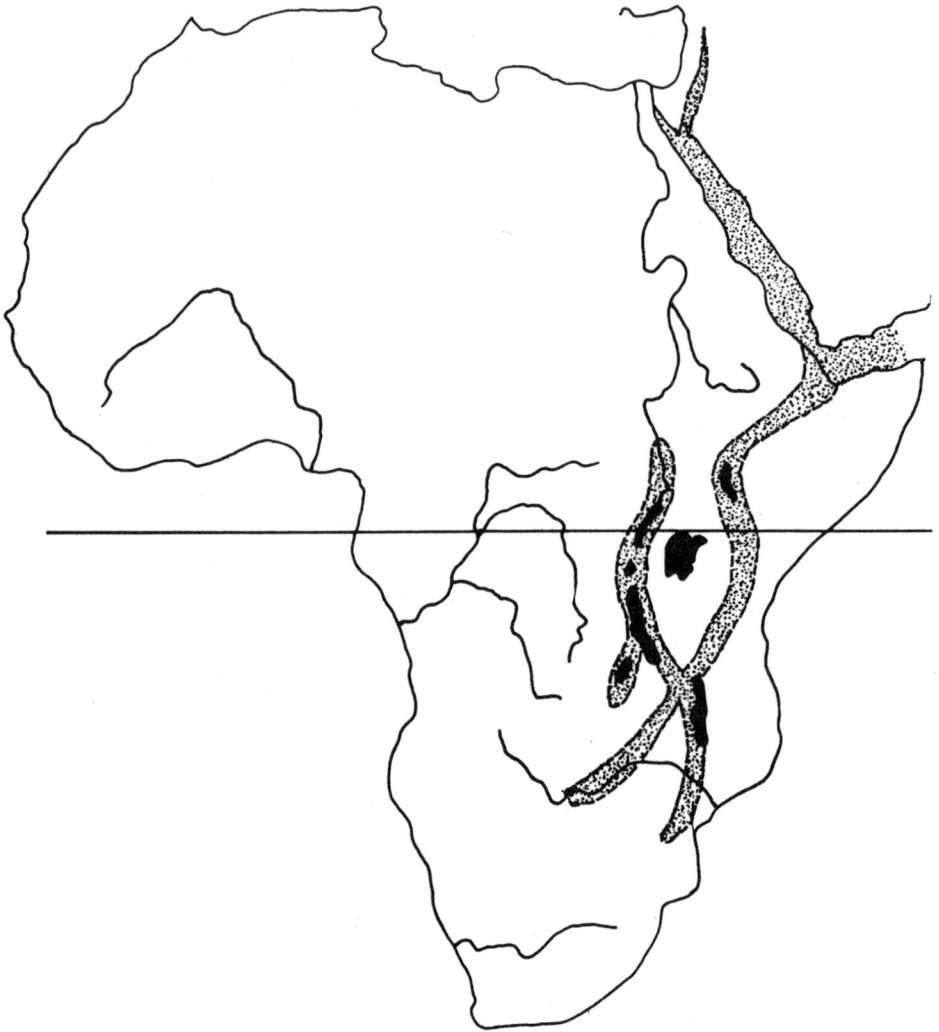

FIGURE 26 — The location of the Great Rift Valley in Africa.

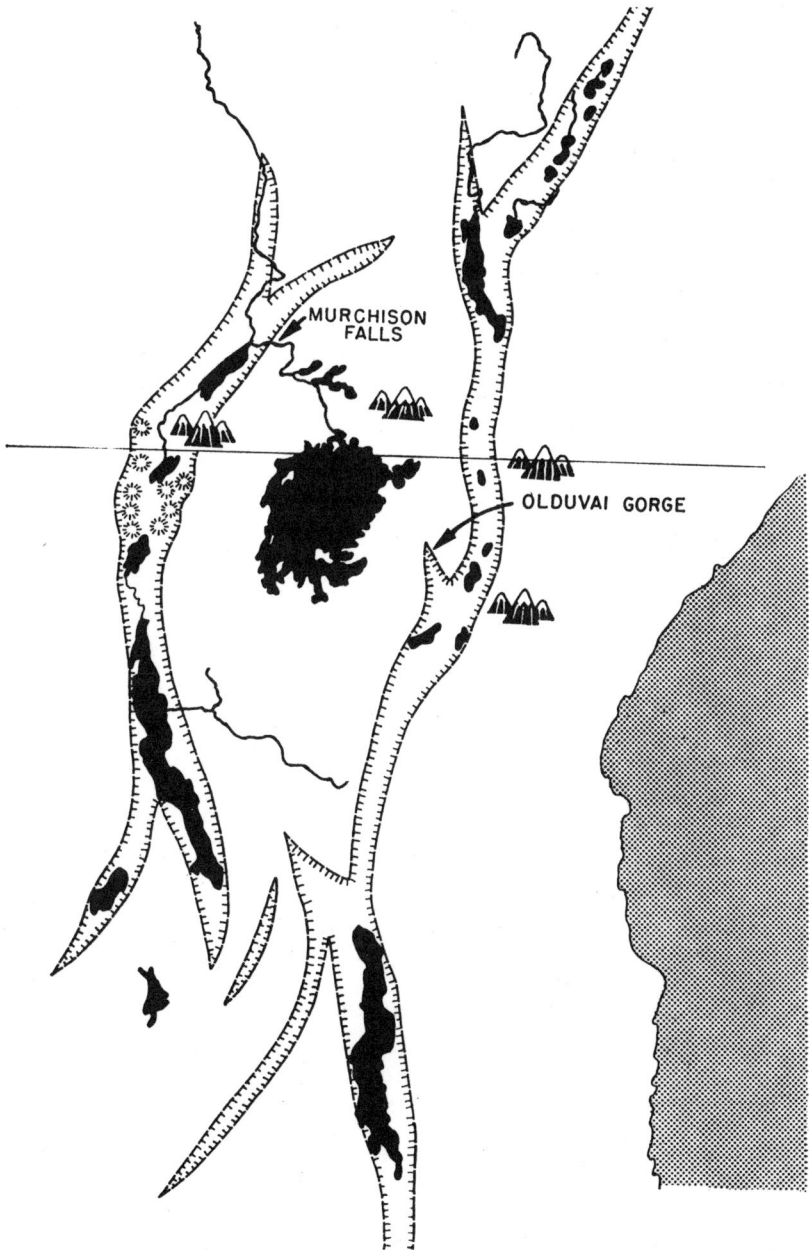

FIGURE 27 — A regional location of the Great Rift Valley and Lake Victoria in Eastern Africa, astride the equator.

sponses? Could the catastrophe which terminated that atmospheric regime also be the same cataclysm which buried the fossil
men? Could it be, for instance, that man in that age lived much
longer, and thus had much more skeletal time in which acromegalic bone growth might occur, as is suggested by Figure 25 on
antediluvian longevity?

mendous velocity. The lack of erosion at Murchison Falls is a further indication of the recent uplift of this region, which again offers evidence of
the recent dating, the recent new oblateness, and the celestial nature of
the Flood crisis.

If there had been no Global Flood, there would have been no series
of water-laid alluvial, vertical, compressed stratigraphy on the surrounding plateaus. And if there had been a Global Flood after the rifting of the
Earth's crust, there would have been diluvian stratigraphy in the bottom
of the valley, which is not the case.

It was on the edge of one of the clefted spurs of the Rift Valley in
Tanganyika where alternating layers of shales, sandstones and pumices
were laid down, that Dr. Leaky found his rich fossil deposits, including
Zinjanthropus. Any explanation for Zinjanthropus must include an explanation for his manner of entombment. Zinjanthropus, dated arbitrarily
at around 1,700,000 B.C. (a little extra beyond Lyell's 1,000,000 B.C. for
margin), has been found in strata which was alternately laid down and
compressed about 4,500 to 5,000 years ago. Then, some 500 years later,
due to the requirement for a new bulge zone, and a new isostatic equilibrium, rifting occurred and the Great Rift Valley was created. Zinjanthropus was found at the Olduvai Gorge, on an edge of the cleavage. It would
be highly interesting if all of the fossils in Tanganyika (and not merely a
handful at one section of the edge of one spur of the rift) could be located
and examined.

Further, this story sounds suspiciously like a wrenching of the
Earth's crust, recorded about 500 years after the Flood, during the time
of Abraham in the vicinity of Sodom and Gomorrah. Here is a zone of
crustal weakness similar to the subsequently shattered Jericho. However,
the Biblical description of this region prior to the Sodom-Gomorrah catastrophe does not indicate that of a Rift Valley. Genesis indicates that this
was a valley (the Vale of Siddim, Genesis 14:10, 17, full of slime, or bitumen pits). Genesis indicates that it was a well-watered (well-irrigated)
valley, and quite productive.

Subsequently came the seismic holocaust which almost engulfed the
fleeing Lot, and did engulf his wife. Perhaps Lot's wife, being more attached to Sodom, her home town, and being more reluctant to leave, became engulfed in hot, toxic sulphurous fumes like Pliny the elder, when
he was investigating the volcanism of Vesuvius as Pompeii was being
destroyed.

The location of Sodom and Gomorrah is in the Rift Valley. This, in
Genesis, is a description of a major physical disaster for that region. The
time is five centuries after the Flood, sufficient time for the Earth to
develop intense internal pressures in a new zone of oblateness. The local
picture interweaves into the total web of reasoning, increasing the understanding of the Flood as an astral catastrophe, recently dated. Hence our
suspicion is that Noah and Zinjanthropus were contemporaries. Noah, a
shipwright, escaped; Zinjanthropus didn't.

Zinjanthropus had skeletal features which seem mildly deranged when compared to the norm of this age, but they do not particularly reflect a transition from apehood to manhood. Rather, they reflect acromegalic disorders coinciding with other major endocrine maladjustments. For instance, Zinjanthropus had some inexplicable dentition. The incisors are underdeveloped, whereas the molars are overdeveloped. This is a malfunction of growth hormone and is a different pattern or sequence from the current norm. Evidences of differing waves, periods or sequences of growth hormone in the antediluvian environment were not limited to man.

All mammals, and seemingly all animals, experienced comparable variations of growth hormone. The imperial elephant, the mammoth, and the mastodon had extremely long tusks, which often curved 180° and often crossed. Modern elephant tusks (pachyderm dentition) do not achieve this, but then modern pachyderms may not live as long. Similarly, one may compare the saber-toothed tiger to the modern tiger, the saber-toothed mesonyx to the modern wolf, and the saber-toothed smilodon to the modern panther. All had oversized incisors, compared to the norm of our current age. Zinjanthropus, rather than having oversized incisors, had oversized molars. This suggests a different sequence or wave of growth hormone, possibly related to certain dietary fluctuations. He also possessed other variable proportions of cranial malformation. Here is a reverse parallelism between the dentition of Zinjanthropus and the more common pattern for dentition of the saber-toothed mammals, neither of which are normal to modern standards

Acromegaly, like oversized dentition, is a proper function of growth hormone at an improper time or in an abnormal amount. When acromegaly occurs in our age, it is the abnormal, but it may have been the normal in the earlier age. When it occurs in our age, the lower jaw begins to expand, becomes prognathous, and overrides the upper jaw. The dentition becomes more widely spaced. The posture sags as the clavicle thickens. The supraorbital ridges expand and the eyebrows protrude. The zygomatic arches thicken. The temporo-mandibular joint and cranium expand. The vertebrae thicken, as do the metacarpals and metatarsals (fingers and toes). In addition to skeletal changes, the hair coarsens, metabolism changes, and the psychology of the person may change although the intellectual powers may remain acute. The basic genetic material has not changed. There has been no transmutation of species, as Darwinians intuitively assert.

Again it is recalled that Darwin knew nothing about genetics and nothing about endocrinology, and he rejected what had been suggested concerning catastrophism, Creationism, the antediluvian canopy, the earlier longevity and related matters which are evidenced in Genesis. In proposing his new view of man, via continuous emergence from lower forms, he showed an element of genius but also an element of rather arbitrary guessing. His genius is shown in his ability to organize and reorganize items into new patterns; his arbitrariness is shown in his lack of critical testing and in his refusal to recognize either possibilities or probabilities of his error.

(B) GIGANTISM. Acromegaly, a thickening in bone structure *after* maturation, is one phase of the function of growth hormone. The other phase is gigantism, which is caused by an increase in the rate of growth hormone *before* maturation. Antediluvians matured more slowly than men in the present age, but after maturation, they degenerated even more slowly. Growth hormone, either in excessive amounts or over greater lengths of time before maturation, results in gigantism, whereas growth hormone in excessive amounts after maturation results in acromegaly.

Many mammals in fossil form exhibit a tendency to gigantism; they often are twice the size of their current counterparts. Among examples are bears, camels, panthers, pigs, rhinoceroses, elephants, tigers, and wolves. Fossil birds were much larger than their modern counterparts. Insects also were larger. Dragonflies with twenty- and thirty-inch wing spreads have been found, and the examples of the fossil reptiles (dinosaurs and turtles) also show great extremes. Furthermore, fossil flora (plant life) also exhibit these same tendencies toward gigantism.

Although generally speaking, gigantism was common in the earlier age, it was by no means uniform. Sometimes a rule is proved by exceptions. Two exceptions are the horse and the sloth. Fossil horses (eohippuses) have been found, some 15 to 20 inches high. This is an example of an animal, large in our age, but small in the previous age.

On the other hand, there are fossil forms of sloths which

weighed 10,000 pounds. This is an example of an animal, small in our age, but very large in the previous age. Thus, there are exceptions to the general rule of antediluvian gigantism, and the exceptions run in both directions.

In the matter of gigantism, dimensions can be somewhat deceptive. Brachiosaurus, for instance, was twice as tall as the imperial elephant. But he outweighed the elephant by about 45 tons—some 50 tons to 5 tons. Gigantism in the earlier age can be illustrated by the following list which gives the length of fossil reptiles. A list of large fossil mammals is also given:

TABLE 7

Reptiles	Length	Mammals exceeding 10 ft. in height at the shoulders.
Diplodocus	87½ ft.	Agriotherium
Bronosaurus	67	Alticamelus
Bachiosaurus	65	Amebelodon
Icthyosaurus	40	Baluchitherium
Allosaurus	35	Brontops
Trachodon	30	Megatherium
Triceratops	30	Mammoth
Pteradon (wingspread)	25	Promerycochoerus
Stegosaurus	20	Subhyradocon
Tyrannosaurus	20	Teleoceras
Tylosaurus	20	Tritemnodon
Archelon (turtle)	12	Uintatherium

It can very well be assumed that many species and varieties of animals in the fossil record have yet to be unearthed. But enough fossil animals exist to support the conclusion that different patterns of growth hormone, and probably also longevity, occurred in the previous age. Among its results were both acromegaly for some forms, gigantism for other forms, and both for yet other forms. This occurred not only in man and in other mammals, but in reptiles, birds, insects and apparently all fauna, and flora also.

Growth hormone and acromegaly are one endocrine imbalance which is suspected as being common in the previous age. Another is hypothyroidism, an undereffectiveness of the thyroid gland. While growth hormone and hyperpituitarism contribute to acromegaly and gigantism, hypothyroidism contributes to dwarfism. These factors seemingly were all inextricably tied in with the principle of differing rates of maturation and longevity in the earlier age, and the Greenhouse Effect.

(C) HYPOTHYROIDISM (CRETINISM). Another hormone malfunction, hypothyroidism, involves the thyroid gland, the controlling mechanism of body metabolism. In the earlier age, there was a lack of winds, due to the heat equilibrium. The resultant lack of both horizontal and vertical mixing of the atmosphere meant no rains or mature river systems. But the abundant water vapor and diurnal dew resulted in plenty of moisture, and abundant swamps. These factors imply that soluble minerals (salts of bromine, cadmium, calcium, chlorine, cobalt, copper, fluorine, iodine, manganese, potassium, and sodium) would not be dispersed very widely in nature and there would be little in the way of leached soils, a circumstance which would contribute to soil structure. Some of these minerals are required by the human physiology, if only in trace amounts. Iodine deficiency would be likely in soils scattered across the Earth's surface in that earlier climatological regime. Fluorine, an important element in bone salts, including dentition, perhaps was even more poorly distributed.

Iodine in trace amounts is vital to the proper functioning of the metabolic processes. When iodine is lacking in the diet, or when the gland itself malfunctions, hypothyroidism results. Following is a description of the effects of this disorder:

> The enhancement of skeletal maturation by thyroid hormones alone has also been applied by Walker in comparing skeletal age and chronological age in newborn rats. The influence of thyroid hormones on bone growth is of clinical importance because of the abnormal osteogenesis in cretinism or juvenile myxedema. Thyroid hormone therapy restores ossification in children, but hyperthyroidism in adult life may cause osteoporosis.[24]

> In general, thyroid deficiency in the young cretin will result in stunted brain development. It is for this reason that so many cretins are of low intelligence. Since the damage once sustained is at least in part permanent, they rarely attain their full mental potentialities . . .

[24]Gerald Litwack & David Kritchevsky, *Actions of Hormones on Molecular Processes*, New York: John Wiley & Sons Inc., 1964, p. 123.

> The adult cretin is a dwarf, rarely being over 4 feet tall. He walks with a waddling, shuffling gait, in part due to the laxity of the hip joints and the bent legs. Curvature of the spine tends to shorten his erect height. The head is that of a normal-sized individual, but appears large when resting atop a dwarf . . .

> The orbits are large, the nose is broad and flat, the bony part being underdeveloped and the cartilaginous portion flabby. . . . The head is large and there is a wide open anterior fontanelle and frontal suture. The nose is broad, flat and depressed. The cheeks are prominent.[25]

> The typical hypothyroid child is dwarfed, and the ratio of the upper and lower skeletal segments remain that of a younger child. The naso-orbital development is infantile, so that the bridge of the nose is flat and broad, causing the eyes to appear wide-spaced and the nose is short and underdeveloped. Osseous development is retarded, dental development is retarded and defective, and epiphyseal dygenesis is frequently present. [26]

Even in our age, with the soils of the Earth having been washed with mineral-dispersing flood-tides, there are areas in which iodine is lacking in the soil, and in the diet (without iodized salt). These regions include the glaciated Alpine region of Europe, the Himalayan-Tibetan region of Asia, the glaciated Scandinavian Upland of Northern Europe, and the glaciated Canadian Shield and Great Lakes Region of North America. Cretinism was a common condition in Switzerland up to and even into the twentieth century. In World War I, 3% of the draftees in the Swiss army were rejected for some degree of cretinism.

Cretinism, if related to lack of iodine in the diet, becomes increasingly prevalent in successive generations. For instance, a mother with a degree of cretinism will carry a cretin-oriented fetus. This fetus, when born, will already have incipient cretinism, which it may or may not overcome following birth, depending on the diet. Thus, the degree of iodine deficiency in a mother's diet is particularly important because it not only affects the mother but the unborn fetus as well. Thus, children can be born

[25]Louis J. Soffer, *op. cit.,* pp. 832-833.

[26]A. T. Cameron, *Recent Advances in Endocrinology,* Philadelphia: The Blakiston Co., 1940, p. 41.

both with cretinism, and can develop it after birth. The degree of iodine deficiency will fluctuate as the diet may change, and trace amounts of iodine become available. Hence, the degree of the affliction of cretinism will change and, depending on how early it is caught, many of the conditions, including skeletal deformation, can be partially corrected or reversed.

Based on the climatic equilibrium and the lack of rain and running water in the previous age, it is postulated that a lack of iodine was common in the soils of many of the regions of the Earth. In marine locations, this would be partly offset by the availability of iodine from the oceanic reservoir. Iodine deficiency is considered to have been particularly common in heartland (non-marine) locations, at a substantial distance from the oceans.

Hypothyroidism further complicates the skeletal system, with its tendency to produce a particular type of dwarfism. Thus acromegaly, related to gigantism, and hypothyroidism, related to dwarfism, are considered to have been simultaneous factors in the earlier age.

The relationship between the endocrine glands is complex, including a series of feedback (reciprocal) relationships. When one gland does not function sufficiently, the master gland, the pituitary, which secretes at least 14 distinct hormones, will proceed to secrete a hormone which will stimulate the particular gland involved in the malfunction. Thus, when the thyroid does not function efficiently, the pituitary will produce an additional amount of thyroid-stimulating hormone in order to maintain the needed balance. In this way, hypothyroidism (too little thyroid, caused by a deficiency of iodine in the diet) *will cause* hyperpituitarism. Hyperpituitarism, including additional amounts of growth hormone, may be correlated with acromegaly. In this indirect way, a lack of iodine in the diet while causing hypothyroidism may also reciprocally cause hyperpituitarism.

Gigantism, already noted throughout the fossil record, was apparently related to longevity in the earlier age. It has already been proposed that longevity was the norm in the previous age. The Biblical record takes considerable pains to make this point clear. Scriptures log the lives of antediluvians in such a way that 10% of their lives were lived prior to maturation (when the epiphyses seal), and 90% after maturation. This compares with a 25-75% ratio in the present age.

In Genesis (6:4) the record states that "there were giants in the earth in those days." Whether this refers to giant animals or a large race of men is not clear; this writer presumes the former.[27] However it has been posited that cavewall art in New Mexico includes reproductions of dinosaurs, even as cavewall art in France and Spain gives reproductions of bison, mammoths and reindeer. Whichever way it is taken, it does nothing to contradict our proposition that more growth hormone, throughout the animal kingdom, was one feature of that age. Another Genesis statement in a similar category is as follows:

> God created the great sea monsters and every living creature that moves (Genesis 1:20, Amplified).

Although the great sea monsters are not elaborated upon, it is striking to recount how impressive some of the aquatic dinosaurs must have been.

Thus it is believed that in mammals, both acromegaly and regional cretinism were normal for that age, even as gigantism was also normal among birds, fish, reptiles, plant life, and numerous oversized mammals, including ostriches, pigs, pachyderms, rhinoceroses, and many others.

For gigantic animals in that age, a long list can be cited, and it might include such interesting specimens as the agriotherium, the alticamelus, the amphicyon, the baluchitherium, the brontops, the moropus, the syndoceras, the psittachtherium and the teleoceras among others. We do not consider that uniformitarianism

---

[27]Gigantism, related to hyperpituitarism and very likely also to longevity, seems to have been a near-universal phenomenon among mammals in the Antediluvian Age. However, this phenomenon was not limited to mammals; in the animal kingdom it also included birds, fish, insects, reptiles, etc. Furthermore, this phenomenon was not limited merely to the animal kingdom; remains of vegetation such as palm leaf impressions, petrified forests, etc., indicate that this phenomenon was universal in the plant kingdom also.

This study presumes that gigantism was rare if at all existant in homo sapiens in the Antediluvian Age; its alternative, acromegaly, however, was common. Yet this study does not preclude the possibility of giant men in the Antediluvian Age.

Geologist Clifford Burdick so suspects. His appeals are to purported discoveries of giant human tracks in four states. The locations are (1) Texas—the Paluxy River, (2) New Mexico—the White Sands district near Alamagordo, (3) Sonora—the Mayo river, and (4) Arizona—both (a) near Ashfork, and (b) on the Hopi Reservation. These findings are given in the following work: Walter Lammerts et al, *The Challenge of Creation*, Caldwell, Ida.; Bible-Science Assn., 1965, pp. 24-40.

has to explain the manner of the life and the demise of the hundreds of extinct species locked into the fossil record. If they can do an adequate job of explanation on 50 or 75, this should be sufficient.

Concerning the Darwinian proposition, one thing is clear from the fossil record. It is this: the number of species which exist has not increased in number since the Flood Catastrophe, as Darwinians would suppose. Clearly there has been a decline in the number of species which presently inhabit the Earth, compared to the previous age. This observation is merely one of many dozen but this too does nothing to bolster the Darwinian case.

Evolution has already experienced two solid strikes, the first from genetics and the second from astral catastrophism. The second strike is not the final one. It is not claimed that genetics and astral catastrophism, alone, refute the Darwinian mythology. However they do open the way for the third strike which is *Catastrophic Environmental Determinism,* or a comparable term, *Antediluvian Endocrinology.*

4. Catastrophic Environmental Determinism (Antediluvian Endocrinology)

This subject of *Environmental Determinism* becomes quite ironic. This was supposedly Darwin's great stroke. It was his strongest thesis. It was his biochemical mechanism. And it was the first to be disproved and rejected. Now, through *Catastrophic Environmental Determinism (Antediluvian Endocrinology),* understood within the framework of the Greenhouse Effect, this last subtheory of Darwinism rapidly disintegrates. Darwinism indeed is not proven by *Environmental Determinism;* it is disproven by it, when catastrophically cast. If this is true, then the logical conclusion is that the supposedly best part of Darwin's theory was actually the worst part.

This is something like Scipio (Scipio Africanus), who defeated the redoubtable Hannibal with the redoubtable Hannibal's own patented set of tactics, in the Second Punic War between Carthage and Rome. Darwinism has stumbled across its own ladder. It has taken a third strike right down the center, leading across its area of supposed strength.

Thus genetics has rejected two of the Darwinian subtheories:
  (1) Environmental Determinism (Uniformitarianly Cast)
  (2) Natural Selection (Random Inbreeding)

Thus astral catastrophism has rejected two more Darwinian propositions:
  (3) Geological Uniformitarianism
  (4) Survival of the Fittest

And a fifth assumption has been classified as empirical and not scientific:
  (5) Recapitulation

And a sixth assumption has been found to be faulty:
  (6) The Alleged Apemen (Missing Links)

5. The Requirement of a Biochemical Mechanism

There is a seventh subtheory, an elusive one. At the present time it must be considered a negative rather than a positive one. It is the lack of biochemical mechanism. Neither genetics nor endocrinology seem able to supply a mechanism for Darwinism. Astronomy, when viewed from our solar system's catastrophic past, is no help either. And any respectable theory needs a mechanism. Evolution has none, and never has, although it seemingly had one before Lamarckianism became discredited. Why hasn't one been generated (or should we say, evolved)?

Is it because Darwinian proponents have not had sufficient time? Will another 30 or 50 years be required to fill this vacuum? Until something better is brought forward as a biochemical mechanism, Darwinism, like alchemy, must be considered a fact of history, but not a fact of science.

The day may come, perhaps not soon, when advocates of Darwinism will closely re-examine the facts. They will scrupulously sift uniformitarianism. They will perhaps be driven toward one of two conclusions:

  (1) Uniformitarianism and emergence are invalid as principles, or
  (2) Emergence might conceivably occur through and because of primordial catastrophes.

Thus some may very well conclude "evolution by catastrophism."[28] This would be quite a change from the current outlook. The present outlook of the humanistic hierarchy is that catastrophism is a very dangerous principle.

While some may propose the idea of emergence by jumps, through catastrophism, any logic for this idea has yet to be laid down. Over and against this, there is always the principle of Creation. This principle is, in the writer's estimation, the most reasonable. And if man, along with the rest of the animal kingdom, has been created, then the Master Architect has achieved some-

[28]Immanuel Velikovsky, a Freudian catastrophist, has come forward with an interesting and unusual view relative to catastrophism and biological origin. Velikovsky rejects the uniformitarian premise, but he adopts the evolutionary premise, a view which requires considerable explanation. While he rejects Lyellianism, he declares his adherence to a revised form of Darwinism. His revision postulated emergence, not by the slow and gradual process, relied upon by Darwin and modern Darwinians. Rather he posits bursts and jumps, synchronized with catastrophes, and caused by catastrophe-induced mutations by clusters. He makes no endeavor to describe any genetical mechanics; neither does he erect any other defense for this idea.

Velikovsky's view, embracing much of Darwinism while rejecting all of Lyellianism, leaves this reviewer with the impression of incongruity and semi-conformity. His views are set forth in his work, *Earth in Upheaval*, pp. 243-259. His seemingly incongruous view is reminiscent of the compromise of Tycho Brahe.

Tycho, publishing about 50 years after Copernicus, and publishing prior to the age of telescopes, adopted parts of both the Ptolemaic system and the Copernican system. He accepted the Copernican proposition that five planets revolved around the Sun (Mercury, Venus, Mars, Jupiter and Saturn). However he rejected the propositon that the Earth did also, preferring to maintain that the Sun with its five planets revolved around the Earth, as did the Moon. Tycho's views were subsequently adjudged as an unworkable compromise; it must be said in Tycho's favor that in his age prior to telescopes, many of the observations in the Tychonic system and the Copernican system were virtually identical.

Similarly it is felt that Velikovsky's views, coming some 30 years after George McCready Price's, are a compromise between the Creationist-Catastrophist view and the Evolutionary-Uniformitarian view. This reviewer doubts whether Velikovsky's seeming compromise is either consistent or stable; nevertheless to Velikovsky's credit, it must be realized that his view is an advance over the uniformitarian proposition. It is not really distant from the Genesis view of Creation in stages, or serial creation. Velikovsky summarizes as follows:

> The theory of evolution is vindicated by catastrophic events in the earth's past; the proclaimed enemy of this theory proved to be its only ally. The real enemy of the theory of evolution is the teaching of uniformity, or the non-occurrence of any extraordinary events in the past. This teaching . . . almost set the theory apart from reality. (p. 259).

thing more complex than the wonder of our galaxy, or even the stellar universe. And if man is created, then this implies he was created for a purpose, which in turn is suggestive of man's responsibility to his Maker. This is against the very grain of anti-spiritual humanism. Thus there are dilemmas which the humanist needs to face. And one possible way out of this dilemma is to return to a pro-spiritual type of humanism. Concerning this subject, more is discussed in Chapter XII, our final chapter.

Before coming to the closing chapter, there are two more uniformitarian propositions which merit scrutiny. Thus far, uniformitarianism has been discussed relative to

(1) the Earth's hydrography, and the evidences of a global Flood

(2) the Earth's lithography, and the evidences of global mountain uplifts

(3) the Earth's Ice Epoch, and the evidences of cascading celestial ice

(4) the Earth's celestial motifs in literature, as recorded by its ancient peoples

(5) the Earth's primordial climatology, the Greenhouse Effect

(6) the Earth's biology and the evidences of regional and serial Creation

Our next discussion of uniformitarianism will view regions beyond our planet, Earth, even as previous discussions have been mostly centered within the Earth's triple-fluid anatomy. The regions beyond our Earth may be classified in four ways: (1) the zone of the Earth's gravitational domain, including the region of the Moon, (2) the zone of the Sun's gravitational domain, including the region halfway out to the nearer stars, (3) the region of our Milky Way galaxy, with its many diversities, and (4) the universe of galaxies beyond. It is to these celestial regions toward which attention is now turned.

XI chapter

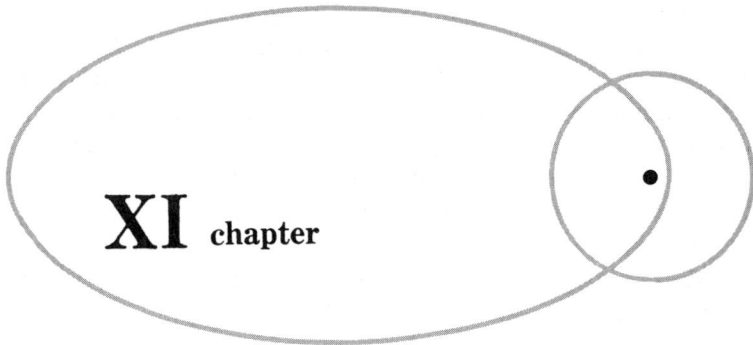

Cosmogony and Uniformitarianism

THE ANCIENTS experienced occasional celestial havoc, and endeavored to understand their situation and their origin in terms which often took fanciful modes, related to such forces as Zeus, Jupiter, Dyaus Pitar, Ra, Marduk and associated pantheistic views.

Science-oriented hypotheses had to await modern knowledge associated with higher mathematics, the telescope and related tools. Modern cosmologies, appealing to science for their basis, have developed only since the era of Newton (circa 1700).

There have been three principal views on the origin of planets. One is that they came from the outer reaches of space. Newton and Whiston held this view, but few followed their thinking. A second view is that a passing star either approached near to, or collided with the Sun, and the debris or solar tidal material became planets. Buffon propounded this. A third view is that before contracting, a nebular sun spun off the material which later coalesced into planets. This third view, a strictly uniformitarian one, was propounded by Immanuel Kant (1724-1804).

Immanuel Kant **A General Theory of the Heavens** (1755)

Kant, as a youth, was educated as a Lutheran Pietist. In his early academic career, he turned sharply away from his religious heritage, and ultimately he became one of the leading skeptics of the modern age. He founded the school of German rationalism, which has given us such figures as Feuerbach, Hegel, Marx (who in turn influenced Lenin), and Nietzsche (who in turn influenced Hitler). The main thrust of Kant's life was in critical philosophy and theology, and he must be recognized as a highly motivated figure.

Even though philosophy was ultimately the main thrust of his life, this was not so in his early teaching and writing career. Originally he concerned himself with such subjects as astronomy, history, mathematics and physical geography. His early academic development was influenced by such diverse persons as Descartes the cosmologist, Leibnitz the mathematician, Newton the astronomer, and Swedenborg, an apparently insane engineer who claimed to have seances with men on Jupiter and other planets and stars. So Kant was motivated to do better, and at the age of 31, he propounded a view of the origin of the solar system, the so-called Nebular Hypothesis. It was set forth in a work entitled *General History of the Nature and Theory of the Heavens.* (1755).

Earlier in our volume, an interesting tendency or trend was noticed relative to the catastrophist, George McCready Price. Price more or less set the style and established the path in which subsequent catastrophists almost invariably followed. Price was a trail-blazer. So it was with Kant also. Kant's influence upon 18th, 19th and 20th century cosmogenists and cosmologists has been profound, since they have invariably accepted his uniformitarian celestial assumption, usually without any questions, more often subconsciously rather than consciously.

In Kant's day, only six planets and nine satellites were known. An explanation for the origin of these fifteen bodies was Kant's objective. Kant suggested that the Sun was once a giant and diffuse nebula, which shrank due to self-gravitation. Most of the material collected into the central star, but some of it did not. The remnants collected on a thin disc which orbited around the Sun. Some of the details of the problems, such as the motion of the planets, the composition of the elements of the planets, the orbits of the planets, and the presence of satellites, were either unexplained, or discussed in a very loose fashion. Nevertheless this view became established, and has held sway in the minds of the academic world for over 200 years.

Kant's conception of our solar system was like a Swiss watch, in which the mainspring was wound up billions of years ago.

He conceived that the solar system was billions of years old, and was billions of years in devolving to its present state *without outside interference.* Thus he had to posit that the planets and the Sun must have had a common physical origin. The solar system was wound up billions of years ago and has been allowed to run unimpeded and *without* interference of any external kind ever since.

Later astronomers reviewed, tested and tried the Kantian hypothesis, and developed some very serious physical problems. Nevertheless early scientists viewed the disc-like rings of Saturn, and appealed to them for proof of the validity of Kant's hypothesis. Here supposedly, was evidence of the principles under which the solar system itself was formed. Here was the process of formation of another satellite for Saturn. And the thin, disc-like rings were considered just another proof that the Sun, at one time in the primordial past, had also possessed a thin, disc-like ring, from which planets were formed.

Simon Laplace **The Nebular Hypothesis** (1796)

Laplace's ideas of the origin of the solar system paralleled Kant's views in most essentials. Laplace, too, postulated that the progenitor of the solar system must have been a vast gaseous fluid which cooled and contracted, leaving behind particles which later condensed into planets. The ideas of Laplace are sufficiently similar to those of Kant to be co-identified as the Kant-Laplace *Nebular Hypothesis.*

> Because his theory lacked computational and observational verification, Laplace placed little confidence in it. Nevertheless, this became the accepted theory of the origin of the solar system for many years.[1]

The Kant-Laplace hypothesis was considered to be scientific fact for the next 100 years, and these were the years during which the ideas of gradualism were developed and refined. Hutton, the early Scottish geologist, applied this principle to geology, as did Lyell. Darwin applied this principle to biology, as did

---

[1]Norman E. Gaut, *Angular Momentum Flux in the Formation of the Solar System,* Cambridge: Massachusetts Institute of Technology, AFCRL-64-167, 1964, p. 8.

Huxley. However, as in the case of Ptolemy's geocentric hypothesis, the Kant-Laplace hypothesis continually became a stumbling block to the interpretation of observed data.

And as it was with the Ptolemaic theory of geocentricity, so it has been with the Kantian hypothesis of heliogenesis (the assumption that the planets were derived from the solar material). In the Ptolemaic theory of geocentricity, every time a planet suddenly reversed its direction in its procession across the sky, another epicycle was added, which explained the immediate problem but did nothing for the total proposition. So it has been with the Kantian theory of heliogenesis.

Every time an astronomer has come forward with a severe question, an answer has been organized, or rigged, which possibly might satisfy the moment, but has made the total proposition ultimately more abstruse. This is why there is a tradition among cosmogenists that any scientist who accepts a cosmogenetical theory in one generation invariably becomes an academic widow in the next. Yet amid this unsatisfying situation in cosmogeny, an underlying assumption, Kantian heliogenesis, continues to be assumed.

George Darwin **The Evolutionary Tidal Theory** (1881)

George Darwin was the second son of Charles Darwin. Although inbred, George Darwin nevertheless achieved high academic standing in the fields of mathematics, physics and astronomy. He specialized in the problems of tides caused by the Sun and Moon, and in this area, he made some valuable contributions to human knowledge.

G. Darwin kept the uniformitarian or gradual perspective of the Kant-Hutton-Lyell-C. Darwin view. But he introduced the subject of solar tides as a possible explanation for the planets. Darwin, in introducing this subject, also revived thought on Buffon's earlier idea of a collision of our Sun with a passing star. G. Darwin proposed that there had been no collision, but had merely been a close approach. This approach caused immense solar tides to be emitted on a disc-like plane.

Darwin proposed that the approaching star caused a tidal extrusion of gaseous material from the Sun. Thus Darwin, like Kant and Laplace, postulated that all of the material in the planets came from the Sun originally, but G. Darwin held it did not occur until after contraction of the Sun to its present approximate size.

He also proposed not only that the Earth came out of material from the Sun, but with evolution in mind, he also proposed that the Moon was borne of the Earth.

George Darwin postulated great solar tides, catastrophic in nature, despite the total lack of evidence of any star ever approaching the Sun. But never once did he mention the possibility of ancient, historic, planet-sized tides involving the Earth and her oceans, so prominent in the catastrophism of Cuvier and so prominent in the Genesis record. George Darwin's hypothesis on the origin of the solar system commanded some stature in cosmology, due in part to his father's fame. George's hypothesis on the origin of the solar system is laden with physical impossibilities. Yet his ideas accurately reflect the predominant thinking on cosmogeny during the latter part of the 19th century and the early 20th century.

The truly immense problems involved in his proposition are reflected in his discussion of the genesis of the Moon, which he claimed was issued out of the Earth even as the Earth was issued out of the Sun. He knew that the Moon was receding from the Earth at a rate of about 5 inches per year. Thereupon he pronounced that it had departed from the Earth, like a baby from its mother, some 4,000,000,000 years ago; the Pacific Basin was left as proof of an abdominal, scar-making departure. Supposedly it has been receding uniformly ever since. The dimensions of problems in this proposal are extreme, Roche's limit being but one.

Thomas Chamberlin and Forest Moulton
The Planetesimal Hypothesis (1902)

Chamberlin, a geologist, came to doubt the concept that the Earth originally was hot gas, which gradually cooled through the molten to the solid state. Chamberlin's review of Ice Epoch phenomena was integral to the reasons why he rejected the Kant-Laplace approach. For instance, Chamberlin showed that if the Earth was white hot and molten, it would not retain gases with molecular weights such as that of water vapor. Chamberlin traced the idea of an Earth, cooling off from a gaseous state, step by step, in terms of molecular motion, and concluded that at each step, the idea was invalid. Thus Chamberlin's approach was dynamically scientific appealing as it did to such principles as the kinetic speed of molecules, dissipating characteristics of gases, centrifugal force and gravitational contraction.

These factors gradually assumed the proportions of over-whelming evidence, and led Chamberlin and Moulton to seek an entirely fresh approach. They too went back to the collision ideas as proposed by Buffon, some 150 years before. They suggested not quite a collision, but a close approach between an intruding star and our Sun, which resulted in violent eruptions and the ejection of solar material which ultimately condensed into small bodies, called planetesimals. These small, cold planetesimals then coalesced into what ultimately became the various planets of the Sun's family.

James Jeans
Problems of Cosmology and Stellar Dynamics (1919)

James Jeans, an English astronomer, later modified the ideas of Chamberlin and Moulton into the idea that a passing star pulled out a filament from the Sun. The filament was thicker at the center than at the extremities, and was cigar-shaped. According to his concept, this helps explain why the larger planets Jupiter, Saturn, Uranus and Neptune, are the more remote.

Harold Jeffreys The Collision Hypothesis (1924)

Jeffreys, along with Jeans, tried several variations of collision, or near-collision (grazing) hypotheses, discarding one in favor of another as new problems were brought to his attention. Jeffreys' idea, going back to Buffon's, proposed that an approaching star actually hit the Sun, not directly but tangentially, a glancing blow, distending the Sun. This, he hoped, might explain the distribution of matter in our solar system. What it actually accomplished was to emphasize the acute problems involved in trying to explain the planets as originating from the Sun.

Among the problems which came to be recognized was that of angular momentum. This problem has come to be considered as the thorniest of the whole group in explaining a theory of the origin of the solar system.

Angular momentum is defined as the product of (1) the

mass of a body, and (2) the velocity of revolution (tangential), and (3) the distance of the body from the center of the Sun. If the body is rotating, the following product is added to the first product: (4) the mass of the body, (5) the average distance of the mass from the axis of rotation, and (6) the average rotational velocity. The sum of these two products (1, 2 and 3 plus 4, 5 and 6) is the angular momentum, and it cannot be changed internally, but only by an outside force.

The distribution of the angular momentum in the inner reaches of our solar system is as follows:

TABLE 8

1.	Jupiter	59.6%
2.	Saturn	24.4%
3.	Neptune	8.2%
4.	Uranus	5.3%
5.	SUN	1.9%
6.	Pluto	.4%
7.	Others	.1%

The question which kept being raised was: How did the planets derive 98% of the angular momentum of the solar system from the Sun's 2%, especially since the Sun possesses 99.85% of all of the mass in our solar system? This problem is not overcome by wishing it away. It called for fresh approaches. Again one is reminded of the problems which kept arising in the Ptolemaic system, when each new and unexplained reversal of the orderly procession of the planets was explained by a new and somewhat arbitrary epicycle.

H. N. Russell The Binary Star Hypothesis (1935)

The binary star hypothesis was first promoted by Russell, and later modified by Lyttleton (1938). Russell desired to avoid the difficulties in the nebular, tidal and collision theories. But he continued to maintain their assumption that the Sun's material was the original material from which the planets were constructed.

He noted that many, indeed at least half of the stars in our galaxy are binary stars. Binary stars are couples or multiples of stars, revolving around each other, but more technically are revolving around a common center in space.

It occurred to Russell that if the Sun was at one time not just a single star but rather a binary, and if a third star approached these two, tidal phenomena could be postulated, but the requirement of angular momentum might also be simultaneously satisfied.

One of the several problems with Russell's idea was that if a third star passed that close to the Sun, why did it not come permanently under the Sun's influence, and become another member of the binary, becoming now a theoretical triple binary. Another problem is to demonstrate how a filament would be pulled out and escape the Sun's gravitational control. A third problem is to demonstrate how such a passing star maintained a hyperbolic orbit, and moved out from beyond our solar system, and then where did it go?

Our nearest star is 4.3 light years away, and gives no evidence of having been in a near collision with the Sun. Neither is there evidence of any other star ever being near the Sun. In fact the chances of such an occurrence can be calculated. The chances are substantially less than 1 in a trillion over a billion year span of time.[2] In fact the chances are fair that such a chance approach has not occurred within our entire galaxy, containing over 100 billion stars, within the last billion years, let alone in our tiny part of the galaxy. Thus there are substantial problems with all theories of the approach of a star.

R. A. Lyttleton
A Variation of the Binary Star Hypothesis (1938)

Lyttleton endeavored to improve on Russell's model. He proposed that the Sun originally had a binary partner, a small companion, which was broken up by a passing third star. The specifics from there become increasingly complicated, partly due to the fact that Lyttleton presented several variations of his original model.[3]

[2]Otto Struve and Velta Zeberges, *Astronomy of the 20th Century,* New York: MacMillan Co., 1962, p. 173.
But the sun, as seen from a distance of 4 light-years, occupies only about 10/16 of the entire sky; the other star, as viewed from the sun, may be regarded as covering an equal angle. Thus the probability of the two objects striking one another after 100,000 years is only 2 x 10/16.

[3]Norman E. Gaut, *op. cit.,* p. 42

These variations of Russell's *Binary Star Hypothesis* did not serve to simplify the problem. Others kept bringing up increasingly severe problems. To cope with some of these, Fred Hoyle suggested in 1944 that the planets were remnants of a former companion to the Sun which exploded as a supernova.

There have been a series of others who have suggested ideas as to the origin of the solar system. While Russell, Lyttleton and others relied on passing stars, which are very difficult to substantiate, appealing to the concepts of Buffon, yet other modern cosmologists have returned to the nebular approach of Kant and Laplace. Gerard Kuiper's hypothesis of *Tidal Stability*, C. F. Von Weiszacker's hypothesis of *Turbulence* and H. Alfven's hypothesis of *Magneto-Hydrodynamic Forces* are examples.

In Chapter X, it was stated that one protein molecule within a cell, or the simplest one-cell animal, is infinitely more complex than our solar system. The simple amino acid molecules contain an extremely complex chain-like architecture with molecular weights ranging from 12,000 to 750,000. DNA and RNA molecules range up to 2,000,000 molecular weight. Explaining the origin of the solar system ought to be much easier to do, and it ought to be achieved sooner than the explanation of the origin of biochemical life even on the simplest level. Observe, however, the great diversity and lack of unanimity which exists among current cosmologists, of which four (Alfven, Hoyle, Kuiper and Von Weiszacker) have been mentioned. There are others, with divergent approaches.

In our chapter on Orogenesis (Chapter V), the near despair of Scheidegger was observed, in reviewing the lack of effectiveness of uniformitarian approaches to orogenesis. Observe, somewhat similarly, the near despair of H. Spencer Jones, and his penetrating review of efforts in cosmogeny.

". . . each new objection raised against any theory of the origin of the solar system has to be overcome by the introduction of some new additional assumption, making the theory in itself less probable."
Appearing to be near total despair, Spencer Jones concluded:
"The solar system must have had an origin; if we cannot account for it except by the introduction of many special and somewhat artificial hypotheses, we shall have to con-

clude that the probability of other stars having systems of planets is very small."[4]

The near total despair of Scheidegger on orogenesis, also held by Hartshorne, is not unlike that which Jones displayed on cosmogeny. Scheidegger was evaluating only theories of orogenesis which have issued out of uniformitarianism. Similarly, Jones has been reviewing theories of cosmology which, at least in the majority of their elements, have issued out of Kant's heliogenetical uniformitarianism. It was demonstrated that Scheidegger's evaluation of orogenetic (mountain-building) theories was commendable, if negative. It was also pointed out that a theory of orogenesis involving astral or celestial catastrophism is badly overdue. Could the same be true of cosmology? It was held, in Chapter V, that the failure to conceive of planetary catastrophism as an explanation for orogenesis hardly was logical. And this failure was related to the current monopoly of uniformitarianism in geological thought. This then, can be classified as one major academic blindspot; it is only one among several.

Six Academic Blindspots

This study has presented a series of academic blindspots, of which six of the more important ones are given below. Each revolves around uniformitarian assumptions.

(1) Disregarding Genesis and Job as history
(2) Disregarding the stratigraphical evidences of a global Flood
(3) Disregarding the indications of astral upheaval as the cause for mountain-building (orogenesis)
(4) Disregarding the indications of celestial havoc for the origin of the Ice Epoch (glaciogenesis)
(5) Disregarding the thrust of genetics, endocrinology and catastrophism in the origin of biochemical life (biogenesis)
(6) Disregarding celestial mechanics as an explanation for ancient folklore and mythology

Of the six points herein listed, they all emanate from the

[4]Struve, op. cit., p. 172-173.

first, which was basic in Kant's uniformitarian celestial (nebular) assumption. Since uniformitarianism was accepted in cosmogeny, it also became accepted in astronomy, in biology, in classical literature, in geology, in history, in paleoclimatology, in theology and in other areas. Thus, uniformitarianism can be termed a "cosmology" since it is a super-philosophy. It has been the essential foundation for anti-spiritual skepticism, and the rationalism which followed in its wake.[5,6]

One may prefer to disregard Genesis and Job as to their spiritual content; this in no way requires that they be rejected

[5]Kant, like Voltaire, Darwin, Marx and others, was interested in aggressively promoting anything which was anti-Genesis and yet sounded scientific. He was the originator of the school of "higher criticism" or skepticism in philosophy and theology in Germany. In this school of skeptical thought, virtually any remarkable or extraordinary narrative in the Bible was challenged, always on scholarly grounds. The skeptics in this school maintained that the Biblical Flood never occurred because rain couldn't have accomplished such an event, and because planetary catastrophes were unthinkable. This same school of thought maintained that the walls of Jericho couldn't have fallen in front of Joshua's armies, even though it was subsequently realized that Jericho is in the middle of the Great Rift Valley, a zone of crustal instability. In spite of such cosmological stories as the Phaethon story from Egypt and numerous corresponding stories in other ancient sources, they maintained that the normal procession of the Sun and Moon across the sky could not have been interrupted because uniformitarian cosmology had no room for such a possibility. This school of skepticism also has told us, in the name of scholardom, that Ecclesiastes must have been written after 100 B.C., although Dead Sea scrolls have been subsequently discovered, antedating 150 B.C., at which time Ecclesiastes had long been in the canon of scripture. Similarly this school of skepticism maintained that the Book of Daniel must have been written about 150 B.C. because of the high accuracy of the prophecies contained therein, and not even Nostradamus was that good. Thus Kant's school of "higher criticism," in constantly appealing to 'intellectualism' and 'scholardom', has successfully perverted scholardom for the purpose of undermining the history of, and the merit in the Judeo-Christian heritage.

[6]Rationalists, in their almost overeager desire to discredit the scriptural record, have made academic assaults upon the assemblage of the scriptures along two fronts, the historical front and the scientific front. Their assault, which has frequently been on the assemblage of Scripture in general, nevertheless has been on the book of Genesis in particular, the book of beginnings or origins.

In founding the school of "higher" criticism, Kant did something more than merely formulate the intricate and systematic anti-spiritual view. With his critiques, he did propose a seemingly impressive proposition. But with the school of "higher" criticism, he joined his intellectual program with an intellectual organization to implement that program. And in so doing, he became a figure of truly major import in the historical phase of this assault upon the Judeo-Christian scriptures.

The fact that archaelogists have frequently verified scriptural history, even in minute details, has blunted this historical assault of the "higher" critics from time to time, but it has by no means brought it to a halt or

for their historical content. Yet this is what has been done, and it illustrates a system of fuzzy thinking engaged in by those who describe themselves as "rationalists." This brings to mind a famous statement by our late President, Mr. Kennedy, on myths.

> For the greatest enemy of truth is very often not the lie— deliberate, contrived and dishonest—but the myth, persistent, persuasive and unrealistic. (Yale University, June 11, 1962.)

These six academic blindspots, hardly credible, hardly logical, but so persistent, begin to merge into a syndrome. Medically, a syndrome is a group of concurrent symptoms of a disease or disorder. This syndrome suggests the rejection of the Judeo-Christian heritage by the academic world may be the basis for uniformitarianism. Whether or not the spiritual rejection of Genesis is justified is a matter for each person to make his own conclusions. However, the rejection of history, especially such basic history relative to an understanding of the past of our planet, is not justifiable. Therefore, this rejection must be rejected.

Rousas J. Rushdoony, in a book on education, discussed the habit of modern society to exhibit academic blindspots.[7] He entitled his volume, with appropriateness, *Intellectual Schizophrenia*. Schizophrenia is a loss of contact with reality of one sort or another, but in the case under discussion, we are only considering a loss of contact with historical reality. If catastrophism and Creationism are facts, as the evidence strongly suggests, then the modern intellectual world is schizophrenic, and the case is not

---

put it on the defensive.

However in organizing the Kant-Laplace nebular hypothesis, and the cosmological uniformitarianism contained therein, Kant also became a leading figure in the scientific phase of this attack. The fact that Kant's uniformitarianism may be pseudo-scientific and not genuinely scientific has not even blunted, much less halted the assaults on this front. His uniformitarianism, supposedly scientific, was seized upon and promoted with extreme success, first by Lyell, then by Darwin, and then by many others.

Very few figures in modern history have been bi-professional, as were Benjamin Franklin, Leonardo da Vinci or Theodore Roosevelt. However Kant achieved the unique position of being bi-influential, a major figure in both the philosophies of history and of science. No other figure in the modern age, to the knowledge of this writer, has achieved a dual influence to such a marked degree. Each fact separately would be noteworthy; taken together in one person, this duality is remarkable to say the least.

[7]Rousas J. Rushdoony, *Intellectual Schizophrenia* (Culture, Crisis and Education), Nutley, N.J.: Presbyterian & Reformed Publishing Co., 1961.

a mild one. Uniformitarianism is taught to the near total exclusion of catastrophism and Creationism in 99% of the college classrooms of Western Civilization, and it prevails to the total exclusion of catastrophism and Creationism in Russia and China.

Six academic blindspots have been reviewed, but this basic list is not complete. There are at least two more, and both are related to Kant's and Laplace's uniformitarian assumptions in cosmology.

Our seventh academic blindspot is the blithe hypothesizing of historical solar tides with a complete lack of substantiating evidence. This lack is coupled with the failure to acknowledge the overwhelming evidence for historical, geophysical Earthian tides of enormous magnitude, both in the oceans and in the oceans of magma within the Earth's crust.

Academic Blindspot 7—Planetary Tides and Solar Tides

A review of the important theories of the origin of the solar system has been given. They include theories by Kant, Laplace, G. Darwin, Chamberlin and Moulton, Jeans, Jeffreys, Russell, Lyttleton, and mention was made of several more recent cosmologists, including Alfven, Hoyle, Kuiper and Von Weiszacker. These theories all assume (with the exception of Hoyle) that the matter which now comprises the planets once was part of the Sun, or its primordial nebula. This is an assumption which shall shortly be questioned on several grounds.

Notice how many of these theories suggest that another star approached our Sun. Some posit a direct collision. Some posit a grazing collision. Some posit a near approach to the range of Mercury's orbit. Some posit a near approach to the range of Saturn's orbit. Some posit a hypothetical binary partner for our Sun. Some posit a third hypothetical solar visitor.

Some posit that the gaseous material of the Sun was pulled out in a disc-like swirl. Some posit that it was pulled out in a filament. Some posit that it was pulled out by solar eruptions. Some posit that it originally condensed from a thinner nebula in the present locations. The Sun is composed mostly of hydrogen, with some helium. Are the planets composed similarly?

Our Sun is located toward the rim of our galaxy, which is shaped something like the elusive Flying Saucer. It is in a fairly remote section of the Milky Way. The nearest star is Alpha Centauri, some 4.3 light years away (26 trillion miles), observable in the Southern Hemisphere. In the Northern Hemisphere, one of the nearest stars is the giant binary, Sirius A and B, some eight light years away. If a solar body passed near our Sun, where is the evidence of it? What receding star might it be?

The chances of any two stars in our galaxy colliding or nearly colliding with each other is remote during a period of a billion years. And the stellar population in our galaxy is much more dense in the more central regions than in the more remote regions, where the Sun is located. To postulate that another star approached our Sun is perhaps not impossible, but it is stretching the limits of credibility.

> Since our galaxy contains roughly 2×10^{11} stars, perhaps only one or two collisions have occurred during the past 5 billion years . . . If the Sun had been one of the partners in such an encounter, our solar system would be practically unique. However, evidence from other solar-type stars indicates that planetary systems are common in space. *Collision theories, therefore, should be discarded.*[8]

Despite the extreme improbability, and despite the total lack of supporting evidences of solar tides, this approach has been common as an operational hypothesis.[9] One good reason why so many have endeavored to set forth newer theories on the origin of the solar system is because the others have been so problematical.

Cosmologists have consistently suggested ideas of solar catastrophes and solar tides, for which evidence is not only feeble, but in fact is non-existent. At the same time, cosmologists have consistently been closed to ideas of historical Earth tides and Earth catastrophes, for which the evidence becomes increasingly overwhelming. Do we have here an academic blindspot? The evidence is sufficiently consistent and strong, that here occurs a seventh symptom in the uniformitarian syndrome previously mentioned.

[8]Struve, *op. cit.*, p. 173

[9]W. M. Smart, *The Origin of the Earth,* Baltimore: Penguin Books, 1949, p. 200. It must be concluded that, despite its ingenuity, the binary hypothesis in the form stated above and in its subsequent modifications is no nearer a tolerably satisfactory solution of the origin of the planetary system than its predecessors.

Academic Blindspot 8—Heliogenesis

Ptolemy's Geocentricity
Copernicus' Heliocentricity
Kant's Heliogenesis

Ptolemy's conclusions, something of a consensus of ancient thought, was codified in his *Almagest*. Ptolemy had adopted in bulk the astronomical views of Hipparchus (circa 150 B.C.-100 B.C.). He agreed with Hipparchus that the Sun and the planets, like the Moon, revolved around the Earth, which was so central to the viewpoint of man. Copernicus, in his studies on revolutionary movements, and without the aid of a telescope, developed the conclusion that the Earth and the planets revolved around the Sun and only the Moon revolved around the Earth. Ptolemy's view was geocentric. Copernicus' view was heliocentric. The reaction against the Copernican view was great. In some cathedrals of medieval learning, where those installed at the time of Copernicus assumed they already possessed a near monopoly on truth, this became a rather painful situation in the long run.

A reaction to Ptolemy's geocentricity was in order; however, it is maintained, the reaction developed into an overreaction. It is something like a pendulum of a grandfather clock, which swings from one extreme through center to another extreme.

Subtly, usually subconsciously, and without even stating the details of the assumption, the post-Newton cosmologists, beginning with Kant, appealing to heliocentricity, assumed that the planets not only revolved around the Sun; they also originated from the solar material. This assumption, usually tacit rather than explicit, is *heliogenesis*. It is something quite different in order and in kind than the heliocentricity of Copernicus. For instance, in a family organization, all of the children who orbit around parental authority were physically generated from the parents. However, in a business organization, all of the employees orbit around the manager, but usually none of them are generically derived from him. They are adopted into the business family. This illustration is given to demonstrate why heliocentricity need not require heliogenesis. But such a tacit transition has occurred in modern cosmology. Kant blazed the way for this erroneous path, and most cosmologists are still making the same assumption. Why do we need to assume that the planetary material originated generically from the Sun, as even such great modern astronomers and astrophysicists as Alfven, Kuiper and Von Weizsacker still assume? The problems associated with this assumption are immense.

Planetary Elements from the Sun?

We do not know the composition by elements of the various planets, although some general estimates have been made. However, the composition of the Earth is known. It contains several dozen elements in trace amounts. The following fifteen elements are estimated to comprise in bulk the composition of the Earth's crust.

TABLE 9

Oxygen	46.60%	Titanium	.44%
Silicon	27.72	Hydrogen	.14
Aluminum	8.13	Phosphorus	.12
Iron	5.00	Manganese	.10
Calcium	3.63	Sulphur	.05
Sodium	2.83	Carbon	.03
Potassium	2.59	Chlorine	.03
Magnesium	2.09	All others	.50

The Earth's magma is considered to be composed similarly to the Earth's crust. The Earth's oceans are composed primarily of oxygen, hydrogen, chlorine, sodium, and trace salts. The Earth's oceans comprise less than 1/30,000 of the Earth's mass and the atmosphere less than 1/1,000,000 of the Earth's mass.

Is the composition of the Sun or the other planets similar to the Earth? If the presence of most of the Earth's elements has been identified in the Sun in trace amounts, does this indicate that the Earth's material came from the Sun? The density of the small Earth, 5.52 (water=1) is the densest of all the planets. Saturn, with its far greater gravity, has a density of but .071, and the Sun, with its immense gravity, has a density of but 1.41. The composition of the Sun is quite different from that of the Earth, the Moon, Callisto, Neptune and other members of the solar system. The composition of the Sun is indicated from the following source:

> The first extensive investigation of the solar spectrum was carried out by Russell in 1929. His most important result was the establishment of the fact that abundance of

hydrogen is much greater than had been thought possible.
Russell . . . concluded that, the solar atmosphere contains
60 parts of hydrogen (by volume), 2 of helium, 2 of oxygen, 1 of metallic vapors, and 0.8 of free electrons practically all of which comes from the ionization of metals. [10]

One problem in the assumption of heliogenesis is to explain
how the earth-abundant materials are derived from the Sun.
A second problem arises in comparing the other densities of the
various planets, ranging from the heaviest (Earth, 5.52) to the
lightest (Saturn, 0.71), each issuing variously from the Sun
(1.41).

Angular Momentum from the Sun?

Any hypothesis which considers the Sun to be the source
of the planetary material must necessarily cope with the principle of motion, and must ascribe or attribute, somehow, the momentum of the planets to the Sun. It has already been demonstrated that the Sun comprises 99.8% of the mass of the solar
system, and yet it contains less than 2% of the angular momentum.

It is the problem of angular momentum, more than any
other single problem, which led cosmologists of the early 20th
century to discard Kant's gradualistic nebular approach for Buffon's collision or near collision approach. Yet other problems,
equally severe to the collision approach have been raised.

George Darwin introduced the idea of solar tides and a near
approach to the Sun to avoid some of the problems in the Kant-
Laplace idea. Chamberlin and Moulton introduced the idea of
erupting ejections to improve on the previous ideas. Jeffreys,
revising earlier ideas, tried to account for angular momentum
by a grazing collision rather than a close approach. Jeans, Russell, Lyttleton, and others have wrestled with the ever-increasing
number of problems which have emerged from either of assumptions of nebular origin or collision or near-collision approaches
to the Sun. Perhaps it is these assumptions which need re-examination, and not the particular details of this heliogenetical
hypothesis over and against that heliogenetical hypothesis.

[10]Struve, *op. cit.*, p. 228

Ellipical Orbits from the Sun's Rotation?

In Table 1, Chapter III, page 36, the eccentricities of the 9 planets were given, along with such remarkable examples as Hidalgo (an asteroid) and Pluto's Nereid. The eccentricities of the planets are quite diverse. They range from the extremes of Mercury (.206) and Pluto (.249) down to Neptune (.009) and Venus (.007). Here again, as in the case of angular momentum, and as in the case of planet densities, diversity rather than similarity is a fact. And this leads toward the suspicion that diversity rather than similarity is a principle in understanding the origin of the planets.

The two planets with the least eccentricity are Venus, second from the Sun, and Neptune (at present second from the outermost, but soon to become the outermost). The two planets with the greatest eccentricity are Mercury, the innermost, and Pluto, the outermost (but soon to become the second from the outermost). The eccentricity of Venus is 1/12th that of Mars, while the eccentricity of the Earth is but 1/5th that of Mars. Why?

Any heliogenetical explanation of the eccentricities of planetary orbits must also account for the eccentricities, and origins, of the satellite systems. Why is the orbit of our Moon 5 times as eccentric as the orbit of the Earth? Why is the orbit of Nereid 83 times as eccentric as the orbit of its home planet, Neptune?

The Angle of the Axis of the Various Planets and the Sun?

The non-uniformity of the eccentricities of the planetary orbits may be one significant variable. Another is the non-uniformity of the planetary plane with the Sun's equator, and the Sun's axis. If the Sun spun out the planetary materials at an ancient date, it would be reasonable to conclude that they were spun out parallel to the Sun's equator, and perpendicular to its rotational axis. But this also is not the case. The disc-like plane of the planets is oriented. But its orientation is not to the Sun's axis. Rather it is to the Sun's galactic orbit. The plane of the planets almost coincides with the galactic plane, another anomaly in any heliogenetical proposition, especially when coupled with the difference of this plane and the Sun's rotational axis. Following is the inclination of the axis of the Sun and the several planetary orbits.

TABLE 10

INCLINATION OF EQUATORS TO ORBITS

Sun	7° 10′
Mercury	no axis
Venus	?
Earth	23° 27′
Mars	24°
Jupiter	3° 7′
Saturn	26° 45′
URANUS	98°
Neptune	29°
Pluto	?

According to the heliogenetical viewpoint, it is merely a coincidence that the Earth's axis is 23° 27′. Further, it is merely a coincidence that the axis of Mars is about ⅔° greater. And it is merely a coincidence that the Earth's period of rotation is 24 days, and the period of Mars' rotation is 41 minutes greater. While these facts may be coincidences, they may also not be coincidences. Concerning Mars, further data is to be given in Chapter XII where further "coincidences" may be correlated. However, for the moment, this observation of these twin coincidences of the angle of the axis and the rotational period of these two planets should be kept in mind. Neither conform to the Sun's axis, 7°, nor to the Sun's rotation, 24.7 days.

Another problem implicit in any uniformitarian proposition is the problem of the retrograde rotation of Uranus. Most of the planets revolve in direct motion, and their axis varies between 3° (Jupiter) and 29° (Neptune). However, the axis of Uranus is 98°, and it nearly points directly toward the orbital plane, whereas the axis of the other planets is somewhat perpendicular to the orbital plane. Further preliminary information about Venus is indicative that it, too, revolves in retrograde motion. Why? Why is there such a vast amount of non-conformity in a theory which idolizes uniformity, and indeed takes its name from the word "uniform"?[11]

---

[11]John C. Whitcomb Jr., *"The Origin of the Solar System,"* Philadelphia, Presbyterian and Reformed Publishing Co., 1964, pp. 16-17.

A Passing Star?

It has already been discussed that the chances of a collision among any of the stars of our galaxy, within the next billion years, is remote. And chance collisions, if any, will more likely occur in the more densely populated regions of our galaxy, as contrasted with the more remote regions where our Sun is located. This possibility, regarding our particular star, the Sun, is so remote as to be unacceptable, considering the associated lack of other supporting evidence.

Action and Reaction?

The reaction was not limited to the observable conclusions regarding heliocentricity, as posited by Copernicus, and as defended by Galileo and Kepler. The reaction included an overreaction by Kant to the extent that the Sun was not only the center of the planetary movements; it was also the mother of the planets. Kant, like his later uniformitarian disciple, Darwin, was not only interested in ideas which sounded scientific, but was particularly interested in promoting or conceiving ideas which were simultaneously anti-Genesis. Thus part of the reaction to the Ptolemaic system was on scientific grounds, but part of it was on other grounds.

The Judeo-Christian heritage had been identified with the Ptolemaic system, although both Ptolemy and his antecedent, Hipparchus, were neither Jews nor Christians. The Judeo-Christian heritage was identified in part with the Ptolemaic system because of the disposition of the monolithic ecclesiastical system of the medieval age, which had adopted Ptolemy along with Aristotle, Moses, Paul and Peter, and endeavored to defend them all. But obviously this cannot account for the depth or breadth of the reaction.

The propagation of the Judeo-Christian heritage includes such principles as the opposing dualities of (1) the flesh against the spirit, (2) holiness against unholiness, (3) morality against immorality, (4) salvation against condemnation, and (5) the temporal against the eternal.

These principles, whether held correctly or incorrectly, are hard, harsh and abrasive on the "nature of the flesh." Thus we find reaction against this particular ethic, wherever it is propagated. It is of interest to note that in the modern world this ethic was propagated particularly effectively in Germany and England. And it was particularly in Germany, with such figures as Kant, Hegel, Goethe, Nietzsche, Schopenhauer and others, and in Great Britain, with such figures as Blount, Hume, Mill, Darwin and the immigrant Marx that reactions to the Judeo-Christian ethic was most pronounced.[12] This geographical similarity is hardly coincidental.

For these reasons, it is held, the reaction to the Ptolemaic logic was not the only factor in the reaction from geocentricity, through Copernicus' heliocentricity, to the improbable but scientific-sounding view of heliogenesis, as propounded by Kant.

Rejecting the Kantian principle of (1) heliogenesis, an over-reaction of heliocentricity, is in order. Rejecting the parallel principle of Kant, (2) uniformitarianism, is also in order. But rejecting a principle without viewing a superior alternative is not constructive. Therefore what is needed is a newer approach, with more substantive supporting data, to the problem of origin of the solar system. Toward this end, the thinking of Professor J. H. Oort of Leyden, Netherlands, is of value.

Oort has made a study in depth of comet phenomena. He found that the Comet Delavan moved not in a hyperbolic orbit as had been formerly assumed, but rather it moved in an extremely long but closed elliptical orbit. Its major (elongated) axis was found to be some 15 to 16 trillion miles (170,000 a.u.). But it is a regular, periodic member of our solar system, similar to Earth, Hidalgo or Jupiter. However its period is somewhat

---

[12]The reaction against the Biblical ethic is lamented by some and urged by others; however, regardless of the personal preference, its presence may well be a sign of cultural health and dynamism. Weyl and Possony, in their volume *Geography of the Intellect* (Chicago, Henry Regnery, 1963), consider that this contradiction within society is the "stuff" from which a culture's dynamism is derived. They proceed to analyze the people listed in *Who's Who*, and conclude that there is a particularly high proportion of Dutch, Jews and Scotch, all people of "the book," and people seemingly with an extraordinary amount of initiative and motivation. They hold that this is indicative of the distribution of dynamic initiative within Western civilization, and correlate both to (1) the propagation of the Biblical ethic, a highly spiritual ethic, and (2) the reaction to that ethic in its various forms.

It is observed that both Pietist Germany and Puritan England, where the Biblical ethic has been most vigorously propagated in recent centuries, are also the two locations where the most vigorous reaction to it has occurred. And these same two regions have been the ones which assumed the lead in the dynamic development of Western Civilization.

longer. It will return to perihelion (its closest approach to the Sun) in about 24,000,000 years. Oort found the Comet Morehouse had a significantly shorter period than the Comet Delavan. It had a period of only 500,000 years.

The Comet Delavan, with an orbit some 15 trillion miles in axial length, extends out well beyond half the distance to the nearest known star system, the Alpha Centauri triple binary. This means that comets verge on being intergalactic.

Oort proceeded with studies on comets. Over one thousand comets are recorded. The orbits of half are known with some degree of precision. Some are constantly being discovered. Some are perturbed into either shorter or longer orbits as they are influenced by the planets. No one knows how many comets reside in the vast regions beyond Pluto. They may exceed one billion in number. Oort proposes that the true number of periodic comets, regular members of our solar system, may well be numbered in excess of 100 billion. Only a few of them approach within 100 million miles of the Sun, where they might, by chance, be illuminated sufficiently to be detected by man's astronomical hardware. Thus, Oort proposes, there is a comet cloud in the regions between the nearer stars. And this comet cloud, or comet reservoir, includes comets of many different eccentricities, many different perihelions (distances of approach to the Sun), many different angles to the ecliptic, and many different masses.

What Oort has accomplished has been to reorganize our understanding of the extent of our Sun's solar system, and its influence. When Saturn was the outermost known planet, during the days of Kant, Newton and Whiston, it was conceived that the solar system extended out for one billion miles. Then Uranus, Neptune and Pluto were discovered. The recognized limits of our solar system were extended to 3 or 4 billion miles. This is the effective limit of our telescopes.

In Oort's approach, the effective limit of our solar system appears to be some 15 trillion miles, and possibly more. This is the zone of the Sun's gravitational dominance. Of the large number of comets which Oort estimates to be periodical to our solar system (and can be considered as bona fide regular members), he believes that less than one in a million have been identified.

Most do not approach even as close as Pluto, some 4 billion miles distant. Only a very small proportion approach the closer-in planets, where they may by chance be perturbed into shorter orbits, and become classified as cometary members of a planetary family.

It is established that there are only nine planets (ten counting the former Electra), within the inner 4 billion miles of our solar system. But could there be thousands, possibly even hundreds of thousands more out beyond the region where our astronomical hardware can detect them? There is no reason to eliminate this possibility, and there are some reasons to maintain it.

Could it be that a planet-sized body zoomed in from this region in a markedly elliptical orbit, approached Electra, an inner planet, and caused an historical fragmentation? Could it be that smaller, asteroid-sized bodies have periodically swept through the inner parts of the solar system? Could this viewpoint assist in explaining the approach of an icy visitor near Saturn, which fragmentized into disc-like icy rings? And what about the curious Nereid, or Pluto?

Many think Pluto was once a satellite of Neptune. Kuiper thinks it may have formerly been a satellite of Jupiter. Forward made the following observation:

> Apparently Pluto is a stranger which arrived in its present orbit from the regions of space. One suggestion is that it was once a moon of Neptune. There is obviously something wrong out past Uranus. It is as if Pluto had come along, interacted with Neptune, and pushed it into an inner orbit. We actually know very little about Pluto, but it is imperative that we learn more.[13]

We can presume that celestial bodies, on historical occasions, have orbited in an elliptical fashion, into the regions of the inner planets. This helps to understand the origin of the rings of Saturn, the craters of our Moon, and also the principle of Earth catastrophism. This principle undergirds our view of *The Biblical Flood and the Ice Epoch*.

Immediately it should be noticed that we, along with Oort, are back to the cosmological assumptions of Halley, Newton, and Whiston. They assumed elliptical orbits were possible for celes-

---

[13]Robert L. Forward, "Pluto, Last Stop Before the Stars," *Science Digest*, August 1962, p. 73.

tial bodies, large and small, beyond the remotest planet. Whiston, the early leader in this concept, has been forgotten. Meanwhile, the views of Kant (heliogenetical and uniformitarian) and Buffon (solar collisions and near solar collisions) gained numerous adherents. The approach of Whiston, over and against those of Buffon or Kant, is recommended for the reader's consideration. The parallel thinking of Oort is similarly recommended.

The Jovian Planets

TABLE 11

THE JOVIAN PLANETS

Characteristic	Jupiter	Saturn	Uranus	Neptune	Average
Eccentricity of Orbit	.048	.056	.047	.009	.040
Number of Satellites	12	9	5	2	7
Mass (Earth=1)	318.3	95.3	14.5	17.2	111.3
Diameter (Miles)	86900	71500	29500	26800	53675
Density (Water=1)	1.35	0.71	1.56	2.47	1.52
Distance From Sun (⁶)	483	886	1783	2791	1486
Rotation (in Hours)	9.86	10.03	10.75	15.80	11.66
Albedo (Reflectivity)	.51	.50	.66	.62	.57

TABLE 12

THE TERRESTRIAL PLANETS

Characteristic	Mercury	Venus	Earth	Mars	Pluto	Average
Eccentricity of Orbit	.206	.007	.017	.093	.249	.114
Number of Satellites	0	0	1	2	0	.6
Mass (Earth=1)	.054	.813	1.0	.107	.033?	.401
Diameter (Miles)	3010	7610	7927	4140	3600?	5206
Density (Water=1)	5.45	5.06	5.52	4.12	2.???	4.43
Distance From Sun (⁶)	36	67	93	141	3671	801
Rotation (in Hours)	2112	720?	24	24.6	150?	606
Albedo (Reflectivity)	.06	.76	.39	.15	.16	.30

What is the origin of the various members of our solar system? Firstly, there are two general classes of planets. There are the Jovian planets, which include the ones which are large, low in density, and rapidly rotating. These include Jupiter, Saturn, Uranus and Neptune. The other group is the terrestrial planets, which are small, relatively dense, and mostly slow in speed of rotation. The terrestrial planets are also mostly the closer-in ones, with one exception. The terrestrial planets include Mercury, Venus, Earth, Mars and Pluto. Of these, the Earth is the largest, the densest, and by virtue of its particular location, is the only one capable of maintaining life as we know it.

The differences between the terrestrial group and the Jovian group are consistent. The Jovian group, when compared to the terrestrial group, are huge, and are spinning very rapidly. They are also relatively low in density. The terrestrial planets on the average are about three times as dense as the larger planets. The differences in the composition between the terrestrial planets and the Jovian planets is significant; further, the differences in the composition between the Jovian planets and their respective satellites may also be significant.

The Earth is composed of large proportions of oxygen, silicon, aluminum, iron and calcium, plus smaller amounts of carbon, hydrogen and nitrogen. The Jovian satellites are composed mostly of various ices, primarily water ice, plus some rock. However, the Jovian planets are composed mostly of hydrogen and/or helium, plus lesser amounts of carbon, nitrogen, oxygen, and (particularly with Uranus and Neptune) possible rock cores.

Diversity seems to be a principle rather than uniformity between the planets as well as various Jovian satellites. This same principle, incidentally, holds for the Earth and its satellite, both of which are composed primarily of rock. The Earth's density is 5.45 that of water; the Moon's is 3.3.

The terrestrial planets, mostly rock, are poor reflectors, with the exception of Venus and its canopy, and the Earth with its reflective oceans. The Jovian planets, with their methane and ammonia atmospheres, are good reflectors. The Jovian planets rotate with a general uniformity. The rates of rotation for these immense planets vary from 9 hours, 50 minutes through 15 hours, 48 minutes.

Based on similarity in masses, diameters, densities, rotational velocities, compositions, orbital eccentricities, reflectivities (albedos), and distance from the Sun, it is suspected that each of these four Jovian planets may have a common origin quite different from the origins of the various terrestrial planets. At this juncture, this discussion shall reach out beyond our solar system for possible clues as to the origin of these four large, icy, major planets in our solar system.

Stars in the Milky Way

The Milky Way is shaped something like the elusive flying saucer. The Sun is located toward the rim. Our galaxy is one of several billion galaxies and our galaxy may contain as many as 100 billion bright stars together with an undetermined number of dark stars and lesser planet-sized material. Our galaxy is rotating around its center, and faster at the center than the rim, where our Sun is located. Our galaxy is traveling at a rather high velocity through the universe.

One fact about the stars in our galaxy is that there is a great diversity among them. There are many kinds of stars, possessing many characteristics. In terms of diameter, some are as small as small planets, while others are huge in comparison to our Sun. The largest stars have a diameter over 1 billion times that of the smaller stars. Some stars are extremely bright, while others have either a low luminosity, or are completely dark.

Some stars are fairly small in diameter but are unbelievably dense. Sirius, a close neighbor to our Sun, is a double-star system. It was originally believed to be a very bright, hot and large star (Sirius means "The Scorcher" in Greek). But wobbles were observed in its movement, which could only be accounted for by another near star, which was not apparent.

Sirius' partner formerly was considered to be a dark star, but this dark partner has subsequently been recognized; it has a low luminosity. It is a white dwarf. Sirius A, the bright and large one, is sometimes called the Dog, while the small and dim one, Sirius B, is sometimes called the Pup. The Pup is considered to be 27,000 times as dense as the Sun, or about 40,000 times as dense as water. One quart of the Pup weighs about 80,000 lbs., or 40 tons. Some stars are many times denser than the Pup.

Stars also vary in brightness, distance, composition, motion, temperature, pulsation, and in other ways. Surface temperatures of some dark stars are very frosty, whereas on other stars, surface temperatures may approach 100,000°F. The diversity among stars, even within our small galaxy, is enormous.

Particular attention is turned toward one particular feature about stars. Many stars occur in groups, and inter-revolve. Such stars which revolve in pairs or groups are called binary stars. It is estimated that at least half of the stars in the nearer part of our galaxy are binaries.

Furthermore, many of the binaries are not merely double-star systems, but are multiple-star systems, containing three or more which are revolving around a common center. Our nearest stellar neighbor, the Alpha Centauri group, is a triple system. It contains two main stars, which are revolving around a common center in space. A third remote companion of this set is Proxima Centauri, which revolves around the common center of the other two at a distance of about one trillion miles. Proxima Centauri is about 25 trillion miles distant from our Sun. Its period around the inner Alpha Centauri pair may be millions of years. [14]

Also of interest is the multiple system, Zeta Cancri. It contains two pairs of stars. One pair revolves around a common center every 17.5 years. The other pair revolves around a common center every 59.7 years. Each pair together revolves around a common center once every 1150 years. The entire group then revolves around our galaxy, which in turn revolves around the universe. Another double-double (quadruple) system of stars is Epsilon Lyrae.

The Castor system is known to include six stars, including three separate pairs. Each pair revolves around a common center. Two pairs revolve fairly close together around a common center, and the third remote pair revolves around the center of the other four.

Of the 30 stars nearest our Sun, 13 are known to be multiples, containing at least 29 component stars. Thus binary stars are not only common, but are common among our Sun's closest neighbors. In some systems, one partner is dark. In some systems, neither partner is dark. And it must be suspected that in some systems, both partners are dark, and hence are undetected and undiscovered.

In some binaries one star is much denser than the other. In some binaries one star is much larger in diameter than the other.

---

[14]Centaur takes its name from the Centaurus in Greek mythology. The particular Centaur with whom the constellation is identified is Chiron, the greatest of the Centaurs. Chiron was skilled in many arts and was appointed teacher to many of the lesser gods and heroes of Greek mythology. He was killed by Hercules in an accident, and was accorded a memorial by being placed among the stars as a constellation. (James S. Pickering, *1001 Questions Answered About Astronomy*, New York: Dodd, Mead & Co., 1959, p. 215). Observe how parallel are the stories of the Greek Electra, the Greek Centauri, the Hindu Rahu, the Japanese Sosa no wo no Mikoto. the Aztec Quetzalcoatl, and other similar celestial motifs from ancient times.

In some binaries, one star is much hotter than the other. In some binaries, spectrographic analysis indicates that the components are dissimilar. In some binaries, the period of rotation is measured in hours, while with others, it is measured in millions of years. Diversity is a general rule; this leads to a major suspicion.

Galactogenetical Hypothesis

If a small, spherical, planetary-sized body became involved in a two-star binary system, it would revolve differently than does either a comet or a planet around our Sun. If the body had a highly eccentric orbit, it would revolve in two different manners: (1) At remote distances, it would revolve with one of the foci being the center of gravity between the two star partners, a point containing nothing. (2) But at nearer distances, in its pattern of orbiting around the inner turn point, it would be perturbed by first one star partner, and then perhaps also the second. Its orbit would be changed. The change in the orbit would be either to (a) a closed orbit of reduced major axis, (b) a closed orbit of greater major axis, or (c) an unclosed hyperbolic orbit. In being wrapped up within the interacting and counter-dominating gravity of the two partners, many kinds of new orbits would occur in various approaches.

Under such circumstances, hyperbolic orbits would be produced occasionally. If hyperbolic orbits are produced by binaries, they may be produced by the binary star systems which are neighbors to our Sun, including the Alpha Centauri triple binary, the Sirius pair, and the pair known as Barnard's Star. Then, we posit, Oort's view of comets, and his comet-cloud hypothesis may be understated. He thought that the origin of the Sun's comets was the zone halfway between the nearer stars. Rather, it may be the nearer binary stars themselves, and their interacting gravities.

The Sun travels across our Milky Way galaxy at a galactic speed of about 12 miles per second, in the direction of the constellation Hercules. This is in addition to the speed of the Milky Way, which is about 170 miles per second. However, Barnard's star, the Sun's second closest neighbor, has a galactic speed of 300 miles per second, in addition to the speed of the entire Milky Way galaxy. Barnard's Star is a binary in which only one member is luminous, which shows that non-luminous bodies in our galaxy can travel at high velocities relative to our Sun's galactic speed.

> We have already said that there is no reason why solar systems should not be common phenomena, and these revelations of 61 Cygni and 70 Ophiuchi give food for thought.... In April 1963 Dr. van de Kamp, director of the Sproul Observatory, announced the discovery of a third extra-solar planetary system. From a study of photographs taken of Barnard's Star, which is a mere 6 light years away, he inferred the existence of a planet 1½ times the mass of Jupiter, revolving at a distance of about 400,000,000 miles.[15]

There are many binary systems in our galaxy, traveling at many different speeds. Forward has suggested that the slow-moving Pluto arrived from the regions of space, a circumstance which is suggestive that the Sun, in its galactic travels, may have overtaken little Pluto.

Is it possible that, at one time in our Sun's travels around our galaxy, it may have overtaken a group of four, hydrogenous bodies which each contained several cold, icy satellites. Is it possible that these four bodies interrevolved in the manner of a quadruple binary (a double double binary), even though in distance they may have been several hundreds of millions of miles apart? Is it possible that they formerly had physical characteristics similar to Jupiter, Saturn, Uranus and Neptune with respect to composition, density, diameter and satellite systems. But is it also possible that they had orbital or revolutionary characteristics similar to the Epsilon Lyrae group, or the Zeta Cancri quadruple binary?

Is it possible that our Sun, with its immense gravity, and its galactic speed, first overtook such a binary, then seized it, and then, when the binary had moved into the inner phase of its eccentric orbit, is it further possible that the Sun's gravity dismembered it? Is it possible that the dismembered bodies of this binary were ultimately influenced to settle down in their present proximate orbits, due partly to this enormous new fifth factor, the Sun? Is it possible that they were influenced to settle down in such a manner that the largest of them (with the greatest

---

[15]James Muirden, *Stars and Planets*, New York: Thos. Crowell Co., 1965, p. 200.

gravity) settled down as the innermost? And the second largest as the second innermost? And the third largest the third innermost? And the smallest the outermost? And is it possible that these four bodies were later viewed by man on the neighboring Earth, and were named Dyaus Pitar (or Jupiter, or Zeus) and Remphan (or Saturn) and Uranus and Neptune?

If this is plausible and possible, then a galactogenetical approach is superior to the existing heliogenetic systems, which strain logic well beyond the point of reason, and which verge on the impossible. If our galactogenetic approach approximates correctness, then many problems are changed. One does not need to endeavor to attribute the angular momentum of the Jovian planets to the Sun, for their angular momentum preceded their entrance into the Sun's inner family. If this galactogenetical theory is correct, then one need not worry about deriving the satellites of Jupiter or the others from the Sun, for they, too, along with their parent planets, pre-existed as satellites prior to their adoption into the Sun's family. One need not be concerned about deriving their components such as carbon, ice, iron, methane, nitrogen and silicon from the Sun, for the Sun did not generate their components. These components were generated trillions, and conceivably quadrillions of miles from the Sun under circumstances which were far removed from those in our Sun's domain.

This hypothesis is that the Jovian planets, with pre-existing satellite systems, were influenced to assume stable orbits in the inner portion of our Sun's sphere of dominance. This hypothesis does not explain their genesis; it endeavors to explain their arrival. This hypothesis does not explain their date of entrance into the inner portion of the Sun's domain, and it does not necessarily explain their high velocities of rotation. But it does explain their method of arrival.

This hypothesis may be found to have two practical benefits, one negative and one positive. The negative benefit is to ascribe with a reasonable degree of certainty where the various planets did not originate. They did not originate with the Sun, either as a condensing nebula, in stellar collision, or even in a near collision. All the variations of the heliogenetic approach can be dismissed. This includes not a small amount of cosmological speculation to date. The positive benefit is to ascribe, with a reasonable degree of certainty, as to the method of arrival of the Jovian planets.

Early in this chapter, three possible approaches to the origin of the solar system were mentioned. One was the nebular approach, as set forth by Kant. A second was the collision approach, as set forth by Buffon. The third was the galactic approach, of large bodies following cometary orbits, as was suggested by Whiston, apparently with Newton's approval. In reviewing the thinking of Oort and the galactogenetical hypothesis as herein discussed, there emerges something remarkably parallel to the embryonic ideas of Whiston, some 270 years ago.

Perhaps the real structure of our solar system escapes our telescope in the remoter regions. Perhaps the real dimensions of our solar system extend halfway out to the nearest stars. In the binary conditions of our stellar neighbors, perhaps astronomical bodies of varying orders do occur, and are perturbed by the counter-gravities of those star systems. Perhaps some celestial material is occasionally perturbed in the direction of our Sun. Perhaps then the origin of the Sun's cloud of comets is not merely half way out to the nearest stars, as Oort suggests, but is out to the star systems themselves.

If this is reasonable, then the origin of the Jovian planets may not be the immediate issue; rather, the immediate issue is the manner of their adoption into the Sun's family, either as an adoption of a quadruple binary, or perhaps as two adoptions of two simple binaries. Perhaps this explains why the Jovian planets describe a plane similar to the galactic plane, a plane significantly dissimilar to the plane of the Sun's axis. If this is so, then (1) the adoption of the Earth-Moon binary becomes easier to conceive, along with (2) its orbital similarity to the Sun's galactic plane.

First, it is reasonable to suppose that the Jovian planets (Jupiter, Saturn, Uranus and Neptune) along with most of their icy satellites, were formed under similar conditions since their characteristics of composition, density, volume, diameter, speed of rotation, satellite arrangement and so forth are generally similar.

Secondly, it is reasonable to suppose that the Earth, with its rock-like composition and density, generally similar to the Moon's may have been formed under conditions similar to those involved in the formation of the Moon.

Thirdly, it is reasonable to suppose that conditions under which the Jovian planets were formed were markedly different and distant from the conditions under which the Earth-Moon binary was formed. These two regions of origin may have contained different relative abundances of various elements, a condition that is a reality among other stars in our galaxy.

Fourthly, it is reasonable to suppose that the Jovian planets, as a former quadruple binary (or perhaps two independent binaries) have been separated from each other's dominating gravitational influence due to the Sun's greater influence in association with the distances involved between them. In contrast to this, the Earth-Moon binary has not been separated due to the lesser original distance.

By viewing the conditions of the Jovian planets, one may come to a reasonable conclusion as to some of the circumstances surrounding their origin, and their method of entrance into the inner portion of our solar system. By comprehending this, one may attain a better understanding of the method of entrance of our Earth-Moon system into the inner portion of the Sun's domain. This is even though the two groups were formed at different times, of different materials, and in different regions, remote in location from each other and remote in location from the Sun.

We have considered reasons supporting the hypothesis that there were two binaries which entered the inner regions of the solar system in ages past. This study does not overrule a third possibility that a third binary may also have become involved in the Sun's inner family. The characteristics of Mercury and Pluto are sufficiently similar to at least raise the question of a possible similar origin for both.

This hypothesis of GALACTOGENESIS[16] utilizes three concepts: elliptical orbits, perturbations, and the inherent diversity of the galactic conditions. Each of these three concepts broadens the background and undergirds the understanding of *The Biblical Flood and the Ice Epoch,* which was a celestial catastrophe, sufficiently recent to be recorded by man.

This study has endeavored to discuss the manner of entrance of some of the planets into the inner domain of the Sun,

---

[16]GALACTOGENESIS is a term being used to describe this hypothesis of origin, both for the Jovian planets, possibly a former quadruple binary group which was dismembered and also for the Earth-Moon binary. This term is used as an alternative approach, and contrary to the idea of HELIOGENESIS as proposed by Kant and many others.

but has not been greatly concerned with the circumstances and conditions under which the planets were originally formed. However, in a brief consideration of these formative circumstances, the proper perspective needs to be maintained.

It is easily demonstrated that the Moon's revolving motion around the Earth is it most apparent motion. However the Moon also has orbital motion around the Sun, as it follows the Earth's orbit. Hence the totality of the lunar motion cannot be described without relevance to the Sun.

Similarly, it is posited, it is not possible to explain fully the orbits of the Jovian planets without consideration of influences beyond the nearer-in region of the Sun's domain, which is a very limited view.

The Sun is one of the more remote stars in our galaxy, located toward the rim, in the direction of the galaxy Andromeda. If one cannot properly understand the motion of the Moon without bypassing the obvious (the Earth), then one must search for both the non-obvious as well as the obvious. And perhaps one cannot understand the nature of the orbits of the planets without understanding galactic motion and historical captures, the non-obvious. Then further, one perhaps will not be able to understand the galactic conditions under which the Sun's planets were formed without understanding the entire galaxy (rather than merely the more obvious, the near portions). It is all a matter of perspective. The fullest perspective is the best, which includes both the non-obvious as well as the obvious. Hence it is suspected that the more distant regions within our galaxy may yield more information as to the processes and principles under which the Earth-Moon binary was formed, or under which the Jovian quadruple binary was organized, than will a thorough understanding of merely the nearer parts of our galaxy.

Catastrophic Timing

If this binary approach for the presence of the Jovian planets is reasonable, a similar binary approach for the explanation of the presence of the Earth-Moon binary is also reasonable. Then one is faced with two problems of Earth history, and not just one.

One of these problems is the replacing of the Lyellian time scale, which recognizes neither Catastrophism or Galactogenesis. Refuting the Lyellian time scale may be worthwhile, but refuting such a negative approach to Earth history without replacing it with a more positive and more defensible approach is not right.

Heliogenesis must be discarded in favor of Galactogenesis. Galactogenesis implies that our planet Earth, and its satellite, the Moon, both have spent ample astronomical time both beyond our solar system as well as within it. Hence, and secondly, a catastrophic time table must include both pre-solar time (galactic time) and intra-solar time (time spent within the Sun's domain).

Following is Lyell's Geological Time Scale, which fails to credit such celestial considerations as catastrophism and galactogenesis. It is supposedly *the* principle of Earth history for this, our era, and in being simultaneously anti-theistic, it has become a basic but brittle precept for modern humanism.

TABLE 13
Lyellian Time Chart

PRE-CAMBRIAN
Archaeozoic and Proterozoic   5,000,000,000 - 550,000,000

PALEOZOIC
Cambrian	550,000,000 -	450,000,000
Ordovician	450,000,000	380,000,000
Silurian	380,000,000	355,000,000
Devonian	355,000,000	310,000,000
Carboniferous:	310,000,000	225,000,000
Mississippian		
Pennsylvanian		
Permian	225,000,000	185,000,000

MESOZOIC
Triassic	185,000,000	158,000,000
Jurassic	158,000,000	125,000,000
Cretaceous	125,000,000	60,000,000

CENOZOIC
Paleocene)		60,000,000	50,000,000
Eocene)		50,000,000	40,000,000
Oligocene)	Tertiary	40,000,000	30,000,000
Miocene)		30,000,000	15,000,000
Pliocene)		15,000,000	1,000,000
Pleistocene)	Quarternary	1,000,000	10,000
Recent)		10,000	to date

TABLE 14

Catastrophic and Galactogenetic Time Chart

CATEGORY I
> GALACTIC TIME   date of origin -   to date
> A. Pre-solar Time   date of origin -   10,000,000 B.C.
> B. Intra-solar Time   10,000,000 -   to date

CATEGORY II
> PRE-SOLAR TIME
>
> A. Pre-lunar Time   date of origin - 1,000,000,000 B.C.
> (Era preceding Capture of Moon)
>
> B. Post-lunar time   1,000,000,000 -   10,000,000 B.C.
> (Era of Movement toward Sun's Domain)

CATEGORY III
> INTRA-SOLAR TIME
>
> A. Outer-solar Time   10,000,000 - 100,100 B.C.
> (Era wherein Earth-Moon system moved slowly across the Sun's domain, across trillions of miles of space, at a rate of centimeters per second, toward the inner region of the Sun's domain. This period is comparable to the half period of Delavan's comet, which is about 12,000,000 years, in its travels out to the edges of the Sun's domain and back.)
>
> B. Inner-solar Time   100,100 - to date
> (Era wherein the Earth-Moon binary was influenced to take its present proximate location and orbit. During this era, the surface of the Earth warmed, ices melted, oceans filled, and climates were organized.)

CATEGORY IV
> OUTER-SOLAR TIME
>
> A. Invisible Era   10,000,000 - 100,100B.C.
> (Era wherein Earth-Moon system was sufficiently distant, 5 billion to 15 trillion miles, that it was beyond the region of Neptune's and Pluto's orbit, yet was within the Sun's domain.)
>
> B. Visible Era   100,100 - 100,000 B.C.
> (Era wherein Earth-Moon system was sufficiently close to cross orbits of Pluto and Neptune.)

CATEGORY V
INNER SOLAR TIME

A. Pre-Hydrocarboniferous Era   100,000 - 20,000 B.C.
   (Era during which Earth's surface became warmed,
   ices melted, oceans filled, water evaporated, climates were organized, erosion proceeded.)
   (This and previous eras correspond to the Lyellian
   scale defined as "pre-Cambrian" and "proterozoic.")
   (During this era, the Earth and the Moon may well
   have been subjected to massive series of minor catastrophes.
   (During this era, either little or no biological life
   occurred.)

B. Hydrocarboniferous Catastrophic Era 20,000-10,000 B.C.
   (During this crisis era, the formation of the Appa-
   lachian-Caledonian-Herzynian zone of orogenetic
   uplift occurred.)
   (During this crisis era, ammonias, hydroxyls, hydrocarbons and related compounds were deposited
   upon the Earth, resulting in strata of coal, pools of
   petroleum, and additional volumes of nitrogen in
   the atmosphere.)
   (This era coincides with that which Lyellians term
   "paleozoic.")
   (During this era, life in various forms was created,
   probably instantly.)

C. Carboniferous Interlude   10,000-2,800 B.C.
   (During this period, the Earth's canopy and Greenhouse Effect was fully developed, and antediluvian
   climatology was organized.
   (During this period the Earth's climate was based
   on heat equilibrium.)
   (During this period, the major part of the Earth's
   biology was created.)

D. Floodtide Catastrophe   2,800 B.C.
   (Era of recent orogenetic uplift of Alpine-Himalayan
   and Circum-Pacific zones.)
   (Era of glacial deposition in magnetic polar regions.)
   (Era of repeated uplift of oceanic tides of contin-
   ental proportions.)
   (Era of burial and fossilization of vast collections
   of biology.)
   (Era of flotation of Noah's barge.)
   (During this era most strata were formed which

Lyellian thought classifies as "mesozoic" and "cenozoic.")

E. Post-Diluvian Interlude   2,800-1,450 B.C.
(Era of repopulation of planet, with many zoogeographical migrations.)
(Era of rise of Han, Mohenjo-daro, Inca, Mayan, Minoan, Babylonian and Egyptian civilizations.)
(Era of pyramid-construction in Egypt by slave labor.)
(Era of isostatic adjustment, including rifting of Earth's crust in Africa.)
(Era during which astral catastrophes periodically threatened.)
(Patriarchal Era.)

F. Exodus Crisis Era   1,450-1,400 B.C.
(Era of Moses and Hebrew migration from Egyptian slavery.)
(Era of plagues befalling Egypt and the entire world.)
(Era of Hyksos, or Amalekite invasion of Egypt.)
(Era of Hebrew invasion of Palestine.)
(Era of Phaethon story and Joshua's long day.)

G. Post Exodus Interlude   1,400- 800 B.C.
(Era of Hyksos dynasty in Egypt.)
(Era of Judges and Davidic dynasty in Palestine.)
(Era of Philistine, or Minoan settlement of Palestine.)
(Era of the rise of Troy and Assyria.)

H. Amos-Homeric-Isaiahic Crisis Era   800- 700 B.C.
(Era of celestial bards of Greece, led by Homer.)
(Era of destruction of Troy, and founding of Rome.)
(Era of the Hebrew fire and brimstone prophets, led by Isaiah.)

I. Modern Era—or Interlude
(Age of Greek, Roman, Medieval and Western civilizations.)

In contrast to Lyell's Geological Time Chart, a Catastrophic Time Scale has been proposed, one which is to be considered as flexible rather than brittle, one which is indicative for the sequences of Earth history. The Catastrophic Galactogenetic Time Chart, like the Lyellian (Uniformitarian) Geological Time Chart, makes several assumptions. One is that the Earth was formed trillions, if not quadrillions of miles from the Sun's domain. So was the Moon. So was the Jovian foursome.

The Kantian, heliogenetic approach requires not only that the Earth, but that all nine planets, all asteroids, and all thirty-one satellites were derived from the Sun. As originally proposed, this also included all of the comets, which may number in the billions. The heliogenetic approach requires the Sun to be the generic source of all (or at least almost all) of these bodies. In all likelihood, the Sun did not generate a single planet, a single asteroid, a single satellite or a single comet.

A second assumption in the Catastrophic Galactogenetic Time Chart, is that the Moon revolved around the Earth long eons before the Earth revolved around the Sun.[17] Heliogenesis assumes that the Sun is older than the planets and the planets are older than the satellites. In the hypothesis of *Galactogenesis,* the author does not state whether the Earth, Moon, Jupiter or the Sun is the oldest. It is merely assumed that the Earth and the Moon were formed in the same region, and under comparable conditions, long before they entered the inner part of the solar system.

The hypothesis of Galactogenesis does not overlook the galactic motion of the Sun, which is 12 miles per second, in the direction of the constellation Hercules. Forward suggested that perhaps Pluto, whose velocity is 2 miles per second, approached the Sun, and interacted with Neptune. On the other hand, perhaps the Sun, with its greater galactic speed overtook Pluto, perhaps even while Pluto may have had a partner.

Herein is presented a cosmology which directly contradicts the cosmology of Kant. Kant partly contradicted the Ptolemaic view, but also partly accepted the Ptolemaic cosmology. And undoubtedly the Ptolemaic cosmology, in its earlier form under Hipparchus, partly contradicted a prior cosmology.

There is nothing wrong with the Ptolemaic (geocentric) cosmology, as long as it isn't taken too seriously. It is proposed that Thomas Aquinas, Tycho Brahe and Pope Urban, among

---

[17]The use of such terms as "day" or "year" becomes quite ambiguous because, if the Earth has only completed some 100,000 orbits around the Sun, it cannot be more than 100,000 years old, regardless of its age, even though it may antedate either the Jovian planets, the Moon or the Sun. Whether for a Catastrophic Time Chart or an Uniformitarian Time Chart, the usage of such terms as 10 billion years, 158 million years or even 1 million years becomes an exercise in semantical fantasy.

others, took it too seriously. However, for practical purposes, Ptolemy's geocentricity explained many things sufficiently well to be workable.

Kant then proposed a hypothesis, incorporating the eternal regularity of Descartes and Ptolemy, the dreams of Swedenborg and the astronomy of Copernicus and Newton. Kant's idea was that the solar system was set in motion something like a Swiss watch, eons ago. It was wound up, and has proceeded without interruption or *without outside interference* ever since. As long as it isn't taken too seriously, it too explains many things sufficiently well to be satisfying. However Kant himself, along with Hutton, Lyell, Darwin, Marx and many others took it too seriously. The problem seems to have arisen, often decades or centuries later, when leaders of subsequent generations take the earlier viewpoints too seriously.

If Kant was granted the academic latitude to propose the origin and development of the solar system in a word picture, that of the regularly-running clock, proceeding *without outside interference,* perhaps this study can take the academic latitude to propose that the origin and development of the solar system was something like a cowboy punching cattle.

In the pioneer days of the Great Plains, railroads were a new thing, the Indians had just been closed off on reservations, and the buffaloes were killed off. Neither homesteaders nor barbed wire had yet arrived. Spreads (individual ranches) encompassed several counties. The vast, rolling plains were used for grazing great herds of cattle. The cowboys would herd their cattle from range to range, and from water hole to water hole.

In their work, they would occasionally come across some mavericks, unbranded strays. Sometimes the mavericks were in groups; sometimes they were alone. They would then bulldog the stray or strays, apply the branding iron, and increase the size of the herd. Now, instead of wandering aimlessly across the broad prairies, the calves would orbit around the cows, and the cows would orbit around the cowboys, as they were herded conjointly across the endless plains.

This is like the Sun, traveling across the broad, endless region of our galaxy. From time to time, our Sun has encountered a dark, stray, celestial maverick, or perhaps a small group of them. They were adopted into the Sun's family. We do not know how many planets the Sun has, including some possibly out beyond Pluto. But we have reason to think that one inner planet (Electra) got "shot." If the truth were known about the dark, outer reaches of our solar system, some 10 and 15 trillions of miles away, it is possible to conceive that the Sun not only gains a few members now and then, but the nearer stars may rustle a few away on occasion also out near the edge of the gravitational domain.[18]

This concludes the discussion of academic blindspot number 8, the assumption of Heliogenesis. If this erroneous assumption stood alone it would be still a cause for concern. But such is not the case. It stands conjointly amid several other major and related erroneous assumptions. The reality may be as follows:

(1) Genesis, like Job, is a valid historical document, and may be a valid spiritual one, too.
(2) The Flood is an historical, global fact, and is not a fanciful, Sumerian myth.
(3) Orogenesis historically was accomplished suddenly and by tidal upheaval.
(4) The Ice Epoch enveloped the Earth suddenly, and was composed of celestial ice.
(5) The astral motifs of ancient civilization contain a core of historical truth.
(6) The earlier Greenhouse Effect promoted longevity, flourishing fauna and flora.
(7) The major assumptions and hypotheses of Darwin were as mistaken as were his marital genetics.
(8) Historical Earth tides and not the hypothetical solar tides, are the fact.
(9) Galactogenesis, and not heliogenesis, is a reasonable cosmogenetical approach.
(10) Uniformitarianism, to the exclusion of other cosmological approaches such as catastrophism, is ludicrous in formulating a creditable explanation of Earth history.

[18]This example of cowpunching, cattle and mavericks may seem excessively bucolic and not sufficiently pedantic; yet some rather deep and profound truths have been communicated by using simple word pictures of lost sheep, vines, prodigals, foxes, sparrows and mustard seeds. Also an ostentatious, multi-syllabled word picture is not necessarily characteristic of either depth or breadth of thought.

These several erroneous uniformitarian assumptions seem to merge into a syndrome, a group of concurrent symptoms characterizing a disorder. This syndrome, involving heliogenesis and uniformitarianism, suggests a schizophrenic condition of our academic age. Schizophrenia is defined as a flight from reality; in this case, it is a flight from historical reality.

Is it possible that this disorder is also an academic flight from the Biblical ethic, upon which Western Civilization was founded? Is it possible that the reaction against catastrophism which has set in has in reality been geared to reject the spiritual ethic contained in Genesis? Is it possible that, through confused thinking, the rejection of the spiritual ethic also involved the rejection of the historical reality contained in Genesis?

Is there a correlation between uniformitarian cosmology, the rejection of Earth catastrophism, and the increasing intellectual rootlessness of our age? Is the rise of uniformitarian cosmology related to the increasing dominance of anti-spiritual principles in our generation? And is the increasing dominance of the anti-spiritual something new to history, or did Greece also experience this phenomenon of pioneer faith and struggle, followed by growth, prosperity, culminating in moral decline and political disintegration? And did Imperial Rome also experience such a phenomenon? And have the Hebrews experienced one, two, or three separate cycles of this same phenomenon which is gripping Western Civilization at the current time?

Could this mean that we have good grounds to be skeptical of the professional skeptics of our age? Could this mean that the self-styled rationalists of our age have been making irrational assumptions in Earth history of an extensive magnitude? Might this mean that our "Age of Reason" may be something less than that? And if one becomes markedly skeptical of the professional skeptics, who then may be identified as the real skeptic? And if the uniformitarian skeptics have been quick to accuse others, others that perhaps have a pro-spiritual viewpoint, of gullibility, might the question be raised as to just exactly which viewpoint requires genuine gullibility?

And if uniformitarian thinking has been essentially negative thinking, what is the significance of such negative thinking in our stage of civilization? It is to this subject, uniformitarianism and Western Civilization, to which Chapter XII, our final chapter, is dedicated.

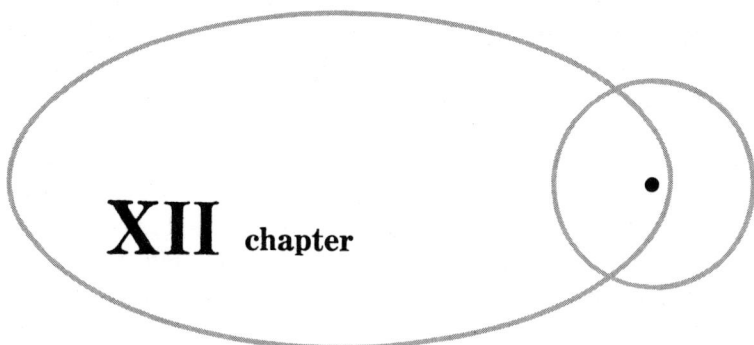

XII chapter

Catastrophism, Uniformitarianism and Western Civilization

ASTRAL CATASTROPHISM (or celestial catastrophism) is a basic view for the history of our planet, and of the other planets in our solar system. It presumes periodically disturbed and conflicting conditions, and those, at least to an extent, have been relatively recent. Evidence is derived not from just one or two planetary systems, but from most, and perhaps from every one of them.

The uniformitarian approach, launched by Kant in the middle of the 18th century, presupposes that all planets, all satellites and all asteroids were formed from the parent solar material, whether by solar contractions or solar catastrophes. The uniformitarian view also presupposes that the current planetary orbits have existed for millions, if not billions of years, rather than thousands of years. The uniformitarian view contends that the Biblical Flood could not have occurred, except as a form of unusual cyclonic weather patterns of a local nature. The catastrophic view contends that not just the Earth, but virtually every planet has experienced astral havoc of one sort or another, and to one degree or another.

PLUTO, with an orbital eccentricity of 0.249, is the outermost known planet, *most of the time*. It averages 880,000,000 miles more distant than Neptune. Nevertheless it does approach the Sun more closely than does Neptune, an observation for which uniformitarianism has no explanation, an observation causing astronomers to suspect a historical interaction. Pluto is not a strong example of uniformitarianism.

NEPTUNE possesses two satellites, Nereid and Triton, both of which revolve in retrograde direction, an extraordinary direction for satellites in our solar system. Nereid, with an eccentricity of 0.749, seemingly almost escaped from the Neptune region. Halley's comet, along with most of the other Neptunian comets, also possesses retrograde motion, like Neptune's moons. If Pluto has historically interacted with Neptune, it no doubt has also interacted with Nereid and Triton. Nereid was unsuccessful in escaping the Neptune system. But some of the comets of the Neptune region, also possessing retrograde motion, may have successfully escaped Neptune. They then may have taken the Sun for one of its two foci, and the region of Neptune for the other. The Neptune system with such satellites as Nereid, is hardly a case for uniformitarianism.

Many astronomers have supposed that Neptune and Pluto formerly interacted; Kuiper and a few other astronomers have supposed that Jupiter and Pluto formerly interacted. Pluto's perihelion is 2,761,000,000 miles from the Sun whereas Neptune's perihelion is somewhat more distant, some 2,772,000,000 miles from the Sun. But Pluto's orbit has two foci. Its aphelion is 4,589,-000,000 miles from the Sun. And its second foci is 1,828,000,000 miles from the Sun.

URANUS, coincidentally, has an orbit ranging from 1,700,-000,000 to 1,868,000,000 miles from the Sun, and Pluto's second foci happens to coincide with the orbit of Uranus, even as Halley's comet's second foci coincides with the orbit of Neptune.

Uranus exhibits other non-uniform arrangements. Most planets possess a modest tilt in their axis, variously between 3 and 29°. Nevertheless the axis of Uranus deviates from its ecliptic plane by 98°. It rotates 8° backwards from the direction of its revolving motion, a most unusual circumstance. Furthermore, the satellites of Uranus also revolve around Uranus' equatorial plane, and not the orbital plane. There is no possible explanation for this in uniformitarian cosmogony; furthermore there is no basis provided to even hazard a guess, because planetary catastrophism and galactogenesis are disallowed.

SATURN, with its brilliant, icy fragments formed into rings, revolving on a disc-like plane, all within Roche's limit for fragmentation, is hardly the best example of celestial uniformitarianism. But it is an outstanding example of icy catastrophism.

JUPITER, the largest planet in our solar system, is considered to be the region of origin for Pluto by the astronomer Kuiper, and for Venus by the cosmologist Velikovsky. Velikovsky supposes that Jupiter expelled Venus by some unexplained mechanism. This writer does not share either of the above opinions.

Nevertheless there is a remarkable aspect of the Jupiter system which leads one to suspect that the influences of Jupiter have been rather extensive, historically. This is the example of the Trojan Asteroids. There are some 12 of these, named after such Homeric heroes as Achilles.

They do not orbit or oscillate around Jupiter like Jupiter's moons. Rather, they oscillate around points some 400,000,000 to 500,000,000 miles distant from Jupiter, some east of Jupiter and others west of Jupiter. They proceed in orbits in such a manner that they, at all times, form an equilateral triangle with the locations of Jupiter and the Sun, the other two corners of the triangle.

Kuiper may be wrong concerning his idea that Pluto once revolved around Jupiter; Velikovsky may be wrong in his view that Venus was the product of an expulsion from Jupiter. Nevertheless, the Trojan Asteroids are suggestive that at least some remarkable conditions have occurred in Jupiter's past.

VENUS is the planet which, according to Velikovsky, may have interacted with the Earth during the 2nd millenium B.C.[1] This author prefers to lay open the suspicion that Venus may have indeed interacted with the Earth, but rather may have been responsible for the primordial hydrocarboniferous catastrophic era. This suspicion is increased with the evidence of heavy and complex hydrocarbons in the Venusian atmosphere. Velikovsky may have confused Venus with Mars.

This writer is not satisfied with everything in Velikovsky's

[1]Immanuel Velikovsky, *Worlds in Collision*, New York: Doubleday & Co., 1950, pp. 39-206.

presentation of this event. However, the writer is most dissatisfied with Velikovsky's destructive critics, professional men and women who have publicly displayed a substantial amount of both ignorance and poor judgment.

The Earth was seemingly engaged in astral havoc at least four times. One era was the 8th century B.C. Another was the 15th century B.C. A third era was approximately the 28th century B.C., the Flood crisis era. Yet an earlier era of celestial havoc, prior to the age of man, was perhaps some 10,000 to 20,000 years ago. And there may be others in the dateless past.

Concerning these specific catastrophes, it would be most likely that the other planets involved are still revolving around in the solar system, and especially in the inner regions of the solar system; it is not likely that they disappeared in the remote regions beyond Pluto. It would be likely that some of these bodies which engaged the Earth would have resultant perihelions closer to the Sun than does the Earth. Venus possesses such a perihelion, some 67,000,000 miles from the Sun, and some 26,-000,000 miles from the Earth at opposition.

MERCURY possesses such a perihelion, some 29,000,000 miles from the Sun. Mercury also possesses an aphelion about 43,000,000 miles from the Sun, and an orbital eccentricity of 0.206, second only to that of Pluto among the planets. How did Mercury achieve such an orbital eccentricity if it were not disturbed and redisturbed? And how did the tiny Mercury achieve such a heavy density, 5.46, second only only to the Earth's 5.52 among the planets? This is much heavier than the Sun's density of 1.41, a major problem for any heliogenetical uniformitarian theory to explain.

The guess of this writer is that Mercury may have been the Visitor which interacted with the Earth during the Flood crisis. It may have subsequently interacted with Venus also. If Mercury is not that Visitor, it leaves only Mars and Venus for leading alternatives. With deference to Velikovsky, this writer agrees that Venus can be eliminated.

MARS is then the only remaining possibility to account for the Flood crisis; it can also be eliminated. Some of the reasons are described by Velikovsky.[2] The reason Mars can be eliminated as

²*Loc. Cit.*, pp. 207-378.

the partner in the Flood celestial drama is because it apparently was the partner in another later celestial drama, the one in the 8th century B.C. Of course the uniformitarian thinkers will give no time to consideration of such a possibility. This means that they have numerous coincidences which they must face, coincidences which they must explain if they genuinely feel they have the superior cosmology. Consider some of these coincidences.

Mars has a rotational speed of 24 hours, 37 minutes in sidereal time. The Earth, coincidentally, has a rotational speed of 23 hours, 56 minutes, in sidereal time. This is a differential of 41 minutes, a differential of but 2.9%. This, in uniformitarian thinking, is a remarkable coincidence.

Mars has an axis which tilts 24° to the perpendicular of its orbital plane. Our planet has an axis which, by way of coincidence, tilts 23½°. This is a differential of about 2%, a second remarkable coincidence.

A third coincidence in uniformitarian thinking, the allegory of Jonathan Swift is now recalled, along with the mythical Lilliputians and Laputans. The Laputans, according to Swift, possessed superior telescopes to the Europeans.[3] The Laputans apparently knew all about the satellites of Mars, their physical diameters, their orbital diameters, and their speed of revolution some 150 years before such was discovered by later astronomers who eventually built better telescopes.

> This is an amazing coincidence. Of course, Swift might have reasoned as follows: It was known that Earth had 1 moon, Jupiter had 4 and Saturn had 7 at the time he was writing his book. It was reasonable to suppose that Saturn might have an 8th moon hidden somewhere and, in that case, if Mars had 2 moons, there would be a nice list of numbers.
> As one moved outward from the sun, beginning at Earth, the number of moons for each planet would be 1, 2, 4, 8. Then too, the moons of Mars would have to be small and close to the planet, or even Europeans with their "poor" telescopes would have discovered them.
> So far, Swift's thinking can be followed. However, his guess that Phobos would rise in the west and set in the east because of its speed of revolution is uncanny. It is undoubtedly the luckiest guess in literature.

[3]Swift wrote *Gulliver's Travels* in London in 1726; Whiston wrote many works between 1696 and 1740, also in London, including *Astronomical Principles of Religion* (1717) and *A New Theory of The Earth* (1696).

Furthermore, this "guess" by Swift was a guess by a literary man rather than an astronomer. *It is described by the disturbed and astounded Asimov in the strongest possible terms describing coincidence which Asimov's command of the English language would allow.*[4]

This paper is not necessarily disagreeing with Asimov. This paper agrees that this indeed is an amazing coincidence, but it is a coincidence many magnitudes greater than Asimov visualizes, if it indeed is a coincidence at all, particularly if the following facts mean anything.

During the 8th century B.C., the Old Testament writers reveal that their world experienced a series of catastrophes, which seem to have had either 15 or 30 year intervals. Amos described one; Micah described one (also described by Josephus and later by Zechariah). Isaiah described the last of these, which was apparently also the worst. He described such phenomena as the Earth wobbling like a drunkard, a blast falling from heaven, and the Sun returning, or suddenly going retrograde in the sky about 10°. This was a time replete with celestial cosmology, disturbed calendars, intense earthquakes, and falling meteorites.

Homer, the celestial bard of Greece, also lived in the 8th century B.C. By way of coincidence he also described the Greek-Trojan conflict as if it were a war among the sky-gods of Greece and Troy. He described it as if it were replete with celestial crises, earthquakes, and extra-terrestrial fortunes. He described this age as if it was a time when Ares in particular (Mars) went to war, and warred with both Hera (Earth) and Aphrodite (the Moon), among others. In this conflict the walls of Troy were destroyed.

Simultaneously, by way of coincidence, the Assyrians described their troubles in terms of astral fortunes, particularly to Nergal (Mars), he who was the "king of battle," the "champion of the gods," and the "king of the chase."

And simultaneously, in terms of uniformitarian coincidence, some Etruscan migrants from Tuscany in Italy founded Rome on the Tiber. With their war-like and "martial" spirit, they established Rome, which they dedicated to the wolf-star, Mars (or Martis, from which our word "martial" is derived). Their wolf-

[4]Isaac Asimov, *The Kingdom of the Sun*, New York: Collier Books, 1962, p. 126

star, so important to them in the era of the founding of Rome in the 8th century B.C., was also seemingly related to the legend of Romulus and Remus who, as infants, were supposedly preserved by the "wolf-star."

Now of course Homer could not have been describing real astronomical conditions of his time, according to uniformitarian thought. But let us suppose that really he might have been, and the modern uniformitarians are the ones who are mistaken about the 8th century B.C. rather than Homer (or Isaiah). Then both Swift and Whiston might have been correct in their interpretation of ancient cosmology. Then Mars may have actually approached the Earth, and wrought havoc in its approach.

Then Deimos and Phobos may actually have been seen by ancient Grecian eyes. Ares, to them, was indeed drawn by two steeds, not two mythological steeds, but rather by two real steeds, at least in their view. Deimos is not really a moon in the general sense; it is a rock about five miles in diameter. Phobos is about 10 miles in diameter. They are moons in the minuscule sense. Apparently ancient Grecian eyes were able to see not only Phobos but also Deimos. Apparently they were not only able to see them, but were also able to measure them, track them, and correlate them to the rotation of Mars (or Ares). How close must a rock of five miles be to be seen, measured and tracked?

Saturn, with a planetary diameter of 72,000 miles, plus a brilliant ring diameter of 171,000 miles, and at a distance of 800,-000,000 to 950,000,000 miles, is just visible to the naked eye. A five-mile rock might be visible at 150,000 miles; measuring and tracking would be more likely at or within 100,000 miles. This is just uncomfortably close, but the ancients in the 8th century B.C. were just that uncomfortable, according to their writings integrated with their cosmologies. This would cause tidal upheavals along the ocean shores, but also in the magma within the Earth's crust, and would cause seismic shocks of major scales. And not only were the walls of Troy destroyed during this era; Isaiah describes the walls of Jerusalem, some 40 feet thick and 100 feet high, as suddenly breached, along with the aqueducts. Their repair became Hezekiah's leading WPA project. And also, Hezekiah found that the Passover festival was gradually becoming later and later in the spring. He found it necessary to add 5 intercalary days in order to make the calendar work.

Prior to the 8th century B.C. the Hebrew calendar included

new moon festivals, celebrated every 30 days, and annual festivals, celebrated every 360 days. (Today the Moon has a 28½ day orbit, and the Earth has a 365¼ day orbit.) And the Hebrew calendar of 360 days looks surprisingly similar to the geometric circle of the astronomical-minded Babylonians, who divided it into 360 degrees, as if it might have had something to do with the calendar. But, of course, all this must be coincidence, if the uniformitarians are not mistaken. Also, according to sundials and water clocks which have been unearthed by archaeologists (those which were constructed prior to 8th century B.C.), it seems as if they failed to measure true east correctly; their architecture was about 1° in error to our true east.

Now if Mars had just happened to approach the Earth within 100,000 or so miles, this means

(a) it passed well within the Earth-Moon system
(b) it passed well within the Earth's gravitational domain, which is some 1,600,000 miles in diameter
(c) it passed well within the influences of the Earth's magnetic field.

And it has already been noticed that Mars has such a sympathetic period of rotation to the Earth, plus a surprisingly sympathetic tilt to the axis upon which it rotates. A slowly turning armature can be accelerated if it passes within the magnetic field of another rotating armature; they needn't touch. Is it not possible that Mars disturbed the Earth's axis and orbit slightly? And is it not possible that the Earth, with a mass 10 times greater than Mars, substantially reorganized Mars' rotation and axis to resemble its own? This study suspects just that; it suspects more.[5]

---

[5]This study suspects that Mars interacted with the Earth-Moon system. This study also suspects that Mars caused the Earth's orbit and the Moon's to shift a little. This study further suspects that the Earth-Moon system caused major changes in (1) Mars' tilt, (2) Mars' speed of rotation, and (3) Mars' orbit.

This does not necessarily mean that there was a net change in the energy potential of Mars. But it does mean that during these crises, especially the last, the closest approach, some of Mars' angular momentum may have been converted. Such a conversion may have been (a) an addition to its rotational momentum, thereby increasing its rotational speed, but (b) a simultaneous subtraction to its revolutionary momentum (and thereby decreasing its orbital semi-major axis, and the eccentricity of its orbit). The Earth-Mars catastrophes are an excellent subject for a model.

One might wonder why Mars is so heavily pocked or scarred with astroblemes. The face of the Moon is fairly heavily pocked, but not so much so as the backside of the Moon. And the backside of the Moon is not nearly as heavily scarred as is Mars. Mars has craters overlapping and/or within craters, overlapping upon craters, in places in a triple overlay.

Today, Mars has an orbit some 140,000,000 miles from the Sun. If it possessed a more eccentric orbit in history, an orbit which had a perihelion of 90,000,000 miles, it came some 50,000,000 miles closer to the Sun at that time than now. Also, one may presume, it may have also receded some 50,000,000 miles more distant from the Sun than is its present orbit. That would be 190,000,000 to 200,000,000 miles from the Sun. The orbits of the asteroids, battered remains of a former planet, are 190,000,000 to 200,000,000 miles from the Sun.

Why is Mars so heavily scarred with astroblemes? Could this be related to a former orbit, of greater eccentricity, which entered the zone of the asteroids? Where did Mars pick up its two rock-like, asteroid-like satellites, Deimos and Phobos? What is this legend of Electra, a former sister planet in our solar system, all about? Surely, according to Lyellian logic, Mars has been orbiting in its current orbit for millions, or perhaps billions of years. But then what planet caused the fragmentation of Electra, if not Mars?

All of these things must be classified as coincidence because Kant's 18th century uniformitarian cosmology has been classified as true science indeed, and allows no room for such a possibility. Therefore, we ask the uniformitarian mind to at least acknowledge that here, relative to Mars, its satellites, its astroblemes, its cosmological position among the ancients, its rotation, its axis, here we have a uniformitarian coincidence many magnitudes greater than that which Asimov realized. And Asimov described but a small portion of these coincidences in the most extreme possible language which he could command.

However, if the catastrophic proposition just happens to be correct, then one may ascribe historical interactions of the Earth

    (1) with Mars in the 8th and 15th centuries B.C.

    (2) probably with Venus in an era verging on the dateless past

and (3) with Mercury in the 28th century B.C., the flood era.

There are really six terrestrial planets, but five terrestrial orbits.

The planets are Mercury, Venus, the Earth-Moon binary, Mars and Pluto. Pluto's interaction with Neptune may have been as recent as the Earth-Moon system's interaction with Mercury.

Beyond the terrestrial planets are the four Jovian planets, Jupiter, Saturn, Uranus and Neptune. If the galactogenetical proposal is reasonable, they may have been a former quadruple binary which also, through ancient interactions, was dismembered and dispersed by the Sun into its present proximate arrangement. Thus, in the galactogenetic and catastrophic approach, there is a beginning of an explanation for all of the planetary orbits, and not merely the orbits of the Earth, the Moon, Mars or Venus.

Uniformitarianism and Modern Humanism

Probably, the Earth-Moon binary, along with the Sun, as a three body system, can serve to illustrate a point relative to science, truth and uniformitarianism. Our moon, perhaps like science, is a reflector of light. But the moon is not luminous; it is not a source of light; it is merely a reflector, and a rather inefficient reflector at that (its albedo is only 8%). Yet the Moon may reflect a full 8%, some light, or no light at all, depending on its particular position. Perhaps this is a little like science, and scientism, which is the idea that science is truth itself. Perhaps science only reflects truth. And perhaps science can reflect the marvels of the Creator. Perhaps science can reflect the miracles of biological architecture, or physical matter. Perhaps science can reflect a full image, though a dim image of our Creator when properly and catastrophically oriented, even as science reflects no light when uniformitarianly oriented. In this way, science is valuable or confusing, constructive or destructive, depending on the way it is "used."

The famous astronomer, Eddington, made a great quip, of some value, when he opined that one is no more able to deduce Divine principles from science than he can extract the square root of a sonnet. Eddington has endeavored to draw no moral conclusions at all from science. This is considerably better than Kant, Hutton, Darwin and Marx, who drew massively negative conclusions from their uniformitarian notions. Yet, Eddington, in drawing no conclusions, perhaps has made some rather general mistakes. One error of Eddington's may be that science is

in fact be a dim reflector of the glory of our Maker. Another error of Eddington's seemingly is, in accordance with uniformitarian propaganda, that Genesis is a sonnet. The fact remains that Genesis, remarkably good source material on Earth history, is something more than a sonnet.

Uniformitarianism In Western Civilization

During man's history, numerous civilizations have been organized, and patterns of cyclical development have frequently occurred. Spengler and Toynbee, among others, have commented, and have traced these stages of development. Development has often started with a small number, possessing a pioneer spirit, possessing a stout faith, and possessing a willingness to migrate if necessary. A small group founded what grew into a civilization. Following the founding stage was that of severe test and trial, tests of foreign powers and trials of nature. The testing tended to refine austere principles into the society. Following survival in the early tests was normally a period of rapid economic and political growth.

Following the period of economic and political growth (and population growth) came a golden age of stability and cultural expansion. Cultural expansion took many forms among the arts. As peace and prosperity continued, the older, austere virtues of faith, morality, sacrifice and patriotism no longer continued to be essential; they no longer continued to be virtues.

Under the protective cover or climate of a successful civilization, hedonism became increasingly dominant.[6] Anti-spiritual ethics emerged and grew at the expense of the earlier views and virtues. Hedonism became first prominent, secondly dominant, and finally overbearing. The population mostly chose the way of "the flesh" and not the way of "the spirit." Civilization became mostly depraved; it collapsed, due partly to a push from without, but mostly from internal moral and spiritual rotting.

Spengler concluded that the majority of civilizations had a cycle of 400 to 450 years, approximately 12 generations. He thought that it took about that long for the lowest values of a society to rise to the top in prominence, something like a period

---

[6]Hedonism: The doctrine that pleasure is the sole or chief good in life and that moral duty is fulfilled in the gratification of pleasure-seeking instincts and dispositions.

of 12 or so hours which are necessary for slag to rise to the top in a blast furnace. Such may be a commentary on collective human nature.

If so, notice the process in Germany, where Western Civilization was founded some 450 years ago. This was the era of Copernicus, Erasmus, Gutenberg and Luther. Germany began to achieve independence and to discard feudalism. It became the place where a Tycho, a Kepler, a Leibnitz, and a Kant could think, organize, manufacture, talk, or publish freely. It became a dynamic society.

Interestingly enough, it has taken Germany about 450 years to pass from the pioneer era of Copernicus, Erasmus, Gutenberg and Luther to the era of Bormann, Goebbels, Himmler and Hitler, and the apparent decline of Germany. England, with its Fabianism and its Beatles, is about 375 years from the days when the men of Cambridge, Puritan crusaders, were forging a new nation. And contemporary America is about 10 generations, 350 years from the Mayflower, and its pro-spiritual foundation.

The Jews apparently have gone through at least two cycles of this same pattern, and if their history in Egypt were better known, perhaps three cycles. In the era, circa 450 B.C. to 70 A.D., they too passed from the era of pioneer faith, migration and from such outstanding leaders as Ezra and Haggai to the era of depravity, and such poor leaders as Caiaphas and the rebel zealot leaders against Rome, who led the nation into such ill-advised policies and horrible fortunes.

Interestingly enough, Kant and his uniformitarianism emerged in Germany about 200 years before Hitler and about 200 years after the era of Copernicus, Erasmus et al. Kant's uniformitarianism was designed to negate Germany's great spiritual heritage, and do so in the name of either "philosophy" or "science." From Kant came Hegel. From Hegel came Nietzsche and Wagner. And from Nietzsche and Wagner came Hitler and associates. From Germany came not only Nietzsche and Hitler's brand of anti-spirituality; it also spawned Marxism, for this was where Marx's values and ideas were formed, in the uniformitarian and atheistically oriented universities of Germany.

It seems like civilizations, when they sow to the wind, frequently reap the whirlwind. The fact that Kant's uniformitarianism came 200 years after Germany's academic and spiritual foundation, and some 200 years before her downfall, may be coincidental; this study suspects it is more than coincidental. It may be a cyclical phenomenon which also has occurred in previous civilizations.

Even as men of anti-spiritual motivation increasingly predominated in Germany in the 18th century, a similar pattern happened in England in the 19th century, in Lyell, Darwin, Huxley, the immigrant Marx, and many others. Here, too, anti-spiritual values metamorphosed into dominance. But this is no different than the age of, say, Isaiah and Jeremiah when anti-spiritual ideas of a pantheistic nature were metamorphosing into dominance in Jerusalem at a rapid pace. The only difference is that the anti-spiritual ethic in that age was pantheism, astrologically related, whereas today it is atheism, uniformitarianly related. But both are essentially views of negation; only their form varies. If these cycles and parallels are a commentary on collective human nature, they are also a reflection of individual human nature.

Before the days of cresting uniformitarianism, Erasmus, Luther, Newton, Whiston, Linnaeus and Agassiz were all considered as humanists, because they were strongly pro-scientific. Being pro-spiritual and simultaneously pro-scientific was normal. But the term "humanism" has changed in definition with the rise of uniformitarianism. Today, rejection of the uniformitarian pseudo-science brings upon one the connotation of being anti-scientific. Rejecting the Darwinian uniformitarianism is considered, by many, beyond the pale of knowledge. Today, to be pro-spiritual and to appreciate the Judeo-Christian heritage, one must, it seems, be anti-scientific. This is a common consensus; it is a mirage. The reality is that the uniformitarian view is anti-scientific; uniformitarianism is also non-historical and anti-spiritual, a pure-bred negative.

Similarly the term "liberal" has undergone a metamorphosis in definition over the years. Liberalism has come to mean generally a tolerance of the anti-spiritual, but not necessarily a tolerance for the pro-spiritual. Liberals[7] are reminded of the fact that these principles of catastrophism and Creationism, with related evidence, require openmindedness, a quality in which most liberals pride themselves.

---

[7]Liberals must not be confused with pseudo-liberals.

And Marxians (not to be confused with Martians), pseudo-liberals who have always advocated the lowest possible spiritual standards along with abundant animal standards, are reminded of the fact that there is no monopoly on revolutionary thought or, for that matter, on considerations of world upheavals. Indeed the catastrophist, studying Earth history, also appeals to revolutions, orbital in nature, and indeed also points to world upheavals, historical in nature, such as the Biblical Flood and the Ice Epoch. And from them one may conclude that both atheism and uniformitarianism are at least mistaken and illogical, and perhaps much worse.[8]

Civilization and Non-Conformity

Normally great civilizations in history have not just occurred; they have been woven and fashioned out by the effort, courage, faith, hope and sacrifice of their early leaders. Dynamic cultures were established by those who were determined, purposeful, stout and rather tolerant. These kinds of qualities are often found in non-conformists. Frequently, history has recorded awards given for non-conformity by declining, disintegrating societies. Abraham's award from Ur of Chaldees was a one-way ticket to the Wild West of that day, Palestine. Socrates, so skeptical of the Greek pantheism and the Greek morality of his day, open and persuasive in his view, especially among the youth of Athens, was given another award, a cup of hemlock. The prophet Jeremiah, in his day was awarded a religious court martial like Galileo; in recent decades another non-conformist, and patriot, General Billy Mitchell, received a military court martial because of his keen military foresight, plus his unwillingness to be silent. Justin Martyr was a most persuasive person among the academic figures of ancient Rome, and his skepticism was profound concerning the Roman pantheon, and the divinity of the Roman em-

[8]The author looks forward to a coming day, possibly in the next century or so, when the merit of catastrophism (and Creationism and galactogenesis) may be looked upon as most logical, even in Russia. At such time, the absurdities of Marxism will be very apparent to Russians, along with the necessity of replacing it. Such a time may well herald the decline of Marxism, and when its decline sets in, it might be surprisingly rapid.
  Such a day might be a step, just possibly a big step toward an age of global peace concomitant with world-wide justice, possibly coupled with an improved ecological habitat, economy, and also a greater longevity for the human race. Such may be a time when the pro-spiritual more than the anti-spiritual, the meek more than the beastly (the praying more than the preying) will inherit the Earth, as is forecast by our Lord in the Sermon on the Mount, when he anticipated something about the meek inheriting the earth.

perors. His award was an appointment in the amphitheatre with some underfed lions. The path of the non-conformist has often been difficult. Nevertheless it is from this kind of men from which new and better civilizations have repeatedly been founded.

Such traits are hardly those of the majority of the cultural leaders of our age. Conformity, enshrined by Freudian thought, is becoming a common thing in our nation, founded by some rather noble non-conformists. And this tendency of conformity (to say nothing of anti-spirituality) seems to be greatest among our intellectual elite, the very ones who are the quickest to decry conformity in others. Conformity, with its associated premium values of security and status-seeking, have frequently been stifling climates for further human progress, or for a dynamic society. Examples are numerous and every profession has them. This study shall cite an example from biological science, the example of Dr. Ignaz Semmelweis (1818-1865), a physician originally from Vienna.

Dr. Semmelweis was an ill-fated but imaginative young doctor who had taken over responsibility for the obstetrical wards in one of Vienna's leading hospitals. He soon noted that women commonly became infected with ailments, particularly after examinations by doctors or their students who proceeded from corpse to patient and back to corpse.

After watching the heartbreaking scenes of death in the maternity wards, and the spreading infections, he concluded that some mysterious element passed invisibly from the corpses to the patients. He established the rule that every physician and student must wash his hands after examining a body. The frequency of infections and deaths declined immediately and sharply. Dr. Semmelweis' guess was a very good one.

However, his guess imposed an added inconvenience upon Vienna's physicians, that of frequently washing their hands. Further, Semmelweis implied that the doctors of Vienna, far from being the protectors of the living, were actually the agents of death, and the deaths of thousands of young mothers. Many Vienna doctors boiled at Semmelweis, even as many other authorities had been angered with a Galileo or a Jeremiah.

Immediate howls of protest were raised against this "nuisance." Dr. Semmelweis was dismissed from his responsibility at the hospital. He was shunned and black-listed by his profession in Vienna, by minds sufficiently warped with professional pride and preconceived prejudice that neither logic nor the needs of humanity could penetrate.

Dr. Semmelweis, being depressed and shocked at his newly acquired disrespectability, migrated to Budapest, where he again took responsibility in a maternity ward in a hospital. Again he instituted the same procedures of sanitation. Again the frequency of deaths among the new mothers markedly and rapidly declined. But his detractors followed him. And again, Dr. Semmelweis was dismissed from his position at the hospital.

Being subjected to the bitterest of sarcasm by his colleagues, and being haunted by the death cries of hundreds, possibly thousands of dying new mothers, he experienced a mental breakdown. He was promptly incarcerated in a mental instituiton. This is one of the sadder case histories of a non-conformist. Every profession has them. Religion has had many; so has the military. On numerous occasions, petty grievances and minor jealousies among the generals were more the issue than victory in battle.

Jeremiah, a magnificently rugged prophet, seeing the moral decline of his people, seeing the enveloping idolatry which they were increasingly practicing, sensed an impending national doom, fast approaching upon the anti-spiritual leaders of his people. Possessing much concern, perhaps too much, he began to proclaim his pro-spiritual message. It gained but few listeners, but it was very successful in rankling the anti-spiritual leaders in government and in religion. Seven kinds of incarceration failed to silence him; stoning ultimately did. His generation failed to heed his message. However, the next generation, humbled by captivity, recognized the value of his message.

Galileo, Jeremiah, Semmelweis, or long lists of other non-conformists illustrate the durability of truth over error, and also of the pro-spiritual ethic over the anti-spiritual ethic. They also illustrate the frequency of dominance of the anti-spiritual over the pro-spiritual. The anti-spiritual ethic, essentially one of simple negation, is inextricably bound up with uniformitarianism, also a doctrine of negation, and this has been so since the days of the inception of uniformitarianism.[10]

[10]Many uniformitarians will no doubt angrily reject our celestial (and pro-spiritual) catastrophism, and partly for the following reasons: It is not easy on the psyches, in fact it is fairly painful for some to acknowledge publicly in front of an audience or a class that they have been mistaken. But this includes a further inconvenience, the necessity of going back to begin studying again. To reject is just much easier.

Conclusion

In the opening pages of this volume, the reader was led to visualize a strange room, well lit, and with a broad-leafed maple table in the center. Lying upon this well-lit table were several thousand pieces of jigsaw puzzle, in random and unsorted fashion. The man endeavoring to complete the puzzle assumed that here, lying on this one table, were the elements of one large, inter-locking, inter-merging puzzle. Intensified effort in working the puzzle led to increasing perplexity and frustration. There were too many corner pieces.

Eventually he wondered, "Might it be that there are, lying on this table, the elements of two, or even three separate and distinct puzzles?" With this, the basis for much progress was laid.

In completing the problem, several puzzles were found. Each contained a picture, separate from the others, and in sequence they each presented different scenes of a single unfolding drama.

So it has been with the historic and pre-historic catastrophes, some more severe, and others, though fearful, were less severe. The Mayans and Hindus were right when they maintained that there have been separate and more or less distinct ages or cycles of human activity, punctuated by catastrophes, even requiring revised calendars. Genesis and Job are similarly found to be correct with respect to Earth history.

This is why a book is written on the Biblical Flood. This is why the subject, although ancient, must nevertheless not be relegated to academic limbo. This is the reason why the correct dating of the Flood is essential to the correct reconstruction of ancient conditions. And this is why it is essential to understand the nature of the Flood, as well as the scope of the effects.

Thus we review the magnificent engraving and etching which has occurred to our planet. Thus we review the ancient celestial motifs, and the Biblical story of a global Flood. Thus we investigate the circumstances of our solar system, and its neighboring stars. Thus we review the structure of our fragile little sphere, as it spirals through galactic space. Review these evidences carefully. Prepare to draw conclusions which may seem amazing, or awesome, and which may indeed lead to new thought. Dare to think. *Sapere aude.*

Selected Bibliography

Abell, George, *Exploration of the Universe*, New York: Holt, Rinehart and Winston, 1964.

Armstrong, H. L. "An Attempt to Correct Radioactive Carbon Dating," *Creation Research Society Quarterly*, Jan. 1966, pp. 28-30.

Asimov, Isaac, *The Kingdom of the Sun*, New York: Abelard-Schuman, 1960.

Aston, W. G., "The Age of the Gods," *The Nihongi* (Chronicles of Japan From Earliest Times to A.D. 697), London: Geo. Allen & Unwin, 1906.

Baker, Robert H., *Astronomy*, Princeton, N.J.: Van Nostrand, 1959.

Baly, Denis, *The Geography of the Bible*, New York: Harper & Bros., 1957.

The Bible

Bondi, H., *Cosmology*, London: Cambridge University Press, 1952.

Cameron, A. T., *Recent Advances In Endocrinology*, Philadelphia: Blakiston Co., 1940.

Colin, Edward C., *Elements of Genetics*, Philadelphia, Blakiston Co., 1949.

Dake, Finis Jennings, *Dake's Annotated Reference Bible*, Grand Rapids, Zondervan Publishing House, 1965.

Dana, James D., *Manual of Geology*, New York: Ivison Co., 1875.

Darwin, Charles, *Origin of Species*, New York: Modern Library.

Darwin, Charles, *The Descent of Man*, New York: Modern Library.

DeBeer, Gavin R., *Charles Darwin*, New York: Doubleday & Co., 1964.

DeHaan, M. R., *The Days of Noah*, Grand Rapids: Zondervan Publishing House, 1963.

Doig, Peter, *A Concise History of Astronomy*, London: Chapman & Hall, 1950.

Durant, William J., *Caesar and Christ*, New York: Simon & Schuster, 1944.

Durant, William J., *The Life of Greece*, New York: Simon & Schuster, 1939.

Durant, William J., *The Story of Civilization*, New York: Simon & Schuster, 1935.

Dyson, James L., *The Geologic Story of Glacier National Park*, Belton (West Glacier), Mont., Glacier Natural History Assn., Bulletin No. 3, 1949.

Freeman, Otis, *Geography of the Pacific*, New York: John Wiley and Sons Inc., 1951.

Finch, Vernor C. and Glenn T. Trewartha, *Elements of Geography* (Physical and Cultural), New York: McGraw-Hill, 1942.

Forward, Robert L., "Pluto, Last Stop Before the Stars," *Science Digest*, August, 1962.

Gamow, George, *Biography of the Earth*, New York: Viking Press, 1941.

Gamow, George, *The Creation of the Universe*, New York: Viking Press, 1952.

Gamow, George, *Matter, Earth and Sky*, Englewood Cliffs, N.J.: Prentice Hall Inc., 1958.

Gaut, Norman E., *Angular Momentum Flux in the Formation of the Solar System*, Cambridge, Mass.: M.I.T., AFCRL-64-167, 1964.

Ginsburg, Norton et al., *The Pattern of Asia*, Englewood, N.J.: Prentice-Hall, 1958.

Ginzberg, Louis, *Legends of the Bible*, New York: Simon & Schuster, 1956.

Halley, Henry H., *Bible Handbook*, Grand Rapids: Zondervan Publishing House, 1964.

Hapgood, Charles, "The Mystery of the Frozen Mammoths," *Coronet*, Sept. 1960, pp. 70-78.

Hartshorne, Richard, "The Concept of Geography as a Science of Space, from Kant and Humboldt to Hettner, *Annals*, Association of American Geographers, XLVIII, 1958.

Hartshorne, Richard, *Perspective on the Nature of Geography*, Chicago: Rand-McNally, 1959.

Henderson, Ernest F., *A Short History of Germany* (Vols. I and II), New York: MacMillan Co., 1908.

Himmelfarb, Gertrude, *Darwin and the Darwinian Revolution*, New York: Doubleday & Co., 1959.

Hooker, Dolph Earl, *Those Astounding Ice Ages*, New York: Exposition Press, 1958.

Howe, George F., "Paleobotanical Evidences for a Philosophy of Creationism," *Creation Research Society Annual*, 1964 (I), pp. 24-29.

James, Edwin Oliver, *The Ancient Gods*, New York: G. P. Putnam's Sons, 1960.

James, Edwin Oliver, *The Worship of the Sky-god*, London: Athlove Press, 1963.

James, Edwin Oliver, *Myth and Ritual In The Ancient Near East*, New York: Praeger, 1958.

James, Preston E., *Latin America, New York:* Odyssey Press, 1959.

Kellogg, Howard W., *The Canopied Earth*, Los Angeles: American Prophetic League.

Kesseli, John E., "Geomorphic Landscapes," *Yearbook*, Assn. of Pacific Geographers, XXII, (1950), pp. 3-10.

Klotz, John W., *Genes, Genesis and Evolution*, St. Louis: Concordia Publishing House, 1965.

Kuiper, Gerard P. et al., *The Earth As A Planet*, Chicago: Univ. of Chicago Press, 1954.

Kuiper, Gerard P. et al., *Planets and Satellites*, Chicago: Univ. of Chicago Press, 1961.

Lammerts, Walter E., "Planned Induction of Commercially Desirable Variation in Roses by Neutron Radiation," *Creation Research Society Annual*, II (1965), pp. 39-48.

Lammerts, Walter E. et al., *The Challenge of Creation,* Caldwell, Ida.: Bible-Science Assn., 1965.

LaPierre, Richard T., *The Freudian Ethic,* New York: Duell, Sloan & Pierce, 1959.

Larrabee, Eric, "Scientists in Collision: Was Velikovsky Right?", *Harpers Magazine,* August, 1963, pp. 48-55.

Life Magazine, "The Fall of Phaethon," Vol. 54, No. 3, Jan. 18, 1963, pp. 56-57.

Linane, Sister Euphemia, CSJ, "The Universality of the Flood Legend," Seattle University, Requirements of Composition, June 1959.

Litwack, Gerald and David Kritchevsky, *Actions of Hormones on Molecular Processes,* New York: John Wiley & Sons, 1964.

Lyell, Sir Charles, *Principles of Geology,* edited by J. W. Knedler, New York: Doubleday & Co., 1947.

Marsh, Frank L., *Studies In Creationism,* Washington, D.C., Review & Herald Publishing Assn., 1950.

Mason, A. Stuart and G. I. M. Swyer, *Major Endocrine Disorders,* Fairlawn, N.J.: Oxford University Press, 1959.

Moore, John N., "The Heritage of Creation Concepts," *Creation Research Society Annual,* 1964 (I), pp. 3-5.

Moore, John N., "The Heritage of Creation Concepts,*Creation Research Society Quarterly,* Jan. 1965, pp. 3-6.

Moore, John N., "Neo-Darwinism and Society," *Creation Research Society Quarterly,* Jan. 1966, pp. 13-23.

Morgan, Kenneth, *The Religion of the Hindus,* New York: Ronald Press, 1953.

Morris, Henry M., *The Bible and Modern Science,* Chicago: Moody Press, 1951.

Morris, Henry M., "Science vs. Scientism in Historical Geology," *Creation Research Society Quarterly,* July 1965, pp. 19-27.

Muirden, James, *Stars and Planets,* New York: Thos. Y. Cromwell, 1965.

Nelson, Byron, *After Its Kind,* Minneapolis: Augsburg Publishing House, 1927.

Nelson, Byron, *The Deluge Story in Stone,* Minneapolis: Augsburg Publishing House, 1931.

Newton, Isaac, *Observations Upon the Prophecies of Daniel and the Apocalypse of St. John,* London: Darby and Browne, 1733. Reprinted from Microfilm: Seattle, Pacific Meridian Publishing Co., 1966.

Nourse, Alan E., *The Nine Planets,* New York: Harper & Bros., 1960.

Peake, Harold, *The Flood: New Light on an Old Story,* New York: Robert McBride & Co., 1930.

Pickering, James S., *Captives of the Sun,* New York: Dodd, Mead & Co., 1961.

Pickering, James S., *1001 Questions Answered About Astronomy,* New York: Dodd, Mead & Co., 1960.

Price, George McCready, *Evolutionary Geology and the New Catastrophism,* Mountain View, Calif.: Pacific Press, 1926.

Price, George McCready, *Geological-Ages Hoax,* Chicago: Fleming H. Revell Co., 1931.

Price, George McCready, *How Did The World Begin,* New York: Fleming H. Revell Co., 1942.

Price, George McCready, *The Modern Flood Theory of Geology,* New York: Fleming H. Revell Co., 1935.

Price, George McCready, *The New Geology,* Mountain View, Calif., Pacific Press, 1923.

Price, George McCready, *Common-Sense Geology,* Mountain View, Calif.: Pacific Press, 1946.

Proctor, Mary, *The Romance of Comets,* New York: Harper & Bros., 1926.

Ratcliff, J. D., "Do Traces of Metal Decide our Fate?", *Today's Health,* March 1966, pp. 34-36, 81.

Rehwinkel, Alfred Martin, *The Flood,* St. Louis: Concordia Publishing House, 1951.

Rushdoony, Rousas J., *Intellectual Schizophrenia,* Philadelphia: Presbyterian & Reformed Publishing Co., 1961.

Rushdoony, Rousas J., "The Premises of Evolutionary Thought," *Creation Research Quarterly,* July 1965, pp. 15-18.

Russell, Richard Joel, "Geographical Geomorphology," *Annals,* Assn. of American Geographers, XXXIX (1949), pp. 1-11.

Sanderson, Ivan T., "Riddle of the Frozen Giants," *Saturday Evening Post,* Jan. 16, 1960, pp. 39, 82-83.

Scheidegger, Adrian E., *The Physics of Flow,* New York: MacMillan Co., 1957.

Scheidegger, Adrian E., *Principles of Geodynamics,* Berlin: Springer-Verlag, 1963.

Schwarze, C. Theodore, *The Marvel of Earth's Canopies:* Chicago: Good News Publishers, 1957.

Smart, William Marshall, *The Origin of the Earth,* Baltimore: Penguin Books, 1949.

Soffer, Louis J., *Diseases of the Endocrine Glands,* Philadelphia: Lea & Febiger, 1956.

Spengler, Oswald, *The Decline of the West,* New York: Alfred Knopf Inc., 1926.

Spengler, Oswald, *The Hour of Decision,* New York: Alfred Knopf Inc., 1934.

Stamp, Laurence Dudley and Stanley H. Beaver, *A Regional Geography, Part II, Africa,* New York: Longmans, Green & Co., 1947.

Stamp, Laurence Dudley, *The Earth's Crust,* New York: Crown Publishers, 1951.

Struve, Otto and Velta Zebergs, *Astronomy of the 20th Century,* New York: MacMillan Co., 1962.

Thompson, J. Eric S., *The Rise and Fall of Maya Civilization,* Norman, Okla.: Univ. of Oklahoma Press, 1954.

Toynbee, Arnold J., *A Study of History,* Fairlawn, N.J.: Oxford Univ. Press, 1947.

Trewartha, Glenn T., *Fundamentals of Physical Geography*, New York: McGraw Hill, 1961.

Vail, Isaac N., *Alaska, Land of the Nugget*, Pasadena: Swerdfinger Press, 1897.

Vail, Isaac N., *The Earth's Annular System*, Pasadena: Annular World Co., 1912.

Vail, Isaac N., *The Misread Record*, Seattle: Simplex Publishing Co., 1921.

Vail, Isaac N., *Waters Above the Firmament*, Cleveland: Clark & Zugerle, 1885.

Velikovsky, Immanuel, *Ages In Chaos*, New York: Doubleday & Co., 1952.

Velikovsky, Immanuel, *Earth In Upheaval*, New York: Doubleday & Co., 1955.

Velikovsky, Immanuel, *Worlds In Collision*, New York, Doubleday & Co., 1950.

Von Weizsacker, C. F., *The Relevance of Science* (Creation and Cosmogony, New York: Harper & Row, 1964.

Ward, William B., *Out of the Whirlwind*, Richmond, Va.: John Knox Press, 1958.

Watson, Fletcher G., *Between the Planets*, Philadelphia: Blakiston Co., 1941.

Weyl, Nathaniel and Stefan T. Possony, *The Geography of Intellect*, Chicago: Henry Regnery Co., 1963.

Whitcomb, John C. Jr., *The Origin of the Solar System*, Philadelphia: Presbyterian and Reformed Publishing Co., 1964.

Whitcomb, John C. Jr., and Henry M. Morris, *The Genesis Flood*, Philadelphia: Presbyterian and Reformed Publishing Co., 1961.

Whiston, William, *Astronomical Principles of Religion*, London: J. Senex, 1717. Reprinted from Microfilm: Seattle, Pacific Meridian Publishing Co., 1966.

Whiston, William, *A New Theory of the Earth*, London: Benj. Tooke, 1696. Reprinted from Microfilm: Seattle, Pacific Meridian Publishing Co., 1966.

Whiston, William, *The Works of Flavius Josephus* (Antiquities of the Jews), 6 Vols., Bridgeport, Conn.: M. Sherman, 1828.

Whitney, George Tapley and David F. Bowers, *The Heritage of Kant*, Princeton, N.J.: Princeton Univ. Press, 1939.

Whitney, Dudley J., *Genesis Versus Evolution*, New York: Exposition Press, 1961.

Williams, Henry Smith, *The Great Astronomers*, New York: Newton Publishing Co., 1932.

Wood, Robert W., "The Age of Man," *Creation Research Quarterly*, Jan. 1966, pp. 24-27.

Woodford, A. O., *Historical Geology*, San Francisco: W. H. Freeman & Co., 1965.

Zimmerman, Paul A., *Darwin, Evolution and Creation*, St. Louis: Concordia Publishing House, 1959.

Index